BEING PRESENT FOR YOUR
NURSERY AGE CHILD

BEING PRESENT FOR YOUR NURSERY AGE CHILD

Observing, Understanding, and Helping Children

Edited by

Jeanne Magagna and Patrizia Pasquini

The Tempo Lineare Project

KARNAC

First published in Italy in 2007 as a self-published book

First published in 2014 by
Karnac Books Ltd
118 Finchley Road, London NW3 5HT

British Library Cataloguing in Publication Data

A C.I.P. for this book is available from the British Library

ISBN: 978 1 78220 141 0

Edited, designed and produced by The Studio Publishing Services Ltd
www.publishingservicesuk.co.uk
e-mail: studio@publishingservicesuk.co.uk

Printed in Great Britain

CONTENTS

To Gianna Williams

The ideas in this book are based on psychoanalytic observational studies according to the Tavistock Cinic method of young child observation.

We are deeply grateful to Gianna Wiliams for initiating Observational Studies of Infants and Young Children, as well as many of the Child Psychotherapy Trainings in Italy. Gianna contributed profoundly to our educaton as well as to many professionals worldwide. Her unique human talent in teaching psychoanalytic observational studies deepy influenced the life and work of Patrizia Pasquini, Director of Tempo Lineare, who collaborates with teachers and parents through observation of young children to help parents, teachers, and children develop relationships based on mutual understanding and trust.

Dr Gianna Williams, psychoanalyst and child and adolescent psychotherapist.

ACKNOWLEDGEMENTS

In 1999, Patrizia Pasquini opened the first service "Tempo Lineare for the child from zero to three years and the family". Because it was so appreciated by the children and parents, she started a continuation of the school for children aged four to six and their parents. Patrizia developed this book in conjunction with Dr Jeanne Magagna and Carla Busato Barbaglio, and now wishes to thank all the parents and children who shared this experience with her.

Patrizia, Jeanne, and Carla owe an enormous debt of gratitude to the Tavistock Clinic and the child psychotherapy trainings in Rome and Florence which formed part of their psychoanalytic training. The Observational Studies form the bedrock of the Tempo Lineare project, which focuses on observing, understanding, and fostering the development of nursery age children and their parents. Patrizia would also like to thank the *Spazio Psicoanalitico* in Rome, which fostered her understanding of group processes.

Patrizia is also grateful to Professor Paolo Perrotti, because he suggested the possibility of her training at the Tavistock Clinic and made the psychoanalytical process alive and interesting to her. Her group analysis with Professor Perrotti and her individual analysis with Dr Sergio Muscetta helped her to understand what is important in life. She thanks them for this. She is also grateful to Emiliana Mazzonis, who taught her that children's play is full of emotional meaning.

There are many people to whom we are grateful for assisting in the production of this book. In particular, Livia Stampa and the board members of "Associazione Genitori e Amici del Tempo Lineare" offered their time, competencies, and financial support in order that both the English and Italian editions of this book could be realised. Many Tempo Lineare parents wrote chapters for the book and translated their chapters into English. Unfortunately we were not able to include all these excellent chapters. The parents who assisted in the collating of the book include Beatrice Colnago, Maria Demolli, Francesca Delaini, and Giuseppe Parigi. A Tempo Lineare parent, Beatrice Colnago, read the entire manuscript and gave many valued suggestions. We are grateful to Karnac books for agreeing to publish the English version of this book.

Assisting in the production of the book were Patrizia's parents and friends: Giovanna Domenici, Agnese Giachetti, Isabella Centofanti, Maria Teresa Giancaterina, and Irma Perrotti. For the drawings, a special thanks also goes to a young painter who assists in the nursery, Cecilia Campironi, who made the cover drawing, and Ankur Sharma. We are also grateful to Isabel Owen, Erin Hope Thompson, Michelle Scott, Rod Tweedy, the Studio, and Ellen Jaffe, who assisted in the editing of the English version of the book.

Finally, we would like to express our gratitude to all the people who made the "Tempo Lineare" experience possible through the affectionate and co-operative climate between children, parents, and the teachers. We also thank the great number of friends, colleagues, teachers, educators, and parents who share with us our passion for this work.

Finally, a special thank you to the local government of the City of Rome and particularly the 1st Municipality, which accepted and financially enabled Patrizia Pasquini's idea for the development of the Tempo Lineare project to take root in the education services of Rome.

Carl Bagnini, LCSW, BCD, is a founding member of the International Psychotherapy Institute in Washington, DC and Long Island, New York. He is the local host of IPI's video-conferencing seminars on couple therapy and Masters' Clinician series. Carl is also a member of the faculties of the Gorden Derner Post Graduate Programs in Clinical Supervision and the Couple Therapy Program at Adelphi University, and he supervises at the Yeshiva University Post-Doctoral Family Therapy Program in Clinical Psychology. He has presented at national and international conferences in the USA, Panama, and the UK and he has written many papers and book chapters on a variety of clinical topics. He has recently published *Keeping Couples in Treatment: Working from Surface to Depth* (2013, Roman and Littlefield). He works privately with individuals, couples, and families, and offers supervision. He is a board member of the Couple and Family Psychoanalysis Division of the American Psychological Association.

Carla Busato Barbaglio completed the Tavistock Model Observation Course in Rome and subsequently qualified as a training psychoanalyst in the Italian Psychoanalytic Society (SPI) and as a child psychotherapist in the AIPPI Child Psychotherapy Training in Rome. She is a teacher at the Italian Psychoanalytic Society, the AIPPI child psychotherapy training, the Adolescent Psychiatry Department, and social work and schoolteachers' training programme in the "Agostino Gemelli" general hospital in Rome. Carla's many publications include: "Nascere, vivere, cambiare: la relazione luogo di tessitura dell'essere", in collaboration with E. Greco, in C. Busato Barbaglio and M. L. Mondello (Eds.), *Nuovi assetti della clinica psicoanalitica in età evolutiva* (Rome: Borla, 2011); "Maternità fortezza da due debolezze?", in: N. Neri and C. Rogora (Eds.), *Desideri di maternità* (Rome: Borla, 2010; "Come genitori e analisti affrontano il trauma", in: T. Cancrini and D. Biondo (Eds.), *Una ferita all'origine* (Rome: Borla, 2012).

Cecilia Campironi has a diploma in illustration and multi-media animation from the Institute of European Design in Rome. With three other artists, she works in Studio Arturo, which organises craft fairs and other cultural events as well as working on the publicity material for these events. Since 2005, she has worked with Tempo Lineare children, helping them to draw and produce material for the Italian edition of this book (Pasquini, 2007). She also designs posters and programmes for other initiatives aimed at gaining understanding of young children.

Jeanne Magagna completed trainings in child, adult and family psychotherapy and has a doctorate in child psychotherapy from the Tavistock Clinic and the University of East London. For twenty-four years, she worked as Head of Psychotherapy Services at Great Ormond Street Hospital for Children. Alongside this work, Jeanne was the Joint Co-ordinator and Vice-President of the Centro Studi Martha Harris Tavistock-Model Observational and Child Psychotherapy Trainings in Florence, Palermo, Trieste, and Venice. Her work also included consulting to Family Futures Consortium, an Adoption and Fostering Consortium in London. Her first career was working as a Head Start Nursery Teacher for Jane Adams Hull House in Chicago, Illinois. Jeanne has edited *Universals of Psychoanalysis*, co-edited *Crises in Adolescence* and *Intimate Transformations: Babies with their Families* (2005) and edited *The Silent Child: Communication without Words* (2012). Her writings on infant observation are collected in *Closely Observed Infants* (1989), *New Developments in Infant Observation* (1997), and *Surviving* Space (2002). She has also published and taught in most continents.

Patrizia Pasquini completed a master's degree in "Observation and Application of Psychoanalytical Concepts to the Work with Children, Adolescents and Families" at the Centro Studi Martha Harris in Rome and the Tavistock and University of East London Degree Programme (1992–1994). She became a member of the Tavistock Society of Psychotherapists following completion of the Centro Studi Martha Harris Florence Tavistock Model Psychotherapy Child and Adolescent Psychotherapy Training. As part of her psychoanalytic training, Patrizia also participated in a Psychoanalytic Group Psychotherapy Training at *Spazio Psicoanalitico* in Rome under the directorship of Professor Paolo Perrotti. Later, she attended a three-year group training on "The Psychoanalytic Meaning of Tales". Later still, Patrizia conducted a two-year experiential group focusing on "Emotional processes in teaching practice" at the Spazio Psicoanalitico. Using the drawings of the Tempo Lineare children, she later published a book of fairy tales, *Da Fiaba Nasce* (2002). Most importantly, Patrizia is the creator and Director of the Tempo Lineare Service in Rome, which is described in this book.

Introduction

Jeanne Magagna

Politics begins in the nursery says Dr Sebastian Kraemer (Kraemer, 2000, p. 115). If all goes well between nursery teachers, the parents, and the child in the nursery, the nursery becomes for the child "his space" away from home. It is his space to make friends outside the family, his space in which he can find care-giving by kind and thoughtful adults outside the family. The nursery is his space to begin creating a sense of being "his own person", with a separate identity as "a person outside the family" who can find his way in a nursery group and, subsequently, in the larger school community of older children (Kraemer, 2000, p. 117). It is for this reason that everyone always asks, what happened when you took your child to nursery?

The position a child takes up in his first peer group within the nursery is influenced by family relationships. The world of the nursery becomes a testing ground for the young child's internalisation of his parents' capacities. These parental capacities would ideally include the ability to be emotionally open and intimate with others, to have an internal capacity for containing and modulating strong feelings, to begin to be able to reflect upon emotional experiences, as well as to pay close attention to what is going on both inside oneself and one's child. The parents have the crucial task of helping the child develop an internal space for holding emotions, phantasies, and dreams and allowing thoughts and other feelings to arise in relation to them.

If the parents have been able to withstand the stress of looking after a demanding and dependent infant, enjoyed conversations with him and loved him most of the time, then the child goes to nursery prepared to trust others, to be curious, to be generous, to be able to share and enjoy things with his peers, to make friends, to stand up for himself when he feels unfairly treated, and, later, to stand up for others (Kraemer, 2000, p.117).

While in the nursery, the child replays his love and hate towards significant family members: his mother, father, siblings, and important members of the extended family. He develops his capacity to lead, to make compromises, to follow instructions; simultaneously, he is encouraged to increase his inner strength to be creative, to be curious, and to think. A containing therapeutic nursery can foster development of the child's capacity to think about his emotions, increase his self-esteem, and help him to become more considerate of the well being of others. On the other hand, research shows that when the nursery functions without containment of the child's emotional and developmental needs, it simply fosters anxiety, which increases the child's cortisol level and the possibility of the child experiencing emotional difficulties. Obviously, sending a child to such a nursery is detrimental to a child's wellbeing. This book, first published in Italy in 2007, as Tempo Lineare: *Osservare, Conoscere, Aiutare I Bambini e I Benitori* (edited by P. Pasquini) is designed improve nurseries' compassionate comprehension of each child's emotional, intellectual, and physical needs.

Bearing this in mind, this book becomes essential reading for any professional group interested in preventative work created in collaboration with parents of children under five years of age. Tempo Lineare is a model of a government funded cost-effective therapeutic nursery which provides typical nursery activities while, at the same time, helping the parental couple and teachers collaborate, from the very first day of a child's entry in nursery, to observe, reflect upon, and support the emotional development of young children. The basis of the work is the Tavistock Clinic Observation Method for thinking about babies and young children.

Tempo Lineare

Patrizia Pasquini, pioneering nursery teacher, child psychotherapist, and group psychotherapist, has dedicated her life to the formation of this psychodynamic therapeutic nursery school programme. Her nursery and school facility, Tempo Lineare, is divided into two units: one for grandparents and parents who come with the babies from birth to three years, and a nursery facility for children from three to six years. Funded by the Italian government, Tempo Lineare is located in the centre of Rome. Patrizia Pasquini has structured the nursery according to three primary aims. The first is to create a therapeutic milieu in which parents and teachers can *observe* the children's interactions with them and, through group experiences, increase their capacity to be emotionally present for the babies and children. The second aim is to develop the parents', teachers', and children's capacities for *containment* of emotional experiences. The third aim is to enable the children *to internalise* the capacities of the parents and nursery teachers in order that they can be more fully present to their own emotional experiences while creatively exploring, learning, and forming important relationships with other children and adults outside their immediate family.

The process of achieving these aims includes Patrizia Pasquini's request for the teachers to write a daily detailed observation of the children's moment-by-moment interactions with parents, teachers, and peers. These observations are then discussed with Pasquini, the head of the nursery. Once a month, the parents and teachers meet for three hours to look at observations of the children's interactions, to study the children's drawings, to discuss their children's emotional and intellectual development, as shown through their play and other communications, and to think about their own experiences as parents and nursery teachers of these children. It is the collaboration between parents, teachers, and professionals that enables Tempo Lineare to function as a therapeutic containing milieu for the social and intellectual development of babies and young children. At times, various psychotherapists, social workers, psychologists, and psychotherapists are involved in the discussions. This book, *Being Present for Your Nursery Age Child: The Tempo Lineare Project*, describes the parents' monthly Saturday discussions in conjunction with Tempo Lineare Director, Patrizia Pasquini, and her colleagues, Carla Busato and Jeanne Magagna. Pasquini, Busato, and Magagna have a long history of learning together, for they spent two years together, with Jeanne Magagna as their teacher, studying infant observation. Also, they have worked with other London-based Tavistock Clinic teachers who formed Centro Studi Martha Harris for the training of child psychotherapists in Italy.

In the Tempo Lineare Saturday Seminars, parents, teachers, and psychotherapists presented their experiences of different aspects of the children and parents' developmental issues. This was followed by two hours of small group discussions of each parent's detailed written observation of nursery age children interacting with each other.

Through reading this book, we hope that you will join us in continuing to find ways of enhancing our capacity to be present for young babies and children.

The book is divided into six parts:

Part I.   An introduction describing how the nursery, Tempo Lineare, fosters learning to observe, understand, share, and develop in the nursery.
Part II.   An observational study of the development of a young mind.
Part III.   Compassionately understanding children's play
Part IV.   From one tale another tale is born: Tempo Lineare's use of fairy tales to help children deepen their emotional understanding.
Part V.   The collaboration between the family, the nursery school, and the wider society.
Part VI.   Contributions of parents writing about "special time" with their children and their parental collaboration with the nursery staff.

In Part I, "Learning to Observe", Chapter One, Pasquini describes the role of Tempo Lineare in developing children's capacities while simultaneously helping parents become curious about their children and their own relationship with them. The new parents bring their young babies to Tempo Lineare very soon after the baby is born. Through sharing their observations and experiences with the staff and other parents they are able to get to know more about what their baby feels, thinks and desires. Through this work the parents develop a reflective capacity. They are given support to deepen their intimacy with both their own infantile emotions and those of their babies. Simultaneously the nursery teachers are getting to know the new babies who, in three years time, may remain in the Tempo Lineare school for four- to six-year-olds without the continuous presence of the parents.

The four- to six-year-old children utilise an already formed trusting relationship with Tempo Lineare staff to support them in separating gradually from secure family attachment figures and to assist them in developing their life with others outside the family. Essential in the work of the nursery is the recognition and acceptance of the parents' and children's anxieties, rage, anger, love, and dependence on key figures, including parents, teachers, and siblings. The nursery uses play, drawings, and fairy tales to deepen the children's capacity for intimacy with, and modulation of, their own current emotional experiences. As all this is occurring, the parents are sharing experiences and building a kind of extended network that sustains them over a six-year period and sometimes longer.

Actually, after leaving Tempo Lineare when their children turned six, the first group of parents rented a facility to meet regularly to discuss their children and to provide an opportunity for the children to play together now and again. This became the Post Tempo Lineare Association, for the parents who left Tempo Lineare realised that their children's imagination and play was so rich when the parents were all collaborating to think about their children's development. The parents also realised that the parents' sense of community supported them as parents. Once a year, Tempo Lineare sponsors a shared study day with old and new parents, teachers, and professionals. Parents present creative videos and discuss ideas alongside other contributors to the study day.

In Part II, "How the young mind is built", the therapeutic work of Tempo Lineare is shown as teachers confront particular relationship issues within and between the children, their parents, and the nursery teachers. In this section, some basic tenets of the nursery are presented in each of the chapters placed in this section. These tenets include an understanding of how the parents' identifications with internalisations of their own trans-generational family relationships affect their own relationships with their children's inner realities. Misattunement between the parents and the baby can prompt the baby to develop protective strategies which then interfere with normal developmental processes of eating, thinking, being intimate with others, regulating his/her own feelings in relation to others, and repairing loving links which have been destroyed.

In Chapter Six, Busato, herself an adoptive parent as well as a grandmother of a Tempo Lineare child, examines the problems inherent in the experience of becoming a biological and/or an adoptive mother. Magagna (Chapter Seven), on primitive protections, describes how traumatised and maltreated children who are subsequently adopted or fostered have distorted pictures of themselves and their care-givers. The children have difficulty developing good self-esteem, trusting their care-givers, and using their intellectual capacities. Their language of trauma and hurt leads the children to develop protections against anxiety which impede the formation of good links with learning, teachers, and with their attachment figures. The children's fear, persecution, and hostility often leave the care-givers feeling hurt, hostile, and rejected. Magagna (Chapter Seven) contrasts traumatised adopted and fostered children's ways of protecting themselves against anxiety with a child who is able to function in identification with helpful parents' introjected capacity for mentalization. The introjection of mentalizing parents enables a nursery child to respond more openly to others with a increased range of more loving and regulated feelings.

In her chapters on emotional and cognitive development, eating difficulties, adoption and fostering, sibling relationships, and self-esteem, (Chapters Five, Eight, and Ten) Pasquini suggests that the task of Tempo Lineare, or any therapeutic nursery for that matter, is to enable the child's primary relationships to develop a healthier course by enhancing the care-givers' capacity for careful observation of interactions between them and the child and to foster the care-givers' capacity for getting to know their own emotional experiences surrounding the baby and the tasks of *being emotionally present* for the baby. To meet this aim, as well as the monthly meeting with the parents in a group, Pasquini meets individually and regularly with specific parents and teachers to think more about each particular child's primary relationships.

Pasquini shows examples of how *by being emotional present and noticing and accepting the parents' and child's unpleasant experiences*, she and the parents can subsequently modify family interaction and the child's interaction with others. Her sensitive exchanges with the parents regarding the teachers' and parents' observations of children's mental states and behaviours with their parents helps the parents understand their children's experiences of love, hostility, satisfaction, anger, hate, and courage. Very beneficial to the child's sense of well being in the nursery is the very early establishment the nursery teachers' and parents' trusting relationship filled with an atmosphere of mutual concern and understanding. It assists the young child and parent to develop dependable and satisfying internalised attachment relationships. The parents' trust in the nursery setting enables the child to feel more secure in the company of the nursery teachers.

Part III, "Compassionately comprehending children playing", includes Magagna, Pasquini, and Busato's observations of the crucial importance of children's play (Chapters Eleven to Fifteen). Play begins in early infancy, when a baby might repetitively drop a toy for mother to pick up, and continues later in nursery, when, through play, the child continues to externalise his deepest emotional states and find ways of creatively elaborating upon important emotional experiences. The chapters illustrate different functions of play which include: to expel emotion, to think about and, thus, regulate emotional experiences, to make creative dramas, to find ways of coming to terms with conflicts, and to develop satisfactory relationships with family and school members. It is obvious that, from the very beginning of life, a child's play activities form narratives about what is central to his or her emotional life. Similarly, shared play activities represent issues and conflicts present in the current emotional climate of the nursery.

Symbolic play suggests that the child has been sufficiently reciprocally attuned to his mother. This reciprocal attunement has enabled him to develop an interior space to form thoughts that can be externalised and expanded upon through play. Tempo Lineare staff and parents attempt to continue this work of attunement by providing a secure, thoughtful space for children's play to develop creatively with a clarity of emotion and complexity of thought. The emotional climate of Tempo Lineare is seen to both inspire and be inspired by the emergence and convergence of each child's phantasies. The chapters illustrate the way in which the parents and teachers carefully observe the play of the children that allows them to connect with parents, teachers, and other children. With the help of Tempo Lineare, the children and parents form a common language through play before they have developed advanced verbal levels of communication.

Part IV, "From one tale another is born" should really be read with the companion volume *Da Fiaba Nasce Fiaba* (Pasquini, 2002). *Da Fiaba Nasce Fiaba* (translated as From the Fairy Tale is Born a Fairy Tale) contains fairy tales and drawings done by the nursery age children in Tempo Lineare. Showing remarkable self-confidence, fifteen of the nursery age children spontaneously clamoured to have the microphone to explain to a shop's book-launch audience why they liked their daily ritual of listening to Patrizia Pasquini reading fairy tales. Their courage in speaking to unknown adults was inspired by extreme enthusiasm for their experience of the fairy tale discussions prompting their own creative narrative drawings. Apparently, within Tempo Lineare at snack time, the children sometimes talk to various other children to campaign for the fairy tale they wish to have read to them on that particular day. On other days, they create their own fairy tales and draw pictures illustrating them.

In Chapter Seventeen, "From tales to life and from life to tales", Pasquini describes how the fairy tale reading, followed by the children's spontaneous drawing of an aspect of the fairy tale, fits in with her belief that children need sufficient emotional space to be inspired and to discover the well of creative imagination within themselves. She challenges the notion of too much structured learning and dictated artistic tasks. For this reason, she allows the children freedom to draw whatever drama comes into their minds after the fairy tale is read to them. Later, the children often participate in a group discussion about how they and others perceive their drawings. Clearly, they are confident in expressing themselves verbally to the adults in the nursery, or they would not have been so keen to present their thoughts to the book-launch audience; however, it is not developing self-confidence, verbal fluency, or creativity which comprises the primary aim of the fairy tale project.

Rather, most important is Tempo Lineare's task of helping each child develop the *capacity to be present in the moment* to his or her own deep and unique emotional experiences. These experiences are stimulated by the children's identifications with fairy tale characters' relationships involving love, loss, jealousy, hate, courage, and hope. As mentioned earlier, on some occasions, after spending some weeks hearing fairy tales read to them, the children ask to write and draw their own fairy tale. "The Queen of the Caramels", which the children wrote and designed, is presented in Chapter Eighteen.

Parts V and VI, "The couple, the family, the group, and society", and "The parents creating and collaborating", respectively, have contributions by teachers, therapists, mothers, and fathers which illustrate the important tasks for mothers, fathers, and teachers to enjoy and participate in the task of fostering the development of young children. In each of the yearly Tempo Lineare Conferences, open to the public, parents wrote and delivered descriptions of their personal experiences of finding their identities as parents and they also presented detailed observations of themselves interacting with their child. Many of the parents have devoted considerable effort to being good parents. They also show how they have mastered the difficult task of setting time aside to be involved with their children within Tempo Lineare. The development of the parents' creativity and thinking is obvious in their contributions to this book.

The book, *Being Present for Your Nursery Age Child: Tempo Lineare Project,* presents an innovative, preventative, mental health programme for young children in nursery and their families. The Tempo Lineare project is in line with many governments' policies that children under five should not have to wait to begin school to be noticed as having difficulties. Tempo Lineare, existing for children from birth to six years, is recognised by parents as a place of support and pleasurable learning. They realise that working together within Tempo Lineare, they can prevent the development of severe psychological problems in later childhood, foster emotional and intellectual growth, and inspire creativity in both their children and themselves.

Many other applications of the observational model of therapeutic work are described in *The International Journal of Infant Observation.* Recently, more detailed descriptions of the value of the observational method have been the subject of an important website: natol.us.infobs. This website describes the methods of infant and young child observation in a way that parents and professionals can use to further their observational capacities and see the purpose of applied observational work with children.

Tempo Lineare demonstrates a model of supporting rather than supplanting "The couple's cradle for the inner child". This concept of the couple creating an emotionally receptive and resilient cradle for the inner child is described by Magagna in Chapter Nineteen. She utilises the sensitive drawings of Tempo Lineare's art teacher, Cecilia Campironi, to depict the need for the parents to become intimate with their own emotional experiences and provide a cradle for each other's emotional experiences. Magagna also shows how working collaboratively, rather than competitively, is a task of the parents' engaging in many dialogues with the nursery teachers.

Included is chapter written by an American father and psychotherapist, Carl Bagnini, who started a fathers' group and interviewed young children about their experiences with their fathers. This chapter was included to emphasise the fact that much more attention needs to be given to the father's important role for the psychological development of the child. Other chapters, by Carla Busato Barbaglio and Patrizia Pasquini, emphasise the value of having more public nurseries' projects similar to the Tempo Lineare project. Tempo Lineare acknowledges and supports the parental couple as being of primary importance for development of their unique young child. We hope that Tempo Lineare will become a model of how nurseries could develop ways of understanding and meeting children's and their parents' need for love, intimacy, security, and a sense of community as well as becoming a containing emotional space for resolving conflicts and developing creativity.

In closing, we should point out that, for the sake of simplicity, the words he and his are used throughout to imply both male and female. Likewise, we recognise that maternal roles are undertaken by men as well as women, but mother is the term often used in the book, rather than "mother and/or father".

References

Kraemer, S. (2000). Politics in the nursery. In: W. Wheeler (Ed.), *The Political Subject* (pp. 114–120). London: Lawrence & Wishart.

Pasquini, P. (2002). *Da Fiabe Nasce Fiabi*. Rome: Genitori e Amici del Tempo Lineare-Onlus.

PART I
ON LEARNING TO OBSERVE

CHAPTER ONE

The Tempo Lineare project

Patrizia Pasquini

T he government-funded project, "Tempo Lineare for children aged 0–3 and their families", is available to interested families in the centre of Rome. Established in 1999, it offers a meeting place where parents and grandparents can play with their children and receive support from psychotherapists and nursery teachers who understand the developmental needs of young children. Parents of young children (from birth to three years) are provided the opportunity to meet each other, to exchange experiences, doubts, and points of view in relation to the growth and education of their children. It is, therefore, a service in which the Tempo Lineare staff work collaboratively "with", and not only "for", the users. The family does not delegate responsibility to the facility, but, rather, is actively involved in the work of the Tempo Lineare service.

Tempo Lineare is situated in an ancient house in Testaccio, a lively working-class neighbourhood in the heart of Rome. Since 1999, when it was founded, Tempo Lineare has become the physical space, the containing space, where this experience, open to twenty-four families each year, has come to life. Since then, over 280 families have turned to Tempo Lineare: 180 regularly attended the service, a hundred more could benefit from the weekly listening space. The creation of a social network sustains this group of parents, children, and professionals through an observational programme that appreciative parents established after the children left Tempo Lineare at age five. Donations by parents were used to rent a facility to support the former Tempo Lineare parents to continue developing alongside their children. Parent discussion groups and children's activity and discussion groups are held there.

Facilities within Tempo Lineare

There are four sections within Tempo Lineare: a space for 0–3-year-olds, another for 4–6-year-olds, one for parents and grandparents, and the consultation area.

0–3 years facility

This facility is similar to a house, to enable the children to identify with a familiar and intimate place. The space is organised with furniture and décor suited to the age of the children, with games and materials to stimulate their curiosity and encourage the fostering of good relationships between the children and adults. The Tempo Lineare service for 0–3-year-olds is open every year to twenty-six families, so that mothers and fathers can spend time together with their young children and babies for two to three mornings each week. Of these twenty-six places, six are for families who are experiencing particular interpersonal or social difficulties. Children aged from one week to twenty months come with their families to the nursery twice a week for three hours, while the group of children from twenty to thirty-six months attend the facility three days a week for three hours per day.

Mothers and fathers spend some time together with their children in the nursery two or three mornings a week. Here, children play, experience their first moments of socialisation, and learn their first competences as they move to and away from their parents. This service has reached families with all sorts of incomes and from varied professions who need support and social contact. In fact, Tempo Lineare has increasingly become a way of getting together socially to work as part of a multi-cultural community in the historic centre of Rome. Tempo Lineare offers families of small children a shared place that enables children and parents, in collaboration with staff, to create the opportunity to think through their various experiences together.

Tempo Lineare for 0–3-year-olds encourages small doses of new experiences in the child's life. It is a place where parents can share the early phases of first-time parenting as well as the fundamental stages of their young children's growth. The mothers and fathers are given dependable support and encouragement to open themselves up mentally and emotionally to the experience of motherhood and fatherhood. It is a service orientated towards socialisation between family groups. It does this by working alongside parents to think together about paying attention to the adult–child relationship and, thus, helps parents to understand their own development as parents as well as that of their child.

When a child moves into the part of Tempo Lineare for children over three years of age, a parents' association is available to continue supporting the development of the parents' ability to listen receptively and to accept a deepening responsibility for their children's emotional development. The role of the psychoanalytically trained staff member within the service involves observing the daily life of the child and parents and listening receptively. The Tempo Lineare staff member is a person whose ability to listen and observe facilitates learning about and meeting the developmental needs of the child and family.

Tempo Lineare facility for 3–6-year-olds

Tempo Lineare 3–6 years is the continuation of the 0–3 years Tempo Lineare project. This project opened in 2003 as a result of the parents' enthusiasm for continuing with the work of the 0–3's Tempo Lineare project. The facility is similar to a house, as described above. An area of the house is fitted out as a workshop, where the children have access to an immense range of materials, including those for play, art, woodwork, and cooking, and an environment with spaces sufficiently large to encourage creative expression.

This service is open to two class-groups, each comprising fourteen children, from Monday to Friday, from 8.00 to 14.00, including lunch. (It is customary that many Italian children do not attend school beyond lunchtime.) The project promotes a "different" way of being for the children because they are enabled gradually to be apart from their parents for a large portion of time. However, the project considers both the needs of the children and their emotional development and the desire of their parents to be welcomed, listened to, and understood. Once a month, the parents meet in a group with a Tempo Lineare facilitator to discuss the emotional development of their children and their relationships with them.

Although physically adjacent to one another, the two Tempo Lineare facilities are very different: in the 0–3 years facility, there are areas for the children and the parents to be together as well as a space for the parents' group, whereas in the 3–6 years service, there is a space where the older children can be together in a large group of twenty-six, or in smaller groups, or in a space alone. There is also a separate space for the parents. In both services, however, there is a space where the child can develop his desire to know himself and his group of peers and to develop his growth potential.

Through providing a service for a longer period, from 0–6 years, the learning path can continue, children can experience true and meaningful, more lasting relationships, and they use their resources without giving up the group's potential for assisting their growth and development. The aim of providing this longer duration service for the children is to help them achieve inner stability and optimism in relationships and to promote access to richer social interactions between children and adults. The lengthier group experience is designed to give greater depth to the emotional experience of meeting the other, which, in turn, fosters vitality and emotional health, inducing change that leads to the creation of a better world for children and families.

All this is also designed to facilitate the children's acquisition of knowledge and the development of their capabilities. In addition, the school programme works to stimulate their curiosity, creativity, and intellectual interest. The children's experience within Tempo Lineare favours introspection as well as the introjection of positive experiences that are essential elements not only of emotional development, but also of mental life and learning. The project recognises and interprets the complexity of the children's life experiences in such a way as to perform the function of filtering, enriching, and giving emotional meaning to the children's experiences with learning and with each other and the adults relating to them. The project involves the parents in the life of the school.

As in the school for younger children, the educational model offered is always that of "participant observation", according to the Tavistock parent–child observation model. "Participant observation" is used to monitor the child's development and the parent–child interaction, and, as such, it is the essential instrument for verifying the validity of the Tempo Lineare educational project. The observation work forms the basis of the training of teachers. It helps the teachers to build a working model useful for the staff and children's groups and for the aims of the Tempo Lineare project. It is further described in Chapter Two.

Interviews with parents and the children's first contact with the school

Before a child is integrated into the Tempo Lineare project, a group meeting is held with the parents to reflect upon the transition from the Tempo Lineare 0–3 years' service to the Tempo

Lineare school for older children. This meeting with the parents enables the teachers to get to know the families of the children entrusted to them. Particular attention is paid to the way in which each child integrates into the school, and this is a central point of observation and discussion in the staff work group. The child's reception, therefore, involves discussion between children, parents, and teachers which enables the sharing of experiences of the transition to the service for older children. It is also the first moment of acquaintance between the children and some new adults in their life. The integration of the children into the new school is facilitated by the presence of some familiar teachers who have shared with the parents the children's fundamental growth stages up until three years of age. It is believed that this style of reception of the children is a very important moment, for it helps all of the parties involved—children, parents, and teachers—to get to know each other with the aim of gaining confidence in the experience that lies ahead.

Reception method

Reception takes place in the presence of the parents, with gradually increasing and personalised times of attendance. This working approach helps to increase the degree of responsiveness of all the parties involved. It also enables better observation and subsequent understanding of the needs and requirements of the children and their families. During the period of integrating the child and getting to know his/her family, it is considered important to carry out observations and video recordings of those moments. At this time, a first meeting with the parents' group, composed of new and old members, takes place to think about this new experience. Also, a discussion group is organised with the teachers to reflect on the methods of integrating the children into the already existing group of children. It is thought that paying particular attention to the children's different personalities enables the teachers to get to know the group with which they will be actively participating in co-operation with the children's families. In this way, full importance is given to the significance and value of a child's infancy and ongoing development. The child's voice represents the shared belief that the child has the right to make his voice heard in this very important transitional phase of entry into the new situation.

The children's groups

The project is made up of two different age groups, each comprising fourteen children. Each group has its own room and a workshop area in which to share some of the time in the day. Particular attention is paid to observation of the group in order to help the children to regulate their emotions thoughtfully, especially those children with interpersonal, emotional, or physical difficulties.

Recurring daily activities

The project centres its work on play activities and observation of the games of both individual children and the group, and involves games and activities that help the children in their development and growth. The two groups jointly manage a reading area, which consists of a corner used as a library where the children can freely choose their books. Each child has a personally labelled drawer containing paper, coloured pens, scissors, modelling dough, and other play equipment that he/she uses at the start of the morning. In the rooms, toys kept in boxes and on shelves are available to the children, who are also responsible for putting them back. Through playing, the children manage and share the areas of the school: they set the tables for lunch, and help the adults to clean and reorganise the room and objects within the room. Thus, they experience the school facility not simply as "cared-for children", but also as active participants holding responsibility commensurate with their developmental levels. This generally helps the children to feel capable and expert in all activities that are possible at their age.

Every day, after I describe a fairy tale or story, the children create an imaginative picture inspired by the story that they have just heard. Each child can, therefore, identify within him/herself the emotions that the story has stimulated. Each child's imaginative phantasies inspire the creation of a new story that is expressed symbolically on a large sheet of white paper.

Once a week, the children play in a group with the "school–family box". This game is used to allow me a moment of observation of the children's "work through play". Through watching the children's play, the teachers and parents understand the children's experiences of the present moment in the nursery. This method is described in greater detail in Part III, "Compassionately comprehending children playing".

The school workshop

In the workshop, the intention is to create the conditions necessary for the child to gain confidence in his communication and expressive abilities. Here, tasks consist of helping the child to express his emotions creatively. The project has two workshops:

- the linguistic and musical workshop;
- the colours and materials workshop.

Linguistic and musical workshop

Through getting to know books, fairy tales, stories told by adults, conversations, nursery rhymes, and plays on words, and through inventing stories, the children are helped to exchange linguistic meanings and usages, enabling them to acquire forms of narrative thought and, in time, to build a personal way of expressing themselves. For children aged three to six, talking to each other and to adults during the various moments of the day is a fundamental tool in the development of thought and learning. The reading corner is also considered as the conversation corner, in the sense of listening, exchanging, having a dialogue, or remaining silent. The children become very confident in talking to each other and adults through this experience. The musical workshop consists of two groups led by an external music teacher with specific expertise in facilitating musicality in the children.

Colours and materials workshop

The workshop is equipped with a single water trough and several taps designed to allow the children to use the water to mix different materials. Water is felt to be an important element in the nursery. It makes it possible for the children to play together around a washbasin and to use sponges, small and large containers, and spoons. Observation of play using water provides an in-depth view of the "oral and anal desires and phantasies" that the children have at this age. Moreover, play using water and the containers helps the children work through methods of containing their emotions. The spontaneous play with water, dough, clay, salt, paste, maize flour, and many other materials also allows the children to satisfy their exploratory needs and maximise their manipulative abilities. They work with their hands, either alone or in a group, with materials such as water, flour, sand, and wax. They also carry out culinary activities such as making bread, pizza, puddings, ice cream, fruit salad, jam, or engage in activities of organic interest such as planting seeds, and growing and caring for plants.

The colours workshop takes place in an area equipped for drawing and painting activities. Available to the children are felt tipped pens, crayons, watercolours, pastels, and poster paints. They can paint on different materials: paper, cardboard, fabric, recycled materials, outlines, glass, wood, and polystyrene. In time, the children express their curiosity, give shape to their feelings, and find increasingly creative ways of showing their thoughts intermingled with their emotions. The colour workshop area is organised by a teacher with specific expertise in illustration techniques, drawing, painting, and the visual arts in general. An artist visits the project regularly to assist in the spontaneous expressiveness of the children.

The school, the neighbourhood, and the city

Tempo Lineare is situated in an ancient house in Testaccio, a lively working-class neighbourhood in the heart of Rome. The environment outside the school is a subject of interest for the children and their parents. Outings are organised to places where it is possible to walk, run, cycle, skip, and jump. The outings are also used to observe the acquisition of co-ordination and motor skills that the children can use within the environment. Children and parents have visited the immediate neighbourhood, the local market, and other significant places in the historical centre of Rome where the project is located. Some parents accompany the children and teachers on visits to exhibitions and archaeological and botanical sites.

Space for family members

There is a space reserved for grandparents and parents who attend with the babies from birth to three years. This is a meeting space for parents and grandparents where they can play with their children and receive support from me and the nursery teachers who understand the developmental needs of young children. Parents of young children (0–3 years) are provided the opportunity to meet each other, to exchange experiences, doubts, and points of view in relation to the growth and education of their children. Parents meet, tell each other their stories, and empathise with one another. Lively, deep exchanges in a group promote the members' ability to understand, listen, and imagine. Tempo Lineare staff work collaboratively "with" as well as "for" the users. The family does not delegate all responsibilities to the nursery, but, rather, is *actively involved* in the work of the Tempo Lineare service.

Consultation area

Near the Tempo Lineare centre there is a consultation space available to families from the nearby central Rome neighbourhoods. This is a free, brief consultation service involving five meetings with parents who may request an appointment to discuss problems of infancy, or questions about the growth and development of their child, with a child psychotherapist who works within the nursery. The parents discuss topics such as the role of play in psycho-affective development, rates of growth, eating, sleep, the significance of crying, and relationships with peers and siblings.

The five meetings involve:

- a first meeting with the parents to listen to their needs;
- three observations of the child with his/her parents at different moments, to observe the child playing and the relationship with his/her father and mother;
- a final meeting to discuss with the parents the issues raised and the observations from the previous meetings with the family.

It is worth noting that the families who have requested help have maintained contact with the service by providing news about the child's development, requesting subsequent meetings, or joining the Tempo Lineare project. It is deduced from this that the consultation area constitutes a first important point of contact with families who feel the necessity to question their parental function and to share with somebody their doubts and uncertainties regarding the growth of their child.

There is also another consultation facility offered to pregnant women and their partners, in order to create sufficient mental space for the couple to consider the birth and ongoing life of the baby and the implications of becoming parents.

The reflective groups and Saturday morning seminars for both schools

There are two separate *reflective groups* that meet for two hours monthly on Saturdays at Tempo Lineare. In these groups, mothers, fathers, teachers, and psychotherapists present their observations and experiences of different aspects of child and parent intrapsychic and intrapersonal interactions. The aim of the reflective groups is to facilitate observation and communication about problematic moments with a child. The presentation of observations of a child interacting with toys or others invites the parents and teachers to be curious and to bear "not knowing" in order not to rush to preconstituted and stereotypical answers to parents' searching questions about problematic areas. The task of the staff member is not simply to give instructions, advice, and solutions, but to favour parental introspection and the interchange of thoughts and emotions that exist within the relationship between the parents.

Thinking together within a group, accompanied by a trained and accessible staff member, allows parents to bear the anxieties that they feel, and, above all, to share with the group their experiences of interaction with their children. Most importantly, the work in the parents' group enables the parents to question themselves about what happens in their relationships with their children. In this way, the reflective group encourages the parents to develop further thoughts about their parental functions. The group process itself is also intended to develop a trusting space in which the parents can develop confidence in the child's developmental process as well as trust in one another and the Tempo Lineare staff. Developing trust within the group takes time and evolves through regular meetings with each other and staff. The process of sharing a sequential, detailed observation of a child's interaction with another and one's emotional responses to it can be imagined as a long journey that is just in the process of beginning in the parents' reflective groups and, one hopes, will continue throughout the child's development within the family.

In some years, instead, there have been a series of talks for the large group on a certain psychological topic, followed by the mothers and fathers, teachers and psychotherapists dividing into groups of eight to read out detailed written observations of the nursery age children interacting with one another or the teachers. Through working together in these observation seminars, parents and teachers have enhanced their capacities to compassionately comprehend the babies and young children.

The Tempo Lineare Conference for the community

The teachers, parents, and psychotherapists create film and written presentations for the yearly Tempo Lineare Conference which is attended by parents, teachers, and professionals from Rome and other parts of Italy. The children's drawings have been published in a Tempo Lineare book of fairy tales. Some films of the nursery have been presented to other audiences, and this book contains presentations by parents and colleagues for some of the parents' monthly Saturday Seminars and yearly Tempo Lineare Conference for Parents and Professionals in Rome.

Characteristics of families participating in the Tempo Lineare trialogue service

Our experience over the years has brought to light a series of issues that have become important for observation. These include pregnancy, childbirth, breast-feeding, weaning, physical separation from the parents, playing with other children, language development, and the birth of a new baby. Anxieties surrounding these nodal points of a child's life have often interfered with his emotional development. When everything goes fairly smoothly, the parents begin to feel satisfied with their roles as parents from the outset.

The majority of the families who have joined Tempo Lineare did so because they wanted to be helped in bringing up their child. There is also a significant proportion of newly adopted children who have attachment difficulties with their new family, and other children who have serious developmental and interpersonal problems. Other problems that emerge are in relation to complicated pregnancies, IVF pregnancies, and caesarean deliveries. Difficult childbirths have created feelings of exhaustion and emptiness in the mothers, caesarean births accompanied by a general anaesthetic have made mothers feel cheated, perceiving the birth of their child as having taken place outside their control and, therefore, without their involvement.

Most prominent is the high incidence of family bereavement that arises from miscarriages, abortions, still-births, and the deaths of grandparents and other family members. The whole relationship between the parents and the baby, from conception onwards, is noted in considering these issues. This makes it possible to reflect with more depth upon the particular phase in the child's development.

There are some very young, unemployed single parents and some young parents might still be studying; however, the majority of the parents work and many have roles of considerable responsibility. Most frequently, parents have discovered that it has been important for them to choose jobs that allow a certain flexibility to cope with raising very young children. These are generally part-time jobs or self-employed professions. There are many parents with upper to middle level occupations, not only in financial terms, but also culturally (journalists, architects, teachers, university lecturers, politicians, directors, and actors). Some, but certainly not all, of the parents' professions involve and encourage greater openness, creativity, and curiosity. Most important, though, is the fact that the group of parents is a very mixed one, for alongside one another are single and divorced parents, aged 18–45, from different cultures and educational and economic backgrounds.

Parents' evaluations of their participation in Tempo Lineare

Tempo Lineare is a pilot project of Rome's First Township. Feedback was recently obtained regarding the degree of satisfaction parents past and present have felt in participating in the Tempo Lineare project. About 120 parents, mothers and fathers, who had or still have one or more children attending the schools, either Tempo Lineare 0–3 (23%) or Tempo Lineare 3–6 (13%), or both (64%), completed a written questionnaire.

One child out of six had some certified medical problems, physical disabilities (8% of the total), psychological (25%), or neurological problems (17%), while half of them were adopted children. For the parents of this group, Tempo Lineare was considered to have helped them very much (75%) or enough (25%) in the task of supporting their children, and almost all of the parents agreed with the project's choice of not separating disadvantaged children from the children without defined difficulties.

All the parents showed a good level of satisfaction (60–90%) with how Tempo Lineare supports children's growth by means of selecting a choice of toys and games aimed to work out any child's difficulty and through fostering both parents' discussion groups and children's discussion groups.

Although more than half the parents found it hard (63%) or very hard (12%) to comply with the demand of attending school with their children for several days a week, 84% of them were glad to have spent this time with their children. The parents felt they had developed a high level of emotional and intuitive ability to observe and understand their children (67%), and great (63%) or sufficient (33%) improvement in their mutual relationships. Only 4% of the parents felt they received insufficient help.

Families, too, found it easier to weave relationship and create bonds between newly born or newly adopted children (40% very much, and 32% enough). There were 8% who answered "little" or "not at all".

Everybody felt that their experience of collaborating with Tempo Lineare greatly enabled their children to make friends among peers and also to achieve good results at school after leaving Tempo Lineare (20% did not answer this last question, as their children had not yet gone to any other school).

Finally, most parents think that the Tempo Lineare project reached a high level of academic and social skills training (68% said "very high", 26% said "high"), that the teachers and staff are good or very good (93%) and that schoolrooms, facilities, and toys are of superior (66%) or average (26%) quality, while there were some complaints regarding the public authorities who were appointed to support the project because only 11% experienced them as helpful.

We can, therefore, claim that Tempo Lineare is an important and useful resource in actively supporting parents and their children towards an improvement of their capacity for mutual love.

CHAPTER TWO

Listening to, and sharing, the experience of growth

Patrizia Pasquini

"The man for whom time is lineare (*tempo e lineare*) will venture towards the infinite and every time, he will leave behind what he laboriously managed to conquer . . . man knows that the world's meaning must be created through imagination, which in turn must be based on reality; therefore he will have to make a long journey and many observations, both in his inner world and outside, to be able to enjoy his brief life-span, heir to a wonderful heritage that he feels he has to leave in better condition for those who will come after him"

(Meltzer, 1983)

In this chapter, I would like to describe the work done by the Tempo Lineare project for the child and the family in its two services for children from birth to three years and from three to six. My experience is so special that I would like to share it with you. I found that people working with children in institutions, schools, and social services often feel frustrated and powerless, but also that many of them had a genuine wish to experience new ways of relating to children, parents, and colleagues. I myself have felt frustrated and powerless, but this fact never restrained my wish to discover new possibilities and to "invent" a world for children where love could facilitate health and growth, and where children and parents could grow together in a shared space. This wish, almost an intense need, to develop such a facility became apparent while observing children and parents' desires, feelings, and behaviour.

We all know that a good relationship between parents and their child facilitates the physical and psychological growth of the child. Becoming a mother or father is an experience that some women and men live through with ease and curiosity, while others live it with difficulty and anxiety. It is, in fact, perfectly normal to feel confused and uncertain when facing a significant role change from being a childless individual to becoming a mother or a father. The responses that a mother and father give to the child depend on their own personal experience as children, but also on the desire to understand the child's behaviour and the ability to identify with his feelings. To help their child develop to his fullest capacity, parents are required not only to share the love they feel for their newborn, but also to understand what they feel and what happens in the child's mind.

The emotional life of very young children and their parents can be met most cost effectively through an approach in the nursery such as the Tempo Lineare *trialogue approach*. This approach is designed to improve the quality of the emotional relationships existing within the triangular mental space created between these three bodies (Figure 2.1)

In a book titled *The Family and the School* (1985), Dowling and Osborne describe their Tavistock Clinic based research. They suggested that facilitating a trialogue collaboration between home and school is the mainstay of a successful approach in helping children develop cognitively, socially, and emotionally. The implications of their research is that it should be a requirement for nursery schools to create joint problem-solving efforts between parents, teachers, and children. In their chapter in *The Family and the School*, Dowling and Pound (1985) described a joint intervention project involving parents, teachers, and children in which nearly all the children who previously were not functioning well socially and intellectually were functioning satisfactorily. The Tempo Lineare trialogue approach described involves a similar ongoing joint commitment involving the families and Tempo Lineare staff to help children improve both the quality of their physical and emotional life and their cognitive development.

Three basic aims and methods of work within the Tempo Lineare trialogue project

The first aim is to create a therapeutic milieu in which parents and teachers can observe the children's interactions with them, understand their emotional experiences when present with the children, and, through group experiences, increase their capacity to be emotionally present for the babies and children.

The second aim is to develop the parents', teachers', and children's capacities for containing their emotions, which involves observing, holding emotions, and thinking about them.

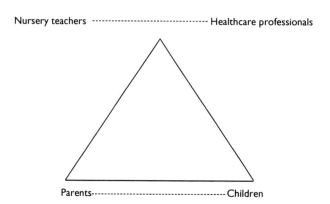

Figure 2.1.   The trialogue approach.

The third and last basic aim is to enable the children to internalise the capacities of the parents and nursery teachers in order that they can be more fully present to their own emotional experiences while creatively exploring, learning, and forming important relationships with other children and adults outside their immediate family.

The process of achieving these aims includes a request that the teachers write a daily detailed observation of the children's moment-by-moment interactions with parents, teachers, peers, and their play materials. As a qualified child psychotherapist and nursery teacher heading the nursery, I then discuss these observations. Once a month, the parents and teachers meet for three hours to study observations of the children's interactions, to look at the children's drawings, to discuss their children's emotional and intellectual development, as shown through their play and other communications, and to think about their own experiences as parents and nursery teachers of these children. It is the collaboration between parents, teachers, and other professionals that enables Tempo Lineare to function as a therapeutic containing milieu for the social and intellectual development of the babies and young children. At times, various other psychotherapists, social workers, and psychologists are involved in the discussions.

The Tempo Lineare ongoing preventative therapeutic work with children aged 0–6 was created to serve the following set of ideas:

- promoting parents' curiosity towards themselves within their relationship with their children;
- supporting harmonious growth of strong emotions;
- observing, welcoming, containing, and helping with these emotions when needed;
- working with mothers and fathers in the interactive process of encountering their child while using improvisation and adaptation to the children's needs and creativity.

Aspects of a typical nursery are coupled with helping the parents and teachers to observe, reflect upon, and support the emotional development of young children.

Early relationships of children to mothers, fathers, and families are developed within a group. This experience is crucial for children's growth. Participating in Tempo Lineare allows mothers and fathers to think about their maternity and paternity and to reach awareness of the common experience they are sharing with other parents. Solidarity arises among parents who try to express their feelings. Parents understand that emotional storms brought about as they greet a newborn can be shared. They also learn that daily life with their children is based upon recurring interactions that have enhanced meaning if they follow their sequence one after the other, moment by moment.

Stern (1985) says every child needs to eat, to be changed, to sleep, and to play. The early years in a child's life are not predictable because they are marked by a daily struggle in interactions that can become problematic for the child and the parents. In Tempo Lineare's reflective groups, parents feel free to express fears, hopes, fantasies, and memories from their own childhood. Learning about oneself and about others helps parents to succeed in their new parental role and to feel pleasure in their new identity. Sometimes, this group learning process helps parents find the right solution to specific problems. At Tempo Lineare, parents can think about their similar experience in their own unique personal situation. They can build a path of knowledge that enhances the development and growth of every child and that supports the ability to think and elaborate on emotional experiences. This task is part of the role of being a mother or a father.

As part of my working philosophy at Tempo Lineare, I use a method of welcoming, listening, observing, sharing, and signalling both a good relationship between parent and child and the problematic aspects of their relationships. In working with families, I try to foster the ability to observe and to think about everyday life. This work with families is shared within a group, which becomes a sort of sounding board for feelings and emotions that, in turn, can be further considered by the parents when they are at home. I know that speaking about welcoming and listening can create misunderstandings, as one could think of simply a friendly support for the parents and children. On the contrary, the "welcoming" I am describing here comes from the Tavistock model of psychoanalytical observation of the mother–child relationship (Bick, 1964).

Participant observation as a model for Tempo Lineare

The role of each staff member within the service is that of a nursery teacher who is a psychoanalytically trained observer of the daily life of the child and parents and a receptive listener. The role of a Tempo Lineare teacher is that of a person whose ability to listen and compassionately observe facilitates getting to know and meet the developmental needs of the child and the family. The teacher is encouraged to follow and observe rather than direct the parent–child interactions.

The Tavistock Clinic psychoanalytical "participant observation model" forms the basis of the training. This model has evolved in the UK, South America, and France, among other countries. It has been used to gain an evolutionary knowledge of the child and to follow his development attentively. Professor Didier Houzel of Caen, France has researched it and considers it as an important aspect of therapeutic work with babies at risk of autism (Houzel, 1999). The method of participant observation is to observe, to understand deeply, and to abstain from any negatively critical judgement.

Methodologically, the participant observation has elements of greater activity on the part of the observer than does the traditional observation method. The traditional observation is equivalent to listening emotionally to oneself and the family while solely observing. Thus, observation of the child and the family provides an opportunity to pick up a multiplicity of signals and communications, for the most part non-verbal, which are made comprehensible thanks to the emotional resonance that they produce within the observer. The observer's empathic attunement facilitates an understanding of the emotional dynamics that the child experiences. The function of the participant observation is to get to know and ameliorate the child's development within the parent–child relationship. It is not only the members of the nursery staff who observe, for the parents also observe and meet regularly with the staff to discuss their detailed observations.

This educational model is used to follow the baby's process of interaction and internal psychological development very closely. The understanding, linked to feeling, abstains from evaluation and judgement. Through closely observing the child, it is possible to monitor, to think about, and to facilitate the child's emotional growth in his relationships. I believe that this working model of participant observation with children and their families is a useful preventative method that can be used by staff in many types of institutions. Listening to parents, when a new baby is born, can help them to contain their normal anxieties in that particular moment. It is all about helping parents to really "see" their child and to trust in their relationship with him.

Vignettes involving the use of participant observation

I would like to introduce a number of examples of potentially helpful participant observations from my experience with children and parents in Tempo Lineare. By giving voice to a mother's powerful feelings and by describing some observations of the mother–child relationship, I will illustrate how Tempo Lineare offers parents the opportunity to overcome parental anxiety and, thereby, provide a better psychological base for the child's future development.

First vignette: Sofia

Here is the mother's account of her daughter, Sofia.

> I began to attend Tempo Lineare with Sofia towards the end of September 2003, a few weeks after her discharge from hospital. Sofia was born before I ended the sixth month of pregnancy . . . I was told that the chances that our child could survive and that she could lead a life within the boundaries of normality were ten per cent . . . When I succeed in joining her in the neonatal intensive care unit, all of a sudden I am afraid to face her. I want to approach slowly, to have an even longer time to get accustomed to what awaits me. As I see her, the shock is bad: nothing in that little being makes me think of normality or of wellbeing. A long wait has started.

> Day after day the situation is getting worse; there are many complications in the baby's physical health, much suffering and, increasingly, less hope. I feel very helpless at the sight of this small life that is passing away: our main contact is the little songs and lullabies I sing, but now my voice fails me. Then finally I try to reach her with my voice. I sing softly, for her and for me, as I lean against the side of the incubator . . .

> After two months and four days, at last Sofia succeeds in breathing by herself! Two months later she is able to leave the hospital. When Sofia is four months old, I ask myself: "Am I allowed to be happy?" We begin to attend Tempo Lineare; it is the first time I am outside home alone with her. I am worried. I drive the car while holding out my finger for her to grasp quietly. I do not know whether it is more that she needs me or that I need to be comforted by the warmth of her body. When we arrive at Tempo Lineare, it seems they have been awaiting us for a long time . . .

As is our usual way at Tempo Lineare, I attentively observe Sofia and her mother as they come into the group. Here is my observation.

> Mother and Sofia, aged four months.

> Mother and child enter for the first time the room dedicated to the babies' group. Sofia is sleeping in her mother's arms. Her body is closely adhering to her mother's breast and side. After a few minutes,

the baby awakens. Her mother smiles and starts to talk to her in a low voice, describing the room and the objects she sees. Then she puts the baby in a circular cloth basket. Mother sits next to her while observing her attentively. Sofia remains still, keeping her eyelids half-closed, but she turns her face towards the mother. After a while, the mother tells me that she would like to set up such a warm and cosy room in her house too. Then she looks at the baby and says that she has to take the child to the doctor in the afternoon for a brain scan. She is silent for a while, before she mentions that she is not worried about the visit. Mother becomes silent once again. Meanwhile, other mothers with their babies have entered the room. After a while, Sofia starts crying softly, catching her mother's attention. Mother takes her in her arms and offers her breast. Sofia grabs the nipple with her mouth and starts sucking. While she's sucking at the breast, her mother talks to her in a low voice, caressing her all the time.

From this first meeting, I noted that the mother uses her voice to keep in touch with the baby, trying to reach her, without being afraid and without retreating or defending herself. This allows the mother to be in touch with her child at a deep level, making room for welcoming the baby and listening to her. The mother's ability to contain the baby's chaotic experience seemed to help the baby to cope with her distressed emotional states. Indeed, when a pre-term baby is born, she has very anxiety-provoking emotional and physical experiences and she finds herself in the presence of a mother and a father who are very distressed by their own experiences with the baby.

My presence as an attentive observer of the mother–baby relationship and the couple's experience in a Tempo Lineare group represents a helpful "emotional holder" for the family. Such "emotional holding through observation" allowed us to follow the first months of Sofia's frail life while helping the parental couple to keep alive their trust in her growth.

Here is a subsequent observation of the mother–child couple after they had been in the Tempo Lineare group for parents and babies for a few months.

Mother and her baby Sofia, aged six months:

Sofia sits in the specially established babies' crawling path. Her mother is behind her. The child touches various objects in the path. She is particularly attracted by small plastic fish floating in water bubbles embedded in a section of the path. Sofia tries to grasp the fish, initially with her hands, then with her mouth, but when she understands she cannot do this, she gives up. She grabs two soft balls the mother had previously taken from a basket and she throws one of them into the centre of the room. The ball lands close to another baby, who grabs it and throws it back to Sofia. The two children start playing together delightedly while occasionally laughing. Every time Sofia moves towards the ball, she stops, looks at her mother and smiles at her. The two mothers look at their babies playing and comment on the developments their six-month-old babies have made in the last few months.

This observation of play shows the mother's ability to create a world in which her daughter can experience herself as a feeling, thinking, and hopeful child. In this first period of this baby's life, it is crucial that parents share pleasureable experiences with her as a way of mitigating some of the difficulties and uneasiness that are part of life.

Second vignette: Flavia

Parents are emotionally able to assist their children by using more thoughtful and integrated mental and emotional functioning. For instance, a mother once asked the group of parents for help because her daughter was refusing to eat. The mother displayed a great deal of anxiety as she spoke of her daughter Flavia's eating problems. I decided to first observe Flavia, and here is the observation.

Flavia, aged one year, and her mother.

Flavia sits on a carpet, surrounded by a few baskets full of objects. She doesn't play, but starts rapidly crawling away from the mother sitting beside her. After a while, Flavia begins to look at a small boy who is playing with a spinning top. Through crawling, Flavia draws close and steals the toy from him. After taking possession of the spinning top she looks at me, then leaves it and keeps on crawling around the room. At this point I offer a second spinning top to the boy whose top Flavia has taken, but again Flavia tries to take it away from him. Flavia's mother leaves the room to have a coffee. Flavia, who has been left by her mother, keeps on crawling towards some baskets of toys. While looking at me intermittently, she then begins to empty a few baskets by taking out the toys one by one.

Once the mother is back, Flavia does not change her position and her mother doesn't move nearer to her. Flavia continues to crawl without starting to play. When I invite the mother to offer breakfast to her daughter, mother hesitates, explaining that Flavia follows a strict dietary regime and that her doctor told her to stick to a precise timetable for meals.

I have thought a lot about the mother's stance and her unease at joining a convivial moment in the group. During case observations, I recall Magagna's paper (2000) explaining how children with eating disorders use different psychological processes to block out of their minds any desire for knowledge, for intimacy, and for food, which represents life itself. During these observations, I noted that mother and daughter did not look for each other's gaze; there was no constant connection between them. Flavia didn't play with her toys or mother, and neither did she seek either her mother's presence or for security with her which could be obtained through eye contact. Flavia's movements were not aimed at knowing or discovering the place, the toys, or other children. They showed her protective need to hold herself together by using her muscles in the non-stop movement of crawling (Bick, 1968).

A month after the previous observation, for the first time, Flavia's mother decided to feed her daughter at Tempo Lineare. She movingly tells me that since they came to our service Flavia appeared to be having fun and mother said she also enjoyed playing with her daughter. Her remarks convinced me that this "space for fun" between mother and child might be the beginning of a more harmonious relationship between them. Here is an observation for you to see for yourself:

Observation of mother and her daughter, Flavia, aged seven months.

Flavia plays with a basket of fruit, sharing it with another little child. Flavia's mother and the other child's mother start playing a feeding game with their daughters. The mothers and daughters spoon-feed each other; they also exchange different kinds of food that they have brought and then the mothers pretend to pour tea, which they then they drink simultaneously while laughing. At a certain point, other children with their mothers join in. The mothers talk about their experiences of being with their daughters while at the same time sitting in a circle around their children, who continue to play.

Something is changing in the mother–daughter relationship. The bond between Flavia and her mother looks more secure, but I feel they need the group to support them in strengthening their reciprocal closeness.

Third vignette: Matteo, an adopted child

Tempo Lineare often receives newly adopted children and their families who have come to realise their parenthood more fully and to find ways of emotionally accepting their children's difficulties and histories. Sometimes, social services suggest that they might find Tempo Lineare a helpful support. Here is one such family that has adopted a child.

> Observation of mother with adopted baby, Matteo, aged six months.
>
> The first time Matteo came to class, he and his mother entered the room where other children and parents were already playing. Immediately, Matteo starts playing with some toy cars. Meanwhile, his mother sits by me and tells me a brief story about Matteo. She is very worried because she fears that her son's premature birth and the trauma of being abandoned caused brain damage. While mother is talking, Matteo continues to play with cars and some wooden bricks. The group of children and adults in the room keep at some distance from Matteo and his mother. Mother moves and sits nearer to her son, and then starts playing with him. Every time she builds a tower with the wooden bricks, Matteo smiles at her. A week after this first meeting, Matteo starts crawling and playing with every available toy. Matteo is very interested in the toy kitchen: he plays a lot with it, often sharing toy kitchen utensils with the other children. His mother gradually becomes more serene as she watches Matteo play. After a few months, Matteo, at eight months, can walk around in the room, supporting himself by holding on to the furniture as he moves nearer to the toys he wants. His mother remains seated at some distance, watching her son playing.

During my observations, I found that once the mother managed to share her feelings with me and lend some thought to her anxiety about the adoption and birth trauma, her anxiety lessened. She was then able to empathise more with Matteo and he felt more supported. As mother became more confident about Matteo's growth as a person, Matteo relinquished his crawling and found the strength to walk while holding on to the furniture. I was surprised, because I had noted that Matteo might not be able to walk because he suffers from some problem with his feet.

Fourth vignette: Rosa

Sometimes, a child expresses his rage towards the parents or other children by hurting another child. As a result, I am confronted with the issue of how to deal with aggressiveness in a group of toddlers and parents. The way one child, Rosa, used to hit her classmates was similar to many other previous situations in the nursery. Here is an example.

> Observation of Rosa, aged seventeen months.
>
> Rosa sits on a carpet: she is trying to open a toy fish containing smaller fish. It takes her a long time to understand how to open it, but she doesn't give up. When she finally opens the container and finds the smaller fish inside, she is happy. After a while, another child comes close to her and tries to take the little fish away from her. Rosa hits him and scratches his face before I can reach her and stop her from doing so.

For about four months, every time a child got close to her, Rosa reacted aggressively. Rosa's behaviour caused confusion and rage in the parents' group. The nursery teachers and I were in great distress. It was hard for us to contain and transform Rosa's aggressiveness, and it was equally hard to contain the feelings she was arousing in the adults and other young children. Rosa's mother was also distressed and embarrassed. What had happened to Rosa to make her aggressive and what was currently happening in her life? Rosa, seventeen months old, was being weaned and weaning made her feel angry and frustrated. It looked as if she was both punishing and obtaining punishment from the adults.

Noticing that Rosa had a special interest in objects containing other objects, I was reminded that children are often very interested in their mothers' bodies. Those bodies, in their fantasies, could contain other children. She was punishing mother for weaning her as well as looking for punishment to help her contain her aggression and anxieties. Rosa was working through her weaning from the breast; I thought that probably her aggressiveness to other children was, in fact, meant for her mother. The question remained: how could we transform and contain this situation in which other children were being hurt and Rosa's anger remained unmitigated. I tried to talk to mother and support her in accepting that her daughter might feel aggressive towards her. Mother found the idea of her child being at all aggressive difficult to accept, despite what she was seeing in the nursery. I also tried to contain other parents' rage by listening to them and thinking about how to resolve the problem. The mother, the parents' group, and I focused our attention more fully on Rosa. This helped her to feel more contained and allowed her to start a new play theme: every time she came to Tempo Lineare, Rosa played with a teddy bear. She hugged it, she took it around the room with her, she placed it next to her while she had breakfast and later while she played with her other toys. During these activities, Rosa often kissed the teddy all over its body.

Rosa's story is one of receiving thoughtful adult attentiveness and, thus, moving from aggressive to affectionate states of mind. Her story enables us to think about the feelings evoked in children when they make efforts to negotiate separation from their mothers. These experiences of anger and anxiety are normal for young children separating from parents. When the teachers and parents discover and accept the feelings of hurt, anger, and anxiety, and other feelings present in the children's communications, the children can progress through emotionally fraught but important developmental steps. I would like to point out that most children attending Tempo Lineare's 0–3 service are emotionally ready to cope with separation from their parents when they are gradually encouraged to face it. They are not exceedingly dependent on their external parents because they have begun establishing secure internal parents. Tempo Lineare's loving care and time devoted to the child, as well as his internalised good relationship with the mother and the father, mitigates the sense of loss of the primary objects of love, the parents. Children know that their parents will help them get to know and to deal with the new environment. They trust that they can signal for help if needed when they face change and separation. In Tempo Lineare, children from three to six years confirmed that it was important and necessary for young children to develop in their parents' presence during the period between zero and three years. In order to confidently exist in Tempo Lineare's 3–6 unit, the children needed to have internalised thoughtful, emotionally containing parents in their earlier years.

In presenting the vignettes above, I am suggesting that good results in the children's development can occur if we adhere to the following principles.

● The emotional life of a child presents itself spontaneously and it is sufficient to observe it. The chance to observe a child alone and with others allows us to understand the meaning of his growth and to live the experience of welcoming developmental changes. It is necessary to observe with an open mind and allow a degree of uncertainty to accompany curiosity about the meaning of a child's communication.

● It is essential to pay attention to the child's evolutionary development in order to promote potential for growth in each single child. Each child's potential is expressed differently within a group of fourteen children in a three-year age range. The opportunity to place a child with both younger and older children helps each one of them to think about where they come from and where they are going, and it allows the child to accept the richness of developmental and personality differences.

It is useful to support integration of problematic children within groups. Some schools choose to have specialist teachers, the "learning support teachers", who are involved with problematic children. In Tempo Lineare, children with problems or handicaps are integrated without "support teachers"; they are helped and supported within the group, together with the other children and their parents, keeping in mind each child's particular needs. "Learning support" is a notion that should be applied to every child, and teachers should be helped to work effectively by assigning to each teacher *only* the number of children who can be assisted to develop. No more children should be assigned to a teacher than she can manage to help. Colleagues and parents can be invited to help the teachers in everyday school activities. There is a mutual gain for all children and parents by including substantial parent participation in the Tempo Lineare programme that integrates problematic or learning disabled children.

The aim of this book and chapter is not to describe all the details of the specific learning programme of Tempo Lineare; instead, the aim is to understand psychological aspects of the groups and individuals within Tempo Lineare as a means of fostering development. I shall conclude by presenting my observation of a group of Tempo Lineare children, aged three to six, spontaneously playing just a few days after the start of the new school year.

Fifth vignette: a 3–6-year-old group in Tempo Lineare

A group of children is playing with plastic dinosaur toys. They build fences and enact scenes in which they fight and then set up ambushes and eat smaller animals. Many younger children participate in this game. I wonder why they have been repeating this game every day this week since school commenced on the first day in September. While I am observing, a child comes up to me and asks in a quiet voice if the new younger children, who had just joined the older group of children, will stay in the school forever.

This clarified the meaning of the children's play! I recalled how one child had painful stomach ache when the new younger children first came to school. Then I said to this anxious child that he had to remind himself that he used to be small child. He replied that all those young children were not able to play with animals as well as they, the older ones. I replied that maybe he was right, but that he could try to help them be altogether; I added that I understood his worry, because it was as if twelve new brothers and sisters had joined the school. The little boy returned to his game and I resumed observing the older children playing. At this point, I noted that they had put inside a fenced space a calf, a rabbit, a turtle, and a squirrel. Then they attacked these vulnerable animals with savage lions, tigers, and crocodiles. They kept repeating this savage attack. To my surprise, when I looked over to the group of new younger children, I found that in this new school group the younger children and older children had spontaneously divided themselves into separate groups and the younger children had organised an identical type of aggressively attacking game!

I searched for the meaning of these games the children have been spontaneously playing regularly during the first week of the school year. It seems that when the new set of classmates is created, the older children appear to show confusion, anger, and anxiety. In this first week, it seems to me that, rather than being a containing space for their feelings and thoughts, the school had become "a suffocating box" to the children of all ages. I also noticed that the older children used symbolic plays that dramatised their emotions rather than actually attacking the younger newcomers to the group. It seemed important to remember that children had returned to school after a long holiday, that they were separated from their parents again, and that they had found new teachers and twelve new children, who could feel like younger rival siblings, at their school.

I choose a fairy tale daily for the children, but, during this time particularly, I chose a fairy tale to deal with the children's budding emotions. On the morning of this particular observation, I chose to tell them the story of "The Ugly Duckling", because it describes a baby swan chased off by everyone. As always, following the storytelling, all the children make a drawing of the story. The plight of the ugly ducking led them to demonstrate and talk about how they felt about exclusion. Each of them talked about an episode in which he or she was very angry and wanted to exclude somebody, for instance wanted his mother, or a brother or a sister, to go away, but some of them could also speak about how they felt when they happened to be excluded by a brother or a sister. I thought that the children, through their play, showed me an attack on the vulnerable, more infantile parts of themselves that needed protection. With a fairy tale, I could give them an "emotional container" that they could use not only for projecting into the characters, but also for thinking about their own individual emotions. By this process of "metabolising" emotional states through drawings and conversations, the children could be in touch with strong and passionate feelings and lend significance to them. Observation, followed by a suggestion to play out or to read a fairy tale, helps children slowly to transform their feelings, including negative and frightening feelings, and to feel that someone else understands and supports them with these feelings. This, in turn, helps them to build closer ties with other children in the group.

Conclusion

In this chapter, I have described the characteristics of the Tempo Lineare service and presented vignettes showing how using the *participation observation method* enables the parents and children to share emotional experiences aimed at understanding oneself and others. This is the *new level of learning* for which we are aiming. I am convinced that a good emotional experience in the Tempo Lineare setting fosters substantial developmental transformations within both the children and their parents. After our experiences together, we will never be the same. A good experience gives us the hope that change is possible. In order to have a transformational experience involving personal and intellectual growth within Tempo Lineare, we have to give ourselves space to be together and time to observe and think about our experiences.

Tempo Lineare is like a path from A to B along which the families walked. Along the way, they shared the activities and the Tempo Lineare philosophy and methods. By telling their stories, the families ended up knowing more about themselves and those they met. They learnt how to build new relationships, how to deal with their own emotions and discover their own emotional equilibrium and freedom. In doing so, they became different than they were when they first walked through the doors of Tempo Lineare.

References

Bick, E. (1964). Notes on infant observation in psychoanalytic training. *International Journal of Psychoanalysis, 45*: 558–566.

Bick, E. (1968). The experience of skin in early object relations. *International Journal of Psychoanalysis, 49*: 484–486.

Dowling, E., & Osborne, E. (1985). *The Family and the School*. London: Routledge.

Dowling, J., & Pound, A. (1985). Joint interventions with teachers, children and parents in the school setting. In: E. Dowling & E. Osborne (Eds.), *The Family and the School* (pp. 69–87). London: Routledge.

Houzel, D. (1999). Therapeutic application of infant observation in child psychiatry. *International Journal of Infant Observation, 2*: 42–53.

Magagna, J. (2000). Severe eating difficulties: attacks on life. In: M. Rustin & E. Quagliata (Eds.), *Assessment in Child Psychotherapy* (pp. 51–73). London: Duckworth.

Meltzer, D. (1983). *Dream Life.* Strathtay, Perthshire: Clunie Press.

Stern, D. (1985). *Interpersonal World of the Infant.* New York: Basic Books.

CHAPTER THREE

Nursery as therapist: understanding the "present moment" of the child

Jeanne Magagna

Introduction

When parents conceive their baby, they have many preconceptions of what this baby represents as it resides inside the womb. Then the baby is born and, in optimal conditions, the parents lovingly bestow hours of their lives to nurturing the baby and giving the baby a sense that being alive is a good experience. At the same time, the baby is filled with the frustrations of being dependent on adults to nurture him both physically and emotionally. For much of the baby's early life, he has a sense of identity as "the baby in mother's arms".

Going to nursery is a significant life event for the entire family. Parents suffer the anguish of having to find a nursery in which they and their child will feel welcomed and cared for by trustworthy teachers. Both the parents and the child suffer the anxieties of change in which the young child loses the identity of being "mother's baby" and becoming a "child out of mother's arms and in the world". Previously, the young child has expected the mother to help mediate his experiences so that they were bearable (Robertson & Robertson, 1971).

Entering the nursery and interacting with strange new adults and young children brings many challenges and, therefore, potential for growth of the child's personality. Previously, within the family setting, the young child might rely enormously on the *external parents* being present to understand his/her needs and wishes. The challenge for the child entering nursery is that the child is required to use *internalisations of the parents and siblings* as a basis for interacting with people.

The internalisation of the parents is a process occurring from infancy onwards. The young child takes in those moments of parental love and intimacy and understanding as a source of feeling good about the self. However, the internalisation of the parents is also dependent on what the child does with his possessive and dependent feelings when he is frustrated. Anger towards the parents and siblings damages the good internal parents and creates less adequate internalisations of the family members. Then moments of being pleased and satisfied in the relationships with the parents and siblings repairs the damage to the internalisations of both the parents and the siblings. These internalisations of parents and siblings form the child's internal world.

In moments of the intense challenge of entering the nursery, as well as in turbulent moments within the family, the young child might suffer night terrors and nightmares linked with both the anxieties of change and the feelings of being abandoned, forgotten about, or not sufficiently noticed and understood. When the child cries during the first parental departures from the nursery, he can experience a variety of emotions including fear, anger, and curiosity. Each child wonders: "Will I be safe here? Who will look after me? Will mother return?"

Yet, there are also statements of anger: "Why are you leaving me here?" "If you loved me, you would stay with me all the time!" "Why can't I stay in my familiar home with all my toys?" All these angry statements can be linked with protest to the external parents, but they can also be quietly and unconsciously directed to the internal parents, or a new baby still at home with the mother. When unconscious hate or anger occurs, the internalised parents and internalised siblings are damaged and contain aspects of the destructive feelings of anger and jealousy directed towards them.

It is quite usual for a young child to have a least some nightmares about "the big bad wolf" or other monster figures chasing him. This "big bad wolf monster" is often created through hateful, angry feelings and oedipal feelings of jealousy, all of these feelings being directed towards the parents. The internal parents distorted by the child's hateful feelings come back at night, in the form of "the big bad monster", to haunt the child. Incidents with bigger or older children in the nursery who have "taken a toy" or not noticed the child, or made a hurtful remark, or pushed or hit the child can also prompt a sense of insecurity and lead to nightmares of monsters.

Growth of the personality: "hardness" or regression?

Growth of the personality, through the experiences of separating from the family and spending time in the nursery, will occur only if the child feels sufficiently understood and supported as he encounters all the challenges of group life in the nursery. It is so crucial for the parents to take the child's nightmares and fears seriously. It is also important for the parents to empathically accept the child's anxiety and understand how terrifying it is to be alone in the bedroom and awaken not knowing if the nightmare is real or a dream. In the morning following a nightmare, the parents' discussion and understanding of the child's dangerous encounter with the night-monster of the bad dream can repair the damage to the internal parental figure and, hence, strengthen the child's *internal psychic equipment* to face the difficulties of daily life in the family and nursery.

Alternatively, the child can put on a brave front, seeking the novelty of the experience with new people, new toys, and new experiences. However, the "brave front" can mask all the normal anxieties of saying goodbye to one's parents, leaving one's safe space with the family at home. The "brave front" may be accompanied by "I don't need anyone at all! I don't depend on anyone! I can take care of myself! I can play by myself or I can make people do what I want them to do!" Naturally, "this brave front" can lead to a hardening of the self to the "inner child", who is having other emotional experiences linked with departure from the safe haven of home with all its known spaces and routines. The "hard brave front" can also lead to extreme *denial* of inner emotions and a lack of contact with one's inner emotional life narrated through the dream process or through spontaneous play. Extreme denial is present when a child has no memory of dreams or nightmares.

If the child does not feel sufficiently supported and understood, a hardening of "the brave front" can lead to developing a primitive omnipotent self or, in extremely anxiety provoking situations, to emotional *regression* to earlier phases of childhood, with bedwetting and frequent crying.

How does the nursery experience become a beneficial opportunity for the child's inner emotional growth and concomitant development of both friendships and intellectual curiosity? Growth of the nursery child's personality can only occur in the context of well-functioning relationships between the child, the nursery teachers, and the parents who are devoted to understanding silent communications of the inner child. I shall now describe aspects of emotional growth in the relationships between the child, the teachers, and the parents. Can you imagine the trialogue of interaction (described in Chapter Two) in which parents' relationship with the nursery teachers and parents' relationship with their child interact with nursery teachers' relationship with the child and the parents?

The Tempo Lineare trialogue approach is designed to improve the quality of the emotional relationships existing within the triangular mental space created between these three bodies (Figure 3.1).

The growth of the personality of the nursery school child

In the first instance, the nursery must be a place where the child feels contained, where he is known in depth, where he has an opportunity to become acquainted and form friendships with people, and, from their responses to him and his reception of their impingement on him, to get

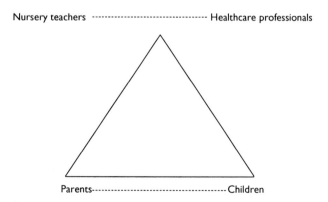

Figure 3.1. The trialogue approach.

to know himself. The child needs to be protected from his own destructiveness and from the destructiveness of others. He also requires the opportunity to develop his creative imagination through spontaneous play, to learn and to develop social skills for getting along with other people. There is also a necessity for him to learn to share in order to join others in activities. In the midst of all this, he has to learn how to manage his emotions (Harris, 1987).

The growth of the personality of the nursery school teacher

Support to do careful observations

In the first instance, the organisation of the nursery must be one in which the nursery teachers are emotionally supported with sufficient time for reflection on their relationships with each other, the nursery child's parents, and the nursery child himself. With this in mind, quite a few nurseries in Italy have had on the premises, or sent a nursery teacher to, "a nursery observation seminar" or a "work discussion seminar". These seminars originated in the Tavistock Clinic in London. In 1948, Dr John Bowlby, a prominent psychoanalyst studying the impact of separation and loss in children, invited Esther Bick, a child psychotherapist, to start the Tavistock Observational Studies Programme. This programme continues in various Italian cities under the auspices of the Centro Studi Martha Harris and internationally within other psychoanalytic, paediatric, psychology, teachers', and social workers' trainings.

Support to become emotionally receptive

Martha Harris (1987), who followed Mrs Bick as Head of the Child Psychotherapy Tavistock Training, describes the unique method of the observational process. She indicates that the value of the observation seminars, apart from learning about the fundamental development of the child's personality,

> . . . is valuable in helping participants discover the value of being, and themselves becoming, a receptive observer. One has to allow oneself to come close to the baby in order to see and retain details, and to cope with the emotional impact and struggle with a great deal of uncertainty in oneself. This is important before understandable patterns in the child's personality begin to emerge. (Harris, 1987, pp. 265–266)

Support to look at the nursery teacher's countertransference responses

By allowing himself to feel his own *countertransference*, by trying to contain it and refrain from action or interference, the observer may learn to comprehend the child's impact on the parents and the nursery school teacher herself. Infant and young child observation also enables the observer to feel the change and vulnerability evoked in him by his own aroused infantile feelings. The observer may learn how his sensitivity to the child and his needs does indeed spring from his capacity to be open to the emotional reverberations of his desires and disturbances, to learn to differentiate among different behaviours and feelings, and to respond appropriately to them. This is the method of learning about the young child, rather than being taught by academic psychology or psychoanalysis.

Allowing sufficient time for observational learning to take place

> This method of learning through observation cannot be hurried. It can be facilitated, encouraged and protected, but it cannot be created or forced. One acquires something of this feeling from observing the wise mother who has learned not to push the baby on prematurely. A wise mother knows that it is illusory to believe that, if she is good enough, she can help him to grow up without any frustration. She therefore allows him to struggle with what is within his capacity. (Harris, 1987, p. 267)

More understanding of this method of learning through the observational process can be obtained through some Tavistock publications, which include: *Closely Observed Infants* (Miller, Rustin, Rustin, & Shuttleworth, 1989); *Surviving Space* (Briggs, 2002); *Developments in Infant Observation* (Reid, 1997); *Young Child Observation* (Adamo & Rustin, 2013).

Both parents and nursery school teachers can participate as observers in the nursery. However, being purely an observer can only occur when some nursery teachers have accepted to take responsibility for the child and participate in a more active relationship with the child.

> If other adults are in fact absent, the child will not see the non-interfering observer as a neutral figure, but as a 'passive parent', who either colludes with what he is doing, or leaves him unprotected against this potential destructiveness and sense of guilt. (Adamo & Rustin, 2013, p. 6)

Without the presence of an *active* nursery teacher, the observer must relinquish her role and accept the child's need for an adult to set limits and participate in some shared activities, while at the same time understanding him.

Being an observer implies that the person watches unobtrusively, respects the child's activities, and leaves the play free to evolve on its own terms because, as Isaacs explained, "play has the greatest value for the young child when it is really free and his own" (Isaacs, 1971, p. 133). "The child can identify with the observer and can find support for his/her own curiosity in seeing the observer's attentive interest in the realm of feelings and intimate relationships" (Adamo & Rustin, 2013, p. 15) The observer can be associated with an image of a friendly adult who can allow the child's exploration of crucial issues through play. However, the observer can also become a recipient of projections of the wish to voyeuristically intrude, to steal glances at people in their private spaces, to punish, as the severe superego does. When the observer is the recipient of such projections, the observer becomes a threatening figure from whom one wishes to escape. "'I want to become a ghost, so you will have nothing to look at!' exclaimed a three-year-old to her observer" (Adamo & Rustin, 2013, p. 16).

Continual support to make observations only of interaction, rather than
of a child's behaviour as though it exists outside the realm of the group

If nursery teachers take the observational method seriously, they will begin to describe situations with children in the nursery in the form of particular moments of interaction between the child, the other children, the nursery teacher, and the parents. There will be no discussions of "Maria did this" or "Gianni did that". There will be no discussion of incidents with only one child described. Instead, a sequence of interactions between a child and others, including the nursery teachers and parents in interaction with him, will be depicted. This can then spur the nursery teachers' group to initiate a thoughtful discussion of the meaning of an interaction between the child and significant others with whom he has been interacting at that present moment.

Example

> "Gianni is listless, doesn't play with anything." This statement is enlarged upon by nursery teachers giving pictures of interaction between Gianni and others. They discover that Gianni is often listless when his mother, an older child, or a teacher does something for him. For example, mother takes some train cars and tracks, shows Gianni where to place them, and attracts his attention so he watches her move the train around on the tracks. What is evident is that Gianni loses interest completely when anyone tries to control what he does. He can play only when someone follows the sequence of his play.

The institution protecting the individual boundaries of the nursery teacher by working on the projections into the nursery teachers

In her paper, "The institution as therapist: hazards and hope", Menzies Lyth (1989) describes the way in which institutions, such as the nursery, have a task to promote psychosocial development of both the nursery staff and the young children. The nursery teachers require a secure, close, supportive group in which they can hold their sense of self and their empathy for the children as they reflect on the effects of the children's, parents', and other nursery teachers' projections. The nursery teachers also need to have a high degree of honesty with one another to confront together the projective systems and rescue each other when the nursery teacher's self is being overwhelmed by various projections. Without an emotionally supportive, reflective group, the nursery teachers run the risk of being too distressed and projecting feelings of incompetence on to the parents, or acting out with the children as a defence against the distress.

Three dilemmas that might engender acting out by the nursery teachers

Three of the many particular relationships that prompt nursery teachers to act out are those with the *deprived child*, the *shy child*, and the *more aggressive child*. The deprived child might project into the nursery teacher an *idealised mother* figure, thereby tempting the nursery teacher to act on the projections and assume the role of an idealised mother who attempts to replace the child's actual mother. In such a situation, the teacher may provide no adequate limits to the child's relationship with her. When, instead of supporting the parents to understand and nurture their child, the nursery teacher *acts out*, becoming the idealised mother with the child, conflict and jealousy between the nursery teacher and the parents arise. In this confusing situation, the nursery child tends to split his feelings and behave more badly with the parents and more lovingly towards the teacher, thus making it more difficult in his relationships with the family.

Similarly, in the case of the shy child, the nursery teacher might be over-solicitous rather than trying to understand the genuine nature of the child's shyness. Shyness can often be contributed to by the child's not having the capacity to acknowledge his aggression and integrate it into his personality. In such a child, the aggression is projected into internal and external figures who are experienced as threatening and untrustworthy. In these situations, the child tends to regress into more infantile behaviour, rather than developing his capacities for the expression of love, hate, and initiative to reach out to do things for himself, such as dress himself, go to the teacher for help, relate to his peers, and show his frustration and anger.

In the third instance, the angry, acting-out child might deal with his anger about being left in the nursery, or being left unnoticed, by evoking anger and subsequent acting out by the nursery teacher. The projection might be so compelling that the nursery teacher loses her own personal identity and acts out the primitive, harsh, projected conscience, or anger, and establishes an excessively punitive way of treating the child or children's group.

Apart from acting out, the nursery teachers' group, without a sufficiently supportive reflective space, can develop *social defences* against making deep and meaningful emotional relationships with the children and their families (Menzies, 1970). When a child *introjects* the nursery teacher's social defences, he becomes blind to his own *inner child*, loses the possibility of finding his own emotions, forfeits the possibility of developing a true sense of himself, and fails to hold on to the emotional point of his existence. The "butterfly phenomenon" (Bain & Barnett, 1986) occurs if the child experiences a predominant pattern of relationships with adults in which there is a series of discontinuities of attention. This occurs if the child's entire time in nursery is spent with a teacher who only momentarily directs attention to the individual child because she is continually being interrupted to give attention to another child. In this experience, the child's "moment of attention" is just part of a series of disconnected episodes.

For this reason, it is important for the nursery to provide something approximating normal family life. This can be achieved by assigning children to a single person, a special carer, who gives special care and attention, but also keeps the child and his family especially in mind. The attachment between the child and special carer means that the assigned nursery teacher can understand the child more deeply throughout the course of the child's stay in the nursery. This assignment of role of special carer develops more of a sense of personal responsibility in the nursery teacher. Along with the role of special carer for some particular children, the nursery teacher can be involved with groups of nursery children during some, *but not all*, of the child's time in the nursery.

Growth of the parents' personalities through a collaborative relationship

Just as the relationship between husband and wife affects the child's emotional development, so do the conscious and unconscious relationships between the nursery school teachers and the parents. The relationship between nursery teachers and parents, like every other relationship, unfortunately, can function as a receptacle into which unwanted emotions can be evacuated, or the nursery-teacher–parent relationship can function as a *container* for thinking about the true nature of the emotional life of the nursery school child. Each nursery teacher and parent might find it beneficial to set some time aside to think about the nature of their relationship with one another at different moments as they accept their shared responsibility for the nursery school child.

In "Shared unconscious and conscious perceptions in the nanny–parent interaction which affect the emotional development of the infant" (Magagna, 1997), I have described six internal images which may also form part of the relationship between the parents and the nursery school teacher. Using a vignette of 2½-year-old Sarah, who is in her third day at the nursery, I shall describe these six types of relationships which may surround her.

Shared internal image: a nursing communion

This is the ideal situation: the primary figure, Sarah's mother, is acknowledged as being particularly important and mother's relationship with Sarah is felt to be irreplaceable. Some of mother's role of cherishing, nourishing, understanding, and protecting the nursery child, Sarah, can also be undertaken by the nursery school teachers, while they acknowledge the crucial importance of Sarah's primary relationship to the mother. The shared image of "a nursing communion" is one in which both the mother and the nursery teacher give emotional meaning to Sarah's feelings in relation to her mother departing and returning; however, both the nursery teacher and mother also both give emotional meaning to Sarah's variety of feelings about greeting the nursery teacher and nursery school children and being with and saying goodbye to the nursery teacher and nursery children at the end of the period of nursery.

Shared internal image: undifferentiated care-givers providing relief

The nursery teacher provides Sarah with relief from her distress in separating from mother by holding Sarah. However, there is an absence of acknowledgement of separation and loss of her mother, who is so important to Sarah. There seems to be little notion of how important Sarah's relationship with her mother is when mother leaves and little acknowledgement of how important the nursery teacher is when Sarah goes home. It is as though Sarah should be happy to be with "a care-giver" rather than have unique relationships with each of her particular care-givers, her mother and her nursery teacher.

Shared internal image: placatory care-giver

The efficient nursery teacher is oblivious to the specific meaning of Sarah's emotions. Sarah's pains are met in the most expedient way, by distracting her with a book or toy and ignoring her pain. Sarah is given the illusion that her needs are being considered, but in fact she is simply being placated. The nursery teacher and/or mother are emotionally distant in relation to any excruciating, intense emotional experiences, of both mother in parting and Sarah in saying goodbye to her mother or her nursery teacher or friends.

Shared internal image: blessed or blamed care-giver

Both mother and the nursery teacher feel each of them should immediately gratify Sarah's needs. It is hard for them to avoid feeling that "the other" is a bad, unkind, care-giving figure, guilty of insensitivity or neglect and, therefore, to be blamed. The concept of developing a capacity to experience, tolerate, and understand Sarah's emotional discomfort does not exist. Idealisation of the "comfort of milk" and blaming of the other care-giver is a replacement for *containment*, which is feared because it involves too much psychic pain.

Shared internal image: coupling cruel to the child

Being aware that Sarah is jealous when the teacher and her mother speak briefly together, just as she is jealous when her mother and father are together, the teacher and mother develop a shared view that liaising and discussing, as a form of handing over information about Sarah, should not occur. It is felt that collaborative discussions between nursery teacher and mother should not occur because Sarah feels it would be uncomfortable and unkind to her to see mother and her teacher conversing.

Shared internal image: the supportive couple

The nursery teacher and the parental figure feel they should liaise, should be allowed to have a few minutes together to work together to "hold in mind" Sarah's infantile needs, her hurt, anger, and fear upon separating from mother, and to think about other emotional issues which might be affecting her. In particular, not only the parental couple, but also the couple comprising parents and nursery teacher feel they have the right and need to talk about and co-operate in helping Sarah with her feelings about being in the nursery away from her family and developing some security in her peer group in the nursery. Even though Sarah is simultaneously experiencing frustration at being left out, she is able to maintain an experience of her parents both emotionally linked in a positive way with the nursery teacher and, at the same time, lovingly concerned about Sarah's wellbeing.

Spontaneous play as an expression of child's relationship to the "institution as therapist"

The nursery school not only has the task of bearing the emotions of the children and thinking about the meaning of the children's, parents', and other staff's interactions, but also has the task of offering the nursery teachers as good models for identification for the children. Through *introjecting* the nursery teachers' capacities for feeling, thinking about feelings, and behaving, the nursery children will be enabled to mature and discover greater personal strength, confidence, and sensitivity.

The matrix of the nursery consists of the web of mental processes existing at any one moment in the life of the nursery (Lawrence, 2003). Observing the free play of the nursery children will establish not only the nature of their personal conflicts and desires, but also will give a picture of how, at that particular moment of spontaneous play, the nursery school institution is functioning as a therapist to the child and being perceived by the child's unconscious. Themes in an individual child's spontaneous play and in the spontaneous play of the group of children in the nursery on a particular day, will elucidate "the present moment" (Stern, 2004) of the child's emotional relationship with the nursery group. The child's spontaneous play offers a potential space, neither inside the world of dreams nor completely outside in the world of the nursery.

The child's spontaneous play can be observed by the nursery school teachers and freely associated to and reflected upon to understand the matrix of emotional–mental processes existing within the nursery. *Free association* to the children's spontaneous play can put the nursery teachers in contact with something unknown that concerns both the young children and the nursery teachers. Thinking about their free associations to the children's spontaneous play can help the nursery teachers get to know more deeply the nature and functioning of the nursery community consisting of the parents, nursery teachers, and children.

Here are some spontaneous play activities which can be freely associated to and thought about by nursery teachers:

Example one: Kirsty, three years, eight months

> Kirsty is holding a baby doll. She moves over to the Chinese take away table and throws down the doll. She picks up the chopsticks and throws them deliberately onto the floor. Then she leans over the table and pushes all the plastic vegetables and utensils off the table. Kirsty then picks up the baby doll and runs off. One of the parents picks up all the pushed over items herself. (Whyte, 2003, p. 135)

Kirsty is able to feel that the nursery is a safe enough place into which she can evacuate her distress. She is thrusting out, into the nursery, her experience of being left "in pieces", feeling herself unheld. So, Kirsty is using *projective identification* to put out into the nursery community her sense of being dropped. The nursery teachers' task is to put this behaviour into the context of "the present moment" of Kirsty's life in the nursery, and this means thinking of what this spontaneous play means in terms of Kirsty's current interactions with parents, teachers, and peers.

As the observer reflected, she became aware that not only was Kirsty not evoking any attention from the nursery teachers, but also Kirsty had lost her best friend, Teri, with whom she had previously spent most of her time playing. Her best friend had just stopped attending the nursery and Kirsty did not know how to put herself back into the nursery group. She expressed her "feeling dropped by her friend" by dropping everything, including the doll on the floor . . . and then she ran away with the doll, trying to preserve some good sense of her self emptied of the unwelcome feelings of rejection. When Kirsty left the nursery and lost her second-best friend, Megan, Kirsty's mother invited Megan over to play on a regular basis. In this situation, the importance of three-and-a-half-year-old Kirsty's developing friendships was understood. Of further importance is that Kirsty now was able to have a continuity of relationships outside the family.

The importance of the nursery as a space in which four-year-old boys and girls can collectively create their own *spontaneous dramas of life* is shown in this vignette:

Example two: Paul, Stephen, Fergus, Daniel, Adam, and Angela, aged four

> Paul, Stephen and Fergus are developing their game in the upper floor of a play firehouse with a pole descending to a lower part of the house.

Angela, Daniel and Adam are talking of marriage. Angela soon emerges dressed in lace and sequins and heads for the firehouse.

Paul says, 'And when the bells go we have to slide down the pole.' Angela responds: 'But don't land on my baby will you, else I'll be cross . . .' . . . Adam, Daniel and Angela now play 'babies' with Adam curling up in a ball on the cushion as though he is a baby. Angela is speaking softly to him. Paul slides down the fireman's pole and Angela says: 'You're not fighting in our house!' Paul responds, 'No, we are firefighters but we don't fight. We're coming to the rescue.' (Bridge & Miles, 1996, pp. 35–36)

Nursery teachers' task is to freely associate to this spontaneous play and think about it as a reflection of the unconscious emotional issues that permeate the relationships within the nursery at that moment in time. Daily observations of this same set of characters in the firehouse drama reveal that the drama changes its form day by day. On some days a nurturing protective function reflecting containment in the nursery is depicted.

At another moment, when the children have been left alone for too long, there is a fight for leadership and pretend play to hurt the baby and then have the play space filled with firemen monsters scaring people (Bridge & Miles, 1996, pp. 35–36). These are the reflections of the group drama of the destructive feelings that emerge towards the children who, at this moment in time, are receiving more of the nursery teachers' care-giving.

However, now there is clearly a group of young children playing co-operatively to elaborate some of their shared emotional issues of the moment. These vignettes illustrate how helpful it is to free someone to observe the details of nursery school interactions.

Conclusion

The position a child takes up in his first peer group at nursery is influenced by family relationships. If the parents could stand the stress of looking after a demanding and dependent infant, enjoyed conversations with him, and loved him most of the time (hate is allowed, probably even necessary, as long as it does not overwhelm love), then the child goes to nursery prepared to trust others, to be curious, be generous, able to share and enjoy things with his peers, make friends, stand up for himself when he felt unfairly treated, and, later, to stand up for others (Kraemer, 2000, p. 117).

If all goes well between the nursery teachers, the parents, and the child in the nursery, the nursery becomes for the child "a home away from home". It becomes a place he knows well, a place where he makes friends, and a place in which he feels he is taken care of by kind and thoughtful adults. The nursery school experience is a crucial foundation for the child's sense of being "his own person", with a separate identity as "a person outside of the family", finding his way in a nursery group and, subsequently, the larger community of a school. It is for this reason that everyone always asks, "What happened when your child went to nursery?"

References

Adamo, S. M. G., & Rustin, M. (2013). *Young Child Observation*. London: Karnac.

Bain, A., & Barnett, L. (1986). *The Design of a Day Care System in a Nursery Setting for Children under Five*. Occasional Paper No. 8. London: The Tavistock Institute of Human Relations.

Bridge, G., & Miles, G. (1996). *On the Outside Looking In*. London: Central Council for Education and Training in Social Work.

Briggs, A. (2002). *Surviving Space*. London: Karnac.

Harris, M. (1987). The Tavistock training and philosophy. In: M. Harris Williams (Ed.), *The Collected Papers of Martha Harris and Esther Bick* (pp. 259–283). Strathtay, Perthshire: Clunie Press.

Isaacs, S. (1971). *The Nursery Years. The Mind of the Child from Birth to Six Years*. London: Routledge.

Kraemer, S. (2000). Politics in the nursery. In: W. Wheeler (Ed.), *The Political Subject* (pp. 114–120). London: Lawrence & Wishart.

Lawrence, W. G. (2003). *Experiences in Social Dreaming*. London: Karnac.

Magagna, J. (1997). Shared unconscious and conscious perceptions in the nanny–parent interaction which affect the emotional development of the infant. In: S. Reid (Ed.), *Developments in Infant Observation* (pp. 33–66). London: Routledge.

Menzies, I. E. P. (1970). *The Functioning of Social Systems as a Defence against Anxiety*. Tavistock Pamphlet No. 3. London: Tavistock.

Menzies Lyth, I. (1989). The institution as therapist: hazards and hopes. In: R. Szur & S. Miller, (Eds.), *Extending Horizons* (pp. 423–439). London: Karnac, 1991.

Miller, L., Rustin, M. E., Rustin, M. J., & Shuttleworth, J. (Eds.) (1989). *Closely Observed Infants:* London: Duckworth.

Reid, S. (Ed.) (1997). *Developments in Infant Observation*. London: Routledge.

Robertson, J., & Robertson, J. (1971). *Young Children in Brief Separation*. New York: Quadrangle.

Stern, D. (2004). *The Present Moment in Psychotherapy and Everyday Life*. New York: W. W. Norton.

Whyte, C. (2003). Struggling to separate: observation of a young child in a playgroup. *International Journal of Infant Observation*, 6(2): 128–142.

CHAPTER FOUR

Weaving bonds: Tempo Lineare, a school for life

Carla Busato Barbaglio

Later in this book, you will find accounts written by the parents involved in the Tempo Lineare project. As you read them, you will discover more about the qualities and potentials of the educational experience present within Tempo Lineare. I would like to emphasise that the definition "a school for life" is not so much an idealisation of Tempo Lineare, but, rather, an attempt to illustrate the importance of the nursery experience on children's development. I shall do this by examining how the Tempo Lineare educational intervention incorporates psychoanalytic and child development theories in order to promote psychological development of the nursery age child and facilitate early detection of the child's difficulties.

The contributions in this book are about "becoming" a mother and a father or an educator and, thus, "becoming" a generator of life. In fact, in the day-to-day life of the parental couple, it is not so easy to create, to continue to nurture and to give life. By its very nature, daily life involves reacting as an adult to different external problems and difficulties and accompanying internal emotional issues while, at the same time, facilitating the child's physical, emotional, and mental growth. The parents' chapters describe the difficulties and joys of becoming mothers and fathers, but also the grievances felt during the course of their lives with respect to personal growth, needs, and anxieties in relationships. These difficulties of parents and grandparents (I myself am a grandparent of one of the children currently in Tempo Lineare) may be linked with painful and problematic experiences such as separations and pain felt by the children due to teachers' and family members' failures to understand and meet their needs. Within Tempo Lineare are families with stories of adoption that describe both the experience of the adopted child and that of the adoptive parents. These stories reveal emotional wounds that, through being observed, described, and empathically understood, can in some ways be healed. Through their stories, families talk about their transformation and their continuous endeavours to become really coupled with a real sense of family. The story of their lives is both enriched by good experiences and fraught with difficulties.

The construction inside a school of a space where it is possible to share these emotional experiences and couple them with careful and continuous analysis appears to me to develop a crucial link between the parents' own deeper emotional experiences and the parental role of understanding their child's experience. This introspective interchange between the parent's inner reality and the child's emotional reality is a requisite for every adult desiring to establish a genuine bond with a child.

Play and drawing giving expression to inner narratives

Children express all their innermost, unverbalised feelings in their play and their drawings. The drawings facilitate viewing the inner self in another, more objective way. Through their artistic representations, the children deal with perceived danger, frustration, and hostility that is so frightening that it needs to be elaborated upon and contained emotionally by the parents and teachers. The same elaboration of inner experiences happens in the Tempo Lineare service for both the younger children and the older children.

The child's method of expression may occur at levels. The reading of a story, the sharing of one's own stories, the awareness of various solutions or possibilities, foster new thoughts, stimulate intuitions and understanding, and, in so doing, make the child feel a little less alone and inadequate. Inner psychological change is made possible through this experience. This occurs because the child is given a different meaning to his sense of existing and, therefore, to his symbolic capacities for representation of his experience.

Baby's birth coupled with bereavement

I shall describe some aspects of a mother's dramatic story that might clarify my point. She describes her psychological collapse when, as soon as her baby was born, she learnt of her mother's death:

A mother's story

My son was born. Subsequently, after about two hours, I received news that my mother had died suddenly in an accident. She hadn't yet learnt of the birth of her grandson. . . . I felt lost, without my past, and for a long time I refused everything: my own happiness and that of my husband and of my son.

It was exactly as if I was watching life from behind a glass without having the possibility to get closer, to take part. I remember my husband pushing a very heavy pram for miles in the attempt to make my son sleep. He pushed the pram up and down along the sand of a beautiful beach, looking for a shadowy place where he could rest. I looked at the beach with a terrible lump in my throat. Every time I thought, 'I must go back to my husband and child, I must stay with them, I must cuddle my baby till he sleeps' but I could not do it. I began to feel increasingly unsuitable for the task.

Things did not improve in my relationship with my husband. I had the impression that my son was the cause of my problems, that he was stealing the love of my husband: I was no longer the only love for my partner. Often, I thought about how a father could feel excluded in those moments such as the breast-feeding, when there is that special bonding of hearts between mother and baby, between the feeder and the one who is fed. For myself as a mother, as for billions of fathers, that special nurturance through intimacy during breast-feeding a baby was not possible.

In the facing of my loneliness there was Tempo Lineare, and the discrete welcome of Patrizia [Pasquini, Director of Tempo Lineare]. While I was surrounded by the parents' incessant and oppressive talking, Patrizia welcomed me in silence. I knew she was very keen not only to be present for Pietro, my son, but she was eager to be present for me as well, but she said nothing. I said nothing, too, but every time I went back to her, to the service where I needed to be with Pietro, for he was a young baby. At the beginning, my time in Tempo Lineare was also not easy for other parents present with their babies. They anxiously scrutinised me. The presence of the other mothers and fathers made evident to me all that I lacked. I did not talk to anyone because I did not want anyone to talk to me, I only wanted to disappear; however, I always went there. Over time, I realised that other parents had their own problems: I was not the only one. With the help of psychotherapy, slowly things began to change. I started feeling stronger and eager to take care of my baby.

That very painful, troubled period is at the roots of my belief that, thanks to our love and comprehension and that of Tempo Lineare, my husband and I have succeeded in creating a peaceful family with deep, intimate relationships. It seems to me that much of my recovery depended on those warm and quiet rooms of the Tempo Lineare service, with all those babies and families, the loving people working there, and Patrizia, who helped me to give some meaning to my story.

I do not think this story that the mother told to the group in Tempo Lineare needs any comment; we can only be very grateful to this mother for sharing her experience. Surely, such an intimate and painful reflection can only be presented to a group of parents who have provided a sort of loving and good safe space. The possibility of sharing such a painful story demonstrates both the kind of bonds that exist between parents and teachers and the nature of the reflective work done by everyone in Tempo Lineare. Such painful stories enable one to come closer to the self and others with less fear in relation to one's own wounds and difficulties.

This mother's contribution was delivered by her to parents, educators, and related professionals attending a Saturday morning monthly observational course on the parent–child relationship. The conference sponsors were the Associatione Genitori e Amici del Tempo Lineare, an association of parents who were currently attending, or had previously attended, Tempo Lineare. This has been an very innovative project, for it has been a shared learning process involving educators, social workers, psychologists, and parents all working together in monthly child observation seminars. Her story shows how, in a good, containing space, very disrupting experiences may turn into a source of new richness for the couple, the child, and the school. Through identificatory processes with thoughtful adults in the group, everyone within the Tempo Lineare development groups may recover more or less unknown levels of self-consciousness which can foster new awareness.

Now I would like to quote from other parents' contributions to Tempo Lineare observation seminars and meetings:

Another mother's story of birth coupled with bereavement

A mother told of suddenly realising that she had never talked about a death in her family occurring almost at the same time her baby was born. She realised this only when Patrizia Pasquini said to her,

"Your son is a quiet child who has no problems in the group. However, when we close the door, he becomes worried about his mother. He does not cry because he does not want to stay in, but because he wants to know what his mother is doing, and how she is."

"Only then", the mother goes on, "did I realise that I had never told anyone about the death I had experienced . . . I cried for a very long time, but from then on I started looking with different eyes at the relationship with my son."

Also, another mother described her astonishment when she experienced her son watching her: "He was seeing me for the first time." Then, over time, she realised that "for the first time I realised that I was watching myself as a mother!"

The watching–seeing process

These two stories are touching, the more so as the most recent child development research continuously hints at the "watching–seeing process" between mother and child, especially at the beginning of the relationship. Seeing, seeing oneself and the other, gives rise to a pre-symbolic interaction which makes children store their experiences in a sort of memory defined as unconscious, *implicit memory*, that comes before the *autobiographic memory*. Seeing one another is not only a simple physical action, but a passage of thoughts, emotions, reflections. Seeing represents a contact between two minds.

Respect for young children and each other

Another mother described her painful separation from her daughter, who remained in the hospital during the first fifteen days of her life. The mother painfully noted that no one could give back those fifteen days, to her, to her daughter, to their relationship, but her pain turned into a new desire to give life to a particular sort of respect for the children which she felt Tempo Lineare fostered in her.

Respect for children seems to be absolutely normal and taken for granted. I wonder, though, are we sure we respect our children? I am increasingly convinced that there is a sort of *dissociation* between what we know about the importance of good quality relationships between parents and children, on the one hand, and, on the other, the proposals for the way we live put forward by society, culture, and the organisational life of institutions, all of which are linked with economic pressures. Respect for children is the essential feature of the educative experience at Tempo Lineare. I say this because Tempo Lineare does not involve simply leaving the nursery age children to the teachers. The parents are *always* involved, even if they leave their 3–6-year-olds in the nursery for six hours. Tempo Lineare calls into question the teachers', parents', and grandparents' own personalities and behaviour towards the children. After leaving Tempo Lineare, everyone will implement the Tempo Lineare interventions according to his own will and ability.

The final form of the relationship between the parents, teachers, and child will depend upon each person's capacity to listen to the other and upon the possibility of allowing the other to be "left to be". In other words, this means that "the other" should be helped "to become himself". Respect is related to tolerance and to recognition of the other as an independent person with a developing mind. In growing children, conflict arises from the incompatibility between the unconscious or pre-conscious child and the child as actually perceived by others.

Parental expectations and capacity to be present for the actual child

Sometimes, the care-giving figure is prevented from accepting the child's spontaneity because the care-giver has a specific "life project" or set of expectations for the child. This "life-project" for the child was elaborated in the care-giver's unconscious prior to the birth of the child. The "life-project", hence, is separate from the child's actual "capacity to become himself". The baby comes into life with a "life project" for him that has been devised without his own participation. The rigidity of a care-giver's "life project" for the child may be enriched and transformed by the experience of a school such as Tempo Lineare, which really listens to the individuality of each child. If the school functions well, it may become a welcoming and supportive structure for the development of child's individuality in the relationships with his parents.

Painful situations, such as those we have just seen, but also tiring ones where the emotional tension is unavoidably very high, could prevent each person in a relationship from seeing "the other" fully with the complexity of his needs and capacities. The birth of a son can cause a huge upheaval in the life of a mother.

One mother's self-reflections

> The first few months are really delicate for a mother upset by the impact and the change in her when she gives birth to a son. A greater risk is not to see herself, as her attention is totally devoted to the new being, to its needs and to the management of the many new inner and outer experiences. Without being aware of it, I had already begun to transmit to my son my unreliability as a mother, my difficulty in being a trustworthy parent.

In the latter part of this book, there will be more contributions by parents describing the impact of Tempo Lineare on their relationships with their child. These writings are important, not because we want to show or idealise the qualities of the school, but, rather, to stress the importance of having within the educative process a containing space where it is possible for the teachers and parents to share experiences and reflections in order to stimulate new thoughts and new ways of being in the relationships with the children and with each other.

Providing a containing space for compassionate comprehension

What is most crucial in the Tempo Lineare project is the quality of the containing space created by Patrizia Pasquini, the parents, the teachers, and the children. One of the most important features for the adults is a kind of shared mental space for thinking together and developing the group's capacity for reflecting upon relationships. The altogether necessary school rules and the didactic nature of some nursery school programmes are replaced in Tempo Lineare in part by a more intense, more intimate human effort of reflecting upon the current problematic issues in the group and individuals and a continuous observation of the emotional life of the various groups and their interfaces within the trialogue of parents, teachers, and children.

Reflection upon the present moment of an emotional experience acts as a modulating container for intense emotions and makes "rules" and "sanctions" less necessary. Winnicott (1956) says that the mother creates in her mind some space where she can comprehend and elaborate upon the anxieties and the worries of a child. This creates the possibility for his individualisation. The Tempo Lineare method of observational work is the basis of this experience of supporting the parents and all the other care-giving figures. It is important to stress that this reflective work needs to include the participation *of everyone* involved. No one, *including the children*, is excluded. One of the teachers told me how much a cleaning lady had deeply understood what was important for a good relationship with some children and how cleverly she intervened and helped in situations of emotional tension. It is for this reason that the cleaning woman's observations are also valued in the discussions.

In every child's life there are some ghosts. They are the visitors from the forgotten past of the parents, the unwanted guests at the christening, a bit like the ugly fairy in the *Sleeping Beauty* tale (Grimm & Grimm, 1823). The intruders can always come into the magic circle, making the parents and their child re-enact a scene of another time, with a different set of players. Fraiberg, Adelson, and Shapiro (1975) describe, in "Ghosts in the nursery", how some people's lives may be obsessed by ghosts of brutality, in the worst situations, or of insensibility met during their infancy. Specifically, they focus upon how crisis situations may be observed, described, and deeply understood in terms of intergenerational trauma. This serves to protect parents and children from the trans-generational transmission of the effects of trauma that have the potential to spoil developmental possibilities both in the children and in their parents' ways of interacting with them.

The importance of reflective functioning

Psychoanalytic, cognitive, developmental, and neuroscience research helps to deeply analyse the development of the mind from the very start of the mother–child relationship, which begins in the uterus, through very specific physical channels. What is important is not just the delivery from generation to generation of specific emotional and genetic characteristics of functioning. In the past twenty years, a great deal of research in the evolutionary and neurobiological field has shown that the human brain is structured by social experiences. The development of the brain, as well as its capacity to realise different modulations of emotional states, depends on the effective presence of a human environment able to establish relationships. Very sophisticated research, such as that of Fonagy and Target (1997), have shown that mothers and fathers with a highly developed reflective functioning have the capacity to have children with attachment ties twice or three times higher than average

Reflective functioning is a very important aspect of Tempo Lineare, as it becomes a sort of extended family, a transitional containing space between family and society. Reflective functioning involves having an attitude necessary to comprehend behaviour in terms of mental states, whether or not they are developmentally normal. It is a sort of interpretation, moment by moment, of an interpersonal situation allowing a mutual adjustment necessary for the reciprocity of interactions. Fonagy (2001) says that mothers who are able to show awareness of their children's mental states favour the development of this ability, enriching the child's infantile model with the actions taken by the care-giver. On the other hand, mothers who are frightened impair the child's capacity to make emotional links internally. The child might later relate to traumatic experiences in a "dissociative way". A frightening mother is a mother who sometimes looks too tired, frustrated, angry, or too bored with respect to needs, messages, and dependence expressed by the child. Such a person becomes threatening. The child's emotional relationships with parents who are calming and reassuring facilitate healthy mental states. The parental relationship and the earliest relations constitute the primary experience of the reflective function.

It makes a significant difference if the parents can talk about their own individual emotions during their conversations, showing the child the different nuances of the single emotions. The quality of the mother–child relationship is also a crucial factor in the development of symbolic thought. The ability to be empathically attuned to the child and to react to his emotional states is a guarantee of the quality and solidity of the security of his attachment. The security of the child's attachment is, in turn, a guarantee of understanding his mental states. Being securely attached is the base for *mentalization*, or reflective functioning, and, therefore, being securely attached is the best basis for the child's learning.

It is clear that reflective functioning in the child can hardly happen if the adults are not very much in touch with their own mental states, and are not on this path towards developing the capacity for mentalization. Each of us sometimes can be frustrated, tired, exhausted, bored, angry, or intolerant, but being aware of these mental states makes a great difference. Awareness always creates modifications and allows *reparation* of misunderstanding in relationships. It enables some experiences not to be detached, too far from oneself, but, rather, to become part of the knowledge of one's behaviour.

Conclusion

The aim of this chapter is to lend meaning to the title: "Weaving bonds: Tempo Lineare, a school for life". Maybe now it is easier to understand why the parents are required to make this huge effort to be present in Tempo Lineare with their children, aged one week to three years, if only for two mornings a week. It is a very demanding effort because it implies a change in the parents' habits of working and going about their daily life. In order for parents of a new baby to participate in Tempo Lineare in the first year of the baby's life, the parents acknowledge their fundamental importance to the child. This is reflected in the centrality of the child in their daily pattern of life. Winnicott (1957) describes how there is no such thing as a baby and suggests that without a mother, an infant cannot exist. He knows that we should also include the mother as part of the indissoluble couple they form. To create a living nucleus of continuous affectivity, the mother and father's love is necessary. Tempo Lineare is devised to include the parents so that this can happen. All the different growth moments between parent and child will be like dance steps with different tunes, from symbolic representation to language.

I conclude with the words of a young mother:

Entering the nursery at Tempo Lineare for the first time, I found myself in the room for the very little ones and immediately noticed a picture of the little prince and his tiny planet. It struck me as a coincidence, because I had read that book so many times. I especially remembered a sentence, so true in my opinion, about how all grown-ups were once children and yet few of them remember this experience (de Saint-Exupery, 1943). Thanks to the magical nursery room in Tempo Lineare, I learnt how to make the most of the time my son and I spent together there. It was in the nursery room, which I visited twice a week, that I found a place where my fears and anxieties could be contained. This enabled me to contain my child's own feelings. Because I realised I was not alone in this experience of becoming a mother, I found it easier to develop more confidence in myself as a mother. This was possible even though I was so very young and so lacking in expertise for the task.

References

De Saint-Exupery, A. (1943). *The Little Prince.* Boston, MA: Harcourt.

Fonagy, P. (2001). *Attachment Theory and Psychoanalysis.* London: Other Press.

Fonagy, P., & Target, M. (1997). Attachment and reflective function: their role in self-organization. *Development and Psychopathology, 9*: 679–700.

Fraiberg, S., Adelson, E., & Shapiro, V. (1975). Ghosts in the nursery. *Journal of American Academy of Child Psychiatry, 14*(3): 387–421.

Grimm, J., & Grimm, W. (1823). In: *German and Popular Stories Translated from Kinder un Hausmarchen Collected by M. M. Grimm from Oral Tradition,* E. Taylor (Trans.). London: C. Baldwyn (2011).

Winnicott, D. W. (1956). Primary maternal preoccupation. In: *Collected Papers: Through Paediatrics to Psychoanalysis* (pp. 300–305). New York: Basic Books.

Winnicott, D. W. (1957). *Mother and Child: A Primer of First Relationships.* New York: Basic Books.

PART II

HOW THE YOUNG MIND IS BUILT

Emotional and cognitive development: from chaotic experiences to experiences made "thinkable"

Patrizia Pasquini

Being a parent does not only mean having a child, it also involves a constant observation and thoughtfulness about oneself in relationship to the child and the other parent. Parenting a child in such a way allows the possibility of a mutual growth of the personality of both the parents and the child. Young child observation enabled Tempo Lineare teachers and parents to study children in the full complexity of their being. We observed and discussed a whole range of relationships between parents and children, including those involving the nursing relationship, the later feeding relationship, bedtime and sleep activities, the meaning of the child's crying in relationship to the parents, and children's play as a communication about their emotional experiences. All elements of children's emotional and social development are considered at Tempo Lineare. Observation gives extraordinary richness of meaning to the child's, parents', and teachers' experience of being together.

Bion (1962a) maintains that at birth the child already has a preconception that the mother will nurture him and that the parents will protect him. Esther Bick, who initiated the Tavistock model of infant observation in 1948, describes how normally developing children, in the earliest moments of life, initially have a need to physically adhere to the mother to feel contained. The child seems to be looking for

> ... an object, a light, a voice, a smell, or other sensual object which can hold the attention and thereby be experienced, momentarily at least, as holding the parts of the personality together. The optimal object is the nipple in the mouth, together with the holding and talking and familiar smelling mother. Material will show how this containing object is experienced concretely as a skin. (Bick, 1968, p. 115)

Indeed, at the beginning of life, the child feels great anxiety at moments of change if the mother does not physically hold him in her arms while reassuring him through compassionately thinking about what he is experiencing and talking to him. The mother has the key role of giving meaning and paying attention to the child's feelings of discomfort, helping him to integrate them with his good experiences of life. Also, Klein (1930) discusses the child's anxiety in separating from the emotionally containing presence of the mother.

She asserts that the child's first fear is one of being annihilated by the terror of death. Bion (1962b) later referred to this as "nameless dread". The child's bad experience in separating from the mother leaves the child experiencing her as bad, and this feeling is then projected in the external world, forming the *phantasy* of the *bad object*. The bad object is then felt to menace the self from the outside. Klein (1930) says that a mother who is able to bear anxiety, without being overwhelmed by it, will enable her child to feel contained. In time, she will give him back his projections in a form modified by her thinking about their meaning to the child. The child seeing that his aggressiveness and his anxiety are accepted, will gradually come to understand that someone else is able to receive his experiences of living with those dreaded aspects of life. Gradually, he will internalise a mother capable of containing both good and bad parts of his self.

Winnicott (1957) describes "primary maternal care" as a state of mind in the mother corresponding to the one in the child, which enables the latter to feel psychologically contained by her. When there is a good encounter between mother and child, the mother can identify with the child and is therefore able to be fully available to him. When there are difficulties in the mother–baby relationship, the mother feels that her sense of self and her identity as a mother are under threat. This experience of being persecuted by difficulties in the relationship prevents her from being intimately in touch with her child.

Bion (1962a) further analyses the way in which a mother is able to get in touch with the mental state of her child to support his psychological growth. He adds to the parental task of containment the task of thinking: that is, not only the ability to take care of different feelings, but also to think about them using a thoughtful and imaginative function that Bion calls "reverie". Bion leads us to realise that, from the beginning of life, one lays the foundations for the building of the apparatus to think, and shows that the mother's reverie is essential in transforming chaotic sensory experiences into thoughts suitable for a deeper understanding to occur.

Supporting parenthood

I would like to share examples of the types of my working with families to understand their children in each of the Tempo Lineare services: from 0–3 years and from 3–6 years. Using observations of children and parents, I shall illustrate the kind of support we offer in parent–teacher groups alongside the children's groups, where they play, with and without their parents, socialise for the first time, and acquire skills and knowledge. The parents come to the nursery when children are 0–3 years. They interact with their very young babies, but also they meet together as parents, without their children, to share their personal stories. The parents are able to experience deep inner changes in a parent's group that develops an ability to listen, understand, and imagine.

We find a very close connection between the parents' and the child's emotional and cognitive development. Alongside the parental couple, Tempo Lineare is a "cradle" for the child, accepting life in its complexity. Within Tempo Lineare is a group of therapeutically orientated teachers working with the parents to promote the vital relationships between the child and the parental couple. This coupling of parents and teachers working collaboratively consists of teachers who, by necessity, are emotionally available to be involved and to be sensitive to every relationship they encounter in the nursery.

Through my work in Tempo Lineare, I have learnt that it is both the child and the couple who need someone able to contain all the feelings they endure, someone who is not afraid to see chaotic situations, who is able to use reverie to understand emotional chaos and to give it a name. Everyone must co-operate if this capacity for reverie is to develop in the triadic relationships between staff, parents, and children.

Developing shared understanding of complex emotions

Here are a few experiences with children and their parents that show what it means to contain and to understand chaotic situations.

Accepting the second-born

Often, parents are surprised by the complex emotional issues which arise upon having a second child and having to create a shared space for two young children. Here is one example of this.

The parents with Lisa, five days old

When I met Lisa for the first time, she was asleep, wrapped in a blanket and gently held in her father's arms. The baby, Lisa, slept in her father's arms while her mother was very engaged in talking to me about her first-born, a son. In subsequent meetings, the mother continued to talk to me about her older child. I wondered what reasons were pressuring mother to be more concerned about her first-born rather than Lisa, the newborn. I was aware that Lisa was regularly entrusted to the care of a babysitter. When Lisa was two months old, she and her mother began regularly to attend Tempo Lineare. At this time, mother spoke with indifference about Lisa, saying that for some reason it was hard for her to grow fond of her child, to hold her in her arms, to take care of her.

Mother and Lisa, two months

After mother came into the baby room carrying Lisa, she introduced herself to the other mothers in the group, who congratulated her on how beautiful her baby was. Lisa was a baby with very regular features and a very delicate complexion. Her mother responded to the other mothers, saying that she was very tired now that she was looking after two very young children. In the meantime, she gently stroked Lisa's hair, continuing to do so when, after a while, Lisa opened her eyes. Mother spoke a little more with the other mothers before she laid the baby to one side on a big multi-coloured carpet. Later, mother looked at her watch and asked if someone would mind warming Lisa's milk in the feeding bottle. She added, "My daughter likes it very hot." Receiving the bottle, Lisa's mother immediately but nervously took the baby in her arms, offering the bottle to her. The baby was very tentative in her approach to the teat and sucked lackadaisically for a while. Then she stopped. Lisa kept her eyes closed and remained still. Responding to Lisa's rejection of the bottle, mother did not offer her any more milk. At this point, the mother came over to me and began talking about how worried she was about her first-born son's jealousy of her relationship with Lisa.

There follows another observation made one month later.

Lisa, three months, with her mother

Lisa's mother walked into the baby room with Lisa sleeping in her arms. Lisa was totally wrapped up in mother's coat. Mother laid Lisa, who was still sleeping, on a big pillow on the floor. Mother decided not to undress her so as not to awaken her. After about ten minutes Lisa started kicking, waving her hands in the air, grimacing, and screaming out. Her mother quickly gave her a dummy, but, although she opened her mouth to receive it, Lisa didn't press her lips around it. Lisa was clearly displeased as she kept shaking her head from one side to the other while opening and closing her eyes. The mother repeatedly offered the dummy and Lisa finally accepted it.

After a while, Lisa fell asleep again for about ten minutes. Then mother moved to sit very close to Lisa. Feeling mother's presence, Lisa opened her eyes, frowned, and looked as though she was on the verge of tears. Her mother offered the dummy to her once again, saying, "Don't cry, don't cry, don't show people how ugly you are!" I was rather amazed to hear this, but I remain silently watching as mother handed Lisa a small round pink rattle with a handle. Lisa looked at it with curiosity, but didn't take it. After a few minutes, she simultaneously moaned and hiccupped before she began to cry.

The mother changed the baby's position and then plaintively questioned me, "Why can't Lisa stop crying?" I responded by saying, "If she is crying there must be something upsetting her." The mother changed Lisa's position again, before offering her the dummy again, but Lisa again refused it. Lisa kept on crying, and her mother began to look anxious. Abruptly, mother told me that maybe Lisa was hungry because she last fed her five hours ago. The mother added that she often forgot to feed her. Together, we discussed this forgetfulness and the difficulties mother was experiencing in taking care of Lisa. When the conversation was over, mother immediately started to feed Lisa. Lisa repeated her pattern of slowly sucking the milk with her eyes closed. After the feed Lisa was quiet and fell asleep.

Following this observation, I felt a great responsibility towards the mother–baby couple and I wondered how I could help the mother to take care of her daughter and remember to feed her. This felt like an emergency, and in the subsequent days I met the parents, who asked to have more regular meetings with me. From this moment, my work was centred on the family and aimed at supporting mother both to understand her feelings that cut her off from responding to her baby and to discover her motherliness towards her. After a month of observations and weekly meetings with the parents, with father giving more emotional support to mother, Lisa's life with her mother substantially changed.

Here is an observation one month later.

Observation of Mother and Lisa, aged 4½ months

Lisa was seated in front of the mirror, near other children in the group; her mother was beside her. Mother handed Lisa a soft stuffed grey toy rabbit that Lisa played with for a while. From time to time,

Lisa fell on her side and, although she didn't utter a sound, her mother helped her to return to a sitting position. Now it was time to feed Lisa. Mother lifted the baby into her arms and rested her head against her breast in such a way that she and Lisa could look at one another. Lisa sucked in a steady, slow rhythm as she almost emptied the bottle. Afterwards, mother allowed Lisa to linger in the safety of her arms. Mother looked at her, smiled, and then hugged her.

From this observation, it is possible to notice mother and child have begun to look for each other. During the three months I have been sharing my observations of Lisa aloud with her mother, trying to help mother and her baby to form a mutual attachment. I do this by accompanying my observation of the mother–child interaction by commentaries, saying, "This is how Lisa begins to look for comfort from you, to smile at you while experimenting with a new toy or a new position." Observing them, I glimpsed a change between mother and baby. I realised that mother is using my conversation with her and beginning to feel supported by me; this, in turn, enables her to greet and nurture Lisa.

Here is a subsequent observation that suggests a better rapport has been established between mother and baby.

Mother and Lisa, six months

Lisa was sitting on a carpet with other children and their parents. The parents have offered the children rattles and baskets full of toy fruits. Lisa looked at all the nearby toys and explored them with her hands. From time to time she uttered a little sound, and her mother commented that her daughter was very curious and active and she added that at home, too, Lisa tried to catch the parents' attention. As mother spoke about Lisa's qualities, I began to perceive the development of an earnest interest in her daughter.

In this period the mother began to wean Lisa, who was able to accept new foods. At Tempo Lineare, often mothers and children sit together at a table set with the children's breakfast. I notice that mothers enjoy watching their children eating together. Lisa, too, ate with pleasure, often smiling at her mother and at me. As the weeks went by, when Lisa was seven months of age, she began to crawl, and her smiling mother watched her movements.

At one year, Lisa was a healthy, smiling, more responsive child. Her development was normal and she showed adequate responses regarding attachment to her mother. In fact, Lisa smiled at her, vocalised, and caught her mother's attention while often seeking comfort from her. Now the mother seemed able to accept and understand her key role in the growth and development of her child.

I, the therapeutic teachers, and the father had co-operated to understand and support the mother in understanding the needs of the whole family. Later, mother wrote to me, saying,

It was thanks to Tempo Lineare that we could have some time for us and no one else, even if at the beginning I was not very keen to come. Sometimes, when I did not want to come, I sent my husband instead. It was only after some experiences of being in Tempo Lineare with the parents that I realised how important it was for me and Lisa to spend some time alone, without her brother, in this place for ourselves. It was not easy: for a long time I felt unresponsive and inadequate as a mother. This led me continually to feel unworthy of her. As time progressed, I watched her playing and responding to my attempts to establish a connection with her. I was surprised to see how nice and loving she was, but I thought of her as someone different and unconnected to me. Finally, when my daughter was one year old, I realised that my feelings were the same as those loving feelings for a baby just born! More than once during the day I found myself thinking about her with love and joy and sometimes I laughed. For me she was really born again, one year later!

According to Meltzer and Williams (1988), at the beginning of life the presence of a loving mother and the effect of her physical beauty, the breast, the face, the eyes, during feeding, have an aesthetic impact on the baby. At the same time, the newborn has an aesthetic impact on the parents, if they look at him in depth. According to Meltzer and Harris, "the newborn's being" brings the possibility of becoming Darwin, Rembrandt, Madame Curie, or simply a human being. Love at first sight, evoked in the mother by the newborn, is the primary condition for the child to be able to tolerate conflict. Meltzer says that if the mother's love is not initially present, the primary emotional bond fails and the baby's subsequent development can be troubled. Lisa and her mother were able to establish an aesthetic reciprocity after we, alongside Lisa's father, helped mother with her difficulties in being present to her daughter.

Now I would like to ask: can this experience of aesthetic reciprocity happen in our work? My experience in Tempo Lineare suggests that we can experience something similar to aesthetic reciprocity: it happens when our perception of the inner beauty of a child stirs up in us the wish to look more in depth and receive his emotional experience more fully in order to understand the mystery of this encounter.

Being overwhelmed by the baby's needs

Another problem can occur when mother feels the demands of the baby are greater than that which she feels she can offer as a mother. To illustrate how Tempo Lineare supports parents' capacity for parenthood, I shall tell you the story of Michela, who entered Tempo Lineare when she was twenty-two months old.

Michela, 22 months, with her parents

From my first meeting with Michela, I was struck both by her excessive movements, running around the room, and by her rapidly exploring objects without lingering for more than a moment. Superficially, Michela appeared confident in this new context, but neither she nor her parents seemed attracted by other children or adults who were in the same room with us. From time to time, Michela interrupted her ceaseless movement to go to her mother. She gripped hard on to her mother's clothes, leaned against her body, and then she left her mother to return to her ceaseless moving around the room. Her sensorial self-excitement made me think about Michela's perception of her body: she seemed to me as if she were always trying to keep at bay something unmanageable. Michela, by touching objects and running from one object to another, thus excited her sensations and seemed to "feel" herself, and this way, perhaps, she managed "to hold herself together" (Bick, 1968).

During her first few months in the group, I noticed that Michela became aggressive with other children when her mother moved away from her. She annoyed other children by hitting them. She also enjoyed stealing toys from them and disrupting their play. Her parents told me about Michela's traumatic birth, of a period in hospital that involved a separation from her mother for two weeks. They also said that it was very difficult to contain their daughter's sudden bursts of rage as well as to help with her difficulties in eating and her sleeping problems. In this interview, the parents also mentioned Michela's eczema, but they did not seem to attach great importance to it.

Here is an example from an observation taken in that period.

Michela, 24 months

> Michela took a doll, put it on the toy bed, and laid a cover over it. Then she remained crouched by the bed. After a while, she took the doll and, while hugging it, began walking to and fro between the bed and her mother, who sat nearby watching her.

Michela showed me that she was able to take care of her doll-baby, providing for its sleep, putting it to bed. However, through her stroll from the bed to her mother and *vice versa*, she suggested that being separated from her mother was very painful.

Every morning when she arrived at Tempo Lineare, Michela ran to the dolls' basket, grabbed one of the dolls by the hand, and let it swing from one hand. She did this while fixedly staring at me and then rushing towards me and putting the doll in my hands, saying she was going to prepare "din-dins" for it. I felt that through this play Michela was asking for containment; I think Michela was giving to me a "doll-self" that I could keep, with the implication that I could be another attachment figure with whom she could feel secure.

After a few months, Michela appeared more open and interested in the children's group, participating in and proposing many different play activities. Here is an observation of Michela's play which seemed to communicate something she felt was important.

Michela, 26 months

> Michela came into the room with her mother, she looked at me and smiled, then she took a plastic piglet from a box, looked at it, then started touching the pig's mouth with her finger and scolding it, saying "spit, spit, bad food". Then she took the pig away, looked at me and ran to find the discarded piglet. She then took it to the dolls' bed, looked at me, and said "pig dummy".

In the first phase of this play, Michela seems to enact a way of splitting good things from bad things: good things can be put in the mouth and bad things can damage. In the second phase, Michela seems to identify with the little pig and, therefore, she is able to express her wishes: indeed, she could be asking about what she was having to deal with when asleep. In order to sleep, she seemed to need a way of having her "bad food"—bad experiences—understood. This play made me think that Michela was beginning to keep in her mind the toys she was using, showing care and attention towards them. She seemed to have abandoned her exciting–defensive, explosive aspects and she showed that she was looking for bodily contact using a relational modality of tenderness and affection. Only during her last month of attendance at Tempo

Lineare did Michela manage to develop a complex and precise language and show pleasure in communicating with children and adults.

I met Michela again one year after the opening of the new service for children from three to six years. Her parents asked for an interview with me, as they were very worried about the irritating eczema present on both Michela's hands and feet. In one of our first meetings, I noticed that Michela's hands and feet were bleeding. She walked with difficulty and hid her hands behind her back. She was very silent and sad as she stood at a distance from the group of children. It seemed that she was afraid to show her torn and bleeding skin.

Michela's eczema made me think of Esther Bick's work (1968) in which she identifies the skin as the earliest boundary and limit to one's own being. Bick describes the formation of the child's self by observing how the personality structures itself from birth. She suggests that physical skin has the function of keeping the various parts of the personality together, enabling the child to have phantasies about a physical space inside and outside himself. Bick further investigates how the internal space of the mind is defined and she theorises the importance of the skin in the child's earliest experiences in his environment. The skin, so rich in receptive organs, enables the child to feel sensations that give him the experience of being inside his skin. This experience, alongside internalising the mother's capacity to attune to his emotional needs and contain his emotional experiences, allows development of "an internal mother" promoting the development of a "mental skin".

Bick maintains that the mother–child relationship is extremely important and the child has to experience his mother as a containing object. In fact, she writes that "the optimal object is the nipple in the mouth, together with the holding and talking and familiar smelling mother" (Bick, 1968, p. 115). She stresses that the object–mother has to provide nourishment, mentally and physically, as well as hold and contain the emotional states that the child is not able to bear. The child, therefore, has to experience and eventually to introject the "containing object". When a child experiences a containing object (an object which is able to give meaning and continuity to his emotional states), he feels that a state of distress has a beginning and an end. He has the feeling of being in his own "physical skin" and also experiences a "mental skin" which will enable him to have inside himself a mental space in which he can think about his emotional experiences and lend meaning to them.

In stressful instances where there is a lack of an adequate internal containing object, the child does not have the opportunity to experience feelings being modulated by thought. According to Bick, the repetition of this distressing experience in the absence of good internal or external containment can lead to the formation of a "second skin". Bick goes on to assert that "disturbance in the primal skin function can lead to a development of a 'second skin' formation through which dependence on the object is replaced by pseudo-independence" (Bick, 1968, p. 115). The function of the "second skin" is self-containment, which the child uses to prevent the feeling of "leaking out". A child experiences the feeling of "leaking out" when he does not find a containing object that gives meaning to his experience.

Therefore, in order to overcome his distress, the child can resort to focusing on a stimulus in the internal or external world that he is able to hold on to and concentrate his attention upon in an exclusive way. Bick (1968) defined this adhesive way of interacting with the environment an "adhesive identification", which is considered a primitive defence mechanism. Meltzer (1974) specified that "adhesive identification" is different from mimicry. Not being able to recognise the object, the child can only stick to it in order "not to fall into a void". This mechanism does not allow for any mental development and, therefore, "learning from experience" is not possible. According to Meltzer, the psychosomatic illness has no symbolic function and, therefore, it is not linked to the representation of emotional life, but, rather, to the lack of the capacity to hold one's feelings in mind and think about them.

After this, for about six months, Michela started showing her hands, only to hide them in mine, not only to adhere to me so as "not to fall into a void", but maybe also to look for a "containing object" which could give a meaning to her painful experiences.

Here is an observation of her playing.

Michela, four and a half years

> Michela played with other little girls at the toy kitchen, preparing "din-dins" for her doll: she spoon-fed it. She kissed it and she hugged it. At a certain point, she came towards me saying that the doll "is ill"; she gave the doll to me, telling me to "Hold it tight in your arms." After a while, she returned to the basket where the other dolls were and she took out the biggest doll. Showing it to me, she says, "mummy cries", and ends her description by gazing intensely at me.

Michela gave me a girl doll, trying to get in touch with me. Michela indicated that the doll cried, but later she showed me that there was a crying mummy, represented by the biggest doll, as well. In looking for emotional contact with me, Michela was searching for containment of her emotions, hoping I would be able to meet her needs. She was able to say that not only is the child troubled, but also there is an unhappy mother who, perhaps, cannot support her.

During the four years Michela was at Tempo Lineare, I regularly met the mother. In the first period, she looked afraid and emotionally detached. She constantly quizzed me about how to take care of Michela and how to deal with her eczema. At the beginning, Michela's mother saw me as an idealised figure, saying, "You know everything about children." She was worried that I would discover her "inadequacy" as a mother and criticise her. She also felt lonely and incompetent in her maternal role. As my work proceeded, Michela's mother realised that I could contain her feelings of inadequacy and support her to get in touch with, and discover ways of, meeting both her own needs and those of her daughter.

When Michela was five, her eczema disappeared completely. She was now more able to express her feelings in a symbolic way through play. Michela began to organise her own form of thought and to establish a dialogue with her infantile parts. In play, Michela managed to express and project her rage to external situations, instead of directing her rage inwards towards herself. Thanks to an initial process of mentalization, Michela had greater awareness of her body and its functions: maybe it was a first step towards the psychosomatic integration suggested by Winnicott (1965). Through greater symbolic abilities, it seemed that Michela could bear and reduce the anxiety regarding loss of her self. This enabled a healing of her psychosomatic illness (Gaddini, 1980).

I often think about Michela's taking care of the doll, and wonder if she was indicating that there was a crying mother. This suggested that in her mind there was a child-doll in need of containment and a sad mother. Michela seemed to come close to the depressive position, living the pain of the separation from her mother; at the same time, maybe she began to be able to face reality.

Conclusion

If we are educating children for life, then perhaps we can believe that the task of a teacher is very similar to the parental function of containment. In other words, the task of the teacher may be to activate curiosity in front of the unknown, both outside the self and also inside the self. Holding an attitude of love for the truth and courage to explore that which one is afraid to explore, but which, nevertheless, requires exploration, fosters a hopeful attitude in the children and parents who come to Tempo Lineare.

References

Bick, E. (1968). The experience of skin in early object relations. *International Journal of Psychoanalysis, 49*: 484–486.

Bion, W. R. (1962a). *Learning from Experience.* London: William Heinemann [reprinted London: Karnac, 1984].

Bion, W. R. (1962b). The psychoanalytic study of thinking. *International Journal of Psychoanalysis, 43*: 306–310.

Gaddini, E. (1980). Notes on the mind–body question. In: A. Limentani (Ed.), *A Psychoanalytic Theory of Infantile Experlence: Conceptual and Clinical Reflections* (pp. 119–141). London: Routledge.

Klein, M. (1930). The importance of symbol-formation in the development of the ego. In: *Love, Guilt and Reparation and Other Works 1921–1945* (pp. 219–231). London: Hogarth, 1975.

Meltzer, D. (1974). Adhesive identification. In: A. Hahn (Ed.), *Sincerity and Other Works* (pp. 335–351). London: Karnac, 1994.

Meltzer, D., & Williams, M. (1988). *The Apprehension of Beauty: The Role of Aesthetic Conflict in Development, Art and Violence.* Strathtay, Perthshire: Clunie Press.

Winnicott, D. W. (1957). *Mother and Child: A Primer of First Relationships.* New York: Basic Books.

Winnicott, D. W. (1965). *Maturational Processes and the Facilitating Environment: Studies in the Theory of Emotional Development.* London: Hogarth Press.

CHAPTER SIX

Becoming a parent of an adopted child

Carla Busato Barbaglio

In this chapter, I would like to present a series of reflections which come from my experience in various roles: as the mother of an adopted daughter, as a psychoanalyst in the consulting room, and as a consultant to social workers working with families who are wanting to adopt a child. As a grandmother of a child enrolled in Tempo Lineare, I have been enabled to explore the subject of adoption more deeply. The thread running through all these experiences is the request to "deal with life", not only seen as a set of behaviours and "educational rules", but also as a series of complex levels of communication. In discussing "dealing with life", I shall focus upon that particular relationship between mother and child that begins in the mother's womb and is the basis of life and of relationships with others. I shall also consider the mother's role, which is commonly perceived as that of a "motherly mother". I shall also describe a "mother's search for her maternal self", who tries to bring joy, love, and understanding while mitigating the effects of possible difficulties and traumas that life can bring. I would also like to discuss the way a mother looks for everything which could create a healthy relationship with the child, paying immense attention to her baby's communications in order to decode them, understand them, and make them meaningful. This does not mean looking for the recipe for the perfect relationship, but, rather, it means being able to tolerate endless pursuit, always questioning, reflecting, and developing understanding and paying attention to her baby's and her own experiences without making them pathological, but also without refusing to face reality.

The mother has to tread a difficult passage to avoid being intrusive or distant, confused or rigid. A mother has to accept learning from her own unique experience with her baby, facing what does not work, did not go well, and that which created, and still creates, trouble. I am going to give further consideration to those mothers who are "preoccupied" with the possibility of being in a good intimate relationship with their children in which they share and bear their babies' emotions while simultaneously reflecting upon them. This implies the capacity to be deeply attuned emotionally to the child in an elastic and simultaneous way, while keeping a space for the individuality of both mother and child. This is the basis of a good and stable union. I am also going to describe those women who take responsibility for their maternality. This word, maternality, represents a woman's capacity and need to become an intimate mother, nurturing the life she and the father conceive. By maternality, I mean not so much a natural or magical talent for taking care of the child, but a particular attitude in being with her child. This attitude should enable a mother to bear conflicts and ambivalence, to keep on thinking, and be loving at the same time: an attitude deeply connected with the body as well as with history and culture, an attitude to be ready to understand and meet the needs of the baby's life.

Moreover, I believe it is very important to highlight how vital it is to think the child has a "mind" from the very beginning of his life. With regard to this, a young mother, after a third difficult and painful miscarriage, told me about her problems with tolerating her two other children, who seemed to have suddenly become particularly attention seeking and naughty. She talked about her need to be on her own to cradle her pain, for she felt irritation towards everybody. At the same time, she had come to me and asked for help. In fact, she felt she could not deal with her children and her husband. She was worried about damaging them all by being physically and emotionally distant from them and by being in their presence when she did not want to be with them.

At the end of our session, having talked to me, she appeared relieved and as though she felt less mean as a mother. Feeling less mean and critical of herself as a mother enabled her to think more about her inner emotional chaos. This enabled her to reconnect to the beneficial maternal qualities she had made use of so far. It was interesting to notice how she could then simultaneously give space to her pain and needs while considering what was happening to her children, how their minds could be affected by her and what they were feeling. She found the capacity to try to help them even in such an emotionally difficult personal situation.

Anthropologist Sarah Hrdy, in her book *Mother Nature* (2000), wrote that what makes a mother motherly is not a magic element inside her, but her continuous presence and devotion to her child, besides her genetic bond with him/her. A mother is the most suitable person to look after her baby, but not the only one. According to Hrdy, it is extremely difficult to find a substitute for a mother, a person who takes cares of another woman's children because, apart from some physical factors, such as breast-feeding, the healthy mother is the most appropriate person to meet her baby's needs through her unique dedication to the child.

I would like to consider "the maternal instinct" as both a description of physical reality and a metaphor to represent the basis of a relationship in which one communicates and thinks. At the end of her book, Hrdy wrote that a good attachment to the mother makes a child confident about his present and future time. The child can bear his mother's absence and become involved with a substitute mother who looks after him, but only if he can be absolutely sure that his mother will never leave him.

To visualise the problem even better, I am going to use pregnancy as a physical–mental model of understanding and attention to those relational levels which seem to be fundamental and consist of not only verbal communication, but also of "physical contact" and "mental understanding" in very close connection with one another. In pregnancy, one is with the other without being the other. An intricate mixture of past experiences and current phantasies are activated by the pregnancy. This makes it necessary for the mother to pause in order to understand the experiences that occur within her. A pregnant woman, who had undergone amnio-centesis, recently told me that in the very moment she had to undergo this investigation, she burst into tears. In the same moment, the gynaecologist's ultrasound scanner showed that the child was rubbing his eyes, as if he was crying himself. The gynaecologist, while reporting the episode to the mother, took a picture and wrote on it," I'm crying too". Who knows what was really happening to the child, but it was clear that both the gynaecologist and the mother were beginning to pay attention to the child, giving a meaning to his movements, starting a dialogue with him, which made more intimate and real what was going on inside her. The ultrasound scan created a new request for attention and understanding of the mother and baby. This is how "the relational alphabet", as I call it, is built up. There was also a need for the mother to under-stand her own tears in order to be able to take care not only of her baby's body, but also his mind.

The development of "a motherly maternality" at the birth of a child is, on the one hand, a natural event, and on the other hand, an intermingling process between the inner life of the baby and that of the mother. The baby's relationship with the mother activates in her deep levels of primitive emotional experiences, rooted in the mother's relationships with her family of origin. These are past experiences, which are still active in the present internal life of the mother, that influence her current relationship with her body, her mind, and with the other people in her life. Her maternality is influenced by how "the significant others" held her in their minds and in their arms, and how they contributed to the formation of her mind.

The relational alphabet instigated at conception

With pregnancy, a new relational alphabet is created. It is new because that child is new, even though he is influenced by his mother's and father's genetic code, cultural background, and inheritance from previous generations. A relational alphabet is activated in the mother's womb from the baby's first cell formation, together with a sensorial sensibility comprising waves of joy, but also emotions of fear, of sweetness, of sadness, and of curiosity. Strong emotions, together with the creation of new thoughts, arise with the announcement of a pregnancy. From the first moment that a mother knows a child is in her womb, through particular hormones in her blood, or nausea, or her new relationship with food, or a different perception of smells, or a special weakness, the baby begins to "talk". The presence of the baby inside the mother is also initially signalled by the way people around her react, because her pregnancy activates shared dreams, fears, uncertainties, reminders of good results, or failures. If the child does not move, alarm bells ring and the mother sends some signals to keep in touch with him. On the other hand, if the baby becomes restless, an adequate mother makes an effort to understand what is making him nervous and what can calm him down. Little by little, the mother remem-bers her experiences and learns to recognise what can generate restlessness in her baby.

The quality of a mother's attention to all this reveals how the evolving process of this new story between mother and baby is going to develop. A mother in her fifth month of pregnancy, in her psychoanalytic session with me, told me that when she was experiencing moments of intense fear or anxiety, her baby would "fall silent". According to the mother, when she was using a particular intonation in her voice to make a sort of request prayer, her daughter was already able to make little movements that reassured her mother that the baby was all right. Moreover, the mother had begun to "feel" what her anxious daughter might need to calm her down when she seemed agitated inside the womb. A deep communication, a relationship between mother and baby, is building up within the baby girl's mind and somehow "reshaping" both the mother's mind, in order for her to be a mother, and my mind as analyst, in order to look at and give new meaning to these mental states. Through our shared attention, gradually the mother began to realise the nature of her anxieties, the effect they were having on her baby, how she could be calmed down, and the risk of using her baby when she, the mother, was having some difficult emotional experiences.

The mother's inner maternality

The mother and her newly conceived baby are in a relationship originated by the body conceiving and based on the experience in which the baby is in the mother's womb, but is hidden. At the same time, the baby is both known and unknown. The baby develops together with the development of the mother's inner maternality (Ferrara Mori, 2014), which starts being communicated to the baby in the womb. During her pregnancy, the mother's mind is reshaped to allow her to become a mother, that is to say, to take care of the child's body, mind, and life. A woman "becomes" a mother in the development of her psycho-physical relationship with her child. Together, mother and baby discover a way of getting to know each other without seeing each other, by activating particular sensorial channels to the point of feeling sensations and emotions. This primitive psycho-physical communication informs the development of the personality of both the woman becoming a mother and the baby in the womb becoming a baby who will live outside the womb.

The mother cannot think only about herself, as she could when she was a teenager, but, together in physical and emotional contact with her baby, she is building up a psychological intimacy which is somehow often given, but must also be worked on by thinking about and understanding what is going on in the relationship. A woman has both to deal with a wide range of real sensorial experiences, sensations, emotions, and feelings in her body and to learn to wait for a response from her baby.

Pregnant women in psychoanalysis with me have made me realise, even more clearly, the particular communication developing at the beginning of the relationship: the deep connection between body, phantasies, and dialogue between two different people, where one person is inside the other; a communication which covers almost unpredictable mind levels, but which also includes all the richness of the infinite ranges of possible physical communications. Verbal contents are, in this case, almost insignificant; what is relevant is the intonation of mother's voice, her body movements, the alternation of silence and words, her being relaxed or nervous, a deep quality of understanding, of "physical" listening to this new being who is, little by little, coming to be known. This is, then, the creation of an inner maternality (Ferrera Mori, 2014) able to contain, to give life and meaning to that new being and to his needs by establishing a relationship "beyond words and physical presence with the person inside", a person who is taking shape and a mind which is developing.

Such a relational level has to do with the building up of a rich range of capacities to develop the mind, to generate and to create particular and secret languages. These are the languages a mother learns to create with her baby when he is still in her womb and "can't speak". These are languages in which body and mind are together, not separated, but united in harmonious communication. When harmoniously attuned communication does not take place, or is stuck, mother and child are both in an endless search for connection. I would also like to add how all the most terrible phantasies which dwell in every ordinary pregnancy, imagining a child with problems, with deformity, fearing one's incapacity to help him, find their container in the mother's body, which opposes all these negative thoughts not only through its expanding tummy but also through the many checks and examinations aimed at reassuring a mother. The mind and the body, with their fears and their reassuring realities, create a good and, paradoxically, definitely symbolic integration. The role of the father in being present for the mother is also crucially important to this process.

Only by analysing the way a mother is expecting her baby can you obtain good information about how that relationship between mother and baby is going to develop, discovering what levels of intimacy she is going to offer and what dark areas she is going to create. All this leads to reflection concerning the necessary emotional space and tranquillity a mother needs to lay the warp and weft of this rich new life and, in such a way, she can go on understanding and supporting her child's "secret languages".

Motherly maternality of the adoptive mother

A mother's attitude to motherhood and the manner in which she cares for the life of her baby does not change according to whether her child is natural or adopted. Despite all the differences between a natural and an adoptive mother, an adequate mother is the woman who is really able to become a mother, to develop her inner maternality.

Adopting a child implies a whole range of realities and deeply intricate phantasies. The adopted child is, first of all, a child who comes to light in the adoptive mother's mind, phantasies, and wishes. Previously, the emotional and physical life of the child to be adopted began in another body and mind, which maybe could not, or did not want to, look after him any longer. Expecting an adoptive child is different from expecting a natural child. The child does not come from the mother's body, which gives life to a baby beyond thoughts, but is based on a relational alphabet the first element of which is actually the relationship between the couple and social institutions permitting the adoption to take place. It is a relational alphabet which often begins with little possibility for "an inner place" and whose space inevitably includes, from time to time, the sometimes very arduous aspects of the world outside: other containers, other mothers, orphanages, psychologists, social workers, lawyers, and the courts.

Life as an adopted child and adoptive parents exposes one to a difficult level of intimacy in a rather acute way. With adoption, there is an accompanying notion of failures to conceive or be kept inside the womb by a mother, rather than a notion of a baby being conceived and coming to life inside the mother, who keeps him. The anxieties connected with failing to become an adequate mother through the body becoming pregnant comes into contact with the feelings of a child abandoned by the mother. This sense of something having failed is one of the essential points to keep in mind when analysing stories of adoption, even stories for those adoptions with a happy ending.

When Roberta, a patient of mine with great talents and potentialities as a professional and as a mother, was officially allowed to adopt a child, she seemed to forget everything she had worked on and understood about the impossibility of her becoming a mother through her own body. As an adoptive mother, she began to suffer from a sense of persecution. People belonging to social institutions appeared to her as dangerous characters, or, at least, people to view with suspicion. She was sure they would never give her a child, and she never received any communication from the authorities with tranquillity. Adopting a child seemed to revive her inner sense of failure. Somehow, she felt she did not deserve to have her wish to have a baby fulfilled. Along with this sense of unworthiness came all the anxieties and desperation connected to it.

Psychoanalysis certainly helped her improve her inner mentalizing capacities and provided more opportunities for supporting her future adopted child's development. Roberta wondered what her adopted child would feel as a consequence of having been given up for adoption. Roberta's first childhood experiences were unhelpful in some ways, because they necessitated that she prematurely grow up through facing difficult experiences without adequate external support and without an adequately formed psychic structure to deal with her feelings. This had resulted in excessive fears, nightmares, and a sense of there being no one to turn to when she felt desperate. Roberta wondered how, with her dominant sense of failure and frustration, she could meet the basic needs of a baby who had begun life relating to a different mother with a different relational alphabet, a mother from whom he had prematurely and painfully separated. How much would that child's emotional difficulties in relying on his new parents make Roberta feel incapable and unlovable, despite her potentially good maternal qualities? How much could she bear the child's aggression without experiencing them as personal attacks? Stories of other difficult adoptions did not lead her to anticipate with pleasure the forthcoming adoption.

Instead, Roberta's mind began to be consumed with investigating and gathering information about other adopted children and their families. She told me about some friends of hers, who were put in a group in which they were asked to discuss children they were introduced to and then they were told they had to choose which child they wanted to adopt. Roberta talked about the couple's inability to understand their feelings, as they were given very little time to think. Instead, they were required to make a quick decision as to which child they wanted. They shouldered the anxiety of remaining sterile, without an adoptive child, if they had a moment of indecision. The child to be adopted at times felt like an object sold at an auction: if Roberta took him, she would cheat the others, and if she did not take him, she would be cheated. In the process, the child himself became more and more desired and seemed more and more a possibility, but, at the same time, he was a completely unknown being, even his age being unknown.

Moreover, her phantasies and the real possibility that she would be given a child with problems seemed to Roberta proof of her difficulties and her worthlessness: maybe she did not deserve anyone but a problematic child. As the time to give the couple a child was officially running out, Roberta was on the verge of madness due to this further miscarriage. She was then asked by the agency to consider a three-year-old child, but, on the very day of the anticipated meeting, he was swapped with a nine-month-old baby. Roberta was extremely happy about receiving a baby rather than a toddler, but she had to change her attitude rather rapidly to greet this new baby on the very day the placement was effected. In all this, it was perfectly clear that the adoption of a child had to do more with Roberta's need to survive as an adequate person.

I have talked only about Roberta and not about Andrea, the child's future father. He was able to bear the complex situation better, perhaps because he was not striving, as "a matter of life or death", for the baby's arrival. As a father, he had a somewhat different attitude to adopting a child. Roberta's story is not only relevant to her, but it highlights the anxieties of many women who are going to adopt or give birth to a child.

Bearing a sense of loss and failure

While a future adoptive mother must face the impossibility of becoming pregnant, whether through her own physical or psychological state or that of her husband, the child will bring with him his own story based on the impossibility of being looked after. For these reasons, the new, helpful relational alphabet is not created from the very beginning, but, rather, it is afflicted by two failures, from two lives meeting at a painful point which may be exacerbated by very different cultural and genetic roots. There is nothing more terrible for a pregnant woman than the experience of the "white eggs", that is to say, the empty pregnancy chamber. Something similar takes place in the mind of a woman "waiting" to be matched to a child to adopt: her hope for something new which is associated with the anxiety of not deserving the child, of sterility, and the potential impossibility of a child being found for her. How can the sterile couple's empty pregnancy chamber be transformed into a loving space for an adopted child? Stern and Bruschweiler-Stern (1998) said that the development of inner maternality in an adoptive mother needs a longer span of time to be structured.

Perhaps the impossibility of having a child stands for the impossibility of generating anything. Perhaps sterility highlights a stop in the growth and psychological maturity of a person and, by its very nature, underlines and activates those levels of insecurity towards life and the capacity to take care of it which are rooted in a not very successful initial holding situation with the maternal grandparents. Both mother and adoptive child, as I have said before, have a physical sense of emptiness. There is a silent mother's body, which does not generate a baby for the mother, and an adopted baby's body deprived of that motherly care which is essential for the child. Between this mother's body, empty or unable to give life to what comes from inside, and the adopted child who comes from outside and has been separated from what was his place with his biological mother, we see the first difference from having a natural child. It is important to think about this difference. The couple that is waiting to adopt a child often have to endure a frustratingly long period of expectation after being officially permitted to adopt a child. The couple feel they are clearly in the hands of others, the institutions, that require them to patiently wait.

The Birth of a Mother, by Stern and Bruschweiler-Stern (1998), is about a very distinct maternal disposition that is going to influence the mother's thoughts, fears, hopes, and phantasies. The book suggests that a mother intending to adopt might need to work particularly hard to develop this inner maternity: this motherly disposition, which cannot be supported by the body, but depends solely on the outside world, tends, at least at the beginning, to activate old experiences which have not been metabolised very well. By this, I mean the relationship with the adoptive mother's own parents and the way they related to the mother-to-be in her childhood. The question then arises: how can an adoptive mother create an inner space when the relationship starts from a fracture? How can she develop a certain level of fusion with the new child and start a communicative work that builds up secret, intimate languages between her and her baby.

How can an adoptive mother create a bond passing from extraneousness to familiarity, at as many levels as possible, tolerating that the two extremes might appear and disappear underground. A familiarity, which as I have widely illustrated before, is based on a failure of the initial psychic incubator and/or the father's sperm, and which has to take failure into account to create good possibilities for emotional intimacy with the child and his past experiences as an orphan. Such familiarity does not come from the body, from the child's "first cells", but from the mother and child's minds intermingling, so that he can emotionally inhabit his adoptive mother and her body, which cannot reproduce anything of itself, and absorb its genetic, social, and cultural structure.

How is it possible to create from this situation, based on a break with the past, a motherly disposition able to connect the cut wires so that life can flow again? This brings to mind an adoptive mother who found her little daughter's smell repulsive. It was a smell she could not get rid of, or mix with her family smells. It is clear that, as the mother rejected the child's smell, the little girl received a message of rejection. How could the child overcome that rejection and turn it into a good fusion with her adoptive mother? How could the mother welcome a baby with different smells, a different colour, different features? The mother had a good disposition to make the child feel loved, yet she found it difficult to accept the baby's smell and all the painful experiences the baby had lived through in her first months of life. One worries, "How will this child be looked upon when she does not follow the family model?"

Similarly, another adoptive mother responded to her child's excessive aggressiveness saying, "Who knows who his parents were and what hereditary taints they had!" Another adoptive parent was asking a social worker for help because her child "didn't work", using the image of a toy that had been broken and needed to be fixed. These words, which convey feelings mirroring the parent–child relationship, will certainly not help adopted children to feel welcome and regarded as loved children. Being adoptive parents is much more complex than being natural ones.

In "Playing with reality" (1996), Fonagy and Target assert that the mother's capacity to contain the child's mental states increases the child's confidence in his ability to cope with emotionally stressful situations. When a child turns to his mother at times when he feels exhausted or overexcited, the child's expectation is to be properly comforted and reassured by the mother. The parents' or nursery teacher's capacity to be present emotionally for the child not only strengthens his emotional bond with them, but also encourages him to pay attention to the person's messages and feelings, thus increasing the child's ability to internalise the capacity to think about his own emotional states. The child's growing capacity to mentalize forms the basis of the child's mental self. At the beginning of this chapter, there was a description of a mother who attributed to her baby girl the ability to calm the mother down. Through this example, we can see that the mother was already thinking about her daughter as endowed with a mental ability. However, an adopted child has rarely had the privilege of being the centre of anybody's interest or consideration; he has been rejected, or, at least, has not been accepted, often from the time of being conceived in his mother's womb. Paradoxically, we expect a more sophisticated mental state from an adoptive mother. She has to work at more complex levels, to go beyond nature to create bonds, to bear a sense of extraneousness and rejection, without feeling rejected. This enables her to start a process from the child's first smells, colour, and linguistic sounds that are going to help her adopted child integrate or to approach somebody with a completely different story. How many implicitly recorded linguistic and sound experiences do African, Asian, South American children, and children from other countries, already have in their memory? At fifteen weeks, the baby in the womb begins to hear the mother's voice and gradually is able to recognise it.

One can go deeper into the study about the constitution of the mind by reading Stern, Fonagy, Target, and many other authors, including Winnicott and Ferenczi. As an adoptive mother, I would also add that an adopted child is often a more demanding child, sometimes extremely demanding, and requires a lot of emotional effort to contain all his feelings. Moreover, the child's psycho-physical–emotional structure might sometimes be deeply psychologically disorganised through higher levels of blood cortisol. Cortisol is a hormone related to stress, which becomes toxic if overproduced and may cause damage to the hypothalamus. Repeated stressful experiences can arouse alert states, supported by the high levels of cortisol, which make the baby more easily frightened.

Such research must be taken into consideration in order to avoid adoption in badly matched parents and children. The adoptive mother referred to above immediately mentioned the biological parents' hereditary traits when considering her child's aggression. She regards this mental state as a concrete reality, and so she cannot change it. If, on the other hand, the mother establishes a connection between her child's aggressive behaviour and the past traumas he experienced, she could intervene and change her attitudes towards the child. The child's inner psychic structure might be influenced by these negative experiences in which he was not comforted. In fact, these negative experiences might have made him more easily frightened and accustomed to responding with aggressiveness to anxiety-provoking situations. A general knowledge of a child's early developmental processes should be the basis for a teacher's in-depth study of children in the nursery. This should be done not to activate new pathologies, but to find as many ways as possible to help promote attunement between the adopted child and his significant others.

Conclusion

I have talked about natural and adoptive parenthood, referring to some specific elements from which both parenthoods originate and how a mother should activate her inner maternity in those cases where life must be taken care of and protected. It seems clear enough that natural parenthood does not imply an innate disposition to motherhood or a parent's greater competence, yet it can offer an easier path to follow from the very beginning. The development of inner maternality, at least at a mental level, is a characteristic of all those people who look after life. I am also referring to fathers, who usually activate their disposition to fatherhood a bit later than women, but cannot avoid creating an intimate language with their child.

Moreover, I also believe that this mental level, that is to say, that inner maternality, must also be an essential part of teachers' characteristics. Let us think about the great number of hours teachers and children spend together. I find the experience of Tempo Lineare very interesting as the focus is on the levels of "good fusion", not only between parents and child, but also between educators and children, alternating this fusion with a good development of the capacity to be separate individuals. "Secret languages" between the children and the group must somehow be activated to create harmony between everybody's past experiences. All this provides a stable basis for children's learning processes, which this school tends to support. From the very moment you enter a school, you come into contact with smells, colours, and different emotions in the group that can encourage or discourage teachers and children working together. The observation of the parent–child, child–schoolmate, and child–teacher relationship becomes subject for research and further reflection and growth for the group and children in particular. The commitment Tempo Lineare requires, for example, the quality and quantity of time parents have to spend at school, cannot be fulfilled without a great deal of effort. Parents work with the teachers, being with them or taking a sideline, according to the teachers' needs. The person running the school obviously needs to have specific qualifications. The head and her teachers, in fact, have to support and help parents develop their reflective functioning, which is the basis of helping their children build their inner psychic capacities. Reflective functioning requires people to monitor themselves, their mental states, and their way of establishing a durable relationship. This experience, which respects children's individual tempos, tells us how much prevention can be carried out, not only to avoid or cure pathologies, but also to enrich children's and parents' life and creativity.

References

Ferrara Mori, G. (Ed.) (2014). *Psychoanalytic Aspects of Pregnancy, Childbirth and Early Motherhood*. London: Routledge (in press).

Fonagy, P., & Target, M. (1996). Playing with reality: I. Theory of mind and the normal development of psychic reality. *International Journal of Psychoanalysis, 77*: 217–233.

Hrdy, S. B. (2000). *Mother Nature: Maternal Instincts and How They Shape the Human Species*. New York: Ballantine.

Stern, D., & Bruschweiler-Stern, N. (1998). *The Birth of a Mother: How the Motherhood Experience Changes You Forever*. New York: Basic Books.

CHAPTER SEVEN

Primitive protections used by fostered and adopted children

Jeanne Magagna

Adopted children may have many different histories, but all have had the experience of leaving the mother in whose womb they lived for the first nine months of their lives, listening to her voice and having experiences associated with her emotional and physical states of being. It is important to explore the life stories of these children who have lost the familiarity of their biological parents and, initially, have fragile links with their adoptive parents. Fragile connections between the children and their care-givers sometimes require repair through some therapeutic intervention.

Patrizia Pasquini, a nursery teacher as well as a psychotherapist, has described some of her ways of intervening with parents and their adopted children within Tempo Lineare. Increasingly, mental health professionals are aware that it is important to support adoptive families, helping them to further the development of their skills as care-givers, understanding and meeting the child's and family members' needs. The aim of such an intervention is to remove obstacles to psychological, intellectual, and, sometimes, physical growth and to help the adopted child form secure attachments with the adoptive parents. Strengthening the attachment to the parents facilitates the development of the child's capacity for reflective functioning. Many children who have been adopted have had some history of emotional, physical, or sexual abuse, and, therefore, have had to erect some protections against anxiety.

In working therapeutically with an adopted child, three key identificatory processes are useful to understand: *adhesive identification*, *projective identification*, and *introjective identification*. In this chapter, I shall describe these processes and illustrate them with vignettes of an adopted child interacting with others.

Adhesive identification

The catastrophic anxiety of falling into space and the fear of annihilation haunts every child who faces change and creates a strong need for sameness, stability, and support from the outside world. Adhesive identification describes a process of searching to adhere to a light, a voice, a smell, or some part of the self, such as muscular firmness, or intellect, or the thumb to provide some kind of a psychic skin to hold the unintegrated parts of the infantile self together (Bick, 1968). Particular types of adhesive identification include denial, muscular rigidity, immobility, non-stop movement, erotisation, primitive *omnipotence*, and primitive omniscience.

A mistreated and subsequently adopted child's use of adhesive identification as a protection against anxiety makes it difficult for teachers and parents to become intimate with him and understand what he is deeply feeling underneath the self-protective behaviours. The habitual attachment to these adhesive mechanisms leads to many of the following symptoms, which Hughes (1997) suggested are common in attachment difficulties:

Lying

Habitual dissociation

Bodily symptoms in lieu of psychological stress

The compulsive need to control others

Increased clinging producing discomfort and resistance

Difficulty in re-establishing a bond following conflict with someone

Interactions lacking mutual enjoyment and spontaneity

Few genuine conversations, but many questions

Lots of chatter as a protection against thinking deeply with another

Lack of empathy

Lack of eye contact

Habitual hypervigilance

Difficulty in learning (pp. 30–31)

Denial: or sticking to the surface of concrete events in the present

> The abused child is likely also *to deny* the existence of his known abuser's mind, since not to do so would be to face the unacceptable fact that those one loves and on whom one depends have malevolent intentions towards one. (Holmes, 2001, p. 71)

Kaspar Hauser had been abandoned, neglected, and imprisoned in a barely lit dungeon. From the age of three until the age of sixteen, he sat, day after day, completely alone—hearing nothing, meeting no one, seeing neither the sun nor the night-time sky. A man visited him daily to give him food and water, but Hauser never saw the man, who only arrived when it was dark. Kaspar's only companions were wooden horses with whom he played all day. When he was too thirsty, he went to sleep. Later, in writing about his life, Kaspar said, "I was always in a *good mood* and content, because nothing ever hurt me" (Newton, 2002, p. 136).

How could Kaspar remain in a good mood when he was starved, thirsty, and completely alone? Kaspar's own rage, fear, or pain were conveniently forgotten or denied because they threatened to engulf him. His diary was full of a delighted acceptance of everything (Newton, 2002, p. 136). In such an extremely depriving situation, sleep and denial enabled Kaspar to survive without people, light or words. Sleep functioned as a massive denial of hunger and thirst. Also, Kaspar's denial of his emotional needs allowed him to survive the sense of being abandoned, the neglect, the lack of human intimacy and the problem of being incarcerated.

Denial allows survival, for it seals off the heart from one's self. Denial is necessary in the service of the self to protect it from unbearable experience and memory of trauma. Denial is used when there is a breakdown in the parents' protective shield, either internally or externally. Denial is necessary when one is being physically and sexually abused. However, denial can be accompanied by an obliteration of both loving and aggressive feelings. With massive denial comes the appearance of what appears as a lack of capacity to use one's mind to focus, to attend, to think. A child can adhesively cling to the image of the biological mother, feeling he loves his mother, while at the same time denying the abuse suffered while the mother was supposed to be protecting and nurturing him.

A child using massive denial may appear intellectually impaired. The child might actually regain some of his mental functioning capacity once the intensity and nature of his previously denied distress is expressed and understood in therapeutic encounters with teachers, parents, and therapists. Here is one example.

> Maria was a five-year-old girl with learning difficulties. Once she was able to express more of her experience of abuse, more of her intelligence returned to her. In one session she tore the head off the father doll. 'Stupid daddy, I've thrown his head away. Now he is only a body. He can't see hear or know. He doesn't know what I am doing to him because he has no mind.' (Sinason, 1988, p. 104)

Maria was not mentally handicapped, but her method of surviving meant cutting her head off, her intellect being destroyed. Sticking to the surface of present events, not-knowing, becoming stupid, became her defence and teachers doubted her intelligence.

'The world understands only talk, maybe the world is blind', said Pia, a mentally handicapped person (Sinason, 1992, p. 205). If time and emotional space is found to consider what the child might have gone through, memory is allowed to return. If a child is mentally handicapped, the child still has emotional intelligence: somewhere the child knows and understands what is happening within and around him. Once the thought is made bearable to the child, some psychological and intellectual growth is possible.

Sinason (1992) describes some traumatised, mentally handicapped children who were thought to be "ignorant and blissful". After some time in therapy, they have "straightforwardly talked of their knowledge that people wished they were dead and hoped that no one else like them should be born" (Sinason, 1992, p. 319). Sinason suggested that one can deteriorate and sometimes die of a broken heart, citing that Second World War orphaned children who were not loved died (Sinason, 1992, p. 208). Denial and not-knowing are necessary defences often over-used by abused, handicapped children who previously needed these psychological protections to survive.

Muscular rigidity, muscular immobility, non-stop movement, and erotisation

Muscular rigidity and muscular immobility

In early infancy, when the baby is traumatised and not supported by the primary care-givers, the infant's method of survival is to retreat both psychically and physically. The infant fears disintegration, falling to pieces, dissolving into a state of nothingness with no *thing* existing, no body, no self. Sometimes the trauma comes from being involved with a jealous, attacking sibling while the mother is preoccupied with her own problems and too identified with her first-born, the jealous, attacking sibling. The traumatised child, lacking an attachment to a protective mother, may fail to cry but rather resort to his own primitive protections against terror. One of these primitive protections is *muscular rigidity*. Here is an example of a terrified child:

> Six weeks old baby Anna is lying on the bed. Her two year old brother James has just recently thrown a book at her, hitting her head. Now when James lunges towards her, Anna's legs are held out rigid and still. Her face is scrunched up with her eyes tightly shut. She hasn't made a sound. She is perfectly still. (Cooper, 2002, p. 73)

Anna is holding her body rigid and "together" and not crying. Anna would appear to be "a good baby", "a quiet baby", "an undemanding baby", yet underneath she is deeply terrified. She does not have sufficient experience of a mother upon whom she can depend. Anna's pseudo-independence, remaining still, not crying, and using her own rigid muscular shell to hold herself together replaces emotional dependence on the mother (Bick, 1968).

There is also Sarah, who, in moments of difficulty, would become extremely quiet and still, with tight, rigid musculature, holding herself together through the stillness like a possum in danger. This happened when there was a discussion of her birth father, to whom she was still attached, who had abused her when she was one. This is characteristic of the "freeze" dissociative responses to stress.

Sometimes, instead of a rigid shell of muscular stillness, a two-year-old child might hold on tightly to hard objects. Such hard objects make the child feel hard, impenetrable, in absolute control, and, thus, safe. The child needs this hard object when he feels solely responsible for his own safety (Tustin, 1990). For example, one child, Andy, held on tightly to a hard plastic Action Man when he went to school or to sleep. This is very different to a child holding on to a soft, cuddly toy or blanket, often representing aspects of his intimate relationship with the mother.

Non-stop movement

The infant is faced with a life or death struggle and, in the absence of a firm, containing mother, who can hold him both physically and psychically, one of his earliest modes of protection is non-stop movement. Non-stop movement is used by the baby as if, in this way, he is trying to stay physically and psychically safe and integrated. He is trying to hold himself together through movement to prevent the terror of a dead end (Bick, 1968). Hunter (2001) describes how, in the absence of a containing mother, non-stop movement can continue to function as a kind of "second skin" container, even when a child is removed from an abusive home and fostered:

Repeatedly sexually abused and neglected, Cynthia, aged 5, exchanged one person or another, constantly chattered, showed her hyperactivity by being restless, fidgety, not able to wait. She was in constant action and this might include anything such as biting, pulling hair, roaring, spitting, screaming, taking one toy after another. Through non-stop movement she held herself together, away from the therapist's looks, feelings or words. Because Cynthia lacked any capacity to contain her emotional experiences, she used non-stop movement to evacuate distress and fend off the arrival of any emotional experience emanating from within. (Hunter, 2001, p. 152)

Non-stop movement forms part of the "fight or flight" physiological responses to stress that, according to Perry (1995), eventually become relatively fixed traits.

Erotisation

Sexual excitement and inappropriate boundaries between the siblings and/or parents or adoptive parents can represent holding on to exciting pleasure to prevent falling into a painful, traumatic sense of loss, boredom, and depression. Sexual excitement and acting out can sometimes be used as defences against the anxiety of emerging dependence on the adoptive parents or nursery teacher. Sexual excitement and searching for enmeshed physical contact can also be used to lessen the overwhelming burden of daily emotional feelings in such a situation. Here is a family situation in which a five-year-old boy, Sam, and his four-year-old sister, Erica, have been adopted following the mother's death through a drug overdose:

At night the two children would sneak into bed together and play mummies and daddies together, touching each other's genitals to get excited until exhausted they dropped off to sleep.

Erotisation was a significant feature of the relationship of Sam and Erica since they had no other ways of blocking their minds and tackling the problems of nightmares, with which they were still suffering. Family therapists were called in to work with the family on this issue of how to help the children with their nightmares, their sleep, and their ability to bear anxieties in another way. The reading, drawing, and discussion of fairy tales in nursery school also facilitated working through some of the aggression and anxiety that Erica was experiencing in her nightmares.

Primitive omnipotence

The cases detailed by Spitz (1945) of children dying in hospital despite being offered food if they had no primary care-taker demonstrate how a child without an intimate attachment can die of overwhelming anxiety. The same thing was known to happen during the Second World War. A child who remains alive through adverse circumstances has somehow learnt to survive and often this survival is due to the use of primitive omnipotence. Primitive omnipotence may involve courage and determination, but also a sense that one has to take care of the self rather than depending on others. Using primitive omnipotence keeps the child safe rather than dying from overwhelming trauma to his self. This is demonstrated in studies of feral children raised by wolves (Newton, 2002).

Primitive omnipotence involves the thought, "I can trust only what comes from me, what I can do for myself. *I must depend on myself.* I can do everything for myself!" This is very characteristic of children described as attachment disordered (Levy & Orlans, 1998). In habitual use of primitive omnipotence, the self becomes idealised as a source of permanent comfort and the other people around can often become the recipients of all the destructive impulses. Gradually, an intense split can occur between the self as "the idealised care-giver for the Self" and "the other", who is felt to be dangerous or untrustworthy. "The other" now holds the destructive impulses transferred from other experiences, regardless of whether or not "the other" is, in reality, loving or hating. "The other", who could be an understanding nursery teacher, parent, or psychotherapist, holds the threat of destroying the omnipotence of the self. This state of mind is aptly shown in stories of abandonment found in *Black Swan* (Anderson, 1999). In these stories, the children initially tend to reject any offer of consolation or love.

A child using primitive omnipotence shows the patterns typical of avoidant attachments. If nursery teachers, or parents, or adoptive parents offer understanding, intimacy, or love, this is experienced as a threat, just as past aggression or abusiveness towards the child was experienced as threatening. The child clings to primitive omnipotence like a shield for protection, fearing that understanding and loving contact could melt his armour of omnipotence that he feels he absolutely must have for survival. When approaching a child who is using primitive omnipotence, a teacher sometimes misperceives the child's response. Often, a teacher or adoptive parent describes the child as being aggressive when, in fact, the child is defending himself by pushing away the terrible threat of love and understanding. The child protects himself in any way he can. He is terrified that if his armour of primitive omnipotence is breached, he will fall into confusion or become overwhelmed with feelings that are too painful and intense and, thus, will disintegrate. This is often present in children with a "disorganised attachment". Below are two illustrative examples.

> A five-year-old boy, John, loved to spend time in his room playing computer games. He seemed to be in a world of his own. He never chose to be with his adoptive parents or sought a cuddle from them. He drove them away if they tried to read him a bedtime story.

> Four-year-old newly adopted Marianne sat in her room playing with her stuffed teddies, talking to them, hitting them, making them go through routines of nursery school life. She slammed the door on her adoptive mother each time the mother tried to come into the room to talk with her, play with her, and try to understand her feelings.

Previously raised in the families in which violence, neglect, and abuse were present, both John and Marianne had resorted to primitive omnipotence as a protection against relationships with people. Primitive omnipotence is also used when there is a lack of caring and protective internal parents. Primitive omnipotence functions as a kind of internal "prison guard", a controlling force which restricts the experiencing of difficult feelings as well as the experiencing of pleasurable moments. The control of the "prison guard" involves an identification with a kind of "super-parent figure", a tough, self-sufficient figure who can obliterate human frustration, vulnerability, and the sensation of having basic physical needs.

In trying to be present for a young child using primitive omnipotence, there are only two feelings: love and fear (Leunig, 1990). Fear can stop the child from loving. As a child utilising primitive omnipotence is developing psychologically and beginning to form a trusting relationship with an adult, he often draws or describes a sensation of the self with feelings being locked inside. For example, one child drew herself crying in a prison cell. Her back was turned to her mother who was looking between the cell bars. Simultaneously, she was experiencing a vicious debate between two conflicting emotions: her love of being understood was in opposition to her fear of being touched emotionally by someone she feared would let her down.

Primitive omniscience

Hunter (2001, p. 156) shows that both boys and girls who have been abused through witnessing of domestic violence, being the recipient of direct physical threat or abuse, or other maltreatment are hyper-vigilant to all cues that might be connected to something which could arouse fear. These cues could consist of a particular smell, or sound, or gaze of a person. These hyper-vigilant children have a raised heart rate and feelings of anxiety in response to minute cues (Glaser, 2000). The hyper-vigilant child is attempting to navigate a sea of potentially terrifying objects who might at any moment hurt him. How does the child survive? The child learns *to watch very carefully* from a distance, while avoiding direct eye contact. He memorises every little detail that signals the possibility of an impending disaster. The child holds on to past knowledge of all facts, auditory, olfactory, and mood states as "danger" signals. Vital details, including perceptions of care-givers' state of mind, are clung on to tenaciously. Every change in the parents' or nursery teacher's state of mind and routine feels potentially dangerous. The omniscient, hyper-vigilant self feels, "I must know everything and rely on myself *because there is no one*, no mother to pick me up and save me" (Magagna, 2002). Primitive omniscience and hyper-vigilance is used to protect the self in lieu of an internal secure parent enabling the self to bear the anxiety of sudden change. The baby-self is terrified of the unknown, fears falling apart, fears dying (Bick, 1968).

Predictability and a sense of security are usually derived from the parents' ongoing reliable emotional state and reliability in care-giving. When the care-giver is not reliable, or nursery teachers are not sufficiently emotionally present for a young child, the child has dysregulated cortisol responses to stress, involving excess cortisol secretions. These are known to interfere with planning and organising of actions, using "working memory" and the inhibition of attention to distractions (Schore, 1994). An abused or neglected child requires that absolutely everything be understood in terms of whether or not it presents a danger to the self.

The primitive protection of omniscience consumes enormous energy in order to scan minute details from faces and body language, read the emotional climate, and try to anticipate situations. The thinking mind almost becomes transformed into storage space: rather than being a thinking space, it is used to store and sort information to aid the search for survival. As a result, there remains very little mental space for thinking about emotional experiences. Change and flexibility in an exploring mind brings the fear of emotional arousal, catastrophic anxieties, and violent phantasies from the infantile self that threatens destruction of the fragile, more adult parts of the personality (Magagna, 2002). An example of such a situation follows.

> For her first two years, a four-year-old girl, Nina, was abandoned at home all day with her only company being a canary and the dog. She was unable to use language; however, she closely watched

her adoptive mother and therapist. When the therapist touched her toy box, or opened the door, or took out a crayon in a different way, or did anything out of the routine, she signalled the therapist, showing her "the right way to do it", which was to repeat the ritual of the past. She was very disturbed by the slightest change in the therapist's hairstyle, room and or mood.

Nina was unable to concentrate and learn in nursery school, or even play for any length of time with one toy, yet she had a prodigious memory for details of interaction. She made no eye contact with anyone, yet she knew and saw so much! (Magagna, 2012, pp. 91–117)

A child who has relied on primitive omnipotence and omniscience to survive in life will feel he needs to know and be good at what he does. While in nursery school, he can feel shattered or persecuted by the numerous learning experiences that confront him with the fact that *he does not know* or requires time to master the task. This can prove equally problematic at home or in nursery school, where every instruction or new challenge can overwhelm him, causing him to "shut down", or freeze, or lead him to escalate his defensive controlling behaviours motivated by "fight' or flight" neurobiological mechanisms.

Before she was removed from her birth parents, Nancy was neglected for several years and hit when she did not fit in with the wishes of her depressed mother. By age five, she was a parentified child who took care of her mother by serving her food and drinks in bed. When she was adopted, at age five, Nancy refused to go to school. She just cried and clung to her pillow and her bedframe.

After considerable discussion, it finally emerged that Nancy was afraid to go to school because she did not know how to read and write! Her anxiety was not relieved when told that the teacher was there to help her to learn to read and write. Nancy felt overwhelmingly threatened by not-knowing, not being in control of a situation.

Working therapeutically with primitive omnipotence and omniscience

It is essential that the nursery teacher and parents recognise that the child's primitive omnipotence and omniscience are being threatened by major anxieties when involved in the learning process. Finding ways of assisting the child to let go of these protective mechanisms in order to learn is one of the primary tasks of the nursery teacher. The adopted child is always looking to see if the parents and nursery teacher value him and support him emotionally. He feels he has to be a good nursery school student to be valued. What seems important is that the child should have the experience of being important in the teachers' eyes, not simply because of performing educational tasks well, but in his own right as a person. It is important not to destroy the child's primitive omnipotence by putting him in situations in which it is clear he will fail to meet the nursery teacher's expectations of him. This can cause psychological problems (Maughan & Yule, 1994).

When approaching Tempo Lineare for the first time, almost every distressed adopted child has a tendency to use primitive omnipotence and distrust the goodness, strength, and adequacy of the nursery teachers. The adopted child can feel simultaneously relieved and threatened by the understanding offered. One sees the underlying approach–avoidance conflict. Essential is the nursery teacher's understanding of the child's conflict between wanting to depend on the nursery teacher and feeling he needs to maintain his omnipotent control. For a child with an early history of maltreatment by loved parents, depending on someone in the new situation of the nursery is terrifying. For this reason, good rapport between the nursery teachers and the trusted adoptive parents is essential for such a child to see that the nursery is a secure place. The child will feel understood if the nursery teachers and parents can recognise the difference between a child simply being aggressive and a child feeling terrified and using hostility in defence of the *"omnipotent self* which he is using to protect himself"* (Cornwell, 1983).

Tempo Lineare has a multiplicity of ways of helping the child through the use of spontaneous play, art, puppets, fairy tales, and drama. Often, group techniques are useful because the child not in the spotlight himself. For example, looking at puppets or using puppets, or drawing a character and describing a character enables the child to feel that people are not penetrating him with their eyes and understanding. Holmes (1993) shows how psychodrama methods can be an effective method of treating attachment difficulties in children. Schore (1994) explores the urge to "avoid the gaze of the world" in a shame-filled child, leading to typical downcast body posture, immobility, and loss of thinking capacity. Schore proposes that the adult needs to use gentle touch coupled with a modulated voice to support such a child. In the initial stage of work with a child using primitive omnipotence, it is often less intimidating and more facilitating to look at the state of mind of the nursery teacher, or a puppet representing someone significant to the child (Alvarez, 1992). Here is an example of creating a narrative for the child to look at another subject, rather than being looked at himself.

> Six-year-old Jeremy refused to leave the waiting room, refused to talk, told the therapist to shut up. Then the therapist started talking to Jeremy's mother and father. The therapist talked about how irritated the mother was when Jeremy soiled his pants and how angry she became. The therapist asked the father and mother if they wanted to find another way of being and another a way of helping Jeremy with the feelings which compelled him to soil. Both parents said yes, they would like to find another way. Jeremy listened intently while the discussion about his parents' relationship with him continued.

Sometimes, playing at the side of a silent child and talking to oneself or a parent or colleague allows the child to observe and get to know the nursery teacher's thinking process. The child is free to attend or not, but his omnipotent control will not inhibit the nursery teacher's thinking about emotional issues.

Projective identification

Projective identification is a phantasy that some part of the self has been separated off and relocated in another person. In this way, there is an alteration of the self with a depletion of actual feelings or abilities. In projective identification, the unconscious primitive emotions are often projected while the child or adult identifies with either a good or bad internalised figure. Described below are various types of projective identification, including identification with an idealised object, identification with the aggressor or victim, and evocative projective identification.

Identification with an idealised object

The "jack-in-the-box" relationship with an idealised "super-competent" person

The "jack-in-the-box" relationship is characterised by one person feeling imprisoned (the jack *in* the box). All sorts of unwanted bits of the personality (e.g., weakness, loneliness, depression, incompetence, neediness, helplessness, rage, and hostility) are *projected on to the imprisoned person*, while the other person is identified as a *"super-competent person"*. This second partner ("jack *out* of the box"), appearing to be super-competent, lacks knowledge of all parts of his true self, which is projected into the imprisoned person. The person who projects unwanted parts of the self to "feel good" suffers from a feeling of emptiness because so many aspects of the self have been projected out into the imprisoned person (Magagna & Black, 1985).

When a jack-in-the-box relationship occurs, it is harmful to the integrity of the personality of both people. The jack in the box relationship is sometimes seen in the nursery when an older child feels hurt and unconsciously attempts to feel strong and proud by destroying the play activity of a smaller child, thus projecting his distress and feeling of vulnerability into the younger child. The younger child feels imprisoned with distress as a result.

"Super-parent" phantasies of the child, parents, or nursery teacher

A nursery child can become identified with an idealised nursery teacher or parent while projecting into her doll the needy parts of herself. Likewise, a mother or father can project needy, vulnerable parts of themselves into their children and then become overwhelmed by the children who are containing many projections of the parents' needy, distressed selves. An example to illustrate this is given below.

> A mother, Rose, had three miscarriages of children conceived with her husband. Desperate to have a baby, the mother then conceived Mary. Subsequently, the mother was extremely anxious about Mary staying alive. For years Rose kept her daughter close by her side at night. Mary had been scripted to alleviate her mother's depression, her grieving for three lost babies, and her profound loneliness.

"Super-parent" phantasies surrounding relating as an adoptive parent or working as a nursery teacher with an adopted child

The urgent need to repair hidden damage to the self can be an unconscious agenda for anyone in a care-giving role. Connected with this agenda is an idea of a "super-parent" who will be marvellous in every aspect of care-giving. Sometimes, because they feared that telling the truth would lead to rejection by a partner or adoption and fostering agency, foster and adoptive parents have concealed their own history of emotional, physical, or sexual abuse or a traumatic experience. The concealment of the previous damaging relationship represents a conscious wish to have the privilege of being accepted by the agency to look after and perhaps love a child. However, unconsciously, there may be a damaged child within the self of the adoptive or fostering parent(s) that is projected into the child to be adopted or fostered. Consciously, parents (or a parent) have a wish to repair both the "damaged child within themselves" and the disadvantaged child whom they are fostering or adopting.

Such parents feel thwarted in their reparative wish and emotionally injured once again when they encounter a child who is intrusively identified with the aggressor from his past and unable consciously to acknowledge his own wish for love and his own hurt. The child might also have a compulsion to re-experience hurt because that fits in with his internal drama. It is not only that such a child projects rage, it is also that the parents can become angry because they feel impotent in their mission to repair damage both within the child and themselves. Moreover, the adoptive parents and nursery teachers can be scripted into responses to the child that re-awaken and amplify the rage and hurt from their own internalised conflictual links with their parents or siblings. As we are all, to a greater or lesser extent, injured by events in our lives, this may apply to all of us, but particularly to adoptive parents and nursery teachers whose rescue phantasies are thwarted by an adopted child.

Working with super-parent phenomena

Words are like a cracked bell; they never give the full richness of meaning. The person speaking the words brings alongside them a feeling state that needs to be understood in the body and psyche of the nursery teachers and parents. Often, the description of a child will include many references to what has been split off and denied in the parental couple's own personalities. This could be seen as "the child in the parent", that is, some sort of unresolved pain from their own past experience of being parented, which remains alive in their current relationships with the children. Likewise, nursery teachers can split off parts of their hurt selves into the adopted child. It is through the experience of narrating or thinking about one's own personal story and developing reflective functioning around one's own emotions that painful, needy, or aggressive feelings projected into the adoptive children can be reintegrated into the parent's or nursery teacher's personality. In this way, both the nursery teachers and the parents will be able to be more emotionally responsive to the multiplicity of needs and vulnerabilities of the adopted nursery age child.

It is useful for adoptive parents to tell their individual histories in order to help integrate sentiments blocked from awareness. Afterwards, it is sometimes helpful to have each parent speak directly *as the child* to an empty chair representing the parent's parents, saying what he or she would have liked to have said long ago as a child to the parents and what they would say to their own parents *now*. In whatever way it is done, it is helpful to encourage parents and nursery teachers to withdraw the inevitable projections of their own infantile self from the adopted child. This will enable the parents and nursery teachers to see a child as smaller than he is, rather than as such a huge, potent, emotional threat to the parents' parenting capacities and the nursery teachers' care-giving and educational roles. Here is an illustration of such a process.

> The nursery teacher and the parents of three-year-old Mark were feeling extremely punitive towards Mark, who was continually inviting them to scold him for hurting another child. Mrs Johnson, the adoptive mother, was distressed and angry about the fact that she had only just recently heard of her son's abusive life in his family of origin. Mrs Johnson then revealed the previously undisclosed fact that her own father regularly beat her. At first, Mrs Johnson found it difficult to acknowledge the

impact of her own experience of abuse. With her husband's support, she was able to show the ways in which she felt very connected to her adoptive son's history. Later, the nursery teachers and parents were able to see that they were being scripted into re-enacting a drama with Mark in which Mark was hitting a child consciously in order to project hurt into another child and provoking the adults to want to hit him.

The parents' and nursery teachers' capacity to face and bear their own emotions, respond to each other's need for mutual understanding and support in helping the adoptive child requires time and space. There needs to be a creation of a therapeutic space for sharing emotions aroused in relation to an adoptive child with difficulties, a space for making careful observations of child–parent–teacher interaction and collaboratively thinking together as parents and nursery teachers.

Projecting distress on to the body as a receptacle so that the body becomes the visible recipient of the projections

There is a *psychological self*, an entity distinct in some ways from the body and there is also a *body-self*. It is important to realise this in trying to understand the various ways in which each affects the other. A baby without a secure attachment to a care-giver can often respond somatically rather than cry out. A young adoptive child might head-bang when angry, feeling that there is no containing parent or nursery teacher who is strong or understanding enough to accept rage.

Neglected, abused children and adoptive children in a very disturbed emotional state attack their bodies rather than scream to someone for help or endure the psychological confusion or pain threatening to overwhelm them. In these situations, the psychological self projects the inner wound on to the body, thus damaging the body, yet claiming psychological relief, as do children who self-harm. An accident-prone child can feel better if his wound is visible on his body: for example, having a visible bandage makes nursery teachers and parents take note. An injury makes inner turmoil tangible, and it can be shared with others, albeit in a dysfunctional way.

Adoptive children may "use self-punishment, suffering and accident proneness to avoid what for them is feared as even greater suffering and danger, namely their perception of the damaged state of their inner world" (Riesenberg-Malcolm, 1999, p. 93). Often, punishment of the body or whole person is a defence against psychic pain. Self-punishment can also be directed to the internalised parents because the child shields the psychological self from this psychic pain. The child feels no one cares and feels internally disconnected from any care-givers.

Identification with the aggressor or the victim

A securely attached child depends on parents to protect him. The child clings to his parents and gradually *introjects* their protective and nurturing care-giving and their reflective functioning. A child whose parents have emotionally, physically, and/or sexually abused him has, nevertheless, introjected these parents. The introjected parents are part of a protective or harmful internal drama with the child. There are various possibilities for *identifications* within a harmful internal drama. One kind of identification results in feeling the passive, frightened child, the victim, leading to depression, despair, guilt, and rage about unmet needs, along with a deep suspicion of any offers of help.

Alternatively, the child might identify with the life-threatening introjected powerful, aggressive and frightening parent in an attempt to rid himself of unbearable psychic pain or out of rage at what has been done to him. He is then likely to abuse others (Williams, 1998). If *identified with the aggressor*, a child needs to obtain mastery and to defy others, and cannot tolerate depression, guilt or shame (Krystal, 1988). Identifications with the aggressor occur most frequently in controlling children with early dysfunctional parenting experiences.

> Newly adopted Andrew, aged five, cut the limbs off his action men and Barbie dolls. Then he denied all knowledge of his actions. Although he is able to symbolize his identification with the aggressor rather than act it out on other children, it is worrying that he disowns his own vulnerability. (Greenmile, 2003, p. 119)

Evocative projective identification

In projective identification, the child disposes of a part of the self by splitting it off and exporting it into a person important to him. Projective identification is part of normal infant development. The mother gives meaning to the baby's emotions and attempts to understand and respond to them. In this way, the baby's distress becomes more bearable to him. A child who has been exposed to unresolved trauma, maltreatment, maternal depression, or prenatal parental drug and alcohol abuse will often use projective identification to control or possess an important person or communicate unbearable states of mind (Fonagy, 2001, p. 88). Here we see a girl using projective identification as a method of communicating unbearable states of mind to her adoptive mother:

> Jenny, unable to bear the pain of abuse and rejection by her biological mother, projected into Jean, her adoptive mother, the hurt, abuse, sense of rejection and lack of love which she felt. She said to her adoptive mother, Jean: "You fat old witch. You stole us. I don't want to be with you." The adoptive mother, Jean, is being asked to receive the projections and identify with Jenny's hurt, much like a mother receives the baby's cries of distress and bears them within herself, giving them meaning. (Vaughan, 2003, p. 174)

The child's self needs to be differentiated from internalisations of abusing and neglectful parents. A child exposed to deprivation and maltreatment is repeatedly confronted with intolerable levels of confusing and hostile care-giving. He is forced to internalise aspects of his care-giver that he is incapable of integrating. In an attempt to experience himself as coherent, he forces the alien, unassimilable parts of himself into others. Through subtle manipulative control of the other's behaviour, the child then maintains the illusion that these parts are now *outside him* (Fonagy & Target, 1997). Attachment-disordered adopted children more frequently need to use this method to establish better internal parents in time.

Of course, the process of using evocative projective identification can backfire in the case of a care-giver being a "super-parent". There seems initially to be an enormous relief of distress on the part of a super-parent who identifies with an idealised parent and projects the distressed part of the self into the baby. Such a parent can take care of her own distressed parts in the baby and experience relief because her own distressed self, when projected into the baby, initially tends not to overwhelm her. However, when the baby cries, as he inevitably will, the care-giver experiences not only the baby's cries, but also her own distressed part that she has split off and projected into him. The baby's cries then become overwhelming and persecutory to the super-parent mother who has projected so much of herself into the baby. For example:

> A deprived woman battered her baby when it cried. She could not bear the cry because she felt it was her own. Everything dependent and fragile in her that she could not bear had been projected into the baby. The baby's cries were then intolerable. (Sinason, 1992, p. 325)

Similarly, faced with the evocative projections of a traumatised, adopted child, the adoptive parent or nursery teacher is likely to feel overwhelmed by unbearable states of mind and might at times need the support of others to meet and understand his needs appropriately. Some of the feelings that maltreated children project into the nursery teachers or parents are those parts of the adopted child that cannot be symbolised, verbalised, or acknowledged by him. The nursery teachers and adoptive parents must hold these feelings within themselves until the child is ready to symbolise them through play, drawing, or discussion and is ready to make sense of the feelings with the care-givers' help. At times, both the nursery teachers and parents need to become more fully acquainted with their inner responses to the child to ask the questions: "What does this feeling I have when with the child tell me about this child? What does this feeling connect within my own personal narrative?"

Working with projective identification

Whether the nursery teachers like it or not, spontaneous activities in the nursery are the forum for the adopted child to externalise an internal situation linked with past or present situations in his life. If careful empathic observations are made in the nursery, the distressed part of the child is subsequently received by the nursery teachers and/or care-givers. The task of the recipients of the projection is to receive the emotions, try to make sense of them, and give them back to the child divested of the psychic pain that the child experienced when his experiences were neither shared nor understood by anyone.

Reversal of the adult–child relationship may be one of the most frequent representations in the child's use of projective identification. The child might dramatise being a parent, doctor, or teacher, while an adult is in the role of "the child" who is to feel the child's feelings.

The extract below is one example of evocative projective identification.

> Marty was given a large sheet of paper to draw his family. He managed to trample on his adoptive mother's drawing, smear her with black paint and he disrupted everyone as they attempted to do the task of drawing. (Vaughan, 2003, p. 132)

The hyper-vigilant child is deeply attuned to the state of mind of the parents and therapist and their capacity to bear the psychic pain and really feel this capacity cannot be counterfeited

(Meltzer, 1967). Eventually, the child will be able to reflect on his emotional state rather than project it into the parent or the nursery teacher, but initially he simply projects unbearable mental states into them. These are traumatic states of mind for which there are often no words, simply unbearable psychic pain and anger about being maltreated that erupts. The risk is, of course, that the parents and nursery teachers become hurt and angry about being mistreated, rather than being emotionally accepting and understanding of the child's unbearable rage and pain and helping him find more suitable ways of expressing his feelings. If nursery teachers and parents are able to observe and understand through using their own emotional responses, they will facilitate understanding of the child's unverbalised state of mind.

> Jenny tenderly looked after a little doll in one of her individual therapy sessions and then she stepped on the doll and treated it with disdain saying, "who cares about the baby anyway". In witnessing this, the therapist felt very distressed. Jenny's history revealed that she had been hospitalized for 65 bruises covering her whole body, including bruise marks and cuts on her face and a sore, infected vagina from having been sexually abused. Here Jenny succeeded in projecting into the mind of her therapist her unbearable mental and physical pain. (Vaughan, 2003, p. 178)

Introjective identification

Introjective identification describes a process of taking in aspects, qualities, or skills of a person in such a way that they are gradually identified with and inform the character of an individual. This forms part of the normal developmental attachment process. In order to introjectively identify with the parents, it is important to acknowledge their separateness and allow them their freedom to come and go as necessary. Eventually, the adopted child can carry his adoptive parents and siblings in his heart and continue an internal dialogue with them. The nursery teachers are also important figures with which the nursery child introjectively identifies.

The internal world, the external past world, and the external present world

Much of the behaviour of children and their parents is more understandable if one gains a detailed picture of both the internal world and the past and present external world. The key components of the inner psychic structure could be described as comprising an internal mother, internal father, and internal siblings.

Much current literature on therapeutic work with adopted and fostered children focuses primarily upon the child's history and how it leads to current problems, including aggression, fear of closeness, perceived rejections, and self-doubts that impede the child's formation of a deep attachment to the carers. However, there is a tendency to avoid and fear looking in detail at *all factors* within the day-to-day interaction of the trialogue of parents–child–nursery teachers. Pasquini, in her chapters in this book, sheds light by observing the child's here and now interactions to get to know the child's mental state and provide a base of reflection as to how the care-givers can ameliorate the relationship difficulties existing between and among the nursery school trialogue of parents, children, and nursery teachers. It seems crucial to look at each member of the nursery school system in the hope that both the parents' and nursery teachers' strengths and difficulties can be understood as part of the continuing enhancement of the child's attachment to the family. The aim of the participant observation approach of this book is to repair broken connections between the child and significant others. Looking at the past and present external world as well as the different types of identifications present in each family member is important.

> Affect regulation includes the modulation of internal feeling states and arousal, as well as the regulation of the intensity and duration of affect expression, according to the needs of the person at a particular time. There is an innate contribution to emotional reactivity and the capacity to regulate one's affect which is however, poorly developed at birth. (Schore, 1994, p. 78)

The mother begins to help the infant to regulate his affect by alleviating distress and reinforcing positive affect. This is a recursive reciprocal process whose efficacy for the infant's development depends on the mother's sensitivity and attunement to the infant's cues (Stern, 1995).

> This includes an accurate appraisal of the infant's feeling state, synchronicity with the infant and the appropriate intensity of the mother's response. Regulated affect allows the infant to engage in exploration of his environment and in learning. (Glaser & Balbernie, 2002, p. 81)

In assessing the parents and teachers in the nursery interacting with one another, it is important to consider the overall atmosphere of the nursery interactions. An important question to consider is: "Is there an overall presence of mature, *loving and thoughtful containing parents* residing internally in the nursery teacher–parent–child trialogue group interactions with the child?" It is this atmosphere that promotes emotional growth and ameliorates inappropriate stress in the child, nursery teachers, and parents.

The meaning of the term "a good internal mother"

When there has been a "good-enough" mother–infant interaction, the child is able to internalise a nurturing mother who receives his distressed and happy emotions, gives them meaning, provides nurturing and physical comfort, security, and the ability to modify pain. The child, thus, has a good internal mother with whom he or she can identify. This leads to a secure attachment. Therefore, the child does not need to resort to adhesive mechanisms to take care of his "baby-self" by himself.

The meaning of the term "a good internal father"

A good internal father enables a differentiation of good from bad, provides limits, and a moral code out of concern for the self and others. The capacity to regulate emotion so that the feeling is not too intense or too restricted is also part of the paternal function.

The meaning of the term "internalised sibling relationships"

The child has also introjected relationships with siblings and peers. It is important to note the way in which conflicts between love, jealousy, and anger are expressed in these relationships. It is also important to note the capacity to acknowledge the existence, the supportive functions, and the needs of these siblings. The importance of facilitating and detrimental aspects of sibling relationships throughout the life cycle has been seriously neglected in our study of children's development (Maciejewska, Skrzypek, & Stadnicka-Dmitriew, 2014; Mitchell, 2000).

The internal couple's relationship

The nature of the introjected parents and their relationship as a couple will be influenced by the qualities of the real parents and by the child's own feelings towards them. A stable sexual identity is based upon acknowledgement of one's gender, as well as upon identifying with both internalised parents performing their task of looking after the infantile self and joining together in creative ways as a couple. The child's experience of his own body and his sense of being "good" and worthwhile or "no good" and unworthy is influenced by these identifications with the internal parents. The sense of the internalised couple is reflected in the child's physical security and physical movements, as well as in the themes of his play, dreams, and stories.

Conclusion

This chapter has examined three identificatory processes, which include *adhesive identification*, *projective identification*, and *introjective identification*. Most important in work with the "child in the parents" and the adoptive child himself is the enabling of the child to release his adhesive identification, involving clinging to the stranglehold of his *primitive omnipotence* and *omniscience*. When the child lets go of his protections against anxiety, he can gradually depend on his parents and the nursery teachers. In this way, the adopted child may introject the capacities of his parents and the nursery teachers, be able to contain his own anxiety, and, thus, achieve freedom to develop into a thoughtful, mature adult.

By being involved in therapeutic participant observation work within Tempo Lineare, the adoptive family is never left as it was ... or it has "loosened its grip and opened its hands" (Leunig, 1990) to possibilities never dreamt of by each family member.

Figure 7.1.   Drawing of the open hand (Leunig, 1990).

References

Alvarez, A. (1992). *Live Company*. London: Tavistock/Routledge.

Anderson, S. (1999). *Black Swan*. Huntington, NY: Rock Foundations Press.

Bick, E. (1968). The experience of skin in early object relations. *International Journal of Psychoanalysis, 49*: 484–486.

Cooper, H. (2002). The sibling link: reflections on the effect of premature triangulation. *International Journal of Infant Observation, 5*(3): 69–82.

Cornwell, J. (1983). Crisis and survival in infancy. *Journal of Child Psychotherapy, 9*: 25–33.

Fonagy, P., & Target, M. 1997). Attachment and reflective function: their role in self-organization. *Development and Psychopathology, 9*: 679–700.

Glaser, D. (2000). Child abuse and neglect and the brain: a review. *Journal of Child Psychology and Psychiatry, 41*(1): 97–116.

Glaser, D., & Balbernie, R. (2002). Early experience, attachment and the brain. In: R. Gordon & E. Harran (Eds.), *Fragile: Handle with Care*. Leicester: NSPCC.

Greenmile, L. (2003). 'A hard day's night': a parent's perspective. In: C. Archer & A. Burnell (Eds.), *Trauma, Attachment and Family Permanence: Fear Can Stop You Loving* (pp. 113–125). London: Jessica Kingsley.

Holmes, J. (1993). *Educating Children with Trauma-Attachment Disorders*. New York: Routledge.

Holmes, J. (2001). *The Search for the Secure Base: Attachment Theory and Psychotherapy*. Hove: Brunner-Routledge.

Hughes, D. (1997). *Facilitating Developmental Attachment, The Road to Emotional Recovery and Behavioral Change in Foster and Adopted Children*. New York: Jason Aronson.

Hunter, M. (2001). *Psychotherapy with Young People in Care: Lost and Found*. London: Routledge.

Krystal, H. (1988). *Integration and Self-Healing: Affect Trauma–Alexithymia*. Hillsdale, NJ: Analytic Press.

Leunig, M. (1990). *A Common Prayer*. North Blackburn, Victoria: Collins, Dove.

Levy, T., & Orlans, M. (1998). *Attachment Trauma and Healing: Understanding and Treating Attachment Disorder in Children and Families*. Washington, DC: Child Welfare League of America.

Maciejewska, B., Skrzypek, K., & Stadnicka-Dmitriew, Z. (2014). *Siblings: Envy and Rivalry-Co-existence and Concern*. London: Karnac.

Magagna, J. (2002). Three years of infant observation with Mrs. Bick. In: A. Briggs (Ed.), *Surviving Space: Papers on Infant Observation* (pp. 30–48). London: Karnac.

Magagna, J. (Ed.) (2012). *The Silent Child: Communication without Words*. London: Karnac.

Magagna, J., & Black, D. (1985). Changing roles of men and women. In: W. Dryden (Ed.), *Marital Therapy In Britain* (volume 1). London: Harper and Row.

Maughan, B., & Yule, W. (1994). Reading and other learning disabilities. In: M. Rutter, M. Taylor, & L. Hersov (Eds.), *Child and Adolescent Psychiatry: Modern Approaches* (3rd edn). Oxford: Blackwell Scientific.

Meltzer, D. (1967). *The Psychoanalytic Process*. Strathtay, Perthshire: Clunie Press, 1990.

Mitchell, J. (2000). *Mad Men And Medusas: Reclaiming Hysteria*. London: Penguin.

Newton, M. (2002). *Savage Boys and Wild Girls*. London: Faber and Faber.

Perry, B. (1995). *Principles of Working with Traumatised Children*. Houston, TX: CIVITAS Child Trauma Programs.

Riesenberg-Malcolm, R. (1999). *On Bearing Unbearable States of Mind*. London: Routledge.

Schore, A. (1994). *Affect Regulation and the Origin of the Self: The Neurobiology of Emotional Development.* Hillsdale, NJ: Lawrence Erlbaum.

Sinason, V. (1988). Smiling, swallowing, sickening and stupefying. The effect of sexual abuse on the child. *Psychoanalytic Psychotherapy*, 3(2): 97–111.

Sinason, V. (1992). *Mental Handicap and the Human Condition.* London: Free Association.

Spitz, R. (1945). Hospitalism. *Psychoanalytic Study of the Child*, 1: 53–74.

Stern, D. (1995). *The Motherhood Constellation.* London: Karnac.

Tustin, F. (1990). *The Protective Shell in Children and Adults.* London: Routledge & Kegan Paul.

Vaughan, J. (2003). The drama of adoption. In: C. Archer & A. Burnell (Eds.), *Trauma, Attachment and Family Permanence: Fear Can Stop You Loving* (pp. 164–188). London: Jessica Kingsley.

Williams, A. H. (1998). *Understanding the Criminal Mind.* London: Jason Aronson.

CHAPTER EIGHT

An adopted child developing within a nursery group

Patrizia Pasquini

This is a story about Sonia, an adopted child from Panama. I met her at the Tempo Lineare 0–3 service when she was 2½ years old, just after she arrived in Italy. She was left with pre-adoption foster parents for a few weeks. The Family Advisory Centre, which was involved in the pre-adoption work with Sonia's parents, referred the family to Tempo Lineare and it was decided that the Family Advisory Centre and Tempo Lineare would work together with Sonia's parents to think about Sonia and how best to help her develop in the context of her family. The plan for the two services and the parents to collaborate arose from the need for a receptive maternal space for reverie, which could hold the emotional experiences of the child and reflect upon her experiences of change and loss. I was aware that, while in the womb, Sonia's lack of an early relationship to a receptive mother could cause a lack of development in her neurological capacity to bear anxieties and also could negatively influence her confidence that her anxieties and feelings could be accepted and endured.

Klein (1930) observed that in optimal family environments securely attached children seem eager to be aware and satisfy their inquisitiveness. This eagerness to be aware and to search for truth from birth is a deep human desire that "promotes psychic health" (Bion, 1962). I am aware that traumatised young children like Sonia need to create some narrative of their previous pre-adoption life in order to plant roots in the soil of new relationships with the adoptive parents.

Here is my first encounter with Sonia.

Sonia, aged 2½ years

As soon as Sonia comes in, she looks around and, while I am exchanging a few words with her parents, she goes to the door of the room where the nursery children are having breakfast. Seeing them, Sonia gives me her hand and we enter the room together. Meanwhile, her parents remain in the room dedicated to families and talk to the other parents. Sonia looks attentively at the children, then sits down, seizes the cereal bowl, lifts it to her mouth and begins to eat the cereal.

All the children look at her a bit surprised, both because Sonia is eating directly from the bowl and because I am saying nothing to stop her. I explain to the children that Sonia does not know our habits and does not understand our language. I tell Sonia that she can have all the cereals she wants, she has only to ask for them. She smiles at me and I wonder if she has understood what I am telling her, because she speaks Spanish, not Italian, which I am speaking. After having had breakfast, Sonia goes on playing in the children's room, without looking around to see where her parents are. I suggest that the parents come into the playroom and they come in and sit down while watching Sonia play.

In the meantime, Maria, another girl, aged 2½, comes near Sonia and starts watching her. Maria, also an adopted child, has been attending the service for over a year now, and she comes from Panama, too. Maria holds out her hand to Sonia and asks her to play. Sonia agrees and they go into the toy kitchen to play. Maria talks to Sonia, again in Italian, showing her all the crockery, and then they begin to dramatise the preparation of a dinner. Then they start taking turns feeding one another as though one is the mother and one is the child, then they exchange roles. From time to time, the two little girls turn towards me to see if I am looking at them. Both girls' parents watch their daughters' games.

I ponder over Sonia being at Tempo Lineare, a new place that she is experiencing for the very first time. Sonia employs a typical mode used when we find ourselves alone in a strange place. She arrives, looks around her, considering the situation. She wonders whether it is a good or a bad place, and, deciding it is a positive space, she starts exploring it, beginning with the food being offered. Sonia, however, does everything by herself; she is working solely according to what she can do for herself and does not ask for her parents' advice or for their help in this new situation. This leads me to wonder if she is using primitive omnipotence (see Chapter Seven). It is as if Sonia is thinking, "I can enter this room by myself, I do not need my parents, I must manage by myself, no matter what happens."

If we did not know her story, we might think that Sonia has worked out a good internalisation of her parents, that she has good self-esteem, and that therefore she can cope by herself. On the contrary, we know that Sonia comes from Panama and that she does not understand Italian; she has never met any of the people she is approaching now, and very probably she has no firmly established internal security, therefore she is using a primitive omnipotence, which is exactly the kind of protection that makes her say to herself, "I can take care of myself, I have to take care of myself, there is no problem."

Nevertheless, Sonia has retained an innate emotional knowledge about how a relationship works, notwithstanding all the times she has been rejected and the psychic trauma she suffered. When she gives her hand to Maria, Sonia shows that she has a memory of what it means to meet and to stay with someone. At Tempo Lineare, the two girls' adoptive parents and I had observed how the two children approached, and how they noticed our watching them. As a result, the whole group felt that it was possible for Sonia to have "good" experience with a peer.

Sonia's play has changed since her arrival at Tempo Lineare. Every week the children belonging to the two- to three-year-old group have their own special box with their own toys with which to play alone for about thirty minutes. I use the special personal box for each child in the younger age group to help them to develop their capacity to play while finding pleasure and relief in doing so. The adults are observing in case the child becomes too anxious during the play. I observed that with the aid of the *special playtime* with a personal toy box, each child begins to give more meaning to his own play, to use his imagination, and to explore his thoughts about his external and internal reality. The special playtime with one's own play box is a useful experience for the nursery teachers to observe carefully. One can notice if the play is disjointed, rough, and without much central coherence, or if the play is cohering around certain themes. One can also note the particular themes and characters of the spontaneous play and what it might be saying about the children's emotional relationships in the nursery (see Chapter Twelve).

Throughout the time the children play with their special toy box, two teachers are not only observing the pattern of the children's playing, but also writing down the specific sequences in the each child's play. These notes are then shared and discussed with all the teachers in a work group designed to foster a deep understanding of the children and their relationships. Certain written observations of the children are also filmed for the parents' group to collaborate with the teachers in observing and discussing the children. One such observation is described below.

Sonia's box contained a folder with blank sheets inside, crayons, glue, scissors, plasticine, pencil, rubber, pencil sharpener, a bit of string, a family of plastic cows, a crocodile, a giraffe, a rabbit, and some rag dolls who formed part of a family: mother, father, grandfather, grandmother, a boy and a girl. As all parents do, her parents had decorated the box and bought the contents in discussion with Sonia.

When she first opened her box at Tempo Lineare, Sonia examined the contents with curiosity and touched everything in the box. Afterwards, she took the scissors and began to cut a sheet of paper into bits for almost the entire time. Then she began to put a considerable quantity of glue on the paper bits and she pasted all the pieces of the paper on to her body.

Immediately after this, Sonia started manipulating some plasticine and asked me to help her to soften it. After handling plasticine for quite a long time, the special time for the play box ended. Sonia had some difficulty in giving up her play and at first she held on to the box, then she agreed to put it away and subsequently she returned to her mother like the other children.

On subsequent days, although there were many playthings within the nursery, Sonia asked to play with her special time box every time she met me, and at home, too, she talked a lot about this wish of hers. During the first month of the special time playing activity, Sonia usually employed glue, scissors, plasticine, and adhesive tape. She cut one sheet after another, handled plasticine, and poured a lot of glue on her paper bits. She seemed to want to stick all the pieces together.

I thought Sonia might be trying to put all of her bits of her experience together and trying to overcome the fragmentation and sense of loss that she experienced internally. Her playing with much attention and eagerness led me to think that she was trying to understand how she could get into the kind of relationship she wanted to have with her adoptive parents and nursery teachers. After the first month, Sonia began to take an interest in the mother doll of the family. She would take it in her hand, look at it, and then she would put it back in the box without playing with it.

By the end of the first month, Sonia is beginning to ask for assistance, for she repeatedly requests that I, her teacher, let her play with her special play box. Asking for help suggests that Sonia is developing a feeling that someone can be useful and helpful to her. Impressively, Sonia, even at home, thinks about her experiences using the special play box, a box that belongs only to her, a box that symbolises a special and privileged space to keep her feelings. Since she began playing with the materials in her special play box, Sonia cut, cut, and cut again repeatedly, as if within this intimate playing space she needed also to express her biting and cutting rage.

It is not clear why she behaves so, or why she covers her body with all the tiny bits of paper she has cut. Perhaps, with these games, Sonia is telling her story, a story of cuttings and separations; perhaps she is also saying that she has been cut away from her mother, from her culture, from her country, and from her language. Also in Sonia's play we can perceive that Sonia is spending much time keeping things tightly together by pasting and sticking bits and pieces to her body. Sonia is showing she is not so interested in playing with toys but, rather, she has a need to possess the bits of paper: the objects to have, to hold together, and to own. The activity of collecting things, joining them together and sticking them, narrows Sonia's possibility of establishing contact with some of her deeper emotions; maybe cutting and sticking together pieces on herself is like building her own safety armour as a way to avoid feeling dependent on her parents or nursery teachers. Another observation follows.

> Before the Christmas holidays, Sonia began to take an interest in every character out of the doll's family: she looked at them, she touched them, but she did not go on to play with them. Instead, she carried on with drawing, with spreading glue, and with handling plasticine. After the Christmas holidays, for the first time, Sonia started to play with the rag dolls: she took the boy and put it in front of her. Then she placed all the rest of the family at a distance one from the other. As I was watching her playing, I remarked that nobody was near the others, and Sonia answered me by showing me another play activity. She started sticking some adhesive tape on every doll of the family; after a while she told me that she wanted to go away and go back to her mother. At that time, apparently, Sonia was telling me that she was sad about the separation there had been for the holidays, so I spoke to her about the disappointment she had suffered and I told her that perhaps her wish to leave me meant that she wanted me to feel the sorrow she had experienced.

> The following week, Sonia, after drawing for a short time, began to cut out a sheet of paper and then unwind a lot of adhesive tape. Then she got up and locked the playroom's door, handing the key over to me. Straight after that she began to tie me up with adhesive tape, winding the tape around my finger and tying me even to the chair I was sitting on. While she was tying me, I told her of her need to tell me she was afraid of losing me, and I reassured her that, even if we could not see each other every day, we could always meet again at Tempo Lineare, and when we were not together we could keep on thinking about one another.

This play activity was a way of exploring her thoughts, and, with my help, a way for Sonia to understand her preoccupation with wanting me for herself, shown by locking others out of the room, and losing people important to her.

> After she had played out her anxieties about forming important attachment relationships and losing them, Sonia began to play with the "mother" of the doll family and also with the cow's family: the cow, the calf, and the bull. She brought the calf and cow close together and then became very upset, very much as though she was terrified of emotional closeness. Getting close brought memories and fears of being abandoned. Also, her play with mothers and babies seemed always to lead to an excited a game with scissors, as if she needed to cut something very quickly. At a certain point, Sonia started opening and closing the scissors without stopping, and this put her at risk of hurting herself or falling down and cutting herself. I was talking to Sonia about what she might be feeling as she played: the wish for an exclusive relationship with me and cutting as a way of showing her rage that she was

having to share me and her mother with others. My hope was that I could contain some of her anxiety about closeness and separation by giving meaning to her play.

Sonia showed excitement, rage and anxiety mostly when playing alone with her special play box in the presence of a key nursery teacher. Sonia was also very keen for her mother to join in with her play. Within the children's group, she talked, played, and joined in with the different play activities in which they were engaged.

Towards the eighth month of her stay in Tempo Lineare, Sonia began to show her feelings about being abandoned more clearly through words and more direct play with "the mummy".

> For the first time, she started to play with the crocodile and the bunny. With quick movements she kept on putting the bunny in the crocodile's mouth, and, after glancing at me, with an equally quick movement she took the bunny out of the crocodile's mouth. During that period, I started to talking about her rage, represented by the crocodile biting the bunny. Once she directly expressed a strong feeling of rage against the mother doll in the doll family, and afterwards she began a new game.

> She brought the girl doll to the mother doll and then, with a quick gesture, she mimicked a mother's voice saying, "away baby!" When I spoke to her about her feeling of be sent away by her birth mother and her fear it would happen again, Sonia responded, "Ugly mummy face", and started to cover the face of the mother doll with bits of adhesive tape. I told Sonia that, perhaps, she was not sure whether there was a "nice" or an "ugly" mother for her, and she answered, "Nice mummy."

I suggested that there was a "nice mummy" when she had a mummy near her, but when away from her the good mummy turned into an "ugly mummy". This occurred when she felt abandoned or left by the adoptive mummy, for then the "good mummy" became filled with Sonia's projections of rage and frustration. After hearing my words, Sonia started to play with the mother and the baby characters: she kept on putting them together, then at a distance, and then together again. It looked as if she were trying to elaborate upon the experience of being together, then separating, and was trying to reassure herself that she could trust the mother to return to the baby.

> After this play with the themes of separation, loss, and reassuringly being reunited again, Sonia tried to cut her finger with the scissors. I stopped her at once, and Sonia came into my arms. I noticed that her face looked upset and her body had stiffened as if frozen. I told her that she seemed afraid of something and slowly Sonia recovered her mobility, her face showed less tension, then she smiled and began went back to her chair.

> Sitting back in her chair, she took a piece of red plasticine and put it on my finger as if she wanted to point out her uneasiness to me; then she took the adhesive tape and started to stick it on her chair as if she wanted to communicate that she would like to stick herself to a place. I spoke to Sonia about her wish to plant her roots and to find herself a place. Immediately afterwards, Sonia took a piece of adhesive tape and put it on the face of the girl baby doll and gave it to me. I told her that we should give a face to the doll because with such a covered face it was impossible to know who she was. Sonia immediately removed the adhesive tape from the face of the baby doll and went back to play quietly.

A developmental sequence was present in Sonia's games: first, the rag-dolls are neatly placed, well apart and at a distance. All are frozen in place, all are separated, and there is no emotional link between the family members. Later on, with my help, Sonia starts to symbolise her different feelings about connections between mothers and babies. Her need to cut and to separate is showing the presence of strong aggressive feelings about being abandoned by her biological mother.

As well as aggression, there is longing. Sonia reveals how much she wishes to be kept close, by her birth mother, by her parents, and by me, but she also reveals how all those feelings stir up a fear that if she feels love she will feel loss, as happened before in her life. Sonia is also feeling a huge fear, a deep anxiety, due to the fact that her protection against emotional links with people is thawing. She is moving from her hard primitive omnipotence, dictating "Do it by myself, for myself, I don't need anyone", to feeling more anxiety-arousing love and dependence on her adoptive parents and the nursery teachers.

For Sonia, who has lost her birth parents, moving towards dependence implies the enormous risk of experiencing that people can come and can go away. She is finding it difficult to let go of the psychic protection of "do it by myself" primitive omnipotence and allow herself a relationship in which she depends on the important adults in her life. Sonia, it seems, is asking herself, "Can I give up a protective system, which is a part of myself, which allows me to survive turmoil? Will my care-givers take care of me or will they neglect and abandon me as I was abandoned in the past?" Sonia's symbolic play expresses a depth of feeling accompanied by courage to think about the truth of her emotional life.

When Sonia became three, her parent had to take her to a different nursery school for 3–6-year-olds. Just before she parted from Tempo Lineare, Sonia and I participated in this special time play session.

> She introduced a new game that lasted the whole period of our staying together. She began to take the dolls of the family one by one and to cut a lock of hair from each of them. Then she played with the crocodile, placing it in front of the family characters as if she wanted to show that she felt a biting rage inside her. She then started handling plasticine and glue and from time to time she ran to wash. It was obvious that she was experiencing a lot of anxiety.

> During one of our special time play sessions, I told Sonia that she had been showing me for a long time how very angry she was. Sonia, looking at me, said, "I really angry." I added that she probably was so angry with me because we were going to say goodbye in a month and she would be changing schools to go to another nursery school for older children. Sonia answered me, "I really angry with Patrizia." Immediately afterwards, she began to make a drawing which she folded and tied with string. Then she got up from her chair, came near me, and handed me her parcel, saying "Gift for you." I took the gift, telling her that it was clear that she was beginning to feel I saw her and was with her: I told her she was showing that she was no longer only the girl who cut and glued, but she was also a girl able to be in love with her mother, with her father, and with me.

Observing Sonia's play created a wish in me to understand her more profoundly. Ours was an implicit communication process relying not on words but, rather, on voice tones, glances, body positions, and the play using her hands. This special time play space for Sonia evoked in her a wish to elaborate her feelings and, gradually, over the year, she began to form more intimate attachments with others. It is as if we started to build a bridge of links with experiences within herself which were not previously shown explicitly. The observing work during the daily life of nursery, if properly done, already changes the ways of communication between the thinking and feeling self of the child. Detailed observation of the children's play also changes our way of looking and being with the children and, by its very nature, modifies the interaction between and among the teachers and children.

Conclusion

I have tried to highlight what happened emotionally inside an adopted nursery age girl, Sonia. Observation of her play acted as a kind of spotlight on her internal world, which is the private space where the most significant part of our thoughts and feelings unwind and reveal themselves. During the special time with Sonia, I tried to contain her anxiety by means of turning my attention to her internal world to help her to feel more aspects of herself and to realise her potential capacities for love, hate, and gaining understanding.

Tempo Lineare helped Sonia to overcome and to work out her difficulties. It also helped her parents to understand that some anxieties are reopened in Sonia's mind every time a change takes place in her life, and that those anxieties are a reproduction of her previous childhood experiences that are still unconsciously present. During her years at Tempo Lineare, Sonia developed inner security and her parents further developed their capacity for reflective functioning in their roles as mother and father. Working through her anxieties and letting go of her defences in the secure setting of special time in the nursery allowed Sonia to develop intimate and more secure attachment relationships with both her adoptive father and mother and permitted her to establish new friendships with teachers, other parents, and the children in Tempo Lineare.

References

Bion, W. R. (1962). *Learning from Experience.* London: William Heinemann [reprinted London: Karnac, 1984].

Klein, M. (1930). The importance of symbol-formation in the development of the ego. In: *Love, Guilt and Reparation and Other Works 1921–1945* (pp. 219–231). London: Hogarth, 1975.

CHAPTER NINE

Feeling good, feeling bad; being good and being bad

Jeanne Magagna

How does one differentiate *feeling bad* from *being bad*? Is there such a thing as a bad emotion? Or is one bad simply when one behaves badly? Is one good simply when one *behaves well*? My exploration in this chapter has been provoked by hearing mothers say, "The baby was very good today", coupled with hearing a psychotherapist say, "There is no such thing as a bad feeling." Now I would like to initiate a process of thinking about this variety of emotional experiences: *feeling good, feeling bad, being good and being bad* in the context of being a child or being parents with a child.

The couple's cradle of mentalization

In "The couple's cradle for the inner child" (Chapter Twenty), I have described how the couple create a cradle for each partner's *inner child*. How the couple cradle each other's *inner child* significantly influences how husband and wife provide a *cradle of mentalization* for their actual child's emotions and help their child to develop. Sometimes, the husband and wife remain together, sometimes they separate, but in either instance the couple still remain responsible for creating a cradle of mentalization (Fonagy, Gergely, Jurist, & Target, 2003) for the physical and emotional life of their child.

The cradle of mentalization involves four steps:

1. Experiencing the emotion.
2. Identifying the emotion.
3. Thinking about the emotion and giving it more meaning.
4. Finding a way of expressing the emotion which has been modulated by thinking about it. This can involve choosing to express the emotion directly to others or choosing to contain the emotion in symbolic form to further understand oneself.

The couple's cradle of mentalization is required for all the parents' and child's emotional experiences. Many of these experiences are labelled by family members in the following way:

being good,
being bad,
feeling good,
feeling bad.

The cradle of mentalization, intermingled with respect, love, and forgiveness, informs the essence of good parenting, good education of the child, and healthy emotional development of each family member.

The parents

Parents often feel good and have the experience of being good in relation to the new baby who has been conceived. This experience of being good to the baby inside the mother often continues until the birth of the baby. At this point, the task of parenting presents itself as a twenty-four hour task of bearing, empathically receiving, and meeting the baby's overwhelming dependency needs for intimacy, love, and emotional and physical containment. New parents undergo a *transformation of their sense of identity* as they realise how their new baby is totally dependent on the parents for survival. The parents also become aware of how the baby will regard them *as parents* for the rest of their lives.

This realisation of the baby's total dependency on the parents can be accompanied by the most beautiful moments of attunement between mother–father–baby. Sowa (2002) describes the beautiful moments of attunement in these words:

Can one dare to say that aesthetic sensibility is the first experience of the infant? That it represents the moment in which the mind is set free to begin its lifelong search for beauty and form as well as for other minds? That the mind in order to survive will seek it in whichever way it can. Can one posit that aesthetic sensibility stands in for what we cannot fully contain or express in other forms from our life in the womb, those remnants and reverberations that each of us carry where we were given first rhythm, then sound and eventually light and taste, and finally smell of the first live being into whose arms we were placed? (Sowa, 2002, p. 11)

These are beautiful moments of intimacy in which the parents feel good and the baby feels good. These moments of passionate intimacy create anxiety and, thus, are hard to sustain. They are rather frightening in their emotional intensity. The beauty of intimacy might feel like a brilliant sun shining too intensely. As a result, the intimate attunement between the parents and baby is often broken by either the parents or the baby. As strange as this may seem, there may be a fear of the beauty of the moment. Exacerbating this fear is mother's realisation that the baby needs her to be emotionally present *all the time*. This realisation awakens and enhances the mother's own infantile needs for love, comfort, and thoughtful understanding.

Feeling bad

It is natural for a mother to feel bad at the very same time she is being good to the baby, for early in the baby's birth she may experience moments of depression. A new mother is often surprised by how she can feel bad within herself even though she was so keen to be a mother, to have a baby. The statement, "I need some sleep, some rest", is one of the first signs that the mother does not have an emotional balance between *giving to the baby* and *receiving emotional support* from her own internalised parents, her partner, and friends. She may feel that the couple's cradle of mentalization is not adequate to look after her own inner child. When the mother's own unmet needs rise to the surface, dominating her maternity, she feels bad. Obviously, this is a sign that she needs someone to be with her, someone to bear her ambivalent feelings, someone to think about her experience of having a baby who is *totally dependent* on her.

It is at this point the mother might say, "The baby is *being so good*", or "The baby is *being bad* today." What does being so good mean? It suggests that the baby has not been crying in distress, wanting the mother or father to be with him. It indicates that the baby is not showing hunger, tiredness, pain, or simply an attachment wish for companionship, friendship, and comfort from the parents. Being a good baby refers to a baby not showing distress, not provoking and demanding motherliness or fatherliness in the parents. Being a good baby allows the parents to rest in their old identity of just being a couple without children. Also being a good baby can allow the parents to feel competent and, thus, confident in their new parental identity. Being a good baby allows the parents to feel good. Sometimes, though, parents feel it is only when they are able to comfort the baby who feels bad and is crying, that they are able to feel good as parents.

Being "a good baby" and feeling bad

What is often not initially understood by parents and professionals is that being "a good baby" who does not cry could involve the baby in either feeling good or feeling bad. Not crying could mean the baby is feeling good because he is protected by the "couple's cradle of mentalization". Here is one example of this:

> The securely attached baby is *attuned* to by the mother. The parents' care-giving is sensitive, loving, responsive, consistent, and available. The parents of a securely attached baby are interested and alert to both the baby's physical needs and the baby's state of mind. The mother and father accept the baby's loving need for a friendship with them and the baby's need to be attached to them and dependent on them for his life. The parents also accept the baby's hostile and angry feelings when separation or non-understanding occur. The securely attached baby knows his cries will meet with an attentive parent. The securely attached baby can feel good and be good in a loving connection with the parents.

However, being a good baby by not crying could also be a signal that the baby does not trust the parents to come to his rescue if he feels bad and cries. The baby might avoid crying because of lack of trust in the parents' capacities to parent him. The baby might be a good baby who is not crying while simultaneously *denying* deep inner distress. The baby could be using *not knowing*, *denial*, and sometimes *dissociation* to avoid opening himself to his distress, to his anger, to his crying, to his own feeling bad.

"Being good" and the body or psyche feeling bad

The baby will feel bad if the mother and father become too overwhelmed or persecuted by him or if they become too depressed and unresponsive to his needs. Likewise, the baby will feel bad if the mother and father continue to use omnipotent control or obsessional defences, which they have developed during their own childhood, rather than the couple's cradle of mentalization. For instance, the couple might decide to feed the baby when they want to, rather than when the baby is signalling hunger to them. Also, they might never let the baby grasp the spoon or some food because allowing the baby such independence is too messy. In these instances the baby will feel bad because he experiences himself as too controlled, too much of a burden to the parents.

As a baby, one can feel bad and yet thought to be good because the parents are not experiencing the baby as feeling bad. This happens when a child shows physical symptoms that might be partly psychosomatic. Hiccupping, colic, constipation, not eating, not sleeping, eczema, asthma, and colds are examples of psychosomatic symptoms which might ensue in lieu of the baby crying out with distress and/or protest to the parents. Unconsciously, psychosomatic symptoms may exist in lieu of a baby being bad, for the baby might rightly intuit that crying out will be too persecutory to the mother.

Often, insecurely attached babies do not cry . . . they are good babies who feel bad. Here is a typical situation that occurs if a baby feels unprotected by the mother.

Example two

Two-year-old James forcefully pushes a dummy into his five-month-old baby sister Anna's mouth. Anna looks stupefied, her eyes glazed over. Her eyes are not focused on anything in particular. Her fists are tightly closed, but her body is limp (see Cooper & Magagna, 2006, p. 26).

This baby with an avoidant attachment downplays and inhibits her emotions and feelings but she needs her mother to come to her rescue. She is compliant while her body soaks up conflict and distress. Later, Anna has hiccups and sleeplessness. Babies with psychosomatic difficulties do not cause trouble . . . they are good babies who feel bad.

Feeling bad and being bad

What determines how a baby is able to feel bad and "have a bad day" or be "really bad today"? What makes it possible for the baby to cry out in protest or frustration? What enables the baby to bite the breast, bang his head against the breast, hit the high-chair table, or, as a child, kick the mother, hit the mother, throw an object at the mother or father, or show some form of aggression to the parents?

Usually the baby both feels bad and is bad to the parents only if he can trust the parents to love all of him: *both his good self and his bad self*, both his loving, accepting, grateful self and his protesting, angry, destructive self. He is able feel safe being bad to the parents only when he is securely attached to them.

Being bad

"Being bad" is a term used by parents when their baby cries. Later, when children are being bad, it is often forgotten that the child's being bad is frequently, if not always, preceded by the child's feeling bad. Being bad is often a defence against feeling hurt and frustrated.

Example three

Three-year-old James pulls his one-year-old sister Anna's hair. Anna cries. Underneath his aggression to his sister is James' sense of loss of identity and sadness because he has lost mother's sole focus on his needs. He has to share a space with his sister forever and, even at three years, he feels that sharing is like being completely dropped as mother's special baby (Cooper & Magagna, 2006).

Example four

One-year-old baby Anna has been unprotected by mother from frequent injuries by her brother James. She lies down on the floor at her mother's feet, wailing softly. When mother does not comfort her, Anna gets up and walks to the toy-bin where she collects a toy. Mother ducks when Anna suddenly throws a toy car towards her face. Anna is *being bad* to the mother because Anna feels bad when her distress is ignored by her mother (see Cooper & Magagna, 2006, p. 28).

Being bad may or may not be solely destructive in intent, but at all times being bad is a sign of suffering. For this reason, it is crucial that the couple's cradle of mentalization is provided for the baby throughout both the day and night. The couple's cradle containing the baby's anxieties is a necessity for the baby's psychological growth.

It is important for the parents to understand that being bad can pertain to *both feeling bad* and *being bad* in the child's internal reality evident in the child's phantasies expressed through symbolic play, dreams, and drawings.

Example five

Three and one half year old Lisa embraces a baby doll, but as soon as the baby complains of *feeling bad* or having some need, Lisa is a bad mummy for she hits him and throws him down again. Laughing, she proceeds to cut up the baby and eat the pieces of baby (Adamo & Magagna, 2006, pp. 105–106).

Example six

Alice has many nightmares of a lion with claws chasing her after she has tried to hit her younger brother being lovingly nursed at her mother's breast. She has felt bad through jealousy, then she has been bad, and then she feels terrorised in her nightmares.

As in example three, above, when Anna tried to hit her mother, being bad can also pertain to feeling bad and subsequently showing unrestrained acting out of bad feelings towards the parents, siblings, and others. Lisa, in example five, above, is showing through her symbolic play how she feels like being bad to the rival baby; whereas Alice, *after feeling bad*, is compelled to *be bad* to her brother.

Being bad symbolically

Often parents ask, "Is it all right if my child is being bad in his dreams and play? The child is not hurting anyone." My response is that we carry within ourselves our mother, our father, our brothers and sisters. Whether they are dead or alive in external life, they remain good figures or bad figures depending on our love and hatred towards them. Think about the situation in which a person is feeling loving towards someone who is dead. In this case, the person may have a loving encounter with this person in a dream. The person feels alive internally.

Example seven

Proust thinks of his mother "bending her loving face down over his bed, and holding it out to him like a Host, for an act of Communion in which his lips might drink deeply the sense of her real presence and with it the power to sleep and dream" (Proust, 1922, p. 15).

On the other hand, a child can feel hurt and/or furious with his parents for separating from him and going out, or saying he should sleep in his own bedroom. In his phantasies, he hits and kills his parents (Figure 9.1).

The result of the boy's rage is actual damage to his internal parents. In the child's phantasies, the *internal parents* can then die. This can lead the child to fear that his *external parents* are actually going to die. At other times, this fury and attack on the internal parents can lead the child to fear that the external parents will be hurt in an aeroplane or car crash. In internal reality, damage

Figure 9.1. Child angry with parents.

occurs to the internalised parents and internalised siblings as a result of angry attacks. Some examples of dreams showing damage to internalised family members are shown in Figure 9.2

Nightmares, sleep difficulties, eating difficulties, school refusal, and extreme social shyness can be the result of attacks on the internalised family members. Subsequently, persecution by the attacked and damaged internalised figures often occurs. Figure 9.3 shows examples of how persecutory anxieties reveal themselves.

Figure 9.2.   (Left) A broken boat representing rupture in capacity to mentalize. (Centre) Children calling for help. (Right) A scolding teacher.

Figure 9.3.   (Left) Fear, a product of aggression projected into the mother and father. (Right) Phobia of school created by aggression to teacher and students and creating claustrophobic fear of being imprisoned in a terrifying space.

The price paid for being bad

Whether an aggressive attack occurs in external reality or in the internal reality of dreams and phantasies, retribution to the aggressor usually follows. This is because a *primitive harsh superego* is usually internally present to punish the aggressor for having destructive feelings (Figure 9.4).

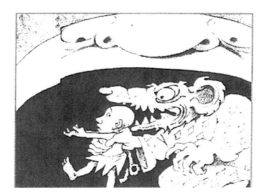

Figure 9.4.   Fear of a monster after hitting one's sister.

A sense of *persecution* is not the only result of phantasised aggression or aggression acted out in external reality. When there is an aggressive attack on internalised parents or sibling, the child identifies with these internalised damaged figures (Figure 9.5). The result of this identification with damaged internalised family members is poor self-esteem and depression (Figure 9.6).

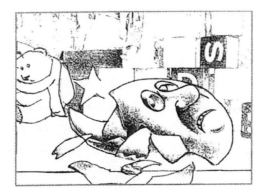

Figure 9.5.   Damaged sense of self created through identification with attacked and damaged internalised family members.

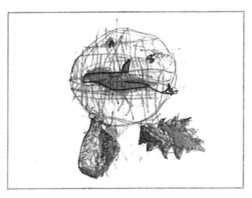

Figure 9.6.   Scribbles on face suggesting lack of self-esteem linked with identification with attacked and damaged internalised family members.

For this reason, it is essential for the child to develop love and concern for the damage done to parents and siblings in internal reality as well as in external reality. Only through the child's development of love, forgiveness, and concern for the family members can damage to these important internalised family members be repaired. Love for the parental figures and siblings reinstates them as good helpful figures, rather than persecutory figures.

Example eight

Alice previously had a dream of the lion chasing her; now she dreamt of her parents having some life-saving equipment to rescue her as she was falling down a mountain.

The couple's cradle of mentalization used for saying no

The child often becomes hurt when the parents place limits on the child's feeling that the world should be constructed according to his own personal wishes. The child might also feel very angry towards the parents for creating a necessary limit on his pleasurable expression of feelings and impulses.

Example nine

Two-year-old James tosses his block in the direction of Anna, who is giggling with delight while playing with her mother. Mother calmly scolds James by saying that he should not throw things. James throws another block in Anna's direction.

If the child is frequently requiring "no's" and stirring up angry feelings in the parents or teachers around him, it is important to understand what the child is experiencing underneath his actions which requires such frequent limit-setting responses. It is often the case that a child feels bad before he is being bad. Frequently, the child is "being bad" because he experiences something painful: a hurt, a humiliation, or some anger. A repetition of making parents or teachers fed up with him could be an anxiety-ridden *re-enactment* of an internal situation in which a child already feels rejected because he already is bad in being angry with his parents or teachers.

Example ten

Three-year-old Johnny runs out of the playroom to grab a bicycle from one of the younger children playing in the garden. The nursery teachers are being continually drawn into a relationship that consists of reprimanding Johnny. They will be forced into this punitive interaction until they give Johnny the immense satisfaction of having the teachers observe and understand his emotional state and individual needs. At this present time, he is beginning nursery just at the time his mother has given birth to a new baby.

This situation is a reminder that as well as maintaining firm limits and saying "no", parents and teachers might need to give the child other experiences which show the child that they understand both the child's aggression and his underlying motivations prompting his "being bad".

The effects of limit setting

The child has the developmental task of moving from the position of thinking only of his own wishes to developing a respectful concern for the rights and needs of others. If the parents do not help the child bear the frustrations of their "no", the parents will deprive the child of the opportunity to develop a healthy concern for others. Parental love, nurturing experiences through play, understanding, *and limit setting* permit the child to have healthy intimate relationships with others and use his capacities to their fullest.

There is often a developmental process involved in the child's ability to accept parental limits. There are two general processes that might be involved, listed below.

1. Limit setting with love and understanding
    In the first process is the optimal situation in which the child experiences a *sufficient balance* of loving and destructive feelings towards the parents and siblings. Initially, in this situation, when the parents insist on limits, the child does not feel good. He has to delay gratification of the expression of his feelings, and he has to put up with the horrid frustration of limits. The child might feel unloved because the parents set limits. He might also feel hurt and angry. As parents or as a teacher, one can feel bad when the child becomes hurt and hostile.
2. Limit-setting that is appreciated
    A child has a different emotional experience and behaves differently when his emotional needs for parental love and nurturing are met and he feels his motivations for breaking limits are understood by the parents. The child will eventually feel emotionally safe and supported by the parents containing his destructive selfishness or aggression and placing limits on him (Figure 9.7).

When the child receives enough love and understanding and develops enough love for the parents help to him, he is able to repair his bond to them, which has been broken through his hostility to their limit setting. The child's love for the parents also enables him to respect the parents' authority in setting limits. He gradually loses a fear of persecutory authority figures and identifies with mentalizing internal parents concerned for others wellbeing. Limits are now felt to be frustrating but reasonable. The child's capacity to delay gratification of his wishes permits a movement from egocentricity to the development *of emotional maturity*. With this

Figure 9.7.   Parents supporting child to bear the frustration of their good limit setting.

capacity, the child is able to share with others, to be generous, to have love for himself, to strive for longer-term goals, and to achieve and form intimate, considerate relationships with others (Figure 9.8).

Figure 9.8.   Love for the parents and remorse for one's aggression.

No limit setting, just letting the child have his own way

It is an unfortunate situation when the child experiences inadequate love for the parents and more hatred of the limit setting function of the father, whether it is in the mind of the mother, in the mind of the father, or in mind of the teacher. The egocentric and immature child hates *the reality principle*, which necessitates that he think about the needs of others and his own longer term needs rather than his wish for immediate pleasure (Figure 9.9).

Figure 9.9.   Child saying "No" to the limit setting functions of the parents and wanting to "be the boss" of everyone.

The child who hates limits feels "my dad is horrid" (Figure 9.10).

The child experiences being bad as easier, for he can immediately have the pleasure of doing things according to his own wishes, can have the pleasure of being selfish, and that of not sharing and caring about the needs of others (Figure 9.11).

A child who experiences being bad as easier gradually finds that feeling good without limits actually makes life harder, for the following reasons.

- The child feels selfish and such a child is unable to develop friendships, for other children do not like his self-centredness.
- The teacher and parents continually scold him. The child in his future adult life has difficulty in his relationship at home and at work.
- The child does not have the capacity to use mentalizing to set limits to his own impulses (Figure 9.12).

Figure 9.10.   Father shouting "No" to his child.

Figure 9.11.   Ganging together in an aggressive act towards the rules of the parents.

Figure 9.12.   A girl overcome by her impulses because she lacks internal capacity to think about her emotional experiences.

- The child has not become used to limits and absolutely hates limits.
- The child cannot sleep because he is continually persecuted by monsters filled with his aggression retaliating against him (Figure 9.13).
- It becomes extremely hard for child to compromise.
- He cannot consider how two wills of two people demand equal consideration.
- The burden of marriage becomes excessively difficult, for in adult life he is having to learn:
  - how to transform *my way* into to *our way*;
  - how to share and make *my way of life* into a *shared way of life*.

The child and/or adult who attacks limits ends up feeling depressed, and experiences low self-esteem. He also feels unable to use his capacities well.

The tasks of adulthood involving intimate relationships becomes an almost impossible journey to make for a child who has not been given the privileged experience of learning to accept limits. Rather than being good and loving to a child, not giving the child love and understanding coupled with clear limits is being bad to the child.

Figure 9.13.   Being persecuted by a monster in the night.

Providing the couple's cradle of mentalization to repair damage to relationships

Before sleeping, the child requires some time with a parent, some time being loved within the couple's cradle of mentalization. Sleep is essential for both growth and repair of the body cells and psychological development. The child needs to be psychologically resting inside the internalized couple's cradle of mentalization in order to sleep. The child's hurt, anger, rage, and conflictual and intense feelings will be played out in his nightmares and dreams during the night.

For this reason, during the day and particularly *before bedtime*, it is important for the child to have *a secure base* of being together with parents who love and understand him. It is important for parents to give each child a separate space for the reading of stories and for the provision of special play where the parents can understand the child's feelings when he is not old enough to speak about them, but old enough to understand stories about other children's experiences (Figure 9.14).

The child needs to repair any damage done to the attachment to the parents *before* going to sleep. Loving encounters with the parents facilitate introjection of loving parents and foster a child's loving self, which can repair hostile damage to the internal parents (Figure 9.15).

If the boy depicted in Figure 9.15 does not feel remorse, he will awaken, for too intense hostile feelings can make him fall out of the couple's cradle. Remember the drawing of the ship cracking in relation to overwhelming hostility within the family relationships. Providing the couple's cradle of mentalization on a daily basis for the child's hurts, frustrations, and passions helps the child to sleep and create dreams replete with meaning (Figure 9.16).

The development of emotional maturity

When, as parents, you understand the child's hurt and anxiety and endure and understand the child's experience of hating you, disliking you, and being angry with you when you place limits, you are helping a child develop maturity within the couple's cradle of mentalization. It often helps the child to mentalize and modulate his frustrated feelings when the parents have a thoughtful, non-judgemental approach to the child's conflict with their authority. It is useful

Figure 9.14.   A father helping his child to begin to think about and express his emotions through story-telling, conversation, and play.

Figure 9.15.   A boy filled with remorse for having been unkind to his sister.

Figure 9.16.   A child who is able to sleep through the night in the boat representing the parents' cradle of containment of his feelings.

for parents of babies and children of any age to identify with the infantile part of the child while talking about the problem to the sensible, more mature part of child.

Example

A parent could say, "I understand, Johnny, that it would be much more fun if you could stay up till late and watch cartoons, but your body needs some rest so that you can enjoy our trip to the park tomorrow." Here, there is an explicit acknowledgement of understanding of the boy's wish coupled with the firm limit: "It's time to go to bed."

Maturity involves accepting *the reality principle*, which involves the child in feeling:

- I am becoming more human.
- I am becoming able to be close to others.
- I need others.
- I love others.
- Their needs and wishes can also be understood and accepted by me.
- I feel good being with others.

For these reasons, it makes perfect sense for parents and teachers to set firm, consistent limits while sharing understanding of the child's feelings.

Problems in setting limits

Why is it difficult for us to set limits? Why is it that one or both of the parents might feel reluctant to set important limits on the child's egocentric pleasures and wishes? What are the interfering motivations that result in not giving the child an opportunity to have respect for limits?

Some of the emotional factors that inhibit the setting of limits are listed below.

- Hating limits oneself and *projecting the rebellious, narcissistic part*, never yet having been able to bear limits, into the child. This results in feeling it is so cruel to deprive the child of what he wants. This can also happen in a couple's relationship where one partner just allows the other partner to narcissistically inhabit the marriage with "let's do it my way", rather than through meeting the needs of both partners.
- *Projecting part of the neglected, abused, harshly treated, or deprived self* into the child and *negatively identifying* with one's own parents. Negative identification involves bending over backwards to behave differently from one's non-understanding, harsh parents.

Negative identifications with one's parents leads a parent to feel kind to the child, but actually this is being blind to the reality principle and supporting selfishness in the child.

Easy parenting involves bending over backwards to be kind to the child and over-identifying with the child, who is like the child one was. Easy parenting avoids conflicts with the child regarding limit setting. Easy parenting handicaps the child's capacity to find a way of working with others, working through conflicts, and establishing intimate relationships.

Being bad as a parent

When your child is able to put his feelings into words, he will be able to tell you what he feels is your "being bad" at being a parent. When the inevitable bad parenting slips out, do not feel to ashamed to say, "I am sorry. I won't treat you like that again" and mean it! Also, before your child goes to sleep, remind yourself to ask him how he felt about you at the time you were unkind as a parent. Ask how he feels now about the situation. Help him express his feelings about the conflict. You, too, can thoughtfully share your feelings about the conflict.

Here are some children's descriptions of an adult being a bad parent.

1. Parents who don't look after you.
2. Parents who shout and yell.
3. Parents who hit and scare you.
4. Parents who say sort out your problems with each other by yourselves.
5. Making the child feel guilty because his mother gives him everything he wants but she doesn't get her own needs met by the dad and herself.
6. Parents who let a child be hit by a more powerful child or hurt by another child (Figure 9.17).

Figure 9.17. A child who is bullying and terrifying his sister.

Being good as a parent, yet feeling bad

Being good as a parent may involve feeling bad as well as feeling lonely as a parent in relation to the child. However, feeling bad as a parent or as a child when limit setting occurs might be part of the child's path to feeling good.

A benign cycle of child development involves giving the child *freedom to be separate* and enables him to integrate his own aggressive and loving feelings. Helping a child enables him with nurturing and limits enables him to be able to say no and be properly assertive in relation to others. Providing the couple's cradle of mentalization to nurture and contain the child promotes the child's capacity to love and to be creative (Figure 18).

Figure 9.18. (Left) A child with a good rapport with the parents feels good in relation to the food they offer to her. (Centre) An affectionate rapport with the parents permitting the child to generously allow a new baby to also be close to the parents. (Right) A child relaxing in a boat, with sun shining, thanks to the love and understanding of the parental couple, permitting child to bear turbulent emotions.

References

Adamo, S. M. G., & Magagna, J. (2006). Oedipal anxieties, the birth of a new baby, and the role of the observer. In: J. Magagna, N. Bakalar, H. Cooper, J. Levy, C. Norman, & C. Shank (Eds.), *Intimate Transformations: Babies with their Families* (pp. 90–112). London: Karnac.

Cooper, H., & Magagna, J. (2002). The origins of self-esteem in infancy. In: J. Magagna, N. Bakalar, H. Cooper, J. Levy, C. Norman, & C. Shank (Eds.), *Intimate Transformations: Babies with their Families* (pp. 13–42). London: Karnac.

Fonagy, P., Gergely, G., Jurist, E. L., & Target, M. (2003). *Affect Regulation, Mentalization and the Development of the Self.* London: Karnac.

Proust, M. (1922). *Swann's Way, Vol. 1.* London: Chatto and Windus, 1969.

Sowa, A. (2002). Sustained thinking and the realm of the aesthetic. *International Journal of Infant Observation, 5*(3): 24–40.

CHAPTER TEN

The observation of children with eating difficulties

Patrizia Pasquini

"No flower or bird of gorgeous plumage imposes upon us the mystery of the aesthetic experience like the sight of a young mother with her baby at the breast. We enter such a nursery as we would a cathedral or the great forests of the Pacific coast, noiselessly, bareheaded . . ."

(Meltzer & Williams, 1988, p. 16)

T he breast or bottle feeding experience does not only concern feeding itself, but also the atmosphere a child assimilates, an atmosphere created by the family's general mood and the mother's mental state based on the relationships she had and is having with the most significant people in her life.

Breast and bottle are given by a mother together with her mental state, and her milk will have approximately the same flavour. On the other hand, what changes at every feed is what the baby takes inside with his milk and this is what is going to create his way of "feeling".

When a mother is breast-feeding her baby, her attunement to the baby will be fostered by her observing and trying to understand the way her baby takes her nipple and relates to the breast itself. Likewise, when a baby cries, his mother will help him develop psychologically if she finds ways of understanding and calming him in other ways as well as or instead of giving him milk or a dummy. Difficulties in doing this may arise when a mother does not realise that the baby wants to be with her and needs her, for she is the most important person in her baby's life. If the mother cannot value herself or bear the child's dependence on her, it might be difficult for her to accept that she is the chief focus of her child's life. Fathers are very important to the baby, too, and their importance as "nurturing figures" should be linked with the word "mother" in much of this book. When the baby cries, the mother might sometimes give him the bottle or her breast without realising that what he really needs is "her", not simply the milk. Babies see friendship with their mother and father alongside everything else they are given.

Bion (1962, pp. 36–37) wrote,

> If during the feeding the mother cannot allow reverie or if the reverie is allowed but is not asso-
> ciated with love for the child or its father this fact will be communicated to the infant. Psychical
> quality will be imparted to the channels of comunication, the links with the child. What happens
> will depend on the nature of these maternal psychical qualities and their impact on the psychical
> qualities of the infant, for the impact of the one upon the other is an emotional experience subject,
> from the point of view of the development of the couple and the individuals composing it, to
> transformation by alpha-function.

The mother's alpha function occurs when the mother is in a state of mind that is calm and
receptive and able to take in the infant's own feelings and give them meaning (Bott Spillius,
Milton, Garvey, Couve, & Steiner, 2011, p. 475). When the feeding is integrated with mother's
understanding of her baby's request for emotional intimacy, then what Meltzer calls "a beautiful aesthetic experience" (Meltzer & Williams, 1988) takes place. Body and mind, sensations
and emotions become integrated through these nurturing experiences with mother. In this way,
mother and baby come to know one another. The mother's capacity to gradually develop her
relationship with her baby depends on her own capacities as well the support she receives from
her husband and environment. Above all, it is important to help a mother feel the centre of
wonder and amazement (while at the same time bearing her own vulnerable feelings). By looking at herself as the focus of her baby's life, by realising what her task is, and by bearing her
inadequacies, a woman will be enabled to become a "mother".

Observations of a boy and a girl with feeding difficulties

In order to think about the kinds of anxieties circulating in the parent–child relationship when
a child stops eating, I am going to describe two children, a little boy and a little girl, and their
parents whom I have met in Tempo Lineare. I have often helped some of the Tempo Lineare
parents explore their children's refusal to eat and disinterest in food.

Carla, aged nine months

When I first met Carla, she looked very small for her age. Carla did not look at me or into her mother's
eyes. She remained still and silent in her mother's arms all the time. In that very first meeting, her
mother asked me to help her understand her child. She told me that she had been very anxious for
the whole of her pregnancy and she began crying as she told me she had not wanted a third child,
but she maintained the pregnancy with Carla nevertheless. I suggested that we meet with her
husband and together the three of us were able to think about their life and the difficulties they were
facing. The lack of rapport with her mother still prevented Carla from speaking and wishing to
communicate. It was almost as though she were the child who was not to be born.

I worked with Carla's mother for about three years, during which she could share with me
all the fears she had experienced in dealing with a daughter who had rejected her so much.
Through my slow but continuous work of observation of the mother–child relationship, mother
and daughter began to face the anxieties they experienced. This enabled them to know each
other and to create a space where they could understand each other little by little.

By the time Carla was two and a half years old, she began to speak and express her feelings through games, often by talking to her mother in a very powerful voice. The little girl showed her wish to symbolise her experiences through play and make her needs known vocally to her mother.

When she was almost three, every morning, when Carla arrived at school, she would take the book, *Nicky and the Big, Bad Wolves* (Gorbachev, 1998), go to her mother, and ask her to read it. I noticed that when her mother was reading to her daughter, the mother kept her eyes glued to the book, never glancing at her child. In the same way, Carla would attentively listen to her mother's story while looking carefully at the pages. Soon after that Carla would begin to play:

> She sat down next to her mother, opened a box with some toys in it and took out a house, a wolf, and three little pigs. The child placed the three little pigs inside the house and started to hit the house with the wolf on the roof. While her mother was looking at her carefully, Carla checked that "all the windows had been carefully closed because the wolf could eat all the three little pigs".

A few months later, Carla started a new game.

> She built some fences and inside them she put some "good" plastic animals, while she placed "bad" animals outside the fences. Animals had to stay where they were. Carla said no animals could move for it was dangerous to stay outside the fences. Carla's gestures showed all the intensity of an inner persecutory situation that might have been connected with the adverse circumstances of her conception, or perhaps, but not necessarily, other negative aspects of her relationship with her family.

> Later on, Carla dramatised another scenario, accompanying it with conversation about a kitten in danger: she took a plastic dinosaur and a plastic kitten and tried to build a house for her kitten. She chose an empty glass as the safest home for her kitten and put the little cat inside. Quickly, she brought the dinosaur near the kitten and looked at me. I asked her whether her kitten was in danger and Carla said that nothing wrong could happen to the kitten inside its home. She also said that "that house was a safe place" and added that the kitten could look at the dinosaur but nothing bad could happen to him.

I sensed that Tempo Lineare had provided a safe space for mother and Carla to begin to address some of the persecutory fears that she had. Three years after Carla and her parents left Tempo Lineare, her parents wrote describing their life in Tempo Lineare and their subsequent journey into her primary school years. Here is part of the mother's letter:

> Now Carla is almost six and she is a very self-assured and self-possessed little girl who never talks nonsense. . . . Carla has learnt how to show her mood through games and drawings and now she can express her worries, fears and anxieties with precision. . . . Children feel great affection for her and want to be with her . . . I discovered that being with her is really nice . . . going to and coming back from school is a pleasant and precious time for her and for me, for we can walk and chat for about twenty minutes, and even if it is a short time, it is a useful way to be together on our own . . . I believe that Carla is now aware that there is always space and time for her inside me and that she can trust me because we have been able to get to know and understand each other.

Carla's father added to mother's note, saying,

While in Tempo Lineare I was required to watch Carla play and to concentrate my attention on her for a time which seemed static and endless ... to observe my daughter, to follow a child's tempo, to talk to her without words ... but I shall never forget those mornings, when I had managed to take some hours off work, and we had our walks from home to Tempo Lineare, hand in hand, describing all the little corners of the Testaccio area with precision ... Carla always describes her moods in an extremely lucid way and so she is able to deal with them, to play with her fears and to communicate her difficulties clearly. Carla can ask for help and she knows that when she asks for it, I will listen to her.

When Carla began to eat regularly, she also started to speak and play. I believe that Carla's capacity to play expressed the change in her relationship with her mother. The observations depict Carla's evolving interest in sharing her feelings, needs, and phantasies with her mother. Through her play, Carla communicated to us images of her feelings. The protective house seemed to suggest that she could hold on to an internal image of a mother who holds and protects her from excessive fears. This space of observation enabled Carla to feel supported and understood. She, like her kitten, had finally found a good container. She could trust her mother and was aware that nothing dangerous could happen to her any more. Still, it would be necessary to integrate within herself hostile feelings and scary internal situations linked with representations of the dangerous creatures. I shall go on to describe a little boy with feeding difficulties:

Max, seventeen months

Feeding and eating difficulties are sometimes linked with external traumas, but they can also be a result of cumulative traumas linked with lack of attunement between mother and child, as seen in the earlier vignette of Carla. Max, like Carla, also had difficulties in eating. Max, on his first day at Tempo Lineare, seemed a very lively and clever little boy, good at speaking and playing. His mother, from our very first meeting, voraciously talked to me, sharing her anxiety about Max's sudden and abrupt weaning due to a disease she had contracted. She asked me if this sudden interruption of his breast-feeding could damage their relationship.

During his first few months at school, Max refused to eat breakfast with his schoolmates. Moreover, I observed that during the break, a time devoted to eating, Max refused to remain seated and left his place at the table very early without eating the food he had been offered. Instead, he ran around the room in an excited mood. On the other hand, if other group activities, such as playing and drawing occurred, Max seemed to be very interested. During these activities, he never moved from the table and was curious about both the games and the children in his group.

When Max was about twenty-two months old, his mother told me she was again pregnant.

This was the beginning of a very anxiety-provoking time for Max. I observed how his movements in the schoolroom became increasingly excited. Usually very anxious anyway, Max now moved restlessly, went out of the room to check if his mother was still there, annoyed his mates, and, above all, he began to refuse all the activities in which he had been previously very interested. The only game in which he showed an interest was a wooden boat with "good" and "wild" animals inside. I observed that he played with all the animals at his disposal, but found it difficult to play with the two wooden crocodiles in the ark; he usually placed them far away from the other couples at the end of his game.

Through playing with the ark, Max seemed to show his need for a safe place, a place where he could hold himself together tightly and feel psychologically contained. At that moment, I acted as a mother would do with a very anxious child and I tried to support him by talking about his dramatisations in his play in order to reduce his anxieties.

During his first year at Tempo Lineare, I observed that Max's eating problems were increasing in the same way as his sense of persecution and irritation against his parents. He often cried and yelled desperately in the schoolroom. In this early period, when Max was at school he kept at a distance from his mother and showed his irritation towards his father, me, my assistants, and the other children. The climax of this crisis coincided with the summer holidays.

When school started again, Max was twenty-nine months old. He seemed anxious, kept on refusing to sit at the table with the other children at the break, and, instead, he tried to eat plasticine or salt paste during plasticine moulding activities. One of his favourite games was "pretending" to eat plastic maize, chocolate, or ice-cream.

I observed that in this early period Max could not speak properly and started to stammer badly. His mother often told me about her child's difficulties and the fear she felt inside herself caused by this new pregnancy. She was afraid she could have the same health problems she had had during Max's breast-feeding. After a talk I had with Max's mother, I began to think about her past anxieties and fears.

I found Gianna Williams' (1999) paper about the introjection of the omega function very useful. She described how children are receptacles of the parents' anxieties that are projected on to them. Children whose parents are unable to accept the child's fear of death activate a mechanism which reinforces that anguish in the child. In this way, the child's fear of death also remains uncontained (Williams, 1997, p. 112).

Exactly when his mother asked me for help, Max began to claim my attention. He began to play with plastic animals, usually preferring "good" farm animals. Sometimes he played with the crocodile, with the big mouth of teeth, which he turned against me. After playing with these toys, he emptied the animal box, scattering the contents around the room. Through games, the child showed the confusion he was feeling about the changes taking place in his life.

When his sister was born, Max did not come to school for a while and then he attended the school again with his father. He was very excited, did not accept any school rules, and even his father could hardly stop him from breaking rules. When snack time came he was the only child who could not remain seated at the table and when he did, he did not eat at all. In this same period he tried to hurt himself, putting some toy nails, colours, salt paste, and other inedible objects into his mouth.

Here is an observation of Max's play.

Max, aged thirty months

Max was reading a book whose title was *Il Bebe* (Bour, 1992). For a long time he paged through it carefully. A little girl came up to him and looked at the book with Max and then handed it to me. I suggested the children should sit in a group in front of me to listen to *Il Bebe* being read. While Max was listening to me, he kept on moving continuously, pulled a face, opened and shut his eyes at regular intervals, and rubbed his face like a baby. When I asked about his new sister, Max seemed excited and shortly afterwards he responded, "My sister is grown up, I'm still a baby."

Max seemed to imply "nobody can understand who I really am . . . I'm a little and unhappy baby." After Max played a game also suggesting these feelings, I realised that we needed to work more closely to understand and support him with his anxieties about being replaced by the new baby. When I met with his mother, she told me that Max was eating very little and the paediatrician had suggested that he was underweight and needed further therapeutic help.

I suggested she, together with the whole family, should come for a talk. During that first talk, I observed Max scattering toys all over the playroom and, at a certain point, he took a set of Russian cows. After the child had looked at me intensely, he threw the set far away, and then he went and cuddled up beside an inflatable baby ring. He looked at me once again and I told him he was communicating his need for continuous attention, as little babies or his sister had. At that point, Max began to take out of a basket all the soft toys and give them to me. Soon after he retrieved them and put them in a line, one next to the other. In that moment, he was expressing his wish to have a baby room. When it was time to leave the room, he asked me for a biscuit, I gave it to him, but while his mother was putting his jacket on him, she unintentionally broke the biscuit in pieces. Max became agitated and his mother picked the biscuit up and said, "Come on, you can eat it all the same!" Max answered that he did not want it. The situation became less conflictual when I gave him a new, whole biscuit, which he took and ate.

After the meeting with mother, I made some detailed observations of Max's play and held discussions with the nursery staff group about ways of understanding his fear of loss of identity, his difficulties in sharing his parents with his new sister, and ways of being more fully present with him in the nursery. Two weeks later, while I was asking the children if anybody wanted some milk, Max drank two glasses of it with great satisfaction. I suddenly remembered that he had not had any milk from the time he had been weaned, but now he was drinking milk again! Not only did he ask for the milk, but also, on some occasions, he felt like taking the glass full of milk with him wherever he went and played.

Later that morning I observed Max:

Max was playing with the "good" plastic animals, a pig family that Max moved from the floor to a little chair. He took two little boxes as food bowls for the pigs and began to role-play a feeding situation. The pig family was made up of a father, a mother, and two babies. While he was playing, Max checked to see what two other children were doing. In fact, they were offering me many plastic ice-creams while I pretended to eat them. A little girl from his group took a cloth lion and, while she was approaching me, pretended the lion was eating an ice-cream. Max looked at the scene with an amused look on his face, then he went and collected a crocodile and while he was approaching me he also made the crocodile have an ice-cream. As he approached, I said, "This crocodile is really angry!" Max smiled and kept the crocodile in his hand, as if it wanted to devour the ice-cream with its jaws. In that period, the crocodile was the animal with which he played most frequently.

Through his games, Max seemed to communicate his current emotions, which included hurt, neediness, and aggression, very vividly. He also spoke to his mother, saying, "I do not want to grow and to eat." Yet, even though he kept on eating very little at home, as though to emphasise his discomfort and need for more maternal understanding, he ate more and with more satisfaction at school.

In that period, I was continuing to work with his parents. Even though Max eventually began to eat at home, his father and mother considered obtaining more psychological support for the whole family, in order to work through some of the difficult crises the couple faced in their own lives. The observation of Max's games had enabled me to recognise his great affection and interest in me as well his loneliness, rage, and fear of displacement experienced in relation to his new sister.

Magagna writes that, in her experience, if the external person with the child provides that which is enlivening, interesting, and nurturing in relation to the actual life of the child, then the child will begin to turn towards the therapist and to have great trust in the primary internal figures and parents. In this way, psychological growth is possible (Magagna, 2002, pp. 100–101).

Competent people with an educational role, such as those teachers working together through the use of careful observations and understanding of the child, can help him to develop his positive potentialities.

Observation of Max's last days at school

Max took a plastic cow from a box and, with the string at his disposal, tried to tie it up. Then he took the children in the doll family and, holding them in his hand, said, "They are all tied." Then he took the cow, which he put with a calf, and, when I asked him what they were doing, he answered that "they were together."

I asked him if he was thinking about his mother a lot at this time and he answered that he was.

Then he put the toy little girl on the calf's back and looked intensely at the scene. He then played with a bull for a long time and tried to make the bull feed the calf. I told him that it was a father. The child looked at me and stopped playing; he later took a pair of scissors and tried to cut the cow's legs. I asked, "Are you angry?" Max did not answer, but he then took the little girl and brought her close to her mother. I talked about how difficult it was for him to see that there was also a little sister next to his mother. The child looked at me and then put the scissors far away from where he was standing.

After this long period in which he refused to eat, Max began to eat again. He had learnt how to convey to his parents and teachers his feelings of jealousy, anger, and displacement by his new sister. Play had allowed him to symbolise his feelings and express them in a safe way while the adults compassionately observed, felt, and thought about what he was experiencing.

Two years after these observations, Max was beginning to move from being "a baby" to growing into a little boy who felt he had understanding, protective internalised adults. This provided him with the possibility of letting go of the young baby position in relation to his mother. Expressing his feelings both through play and words, in a very critical moment of his life, gave Max the chance to rebuild a relationship of intimacy with his parents.

Conclusion

In this chapter, I have described how carefully observing a child's play and helping the parents to understand their child more fully enables the child to express feelings, hitherto repressed, which inhibited eating and drinking of their parents' and teachers' food.

References

Bion, W. R. (1962). *Learning from Experience*. London: William Heinemann [reprinted London: Karnac, 1984].

Bott Spillius, E., Milton, J., Garvey, P., Couve, C., & Steiner, D. (2011). *The New Dictionary of Kleinian Thought*. London: Routledge.

Bour, D. (1992). *Il Bebe*. Trieste: EL.

Gorbachev, V. (1998). *Nicky and the Big, Bad Wolves*. New York: North-South.

Magagna, J. (2002). Severe eating difficulties: attacks on life. In: M Rustin & E. Quagliata (Eds.), *Assessment in Child Psychotherapy* (pp. 51–73). London: Duckworth.

Meltzer, D., & Williams, M. (1988). *The Apprehension of Beauty: The Role of Aesthetic Conflict in Development, Art and Violence*. Strathtay, Perthshire: Clunie Press.

Williams, G. (1997). *Internal Landscapes and Foreign Bodies: Eating Disorders and Other Pathologies*. London: Karnac.

Williams, G. (1999). On different introjective processes and the hypothesis of an omega function. *Psychoanalytic Inquiry, 19*: 243–254.

PART III

COMPASSIONATELY COMPREHENDING
CHILDREN PLAYING

CHAPTER ELEVEN

A way of looking at a child that contains and creates meaning

Carla Busato Barbaglio

A person I know, who treats children affected by serious brain lesions that damage their eyes, showed me his work with a little blind girl. I heard him saying, with a sweet and confident intonation in his voice, "Look towards my voice." After several requests, the little girl smiled and turned her empty eyes to the man's voice, as if this voice had turned into a "sound cradle" which could help her direct her attention. The doctor's capacity to beckon the blind girl with his voice impressed me and greatly influenced my thinking about my work as a psychoanalyst.

A psychotherapist uses her voice. It is this that the patient can perceive and use as an orientating and reference point in her journey towards becoming an individual. A particular tone of voice also helps a child to identify just who the speaker is, not just his name, but also the nature of the feelings present in that person at that time. Psychotherapy and psychoanalysis create a space in which mutual understanding and communication between the therapist and the individual may bring the possibility of unexpected improvements in the person's life.

Several current studies focus our attention on the way a mother and a child look at each other. Their way of looking at one another creates a pre-symbolic interaction between mother and child. This pre-symbolic experience is stored in the child's unconscious, implicit, and procedural memory, which is developed before his autobiographical memory. Looking at each other, mother and child convey to each other their thoughts and emotions, thus establishing an intimate connection between their minds.

By continuing to look at each other, mother and child weave a net that becomes the basis of their relationship. In a similar way, an intimate connection establishes in the child an internalised inner dialogue between mother and child. From this perspective, even the child's way of playing has its beginning in his mother's womb, in the way she holds, thinks about, cuddles, in other words, loves him. Would it be possible to describe this inner attention as a "pre-playing stage"? What really interests me is how the child's eyes are even prenatally "directed" by his mother, as I said before.

Much of the mother–child dialogue, through which the self takes on more particular characteristics, takes place after the child's birth. The first way of playing is through words, and it is based on the contrast between what is real and what is unreal. Although the mother pretends her baby could understand her and know who she really is, only a part of her is convinced of that. She used to talk to her child while he was growing in her womb, as many pregnant mothers do, and she imagined what her baby was like. A part of her thinks her child recognises her voice and she is right, as many studies have proved. A child inside his mother's womb can distinguish his mother's voice from other people's voices. Playing with words is not only based on the contrast between real and unreal, but also on the contrast between being serious and not being serious.

Then the child arrives into the light of the world outside the womb. The way he is welcomed is part of the continuing game of the mother–child interaction. The mother's intonation, her way of holding her child or offering him the breast or the bottle, anything that helps their relationship develop, is the basis of the child's future way of playing. If we listen to ourselves talking to children, especially to babies, we may notice how our voice becomes high pitched, how we start using lallation and how, in case we need to calm down a child, the intonation of our voice becomes a warm hug. All this should make us aware of when, instead of the warm voice, our voice becomes hard, anxious, tense, and stops the child from looking at us with confidence. This is an alarm bell signalling that the *positive communication play* between mother and child is coming to a stop and a more stressful way of communicating is taking its place.

A baby whose anger at home is just "tickled", rather than contained, has repressed anger that pops up elsewhere, sometimes resulting in other children being bitten or hit. Nowadays, we are increasingly aware that a sense of wellbeing makes endorphins and serotonins circulate in our blood. All these substances working on synapses and connections may make neurons more elastic, and, thus, they make the individual predisposed to a sense of wellbeing. We have other ways of calming and soothing through reflective functioning, involving thinking about the baby's emotional state while soothing the baby. What we do know is that it is terribly important to create relationships that support hope and a sense of wellbeing in early childhood, for the effects are felt on a long-term basis.

Bearing this in mind, it is important to consider these questions: how do we look at a child's way of playing? How does the school look at children's play? How do teachers, parents, and children look at each others' play? Does the children's play suggest that we are managing to provide an optimal environment at that moment which permits them to feel a sense of wellbeing, a sense of hope that life is and will be nurturing and good to them?

Psychoanalysis has always regarded dreams as the best means to interpret the unconscious mind. Fonagy (2001) said that some dreams might be analysed with an idea that the patient produces dreams in the context of his relationship with the psychotherapist. Similarly, Freud (1900a) stated that there are recurring anxiety dreams that might arrive at times of exams, separations, and suffering or escaping from a terrible trauma. Something similar takes place when a child is playing. His play conveys the story of his internal relationship with his parents and other important figures in his life, such as siblings, grandparents, teachers, and peers at school. The Tempo Lineare children's games represent not only their own internalised family stories, but also their relationships with all the people present in Tempo Lineare. This great responsibility for the child's emotional life, as reflected in his dreams, play, and behaviour, must, therefore, be shared and assumed by everybody who is part of the school as well as the child's family.

Fonagy (2001) also asserted that the reflective functioning is something a child acquires through a secure relationship with the protective, nurturing, and thoughtful parents. Reflective functioning enables a child to understand another person's behaviour in terms of feelings, attitudes, hopes, and intuition. Reflective functioning implies an ability to define and understand one's inner experiences, and, thus, have some choices and control regarding how one responds to situations. But how does a child's mind deal with our experiences before he fully develops the capacity for reflective functioning? The playing of a child forms part of his developing ability to reflect on his mental states. Likewise, adults' phantasies, dreams, and spontaneous associations interacting with the child's way of being form part of the family and school culture, supporting the child in becoming more fully aware of his own and other people's mental states.

To give you one example of what I mean, a two-year-old child and his mother were talking about Christmas: the Christmas crib, the Christmas tree, and Christmas presents. At one point, his mother asked him, "What present would you like for Christmas?" He answered, "A present." His mother wanted to know more about what he meant by "a present". He responded to her query, saying, "A coloured wish." The child was trying to condense in his few words the essential meaning of what he had absorbed from his environment and he was expressing his idea of a present in an almost poetical way. Something symbolic and real at the same time: a coloured wish. Yet, if his mother had not welcomed and praised his effort and had instead brought the conversation round to toy cars or motorbikes, things would have been very different for him. Welcoming and praising the child's imaginative efforts creates a sense of wellbeing, which is the basis for the child's further growth.

With regard to the importance of parents' and teachers' attitudes to a child, I would like to mention the studies of Badaracco and colleagues (Badaracco, Narracci, & Granieri, 2004), who asserted that if you look at a sick person as sick, you make him feel even sicker. They firmly believed that in every sick person there is always some healthy potentiality. In particular, this happens in a family whose members have experienced a severe psychotic episode. They change completely their way of looking at that mentally ill family member and their attitude makes the family member take on more of the identity of feeling and being sick. We must keep in mind that the outcome of a person who had a severe psychotic episode is strictly linked to the way people interpret what was and is happening to him and relate to him thereafter.

Badaracco also said that in these situations the patient is very afraid, more frightened than all the other family members, and he needs someone to rely on and help him stop feeling afraid.

One of the greatest obstacles to psychotherapy is a family culture of fear. This fearful attitude makes it more difficult for the child to improve. At times, it is easier for a child to cling to his illness to form his identity rather than to assume the frightening challenge and responsibility of his personal growth. In conclusion, Badaracco and colleagues (2004) asserted that *the way of looking at somebody* can be more potent in making a person maintain a feeling of being ill than words. People's words, in fact, can be analysed and interpreted, while it is more difficult to grasp and think about people's ways of looking at one.

You might wonder why I am discussing a person's way of looking at somebody else. This illustration stresses examining our manner of being with a child in school or at home when the child is having a problem and facing an extremely crucial moment of his development. What we think about a child, how we relate to him, imprints upon him his sense of identity in our eyes. If a child feels he is looked at by his parents and teachers as being full of positive potentialities, he will be given hope and vitality, and this will strengthen his self-esteem. This does not mean we do not have to take into consideration those destructive aspects of a child's growth that might worry us. It does mean that it is important to look at children as healthy growing beings who need to be supported to deal with some difficult aspects of their growth. It is important for a child and his parents to feel that asking for therapeutic help is not an indication of failure, but, rather, as an opportunity to give the child and his parents further attention to enhance understanding of some complex situations in the child's development.

Young children are not able to put all their complex emotions into words, but they reveal them through their play. In playing, the child expresses his feelings, his curiosity, his anxieties, and his wishes. The child's choice of an object is made according to the phantasies and emotions the maternal and paternal figures evoke inside the child. Playing helps the child feel and think about his emotions. While playing, the child makes a distinction between imagination and reality. This awareness reveals his ability to think and it is also very useful for him to know that everything is only pretend. Pretending to do things enables him to experience extreme situations such as wars, deaths, or very pleasant situations that he knows will never have any consequences in his real life. He can come back to the external reality of his life whenever he likes and reassure himself, because he has only pretended to do those things. Playing is, thus, a way of dealing with one's intense feelings in order to work through anxieties connected with them and learn how to bear them.

The play in the form of a dialogue between mother and child, which started inside the mother's womb and continued after the baby's birth, is gradually transformed into the child's inner dialogue between his feelings and thoughts. Looking with enthusiasm, affection, and understanding at a child playing enables the child's play to be woven into the parents' and teachers' thoughts about the child's emotional experiences. Baldwin (1906), a pioneer in infant psychology, articulated a theory that proved the importance of playing in human development. He asserted that playing is the basis of culture. He also stated that what is positive in playing is the child's sense of freedom. In Baldwin's opinion, playing is a swinging of the self towards control. By pretending to be somebody else, such as a soldier, a football, a wooden horse, or whatever, the child's real self loses its identity in order to find it. The self can prove what it really is like only by swapping its form.

If we think about playing as the child's most creative and free expression of himself, we must ask ourselves what happens in those situations where games are without this essential freedom and vitality. If the child is playing a game only to please the adults, this does not permit him to have the deeper experience of dramatising his own unique inner experiences. His dialogue between his *inner world* and his parents becomes distorted if they propose the play rather than letting him find what he wants to "play out" from his inner world. A school like Tempo Lineare, which can make children feel a sense of wellbeing by playing, can also encourage the development of a good body–mind interaction, for playing is made up of both sensorial sensations and thoughts.

References

Badaracco, J. G., Narracci, A, & Granieri, F. (2004). *Psicoanalisi multifamiliare. Gli altri in noi e la scoperta di noi stessi.* Milan: Bollatti Borenghieri.

Baldwin, J. M. (1906). *Thought and Things Vol 1: A Study of the Development and Meaning of Thought.* New York: Macmillan.

Fonagy, P. (2001). *Attachment Theory and Psychoanalysis.* London: Other Press.

Freud, S. (1900a). *Interpretation of Dreams. S.E., 4–5.* London: Hogarth.

CHAPTER TWELVE

A special time for playing and thinking together

Jeanne Magagna

A t thirteen, the vast wonders of the inner world opened themselves to me. I accompanied a school friend's older sister to a university class to hear Freud's *Interpretation of Dreams* (1900a) and a lecture on the poetry of Emily Dickinson. Suddenly, the richness of meaning implicit in play, dreaming, and poetry became apparent to me. I likened discovering meaning in these activities to exploring a mountain . . . and I have never stopped my climbing through the interior world . . . trying to make sense of people's actions and children's play . . . *trying to understand the unconscious*. I hope this chapter will motivate you to continue this journey with me . . . to explore meaning present in *your own dream life* and in *your child's play*.

Introduction

In many ways, we play as children and as adults when we create our daydreams and night-time dreams. Play allows us to externalise our deepest emotional state and elaborate upon emotional experiences that are important to us.

A historical perspective on play

Freud (1920g) thought of play as a way to understand how a child made attempts to convey his emotional experience and come to terms with it. Much play is connected to the child's significant relationships with parents and siblings. By observing the free play of the mind, we can perceive the workings of the child's unconscious. Anna Freud, Melanie Klein, and Maria Montessori describe how play portrays the child's loving and destructive feelings, his anxieties and phantasies (Wilkins, 1993). Repetitive play also shows the child's repeated preoccupations that interfere with ongoing development of intimate relationships (Hoxter, 1977).

If your day is busy, and you come home to be with your child, it might be difficult to relate to your child's experiences when away from you unless you sit with him and watch his spontaneous play. Children use play to convey feelings they are not yet able to express in words. Also, a child might fear putting his feelings into words for fear the adults will find these feelings unacceptable and will not love him. In addition, he might have repressed his negative feelings because of an inner critic and they may only emerge spontaneously through the physical activity of playing or drawing. He might not yet have the verbal capacity to put his feelings into words. Play is an acceptable and necessary way for feelings to be shared and elaborated upon. The toys become symbols to substitute for important family and school figures. Sometimes, a toy representing someone on one day may represent someone else on another day.

If you create a regular time each week to play separately with each of your children, you and your child (or children) will have the pleasure of knowing each other better. You will experience your child developing an inner space for thinking in a deeper, more complex and more loving way. You will experience your child's delight and gratitude for having the greatest gift of all, which surpasses all others . . . *that is, a loving parent* having the capacity to be present to accept fully the brunt of the child's emotions. A whole new world of understanding of your child will open up to you through being present, finely tuned to your child playing.

Imaginative, explorative play and the brain system

Sunderland's book, *The Science of Parenting* (2006), gives a further explanation of many of the ideas she originally described regarding the links between the brain and playing. If you provide your child with a loving relationship, filled with lots of imaginative, explorative activities, you will activate the *seeking system* of the brain. When this system is working, your child will have an appetite for life, curiosity, and the drive and motivation to make his creative ideas a reality. It is important not to spoil your child's explorative curiosity by using a kind of discipline that shames your child. If this occurs, he will most likely retreat from exploration.

Providing opportunities for your child to be in a creative union with you and other children through imaginative play can both reduce stress chemicals, and also may increase the number of brain cells available to the child—at least, that is, if the research on rats is anything to go by.

> Rats were given an enriched environment with lots of interesting play activities and lots of social interaction. Two months later the rats had an extra 50,000 brain cells in each side of one of the key learning and memory centres of the brain called the hippocampus. (Sunderland, 2006, p. 96)

Rough and tumble play and the brain cells

City dwellers beware! Children who are deprived of physically and socially interactive play will find it difficult to sit still and focus their attention. One study found that children deprived of playtime at school developed attention deficit disorder and were unable to sit still and focus their attention. Physical play enhances the development of the higher human brain with all its amazing functions, including better management of emotions and stress. The brain's frontal lobes are stimulated by physical play. So, find some time for your child to be involved in rough and tumble play that results in transporting your child into states of joy, squeals of laughter or delight. For example, delightfully rolling on the floor, toppling over each other, playing statue where you spin the child around and then have the child stand still like a statue, playing in the playground, play-fighting, playing hide and seek, leap-frog . . . all these rough and tumble games are important for your child. Do not think that just lessons are important for young children. As well as less active, more thoughtful play in the house, physical play that involves interacting with you and other children is very important, too.

The receptive mind experiencing a child's play

How do you develop receptivity to what you experience in your child's play? Developing an internal mental space freed from distractions of the day and the telephone is such a difficult task. A receptive mind is developed most fully if you have an opportunity to see your own experiences through keeping a diary at least once a week and letting all your thoughts and dreams tumble out on the page. Cameron, in *An Artist's Way* (1995), tells you more about this experience of free-flowing journal writing through which you can see the innermost self more fully. In particular, if you do not see your own jealousy, your own hate, your own needs and feelings concerned with dependency and intimacy, it is difficult to have a mind receptive to the identical feelings in your child. Our blind spots in relationship to children occur when we are disowning and denying our aggression, possessiveness, dependency, and fear. The ideal parent strives to receive every aspect of the child's personality . . . and that means the ideal parent strives to get to know every aspect of his own personality to better understand his child.

Receptively accepting the brunt of a child's mental pain, hurt, fear, anger, distress, love, generosity, thoughtfulness, conflict, and sense of mastery gives the child a greater possibility of inner psychological development. Through the parents' generous receptive minds, the child develops the capacity to bear the pain of thinking and the challenge of exploring his own thoughts and emotions in more depth.

The presence of a flat, denying, parental mind could contribute to a child not being able to mentalize regarding his deeper emotional experiences of love, pain, hate, and fear. For example, in infancy, the crying baby can be crying just to be in the company of his parents, but if parents cannot bear the baby's intense dependency they might offer milk and toys instead of themselves. The suffering child later turns to material comforts, showing an insatiable greed for toys, not even being able to understand that it is a deeper, more pleasurable encounter with parents and friends that is really wanted. Then the risk is that the child turns to his toys *not as a symbol for the relationship with the parents, but in lieu of intimacy with the parents.* This leads the way to pathological development in the personality of the child. If the parents have receptive internal space for the child, the child is able to turn to a toy *as a symbol* for the parents and use it to help the child to tolerate the frustrating experience of being separate from the parents and to find the courage to explore, be curious, and to enjoy people and different aspects of his world.

Creation of a special time for play

How many of you played enough with your parents? If you did not, you might need some opportunities to play yourself and learn from being with others in the nursery about how to create different ways of playing with your child.

First of all, though, why not go home and ask your child, "Do you think you and I play together enough?" If the answer is no, or even if it is yes, it would be good to develop a deeper understanding of your child's play. What I would like to suggest here is that you create spontaneous playtimes with your child. I also think you would be safer if you marked in your diary *at the same time each week*, a regular "special time of half an hour for playing". Do this for one month. You should follow this schedule without fail in the same manner that you go to work or have dinner. If you feel uncomfortable doing this, then think of someone who can do this with your child. Ideally, a child should be engaged in social play and/or communication that directly involves an adult for at least one hour a day. Physical play, such as running, playing ball and other sports, with the parents ideally, would alternate with this special time play that does not involve so much muscular activity.

Preparing for the less active special playtime

I invite you to make a special box 45 × 45 cm, fill it with pairs of mother and father animals with two babies: farm animal families, wild animal families, and human families with four grandparents, too; 15–20 fence pieces, some Lego, some sellotape, a pair of scissors, some felt tips or crayons in good condition, a plastic envelope folder and ten sheets of blank A4 paper, several balls of plasticine, an eraser and two lead pencils, two small balls that can be safely thrown, bubble-blowing equipment, string. Have a few puppets, too, they can be simply two socks with two buttons and red mouths, or you can buy several more complicated ones. Paint and some larger sheets of paper can also be added if you have a place where you feel it is suitable to paint.

Playing for half an hour to one hour, depending on developmental phase of the child

Now, invite your child to spend a regularly scheduled time playing with his/her "special box" reserved just for this occasion. If your child does not want to join you or cannot initiate some spontaneous play, after a while you can try to start playing by yourself. Just be sure to tell your child that this is what you are going to do, place yourself in a conspicuous place, say where you are, and play using talking aloud to yourself to show how you are using your imagination. Again, Sunderland (2006) describes these activities more fully in her book.

A story will be created through the play; watch it as you watch a film. If your child is playing, you can say you will do whatever he/she requests that you do. He can be your director. If you are playing by yourself, because your child has not joined you on this occasion, let your hands take the lead, let them move spontaneously, moving the toy figures around until you have created an action or some actions.

Attitude of the participant observer

For play to be useful in helping to solve problems you need to be:

- a sensitive partner with whom child feels safe and secure;
- a participant observer, who perhaps guides a little, but does not dominate the play;
- a participant who takes pleasure in the activity of shared play;
- a participant who agrees that imagination, cognition, love, and aggression can all be part of the play;
- someone who provides reciprocity between the baby part of the child and the parent so that the child can develop an internal space for thinking about his emotions

The importance of child-led play

Spontaneous child-led play is likely to reduce the level of the child's stress chemicals. It is important to follow and not dominate with conversation. It also helps to reduce the child's aggressive behaviour if you allow your child to bring conflicts that have been inside his head out into external space. This then enables the child to work out the complexity of the conflicts through play. By emotionally participating in the play, you will have thoughts arising within you that will enable you to understand the issues that are troubling him. You need to be prepared to understand the child's painful, not so pretty feelings. Do not try to "cheer him up" or make things better before you have understood the pain. Some examples of play are listed below.

- You can describe what your child is doing: for example, you are putting a fence around the three baby lambs, maybe protecting them so they are safe.
- You can ask to play . . . May I join in . . . what would you like me to do?
- You can offer some affective touch to your child while he is playing, perhaps a hand placed gently on his shoulder.
- You can acknowledge through praise: "That was interesting!"
- You are not permitted in any way to be critical of what occurs.
- You cannot allow any physical hurting of yourself or others.

The play activity

Here is an example of play that we can use just to understand more fully what I am suggesting for special time. First of all, here is an example of baby's play at eighteen months:

> Baby Eric is in the bath; he takes a plastic duck and he throws it out on to the floor. Then he takes another plastic duck and he throws it at mother. Mother says, "Stop!" Baby Eric continues to throw wet toys at mother (Magagna, 2002).

Here is the second example, of play at twenty-two months: Eric's mother is noticeably expecting a baby, which Eric realises through discussions with his parents:

> Baby Eric plays with a basketful of plums and tomatoes, he rubs the tomatoes, holds them gently, squeezes them a bit, and then throws them, one by one, to the floor. He says, "Tomatoes, plums, see! Then he picks them up and throws them to the floor again. He then climbs on a stool and stands on it, and turns around on the stool. He is getting very excited (Magagna, 2002).

The third example of play is at twenty-six months: Eric's mother is due to have her baby the subsequent week:

> Baby Eric brings the pieces of train to mother and puts them one by one on her legs. After he puts each train car on her leg he rolls it off her leg and lets it drop. There were three pieces. He laughs as each piece drops. Then he picks the three pieces up, puts them on his mother's leg, and struggles to connect the cars of the train. He is unsuccessful and says to his mother, "Fix it." She connects two train cars for him (Magagna, 2002).

Discussion of these three examples of play

In these three examples of play, the bath, the tomatoes, and the trains, Eric reveals destructive wishes: he is throwing toy ducks at mother, dropping the tomatoes out of the basket and dropping the train cars. After pulling the train pieces apart and dropping them, he gleefully laughs. Later, though, in the third play sequence, Eric is asking his mother to fix the train, to connect the pieces together. There is a sense that Eric is feeling dropped by mother as the about-to-be-born baby changes mother's capacity to hold Eric physically and, thus, intrudes more obviously into his relationship with the mother. Eric is also cross that the couple have produced a new baby, disrupting his family of three where he is frequently the sole focus of their attention.

However, nothing is definitely clear in these play activities. I imagine that that Eric is frightened of being dropped out of mother's lap and, in the last two sequences, he wants to drop "the baby" out of mother's lap. As time progresses an increased symbolisation of aggression occurs: there is a transformation in the play from concrete throwing of ducks at mother to use of the basket of tomatoes to symbolise mother and her babies. Such symbolic play activity protects mother's body and the baby in the womb from Eric's aggression. In the third symbolic play sequence, involving rolling the train cars off mother's legs, Eric portrays his internalised trust in his mother as a helpful person who can help him mend the train he has aggressively thrown to the floor.

Now let us look at play in an older child

The story is drawn from a Master's degree thesis on "Special time" (Carignani, 1994, p. 45).

> Susanna, four years old.
>
> Susanna takes a baby doll, saying that he must go to hospital for he has burned himself. She puts the baby in the house and asks, "Do you hear the screams?" Paolo asks, "Yes, what is happening?" Susanna says, "The doctors are looking at the baby and the baby is screaming because he is burnt." Susanna then takes a pan and shows Paolo, "This is the pan where the baby was burned in." Susanna then puts the baby back in the pan and says "It's being fried." She puts the lid on the pan and rubs the pan on the pretend stove. There is squeaking from the rubbing of the pan and Susanna says, "The baby is screaming!" Then she puts the baby back into the play-house hospital, saying, "The doctors are going to make him better."
>
> She again asks Paolo, "Can you hear the screams? When Paolo agrees, "I can hear the screams, this is what I am here for, to understand why the baby suffers so much", Susanna then says, "Maybe it is

not a boy but a girl." She looks at Paolo and says, "The girl can be cured if the doctors are not frightened by the screams. If the doctors are frightened they might run away from the hospital and the girl will die of her burns. The doctors put bandages on and Susanna stops crying." She adds, "The pain will maybe go away, maybe not."

Recalling the play activity

Let's see, now, what happened in the play? This is an inner narrative created through spontaneous play:

> A girl is in hospital with pain ... maybe she will be helped, maybe not.

What are the characters feeling in the play?

You can talk about them in the third person, or you could hold one of the characters and speak as though you were the character. For example, I could take hold of the little boy doll, the doctor doll, or the burning pan and talk about the emotions of each of the characters in the play scene in the following way:

1. Identifying an emotion: what are some of the emotions?
2. Describing the emotion: how would you describe the emotion?
3. Amplifying an emotion:
    (i) sharing understanding of an emotion;
    (ii) helping the child mentalize about an emotional experience present in one of characters in his drama, perhaps saying this,

The little girl is worried that no one will stay by her side and help her.

What is the theme of this play?

Look at the way in which power relations are articulated, upheld, and challenged.

> The little girl needs the helpful doctors to stay with her because she is suffering.

What could be the purpose of the child playing this?

Susanna kept repeating parts of the Cinderella fairy tale, which must express a feeling that she is oppressed by schoolmates and/or siblings.

If play is repetitious, what is the anxiety that needs to be played out again and again?

What we know is that Cinderella is ill-treated by her stepsisters, but also she gains the Prince and his riches, leaving the stepsisters in despair. Susanna repeats parts of the Cinderella story, for it dramatises how Susanna feels herself to be the victim of oppression. Finally, in both the Cinderella story and Susannah's play, there is a more certain good outcome.

If a theme is interrupted, what is the emotion that stops the play continuing?

A sense of something better comes with the Prince, who interrupts the scene of the sisters' sibling rivalry.

If theme is completed, what feeling has the child elaborated upon in the play?

The theme of being mistreated and the hopefulness of someone understanding Susanna has been illustrated.

What pleasure and sense of relief could the child be getting from the play?

The relief comes from Susanna seeing Paolo for "special time sessions" at a set time each week, gradually experiencing him as "The Prince" who will understand her psychological wounds and, thus, help her find some relief from the misery in her life.

When a child cannot play

Some children get stuck with a particular issue, particularly when they have not internalised a mentalizing parent who can think about their emotional experiences. In particular, severely traumatised, emotionally abused children or autistic children have difficulty playing. Hopkins (2002), a child psychotherapist, has written very movingly about this:

> Paddy was a three-year-old boy whose mother was suicidally depressed. His parents were unable to play with him. When he was in the room with the psychotherapist his only activity was to drop, throw and bang cars. He had no structure to his play. Juliet just named what he was doing. She said, "dropped car, thrown away car, hit car". Later she imitated his animal noises and the clapping of his hands. (Hopkins, 2002, p. 91–99)

In a similar situation I have talked for the car: "Poor car, it fell down." I would also speak as though I were the car, "Ouch, ouch . . . it hurts to be thrown down, it hurts to be dropped, ouch, ouch it hurts so much, ouch ouch! Ouch, ouch, it hurts to be dropped from someone's mind."

The particular child I saw ran water all the time, so I would talk as though I were her: "I love the water, I can make it come and go . . . I can have the water whenever I want it. There is never a stop to it." Then I would talk as though I were the water: "Here I am for you, I am always here for you whenever you want me." Then I would talk about my being with her (Magagna, 2012, p. 97).

Following a sequence of play through a series of "special play" occasions

These observations of play are taken from a sequence. Let us see what we can discover from observing this play of Paddy, described partially above by Hopkins (1996, pp. 20–27).

Identifying with a good figure

Paddy moved to second stage of symbolic play called "pretend play": he engaged in an imaginary play of feeding the therapist bananas and milk, using the plasticine. He then invited the therapist to feed him (Hopkins, 2002, p. 95).

Projection

Paddy would play hide and seek, the next phase of play in which he jumped out of his hiding place to kick her. In this way he was projecting onto the therapist his fears (Hopkins, 2002, p. 95).

Persecution

Paddy would play crocodiles, he wanted the therapist to play too. The play was repetitive, compulsive and urgent. He couldn't cry (Hopkins, 2002, p. 96).

Identifying with the aggressor and then identification with the good figures

Paddy continued to identify with the horrible monsters and the crocodiles As Paddy trusted his therapist a little more he began to identify with "a good her" inside himself. Soon he was identifying with the good figures in his life (Hopkins, 2002, p. 96).

Reparation and concern for the other

In this chapter, I have previously shown an example of Eric asking his mother for help to fix the trains, a way of requesting help in repairing damage done through his aggression.

Exploration, curiosity, mastery

One-year-old Jerry became curious about the contents of his toy box, emptied them out, held them one by one, looking at them, and then put them back inside the box.

Developing an inner space for creative dialogue with inner feeling

Anna, aged 3½, dreamt of a lion looking at her and she told her mother she was scared.

Initiating spontaneous play when a child is not playing

Ideally, you will be able to follow the activity initiated by your child and get involved in an intimate relationship through the play. You will intuitively feel whether or not the activity is pleasurable for your child. Pleasurable play enables the child's brain to become filled with optimal levels of dopamine that are vital for a child to feel intensely alive. If the child loses interest in playing, then it is not the right moment or the right activity. There is no sense in going on with it.

If your child is stuck on the beach or on a Saturday morning at home and cannot find a way of amusing himself, you might want to help the child get started on some kind of play. For example,

> Suggest that you choose a place in which imagination can be used. For example, one could choose to be in a pretend circus, toy shop, farm, country with with animals, in a fairy tale scene or in a TV cartoon. Once you have chosen a setting, drawings, plasticine, shells, sand piles, buttons or toys could be used to represent the characters as you create a dramatic scene. (Sunderland, 2006, p. 148)

If you are at home during a special play time, you might start off with a few ideas: go to a treasure island and start exploring there, build a farmyard, create a household drama with the dolls, play school with some pretend animal friends and a puppet teacher. You can invite your child into your play. If your child still is not interested after a few weeks, then tell your child you will play once again with the toys yourself.

Play as a way of the child communicating troubles

A young child might not be able to verbally communicate what it is that is giving him a stomach ache, making him feel unhappy, or making him feel grumpy or angry. However, the child can know that something is not right inside. If you develop the notion of special time with the child, gradually he will notice that you "understand the play". After a few months of special time, you could give your child one of the small toys from the "special time play box" and suggest that sometimes things cannot be spoken about initially, but they can be "played out" and you can try to understand. So, suggest to your child that if he cannot tell you about something, but he feels in difficulty, he could bring you the toy and suggest that you "play it out" as in the following example.

Sibling rivalry can be one of the worst difficulties for under fours. Your three-year-old can begin to get aggressive as a sign that things are not right, but not know what to do with the aggression. Instead of stealing a toy from the young baby, the three-year-old could be encouraged to "play it out" with you. You can also talk about the problem: poor little cat, he wants to be with his mummy all the time and mummy is feeding some of the other little kittens. Mummy still loves him and Daddy still loves him. Just as mummy and daddy love you, Johnny, even when we are with baby Bobby. We know you have a pain in your heart.

Repetitious play

The daily repetitious moving of hard objects, trucks, vacuum cleaner pipes forward on the floor should alert you to the fact that there is some misattunement between you and your child. The child is having difficulty developing an internal capacity for mentalization, for symbolic play, and a psychotherapeutic consultation would be worth considering. The child's lack of mental-ization and attunement with the parents could have many precipitating causes. The point is to understand the impasse to symbolic play, discover the child's worries, which could be quite severe, and find ways of diminishing the child's anxieties rather than holding any party respon-sible and blaming them.

Monsters in play

Why do monsters appear so frequently in a child's play? A child may draw them, dramatise them, feel pursued by them in nightmares, or play a game in which monsters are involved (Hopkins, 1996). The repetitive play involving monsters can suggest that a child is preoccupied with something that requires an adult to help the child to understand what the play is about. Such repetitive preoccupation with terrifying monsters can suggest that primitive terrors might inhibit the development of mentalization. Four reasons that children can have for playing with monsters are:

1. Creating and/or using the monster as a scapegoat upon which the child can project aggres-sive feelings in order to maintain a loving relationship to the parents and siblings. This involves a *splitting* process: I love the baby and hate the monster.
2. Playing monster games to externalise an internal drama in which the child feels terrorised by internal monsters because of some traumatic hospital, family, or school event (Hopkins, 1996):

     Hitting parents or sibling, domestic violence, severe bullying in the playground, painful and traumatic physical interventions in the incubator or later in life can all perpetuate monster play in which the child is terrified and a victim.

     Example 1: A child having injections regularly in hospital or surgery in early childhood.

     Example 2: A child who is frequently bullied, hit by a sibling or parent and then projects all his aggression into the hitting sibling can feel terrorised by the monster.

3. Playing the monster can be used to project terror into others so that they can experience the trauma that the child originally experienced.

     Example: A child might play the terrifying lion as he integrates his aggression back into himself. His identification with an omnipotent lion might express a need to have a sense of potency and control over frightening situations. This could represent a step in development in the child, although further development in the play would be needed.

4. Monster games in which child suggests that he and the other take turns playing the monster might involve a replay of experiences where there was conflict between parents and child as in this example:

     Example: The parents say, "Time for bed". The child is angry about the fact that mother and father will be alone together while he has to go to bed and remain alone. The child becomes furious about the parents' bedtime rule. Internal parents turn into monsters who frighten the child in nightmares and daytime play because the child's aggression has been projected into them.

Parents allowing the child to sleep with them leave the child with an unconscious Oedipal phantasy that he has interfered with the couple's relationship. Then the child might experience a nightmare of being attacked by the monster representing guilt for his own destructive possessiveness and jealousy of the parents' coupling.

Interruptions in play sequence

Play is intended to permit the child to work through anxieties, develop identifications with parents, and discover knowledge and skills. Sometimes, though, there is too great an anxiety produced in the play and the play sequence is suspended. The play sequence is interrupted because the child cannot bear the danger or pain produced by the play. Being infused by overwhelming feelings, the play has lost its symbolic value. For example, the pretend "big, bad wolf" has become the real "big bad wolf" and it is too terrifying to continue playing.

Too many interruptions in the play sequence might suggest that the child is very troubled and needs a psychotherapeutic consultation to more fully understand his troubling inner conflicts. Let us observe and compare the levels of anxiety present in these two examples of three-year-old children's play after the teacher suggested that all the children embark upon pretend cooking.

> Example 1: Alex finds some pretend cereal, pours some pretend milk, imagines he is eating the pretend cereal, then he pretends to warm some soup and says he has turned the stove burner down.

> Example 2: George continues his play of quelling fires, battling monsters and pretending to be a cowboy. He gallops on his horse, sings, goes to a wheelbarrow and throws some bricks out from it. Suddenly George says he is making cookies and he gets some imaginary ice cream, throws it to the ground and then he throws a plate.

It is obvious that George's play is characterised by aggression. His impulsive, aggressive acts also disrupt or disintegrate the play themes. Such play, which hardly linked to the teacher's suggested theme of cooking, indicates that George has been unable to consolidate a good internal containing mother that permits a developed symbolisation of his experiences. He also seems hostile to the teacher's instructions for the play. George needs an adult to help him with his aggression, for he has few internal resources for modulating his inner emotional life. Imaginary play filled with aggression can be used as a reflection of poor attachments, which include troubled unrelatedness to others.

In contrast to George, Alex shows sequences in his play, fluidity of symbolic productions and a theme of cooking some soup. Alex has a capacity for a developed symbolic play. He is beginning to develop the capacity for mentalization. This is linked with his being sufficiently lovingly connected to the teacher's mind that he can thoughtfully play along the lines she has suggested.

Stopping play

Once a child is fully engaged in play, the risk is that it is truly difficult for the child to respond to instructions to stop and listen or change to a different activity, such as taking a bath, going to bed, coming to dinner, or going out. This is because the key chemical systems in his brain are undeveloped, making him unable to easily shift his attention from his play to the teacher or parent. The child's attention is virtually locked on the activity he is doing. It is important, therefore, to warn a young child that it will be time to stop playing in five minutes. Then, when the five minutes are up, it is helpful to have a count-down: 5, 4, 3, 2, 1. If the child does not respond then, it is important simply to take the child by the hand to where you want the child to be. Praising for stopping an activity and responding to you is helpful. Too much scolding or nagging of the child desensitises the child to your scolding voice (Sunderland, 2006)!

Using play as ways of spontaneously relating to difficulties during the day

Sometimes, instead of simply being boring and making a rule about what should happen, you could use your creativity to deal with important issues that you and the child are facing.

Play as a way of relating to child's anger about your not being present and attentive to him

If you really analyse your child's behaviour, you will find that so much of it is linked with your child finding it difficult when he is not the central focus of your love, care, and thoughtfulness. Jealousy of your talking to others, being with another child, talking on the mobile, or being at work seems to provoke aggression in your child. You could use play as a way of recovering the empathic connection between you and your child. For example, you could provide a good encounter through creative, warm play. You will need to use your imagination for this. You need to embark on a play sequence in which the animal or human figures show aggression. It is important that you fully honestly receive and acknowledge the brunt of what the child is feeling towards you at some point during the activities mentioned below. These could be followed by generously sharing some of your loving affection. Sunderland (2006, p. 203) is filled with imaginative ideas such as:

- play biting tigers and end by cuddling your child;
- play taking a shower . . . wash out all the anger in your child;
- while simultaneously talking about what the anger is about, give your child a massage with your hands to work out all the tension aroused by the anger.

Initiating play in places where child may be bored (Sunderland, 2006, p. 139)

If you are busy talking on the phone, or talking to a friend at home or in the restaurant, it is likely that your child will get bored. Being in a low state of brain arousal creates a need to satisfy a hunger for mental stimulation. Your child is going to feel the need to do something, as you know. If you provide an interesting activity, appropriate to your child's developmental level, it is likely that you will engage his higher brain in a co-ordinated way that will enable him to focus on the activity and, in so doing, calm his wish to run around. So, for example, bringing a little bag of toys, a drawing pad, some paper and pens and a colourful storybook is likely to result in your child not getting scolded for throwing objects on the floor or messing with food.

Supermarket shopping is another opportunity for your child to have lack of structure, stimulation, and recognition. Shopping can involve your child in a mystery hunt for hidden items. You can wonder which aisle the biscuits can be found in and begin a treasure hunt for the mysterious treasure! Another possibility is to tell your child that you are playing "Champion Shopper", whisper into your child's ear the name of a shopping item, such as plums, needed for the trolley. If the child succeeds in finding the plums, you whisper, then your child is a "Champion Shopper" and deserves a Champion treat! You can help your child choose a little treat for being a champion in this shopping treasure hunt (Sunderland, 2006 p. 141).

It is your responsibility to provide structure for the child, stimulation if the occasion means the child will be bored, and sufficient recognition so that the child feels you are keeping him in your mind even though you are doing something else.

Play as a way of relating to your child when he wants to boss you or bully you

Bad behaviour in a child will occur, but it is important to consider the process of interaction between you and the child that might have resulted in the bad behaviour. If you can spend some time reviewing the day aloud, with your child's assistance in remembering good, fun, difficult, angry, provoking, loving moments, it will help your child develop a capacity for reflection about who he is and what he is doing. If something has gone wrong that requires an apology or some form of reparation, either on the part of a parent, a sibling, or the child whom you are with, it will be helpful to initiate such a process. Hostility towards a child in turn promotes more hostility and difficulties. Understanding what hurts and how that hurt turns into a hostile act can provide a more understanding and, eventually, a more co-operative exchange between you and your child. Sometimes, a child enters "boss mode" because of some underlying anxiety in the relationship with the parents. It is more anxiety provoking for a child who kicks, shouts, or ignores your authority, for the child is left without the very necessary thoughtful, supportive parent figures he needs. He becomes insecure and the person he has attacked, either mentally, verbally, or physically, is filled with hostile projections and becomes the figure of nightmares.

For this reason, there are times that you must simply address a controlling child who is taking over your parental functions. The secret is not to pay attention to your child when he is dominating you with commands. Suggest being with you in a way that will create kindness in you. Sometimes, a child's bossiness may be an imitation of a parent or teacher figure bossing him around in a manner he has not liked. *If this is the* situation you also want to explore the child's experience of being bossed about in a way that is not helpful to his development. Once again, Sunderland (2006, p.131) has some creative ways of responding to a very bossy child. For example:

A child keeps ordering you to let him go shopping for a toy truck. You can say something like: "You really do want to boss me about, don't you? Let's do it together to this can of baked beans: 'Can of baked beans . . . get that toy truck for me now!!! I don't want to wait! I want it now!'" Be as vocal and loud as your child and, through being humorous, you can hope that you might move your child into playing together, being together in a more caring way. The basic point of this play is to give the message that you do not allow yourself to be bullied, but also you want the child to see a mirror of the controlling, bullying behaviour that has been going on.

Playing cruelly with other children

If your child is playing with children and being a child who is hateful in playing, bullying or hitting, then you need to stop and try to understand what is not being sorted out and needs sorting out. There are many reasons for this but some are easier than others to note.

- Hitting and shaming shouting by parents or teachers creates hostility. The child will play a tyrant in identification with a tyrannical discipline.
- The child might be feeling deserted in some way by the parents and has a lot of unworked through rage about this.
- Jealousy of the parents' relationship has incited anger and hatred and there has been insufficient opportunity to work through with the parents by means of play and intensely related quality time with the parents.
- Jealousy of other children in the family unmitigated by sufficient opportunity to be in a one-to-one relationship with a parent. There has also not been sufficient opportunity to work through some of the problems through play and conversation.

Never sharing toys

A child who cannot ever share a toy when playing, or who is continuously involved in struggles over sharing, has some difficulties in internalising a nurturing, generous parent. Anxiety about being dropped out of the parents' mind ensues when another sibling is present. Aggression to siblings, peers, and parents for having other children around leaves the child with an attacked and damaged internal sense of wellbeing. Holding on to toys is in lieu of being able to internally hold on to good relationships with loved ones. Generosity to others comes from feeling loved and understood and protecting that feeling of being loved. Generosity cannot emanate from rules. Rules just make for placatory gestures and peace and quiet. That means that more than rules are needed to help a child feel confident to share the space, share the toys, share the parental love and the teacher's attention with others.

There is also another, more complex, issue which needs resolving when a child feels unloved and possessively clings on to material possessions: when a child experiences two other children or the parents giving affection and attention to one another and leaving him out, he can feel jealousy and hate. The child then could feel bad because he is unloving, but he might also feel bad because his ugly hate and jealousy make him feel he is no good and unlovable. He loses track of the love he is actually receiving from the parents, teachers, friends, and siblings. He might cling to possessions because he can control them, whereas love from others is freely given and freely taken away.

The child's jealousy and hate can be mitigated by your giving adequate empathy and time for understanding your child. It is helpful for the child if you can bear the ugly hate and jealousy, name it, discuss it without criticism, and understand your child's pain in having to share you with the other child.

No rule can create empathy and generosity in your child . . . only love, empathy for your child's pain, seeing, bearing, and understanding his pain and hate can help him feel lovingly connected to you. His gratitude that you understand and accept him will mitigate his sense of being unlovable and ameliorate his hate.

Conclusion: the beauty of play

The beauty of play is that it reveals the child's dialogue with himself regarding his emotional experiences. Through play, the child can think his own thoughts, work through his experiences, and enjoy life. Symbolic play suggests that the child been sufficiently reciprocally attuned with the mother. Through reciprocal attunement with an understanding mother, the child is able to develop an interior space to create thoughts around feelings that can be externalised and expanded upon through symbolic play. Play *gives birth to creative thought*. Play also *allows a connection with others* before language has developed or when multi-cultural experiences are occurring. *Before there is a common language there can be play.* Below is a poem elucidating how communication before words is possible.

> *On the Seashore*
>
> On the seashore of endless worlds children meet.
> The infinite sky is motionless overhead and the restless water is boisterous.
> On the seashore of endless worlds the children meet with shouts and dances.
> They build their houses with sand, and they play with empty shells.
> With withered leaves they weave their boats and smilingly float them on the vast deep.
> Children have their play on the seashore of worlds.
> They know not how to swim, they know not how to cast nets. Pearl-fishers dive for pearls, merchants sail in their ships, while children gather pebbles and scatter them again. They seek not for hidden treasures, they know not how to cast nets.
> The sea surges up with laughter, and pale gleams the smile of the sea-beach.
> Death-dealing waves sing meaningless ballads to the children,
> even like a mother while rocking her baby's cradle.
> The sea plays with children, and play gleams the smile of the sea-beach.
> On the seashore of endless worlds children meet. Tempest roams in the pathless sky, ships are wrecked in the trackless water, death is abroad and children play.
> On the seashore of endless worlds is the great meeting of children.
>
> (Tagore, 1936, pp. 51–52)

References

Cameron, J. (1995). *An Artist's Way: A Course in Discovering and Rediscovering Your Creative Self.* London: Macmillan.

Carignani, P. (1994). Introducing the observational model in school. Master's Degree Thesis, University of East London.

Freud, S. (1900a). *Interpretation of Dreams. S.E., 4–5.* London: Hogarth.

Freud, S. (1920g). *Beyond the Pleasure Principle. S.E., 18:* 3–143. London: Hogarth.

Hopkins, J. (1996). From baby-games to let's pretend. *British Journal of Psychotherapy, 31*(1, part 2): 20–27.

Hopkins, J. (2002). *The Legacy of Winnicott: Essays on Infant and Child Health,* B. Kahr (Ed.). London: Karnac.

Hoxter, S. (1977). Play and communication. In: D. Daws & M. Boston (Eds.), *The Child Psychotherapist* (pp. 00–00). London: Wildwood House.

Magagna, J. (Ed.) (2012). *The Silent Child: Communication without Words.* London: Karnac.

Sunderland, M. (2006). *The Science of Parenting.* London: Dorling Kindersley.

Tagore, R. (1936). On the Seashore. In: *Collected Poems and Plays of Rabindranath Tagore* (pp. 51–52). Trowbridge: Redwood Press.

Wilkins, D. (1993). *Play is the Work of the Child. A Comparative Study of Maria Montessori and Melanie Klein.* London: University of East London.

CHAPTER THIRTEEN

Developing altruistic skills in Tempo Lineare: "The Island of Puppies"

Patrizia Pasquini

Tempo Lineare is a school where children are be helped to become interested in others and develop their wish to be helpful to others. This is connected to the fact that Tempo Lineare is a school that can be "altruistic" not only in looking after all children in general, but also in meeting the needs of those young children who have experienced abandonment, traumatic births, abandonment, or pathologies linked to metabolic, genetic, or relational illnesses. It is a place for preventative work that can activate cultural changes and foster the parents' ability to be present for their child with empathy and understanding. I have exerted a great amount of energy and passion to help children to develop their own personalities, and, at the same time, to support parents and workers in the difficult task of helping the children develop their full potential in every aspect of their lives.

In order to illustrate how Tempo Lineare fosters extremely satisfactory results in promoting development in the children, I shall describe a series of weekly special play sessions with one child Mario, aged three years and ten months. As mentioned before, each week children play for one-half hour using the "School–Family Box", which consists of toys chosen by the children with the assistance their parents. My experience with Mario and other children in Tempo Lineare led me to understand that in order for their explosive anxieties, their disintegrating anguishes, or their desperate loneliness to stop, I had to intervene in a "therapeutic" manner by transforming the school in a place of "healing" and development, where the shared experience of "good" relationships might encourage the wish to help the others. In developing Tempo Lineare's underlying philosophy, I realised that creating such a developmental space was essential for the development of those children who are inhibited by anxieties and defences against them. My sensitivity and resources were to be used in creating a space of generosity to help them develop their potential to the fullest. All this could happen only if the group activated everybody's listening and observing skills. The school as a therapeutic space could rewrite the tale of interrupted vitality in living a good life. I was determined not to have mechanical schemes, such as rote learning, filling in already formed designs, and other such schemes, because they would lead only to automatic responses, not creativity. In Tempo Lineare, I had to initiate an innovative educational journey with the children, helping them to share an experience that might transform them emotionally while leading them to become more self-aware.

My experience with Mario convinced me that children who scream, who require constant attention, who need help but seem unable to accept it, make us feel incapable of reaching them emotionally. Supporting each other with the experience of being perceived as threateningly bad and being rejected was part of our collaborative task as teachers and parents. I began to wonder what a facilitating school should be like in order to look after all the children, including Mario, and offer the best care to all of them. It is important for me to describe my own state of mind and my thoughts because, in order to help children build their own lives, we need to know many things about them which they convey non-verbally through projecting states of mind into us. My attitude was that we could help Mario and others by offering our generosity, love, empathy, and observation.

When he was almost four Mario started coming to our school. He was usually upset: he screamed, he did not look people in the eye, and he constantly tried to run out of the room. His constant movement might have been designed to hold himself together physically in lieu of some internal psychic structure that would leave him feeling safer (Bick, 1968). His language was fragmented, inexpressive, and often incomprehensible. While emanating a sense of loneliness and unhappiness, he did not allow any contact. He felt persecuted by the proximity of both adults and children and when they were near him, he either tried to hit them and push them away or run to a corner of the room to find shelter. There was something terribly desperate in him, but I did not know how to reach him. In order for him to get to know the space and the people around him, we gave him some freedom while observing his experience within Tempo Lineare.

I noticed that when he separated from his parents, he did not show any anxiety. After they left him, he often went into a corner of the room and dropped some objects. Sometimes when they left him he went into an empty space between two sofas which he had separated. Perhaps Mario felt that separation made him lose everything. One day, he dropped a doll, looked at me, and said, "Poor child." When I tried to talk to him, he moved away, putting a great distance between us. I realised that I had to find the "right distance" in order to relate to him.

Every week, the children were given a space in which they could play as they liked with their soft toys, which included rabbits, sheep, puppies, and kittens. The children could also use the toys available within the school. The two groups of children sat before me on two soft blankets and began to play with their stuffed animals while their two teachers observed and took notes on what was happening in the room. The children imagined that the two blankets were the boat taking them on their fantasied journeys.

Playing freely with their soft toys enabled the children to work through their emotional experience. Through creating personalised dramas in their play, each child expressed himself as an individual and in relation to the group. In this way, a sense of belonging and solidarity within the group occurs. The child comprehends how conflicts of love and hate occur when he fears losing people whom he loves. Talking about himself gives him the opportunity to work through the experience of loneliness without danger. This loneliness in early childhood is often linked to an experience of separation from the mother and/or father. When the child feels understood by his "internalised good object" and identifies with it, he becomes more able to adapt himself to the demands of reality: he accepts situations of deprivation and feels less resentful for the frustration he has experienced. Identification with the good internal object gives him hope that he will experience more happiness in his life.

The closely observed play space with the soft toys can help the child make the transition between his concrete external relationships and his imaginary space in which the child expresses different aspects of his love and hate towards the symbolised mother, father, or siblings. In this way, the child's concrete external family survives his possessiveness and his threats without harm. The containment that the group offers for the child's play allows him to face and communicate aspects of his mental life that at times feel impossible to face. Munari (1977) described fantasy as an inspired, boundless thought in which the child becomes the explorer and the enchanted traveller of the kingdom of dreams, of night, of language, of his own life. The fantasy journey belongs to the creation of myths.

Observations of Mario within the group

I shall now present some observations at one-month intervals which illustrate children developing through regular weekly play within a Tempo Lineare group activity.

Observation one: Looking after the soft toys

"We're on the boat! . . . Careful, there is a wave . . . It's raining!" I remind the children that the boat is sturdy and that nothing dangerous will happen. Giulia says that the sea is calm for the storm is over. She adds that we have reached a beach and we can get out of the boat. In the course of this first fantasy game, Mario is isolated from his schoolmates, sitting on a chair, not playing with his soft toy, but with a carrier used to transport the toy. He is interested above all in opening the lid, putting toys in from the toy veterinarian's bag and closing the lid.

Meanwhile, the children imagine they are playing on a beach, moving around in the room. A pretend vet looks after their pet, someone comes to me to have the pet cured, and someone else gathers food to cook and to feed their pets. A girl gives me her baby animal, telling me that it was abandoned, that it needs me and that I must cure it. Someone else comes to me telling me that his baby animal still cannot walk and I must hold it in my arms. Someone else tells me that I must cure it because it is wounded. After a while, the children begin to lay the table with plates, forks, glasses, and food, then they sit holding their baby animals in their arms, feeding them for a while.

Mario takes a few plates, puts them on the table and upon the plates he places nuts, almonds, and chestnuts. A young girl gives me a basket full of eggs, while another child starts screaming that some wolves have arrived on the island. In a lively, frantic mood, everyone hides in the corner of the sofas to protect themselves from the wolves. A sense of persecution and confusion permeates the atmosphere when I decide to invite the children to protect "their babies". The children calm down and once again play more harmoniously. After a while, I suggest the children should go back to the boat because our time on the island is almost over. The children pretend to get on the boat and someone says to his friend to be careful, that he should not leave his foot in the water because it might be bitten by killer whales and sharks. Someone else disagrees with this dangerous idea, saying that around an island there are only kind fish. When one boy, Geraldo, asks another boy, Pietro, what his baby is doing, Pietro answers that it is trying to make friends with the other babies on the boat. I say that if the babies become friends, they will discover many things.

Travelling means knowing about oneself and others. If we open our eyes to new opportunities, each of us can discover new aspects of life and get to know other people. Through their imagined voyage on the sea, the children began to explore and gain knowledge about life. For example, when sailing, you need to know the stars, because you find your correct direction thanks to them. For a sailor, the knowledge of the sky is extremely important. Travelling means "discovery"; often, after this experience, we have changed, we have grown, and we even think differently. If journeys are discoveries, then a "fantasy journey" may signify a journey inside ourselves. There is an internal sea inside each one of us, as the poem "L'infinito" (The Infinite, by Leopardi, 1819) suggests, which is made of fantasy and imagination; when we travel, or when we dream, we set out on a journey which is our own.

Immediately after providing the children with this "play space", I asked the older ones why they were so happy to have made this fantasy journey. One girl said it was nice because they were all together, a boy said that they could imagine a world full of things and friends, and another boy said that they could imagine they could meet many animals and, above all, they could explore an island that they themselves had created. When a child can really be "a child" in a safe place he can enter a "galaxy of fantasies" which is full of ideas, rich imagination, and interests. As one sees, the fantasies become more complex as time goes on:

Observation two: "The breast-island"

All the children sit on the carpet-boat except Mario, who remains a bit isolated, holding a ball he brought from home and looking at the group. A girl says, "The sea's rough, so are we sailing today?" Another child replies, "The captain (referring to me) will take us to the island." I like the idea of being selected to be the "captain" of the boat and, smiling, I say, "All right, but you need to tell me 'Oh captain, my captain, raise the anchor and turn on the engines'." While laughing, the children repeat the phrase and I say, "Engines on, let's go!" Gianni says, "We are going to the island!"; Monica loudly declares, "The name of this island is 'the Island of Puppies'." Pietro beckons me, saying, "Captain, there are huge waves and bolts of lightning", and Jacopo adds, "and also killer whales!" When I ask them if the puppies are afraid, Gianni says "yes" and Pietro says "no". Jacopo thinks that a wave might overturn the boat. I say that it is a good idea to hold the puppies tight so they will be safe and I add, "I see the Island of Puppies, close your eyes and imagine it: it is a beautiful place with pink sand, palm trees, and the sea is calm." We arrive safely and we get off the boat. Maria imitates the bark of a dog, telling me that her puppy is very happy because it is indeed a beautiful place. Everybody clambers off the boat and they all start moving around the beach. Jacopo gives me Mario's soft toy, telling me that he does not want it and that I must keep it. He adds, "You'll see, he will play with it later."

The children, in turn, use the doctor's bag because the puppies have temperatures. A child gives me some sweets, while others take some tote bags to do some shopping. Meanwhile, Mario comes to me and plays with the toy kitchen, pretending to cook some eggs. Some children use the stethoscope and others make injections with a syringe. After a while, Mario takes the syringe, pushing down its plunger several times. For the first time, after several months in Tempo Lineare, Mario is no longer afraid of the closeness of the other children, who play near him and around the room. They lay the table, take some sausages and fruit, and sit at the table, holding their puppies in their arms while pretending to feed them. Some of the younger children stuff their tote bags with food. Maria goes to the toy kitchen to make some cake and to offer me a cup of coffee. Jacopo tells me that his puppy is afraid of sand, Alessandro says that his puppy has a temperature and needs to be cured, and Jacopo remembers that there might be some wolves hidden on the island, recalling the game we played the previous week.

Eleonora suggests that the best protection against such a danger is to build a house. The children gather in a corner of the room, but after a while it is time to set sail again, and once more they are all sitting on the blanket-boat. I ask them if the island is a safe or a dangerous place, and they reply that it is a safe place, but there are some wolves there and they had to build a hut to be safe. Anna says that now they are all sailing across the waves, but Suzanna replies that if they keep quiet, the waves will not come. Pietro says to Jacopo, "Your foot is outside the boat, you're getting wet!" and he helps Jacopo put his foot inside. I then proclaim that we have left the "fantasy island" and we are back in the school.

Each child in the group is now more capable of attending to the other children and more able to remember to whom each soft toy belongs. This game seems to involve taking very important developmental steps, for each child seems to be getting more in touch with the minds of the others and joining spontaneously in an imaginative group journey. The children have started using toys and words to represent internalised relationships between themselves, their parents, and their siblings. Their creative expression was more obvious in those moments in which they were not at the mercy of too intense anxieties, feelings of guilt, or fears of loss. When anxieties overwhelmed them, I noticed a split between the calmer, happier group and the group that felt persecuted by "the bad wolves" and the "hungry killer whales".

Violent fantasies were attributed to these greedy animals and it was almost impossible for the children to take on any responsibility for their own feelings of anger, greed, jealousy, and aggression. Being greedy for the objects in the room seemed to correspond to an omnipotent and inexhaustible wish for food, but also to a wish for freedom from aggressive and persecutory anxieties. The "breast island" which was attacked lost its value as a good object and became a damaged and bad object. The children who were able, instead, to contain their envy through their play and their creativity managed to expand their experiences and acquire more confidence in their effort to stay together and to share an internal experience which allowed them to grow and develop.

To grow and develop, a child needs to learn both from good and bad experiences in order to be capable of love and gratitude towards the good object and to create a stable foundation for his ego. The child can enjoy this only if his ability to love is "sufficiently developed and this enjoyment is the basis of gratitude". Klein (1957, p. 188) points out that

> ... all the future joys of life depend on the realization of a feeling of unity with another person which presupposes a complete understanding for the establishment of a successful relationship of friendship or of love. Such an understanding does not need to be expressed in words ... The evidence of its origins is in the intimate relationship with the mother in the pre-verbal period ... The ability to fully enjoy an early relationship with the breast is essential for the later ability to feel pleasure of any kind.

When the child experiences breast-feeding serenely and the mother and child are attuned to one another, the introjections of the good breast will take place safely. The child will receive from the loved object "an irreplaceable gift" that he wants to preserve and that will be the basis of his gratitude towards the primary object of love. Gratitude is closely linked to generosity to others. Being grateful to the good internal object that has been assimilated allows the child to share his gifts, his love, with others.

Observation three: Looking after the island

The children sit on the carpet-boat ready to play with their stuffed animals. Mario moves from one room to the other, then he sits down and starts playing with some eggs which he puts into a bowl. Maria screams, "My dog fell into the sea!" and everybody tells her to take him out. She reaches over to grab him and holds him tightly. The children call out to me in unison, "Oh, Captain, oh Captain! Are we leaving? Are we going to sail?" Sarah, one of the older girls, exclaims, "Silence, otherwise the sea will become rough." The children remain silent for a while and then start discussing how they are going to behave. Bruno states, "We need to arrive calmly without taking too much food." But Johannes and some of the other younger children claim that they need a lot of food because the puppies are hungry. At a certain point, Sarah says, "I see a palm tree, shall we lower the anchor?" Immediately after that they enter the Island of Puppies. One child, Mark, takes the doctor's bag to treat his puppy; Johannes and another boy start gathering some food in their tote bags to feed the puppies; Pietro chooses some fruit, vegetables, sweets, chicken, sausages, and cheese. They all move in small groups. Some children bring me some sweets, while a few decide to have a picnic with me.

The older and younger children are establishing relationships with each other, disregarding the boundary between the two schools of younger and older children. There is greater freedom of movement between the two school spaces. Mario starts bringing me his toy cars, from which he has removed all the tyres. As a good tyre specialist, I put the tyres back in place and give the cars back to him. He looks at me and smiles. Meanwhile, an older girl, Sarah, has taken by the hand Olga, a 3½-year-old girl, newly immigrated to Rome, who does not speak Italian yet and just joined the school the previous week. Sarah helps Olga choose some fruit and bread to feed her puppy. Then, the two girls become medics, using a thermometer to take their puppies' temperatures and then giving them some medicines.

Some children in the group, instead, start laying the table as if it were a big restaurant table so that everybody can feed their puppies. On the other side of the room, two younger children are laughing excitedly as they empty all the containers and cover the table with lots of food. Some of the older children remind them not to deprive the island of all its food, but the two children do not listen to them. After a while, I tell them that it is now time to return to our blanket-boat and all the children start putting everything in order, except the two younger ones. When they are all sitting down, I tell two children that also this time they have taken a lot of food. Everybody is listening to me, except those two, who respond to my comment by turning their back to me. Johannes says that we are going back to Tempo Lineare and Bruno says that it is necessary to treat the island better and not take so much from it. I reply that that is a good thought and I invite the children to think about what Bruno has said.

In this play scenario, Mario seemed to gain a fuller picture of the group of children, and joined in by asking for his car tyres to be fixed, but he persisted in keeping at a distance from the other children and did not remain on their fantasised journey. I wondered why he saw only closed doors and grey skies everywhere. Although he was slightly less withdrawn, he had limited experience with me as a trustworthy, reliable person. We needed time. His journey inside the experience of Tempo Lineare had just begun. A child like Mario needs an object capable of feeling hopeful on his behalf, since he has not yet developed his own ability to hope that relationships can be good.

The ability to help others and to abandon one's selfishness is not always present in children. Those who have developmental disorders often find it difficult to take the most elementary steps in this process of openness and ability to understand the minds of other people. A child's ability to pay attention to others is also closely linked to whether or not in early childhood there has been the possibility of introjecting parents with good ability to pay attention to his state of mind. Understanding the minds of other people prompts a natural wish to help others. The ability to feel generous allowed the children to be happy to offer their help. In those moments, I felt very close to the children in the group. They were grateful for the work that I do with them every day, which perhaps had contributed to their experience of feeling understood. When children can feel gratitude, they begin to be generous to others. This generosity could be observed in this "play space" with me, in which their destructive impulses as well as their envy and jealousy had diminished considerably. Goodness and love were preserved in their play.

Observation four: Missing the island

Two children who have just returned from their holidays ask me when we will play with our soft toys, but Sarah remembers perfectly the day devoted to this play activity despite a week-long school holiday. Today is the day for our journey and the children prepare themselves by sitting on the carpet-boat. Monica, a child who has just joined the school for the four- to six-year-olds, for whom parents are not present, is crying, saying that she wants to go home to her mummy and does not want to remain at school. Mario is lying on the couch and the other children call him several times, inviting him to join them. The teacher picks him up and sits holding him next to the other children. Mario wriggles away and lies down next to them. Beatrice asks me, "At the end of the year, who will the puppies stay with?" I say that every child can take their soft toys on holiday with them, and then bring them back to school in September. Samuele asks me if the teachers and I will also go on holiday with them and I answer that it seems that they are saying that people should never separate. Sarah, an older child, looks at me with a sad expression and says that she will go to primary school and she will not come back.

The children start a new game, which consists of saying the names of the children who will come back in September and of those who will leave to start the first year of primary school. Daniele, one of the older children, says that they could come back to Tempo Lineare sometimes to play with their friends. When they ask me if we have arrived, I tell them that we have and that we can lower the anchor and get off the boat. The children get off slowly and some of them move towards the baskets holding food, while others gather in small groups. While all the children are moving around, Mario remains sitting next to me. Two younger children start getting a lot of food to put on the table, while others complain, saying that they are exaggerating, because we do not need all that food.

Meanwhile, Mario has stood up and once again has gone away from the group to the couch. I call him, but he does not respond, moving around both rooms before lying again on the couch. Some children place their puppies on the chairs and start laying the table to feed them, while others try to take away some of the food brought by the other two children. Meanwhile, Mario gets off the couch and goes to the other side of the room to play with the "eco-house". After a while, he comes towards me and starts playing with the toy oven as if it were a garage, in which he puts a few toy cars. Two girls crouch under a table telling me that they have found shelter with their puppies in a cave and Pietro offers me some food. The two younger boys start making a lot of noise, which is rather in contrast to the quieter play activity of rest of the group. The young boys' excitement becomes more intense so that I have to stop them from getting hurt.

Meanwhile, I notice that, throughout this play activity, Sarah, an older girl, helps Olga, the child who arrived just a month ago, to choose some food to feed her puppy. I see that Olga repeats the names of the food; after a while, the two girls come close to me and Sarah tells me she is pleased because she has helped Olga to learn many words in Italian. Anna tells me that she is happy about her day on the island, because her puppy played and ate just the food that he needed. Some other children place their puppies as if in a "merry-go-round" and when the circle breaks, they start again.

When I tell the children that it is time to leave, the two groups tidy up the room with great attention, then they sit on the blanket-boat and start talking about their games, telling me how they spent their time on the island. Mario is sitting at his usual place, maybe to show that it is time to have breakfast. Somebody says that it has been a long time since he went to the island and I reply that it is because of the Easter holiday. Susannah tells me that she was very happy to come back because "she felt happy inside". I notice that, as she is telling me this, some other children are holding hands. I remark that one experiences this kind of pleasure when one is able to play with the others in a friendly way, when people help each other, when having fun is not confusing, and when being together makes us feel grateful for the richness we have.

After this meeting, I thought that the children were able to tell me about their anxieties, which they experienced because of the Easter break, the summer break, and because of the departure of the older children, who were talking about their departure from Tempo Lineare to go to primary school in the autumn. Their experience of playing with soft toys enabled them to talk about and contain their anxieties. When children can start to accept that this is the way things happen in life, their play activity can help them become aware of reality, accepting separations as something natural, necessary for their development and growth.

However, I wondered why the two younger children were so greedy and unconcerned about their puppies and their own excited and destructive play. Children who, at an early age, in a peer group, show little openness and little ability to socialise also feel uncomfortable *vis-à-vis* any change, and even more incapable of coping with it because of their rigidity. Therefore, they easily feel very confused and agitated in their social life within a group. It is evident that the experience in a closely observed and supervised group helps a child to "look at himself" and to tell the difference between a behaviour that helps and one that prevents him from developing sensitivity, internal harmony, and good socialisation.

The Island of Puppies is, for the group of children, the representation of themselves as puppies; it is the island where, at the beginning of our work, the children projected only their fears, but which gradually became a place to know one another, to realise that it feels good to like each other, and to be in a place where one can be fed, protected, and looked after. When self-knowledge develops, relationships among children become more profound and their ability to share experiences allows them to develop love for each other. The children also felt contained by my function as a "captain" who offered them a "sturdy boat" where they could strengthen their links with good, security-providing internal parents.

Observation five: On the same sea, in the same boat

Mario is sad, he cries and does not want to separate from his mummy. His mother finds it difficult to separate from him. I remark that it is very helpful for Mario to show her what he feels. The child runs into my room to look at something, but I cannot see what it is. Then he runs towards us, and separates from his mother, crying as the teacher holds him in her arms. In the room, all the children are sitting on the blanket-boat. We sail off. Mario sits beside the group and plays with the pet carrier. The children ask him to get on the boat, and he looks at us even though he does not join us. Somebody says that we are finally going back to the Island of Puppies. A child says that she gave a soft toy to her mother as a gift, after finding it at her grandmother's house. She says: "It belonged to mummy when she was a child! It is a panda . . . even mothers need a soft toy, but as she is my mummy, she often lends it to me." The children are all listening.

We have arrived on the island; the children start playing quietly. Everybody is organised and there is an unusual silence. At a certain point, I cannot see Mario any more. He comes back from the other room after a few moments, holding a colourful abacus. He sits next to the other children, who are playing with their soft toys, and starts playing with his toy. He makes the various rows of coloured balls disappear behind the panel of the toy, then he turns it over and repeats the activity. After a while, I notice that four children of the group have stopped playing to observe him as he plays with his abacus; he seems to be happy to be with the others. For the rest of the time, Mario does not leave the group and remains interested in his toy, while the other children go on playing with pleasure. Towards the end of their time, the four older children, who are going to elementary school soon, come to me and show me a basket in which they have placed their four soft toys. All four of them hold it and sway it in front of me, telling me that they have built a little boat for the puppies. I reply that it is nice to see that their puppies can stay together in the same boat. I add that they are telling me that they have found a way to be together as friends and that this game is teaching us a lot of things about how to be in a group.

It was very interesting for me to observe the four older children as they were playing. The themes in their play gave me feedback on the way in which they had developed through our work with them. Indeed, their emotional needs for love and nourishment seemed to have been met, and the ability to share the cradle-group with the others allowed them to be generous, to love themselves, and to foster the formation of intimate relationships in which they respected the others. When school is an adequate space for the child, the integration that is reached between the "normal" child and the one considered as "pathological" is simply a logical consequence. When school is a suitable place to meet the child's emotional needs, it produces a new way of "schooling" and of thinking about education.

Some schools favour and teach competition, but competition is a social artefact that makes children selfish; there is little competition in a school where love exists in its own right. Helping children use their particular capacities as best they can provides a better model for development. Competition with others distracts them from focusing on what it is possible do with their own skills. When children of different ages daily experience life in a group and are in touch with older and younger children, they can see where they come from and where they are going, so that they can help each other and develop themselves. It is helpful for children to be in a school group where children with special needs are not the object of specific one-to-one attention. This enables them to see that their schoolmates are not "pathological", but, rather, deserving of the same specialised care and attentiveness as every other child.

Conclusion

The child who learns how to tolerate pain is able to love the others despite their limitations and

can internalise the presence of the people who help him because he feels psychically acknowledged. Moreover, a child can turn to the adults with great trust when he experiences carers and
teachers who can take in the painful impact of what he conveys to them and offer him some
mental space which allows him to feel understood and known by them. A condition of a good
education is that it allows all the children to modulate their suffering and to become capable
of accepting some of it. This daily spontaneous sharing, this being "on the same sea, in the same
boat", is something that gives great impetus to the wish for mutual altruism that involves
becoming empathic, kind, curious and able to interact well with other people.

References

Bick, E. (1968). The experience of skin in early object relations. *International Journal of Psychoanalysis*,
    49: 484–486.
Klein, M. (1957). Envy and gratitude. In: *The Writings of Melanie Klein, Vol 3: Envy and Gratitude and
    Other Works* (pp. 176–235). London: Hogarth Press.
Leopardi, G. (1819). L'infinito (The Infinite). In: J. Origo & J. Heath Stubbs (Eds. & Trans.) *Giacomo
    Leopardi: Selected Prose and Poetry*. New York: New American Library.

CHAPTER FOURTEEN

Creating space in the family for imagination and creativity

Jeanne Magagna

This chapter addresses the creation of a space in the family for creativity to flourish. The couple comes together for the ultimate creative act: the creation of another human life, a baby; however, throughout childhood and adult life, our creativity can be inhibited, with serious consequences. For this reason, I describe developing a secure psychological space within the family which acknowledges the value of spontaneous phantasy and supports imaginative activities for all family members. I think about how mothers, fathers, nurseries, and the children's subsequent teachers can all use this creative space to develop freedom: the freedom to use one's capacity for love and work to its fullest.

I address four issues: first, I look at how situations can arise that block a child from developing a creative internal space. I then turn to some solutions, seven different ways in which we can help children to develop their internal space for creativity and imagination. Third, I also give you the opportunity to reflect on what you can do to promote creative thinking, with the help of colourful "thinking hats". I end this chapter by reflecting on the difference that creativity can make in a child's life, and looking at some inspiring acts of creativity.

Impediments to developing an internal creative space

In the beginning, a baby generally experiences sounds of the family, such as voices or the playing of music, and rhythms of the mother's body, such as her heartbeat or her breathing. These sensory experiences become the basis for the baby in the womb's earliest phantasies of pleasure and trauma. We now know, through the work of Mancia (1999), that the baby's rapid eye movements are suggestive of the baby dreaming inside the mother's womb. A mental space for phantasy has thus begun before birth.

If the birth process is not too traumatic, the baby greets the mother and father visually at birth, suckles at the nipple, and cuddles into the warmth of the mother's body. Feelings of wellbeing promote taking in the parents' receptive warmth and love and introjecting secure, loving, internal parents. This secure, loving, internal base provides for the growth of a "house for imagination" to flourish. It is premature to speak of creativity without noting its essence: the use of imagination.

Winnicott (1960) describes how the parents provide a cocoon of receptivity to the baby's wishes and needs, so that the baby's basic genetic need for protective, nurturing parents is satisfied. Target and Fonagy (1996, p. 472) state,

> The child's mental state must be represented sufficiently clearly and accurately for the child to recognize it, yet sufficiently playfully for the child not to be overwhelmed by its realness; in this way he can ultimately use the parent's representation of his internal reality as the seed of his own symbolic thought, his representation of his own representations.

Infancy, however, is not simply a delightful experience. Some of the most traumatic moments are when the infant is in distress and is initially fairly helpless to alleviate the stresses of separating from the mother: a hungry stomach, the wish for a social contact or physical holding. Some of the impediments to the use of imagination and creativity may develop when the baby has not yet sufficiently internalised a secure loving internal base, a house for the imagination, an internal space.

Adhesive identification

Esther Bick, a British psychoanalyst, described how one can adhere to sensory experiences as a way of holding the self together psychologically when there is terror of *falling to pieces*. Bick (1968) states,

> The need for a containing object would seem, in the infantile un-integrated state, to produce a frantic search for an object-a light, a voice, a smell, or other sensual object-which can hold the attention and thereby be experienced momentarily at least, as holding the parts of the personality together.

The "sticking" on to a sensory experience is a normally used psychological protection, in lieu of having either an internalised loving secure base or an external parent containing the baby's anxieties. "Sticking on to sensory experience" should ordinarily be replaced by the parental containment and internalisation of their capacities to love and bear anxieties.

Impediments to imaginative thinking are very obvious when one sees a baby

- banging the head repeatedly in the absence of the mother;
- rocking the self repetitiously;
- holding the body musculature in a stiff, terrified manner;
- engaging in non-stop movement.

In worst-case scenarios, the baby "spaces out" and leaves the external world completely. An example of this is given below, taken from Cooper and Magagna (2005, pp. 25–26).

Anna 5 months, and James 23 months

Anna is seated on mother's lap, facing outwards, having her bottle. She has both hands around the top of it while mother holds the end. James comes over with Anna's dummy . . . and pushes it into [her] mouth . . . until the bottle is forced out. In response, Anna whimpers and cries . . . Crying, James climbs into mother's lap . . . Milk . . . dribbles out of Anna's still mouth. [She remains] motionless, [staring] straight ahead into space. Mother . . . shows she has given up [feeding Anna] by putting the bottle down. Anna rocks herself in an autistic-like rhythm. . . . her eyes [are] still blank and unfocused . . .

This dissociation from the external world does not promote psychological development. Rather, it provides a lack of incentive to have the courage to face the developmental perils causing anxiety. If sticking to sensory experiences becomes a repetitious pattern, what we see is a child holding on to the same old repetitive rituals for dear life, as a protection against the uncertainty of exploration. For example, we might see a child fearing walking and letting go of the table, fearing letting go of the side of the swimming pool, fearing using his inner balance to ride a bike, fearing flying with his imagination beyond the sensory experience of the fuzzy bear, the hard truck, the bead on a string which he is twiddling. I was reminded of this watching two children play.

Day after day, Marco, aged five, uses a toy crocodile's big mouth to repetitiously bite a little lamb and little calf. He does not move into other activities apart from the biting. Eva, aged three, sits at the table playing with some beads on a necklace. She twirls them round and round and looks up only occasionally to see the other nursery children playing with one another.

As I was writing this chapter, I felt that making a list of household tasks, rather than facing a blank sheet of paper on which I would let my imagination fly beyond the concrete, was another form of what Esther Bick calls adhesive identification. I was adhering to concrete activities rather than going into the internal house for the imagination to soar. The anxiety of what I would find in my internal house of imagination was diminishing my courage to go into it and explore.

Hatred of limits, of feeling rejected, creates the critical harsh voice

One of the problems with setting limits and saying "no" to a child's wishes, when the child does not have a secure internal base, is that the child may easily perceive this as "Mummy doesn't love me", or "Daddy doesn't care about me". The child might feel, "Why would they say 'no' if they love me?" Feeling rejected by the parents leads the child to feel hostile. This hostility turns the rule-making part of the parents into a cruel figure filled with projections of hostility. Subsequently, this becomes the perfectionist, cruel voice criticising the self and, thus, inhibiting imagination and creativity. A child might then be heard to say:

- "Nothing I draw will ever be any good";
- "I can't write";

- "I have no musical talent";
- "I don't have a good sense of rhythm";
- "My work is rubbish".

This *critical voice* prevents the spring of life, of imaginative vitality, from arising and developing within the child. Listening to it keeps one safely secure in its prison-guard grip.

Institutional and social inhibition of creativity

The inhibition of creativity is not limited to the individual within their family setting. Torrance (1963) researched the development of creativity in schools. What do you imagine that he discovered? In particular, he noted that these were some of the factors that interfered with creativity.

1. Premature attempts to eliminate fantasy activity.
2. Overemphasis on verbal skills prematurely in child's development.
3. Emphasis on destructive criticism of child's work.
4. Teachers' over-emphasis on conforming too closely to their proposed structure for learning.
5. Coercive pressure to conform.
6. Emphasis on immediate success, rather than on simply using one's capacities as best one can.

The influence of inhibitions

Ultimately, the defences, rigidities, internalised critical voices, and external pressures that I have described lead to a cessation of development, or, in the worst-case scenario, the closure, of the internal creative space. Once the child is older, lack of creativity can appear in various ways. Here are some of the reasons for inhibiting one's imagination necessary for creative acts:

- fear of being out of control with feelings;
- lack of capacity to symbolise because for some reason one was unable to develop a mentalizing internal mother/father inside oneself;
- inhibition of aggression, or sadness because of the lack of a secure base for mentalization;
- lack of a secure attachment;
- lack of a strong sense of self in early years and fear of losing oneself in the phantasies;
- fear of going mad and losing the self completely;
- use of intellect or obsessional behaviour because one is afraid of letting concrete images of things break down inside and be transformed by imagination;
- fear of change, of transformation to something unfamiliar;
- emotional neglect, poverty, and maternal deprivation;
- lack of an internal house for imagination to soar;

- lack of access in the daytime to an internal house for imagination, which may be soaring in one's dreams, in one's unconscious.
- lack of opportunity if families and schools become have too many rigid structures, too many concrete tasks, too many facts to learn, too much input, and not enough meditative space created through "doing no specific task" and *imagining what to do* spontaneously in one's free time.

Seven solutions

An important question is: "How do we help a child to move away from his rigid defences towards a creative, imaginative future?" There is a different path that one can take, although it might entail struggle. It involves enabling the child's resolution to feel "I will try to develop my capacities to perceive, to sense, to listen to inner experience, to symbolise, however limited my capacity, whatever my capacities are." This state of mind involves choosing an unexplored, uncertain, risk-taking path of development. It requires the courage to be open to outer experience and imagination.

We see in early infancy how the baby is naturally inquisitive and has the courage to explore as he searches around for the mother's body and father's voice Magagna (2002, p. 86) describes this:

> [One-month-old] baby [Eric's] arm is wrapped close to his chest with his clenched fingers placed near his shoulder. His slightly bent legs stay still . . . He sucks energetically . . . [for] about seven minutes at the breast, [then he] extends his arm and gradually spreads his fingers like flower petals opening out. With his fingertips he gently moves along Mother's blouse . . . and begins sliding his hand along her breast in a very slow fashion. (Magagna, 2002, p. 86)

We are all born free to explore, to be curious, and to imagine. King (2011) tells us,

> Open is a deeply soulful word . . . Openness, openheartedness, openhandedness are the richest nutrients we can grow our lives on. To be fully open, to experience world afresh to be open is to be fully human, to be receptive, to empathise, to love, to experience all the world's wonders, to experience that variety moment by moment as it comes. It is a challenge to remain open in a world doing its best to close you down. Being able to obtain openness makes living an adventure.

Too often, we delegate to teachers the entire task of helping the child use his imagination when, in fact, the family can also play an extremely significant role in fostering imagination while being together. Let us learn from some creative people how we can foster in family life the development of the internal house for imagination to soar. I will present seven different solutions in turn.

The seven solutions

1.   Using imaginative identification with other family members as well as with fairy tale and storybook characters

All the family can listen to a fairy tale. They can then enact roles in the fairy tale and describe how it feels in that role. This can be a fun activity for the whole family, not just for the children in school.

Children often spontaneously play as if they are the mother or the teacher. Family members can take turn taking roles in the family and saying what they would do in the role of the mother or father. Pretend games such as this may enable family members to imagine another reality in which their feelings and needs are communicated without the child having to be so explicit or verbal about what it is he feels.

Another creative activity is the "empty chair technique", in which a family member might sit on the chair and imagine what it might feel like to be Maria. This might be particularly helpful on a day when a child is refusing to eat, is sulking, or is unable to be come out from retreat and speak after a temper tantrum. The family might sit in a circle around the child and the parents might suggest that family members, including themselves, imagine how it might feel to be Maria today.

*2.   Underlining the value of dreams, helping family members become familiar
with capturing them in the morning, and discussing the dreams and
the theme represented in them*

Drawing dreams, writing down dreams of the past, thinking of dreams for the future, and talking about dreams in the family can foster more connections with the root of phantasy: the unconscious processes. Perls and colleagues, in their book *Gestalt Therapy: Excitement and Growth in the Human Personality* (Perls, Hefferline, & Goodman, 1951, p. 27), say,

> The dream is a message of yourself to yourself, to whatever part of you is listening. The dream is possibly the most spontaneous expression of the human being, a piece of art that we chisel out of our lives ... Every aspect of the dream is part of the dreamer, but a part that to some extent is disowned and projected onto other objects.

Bion (Schneider, 2010) says that dreaming involves the pursuit of truth by means of thinking and feeling; the mind is enriched and developed though creating pictorial dramas of lived emotional experience and, thus, finding another opportunity to look at different ideas about, or solutions to, an emotional issue. Ways of eliciting discussion about dreams are:

1.   We can encourage children's drawings and telling of their dreams as a way of beginning discussions about feelings which they do not have sufficient words to describe. Like the Senoi Tribe children, your children could be encouraged to assume that dreams could be a part of normal conversation about what happened "last night".
2.   If there is a monster in the dream, such as a bear or burglar or bully, family members can discuss ways of using one's personal strength to find safety, to fight back, to own one's aggression rather than project it into the monster.
3.   In telling a dream, there is a request to make something mentally creative out of elements of the dream. It is often a relief for a family member to simply write down a dream, draw a picture of the dream, or write a poem or story using the dream. The creativity of producing imagery connected to the dream allows the person to transform some underlying emotional experiences so that they become more bearable.

3.   *Having openness to hear the heart and mind of oneself and others in the family*
and finding ways of spontaneously symbolically expressing those experiences

"The Family Squiggle Wiggle Game" (Jongsman, Peterson, McInnes, & Berghuis, 2004, p. 47). Have the child pick a family member to draw a squiggly line on a sheet of paper. The child is then instructed to draw a picture out of the squiggly line and then tell a story about his or her picture. Family members and the child will then talk about the story and the characters in the child's story, how they are feeling, what they are doing. Once the discussion is completed, the child will then be asked to draw a squiggly line on another sheet of paper and pick a family member to create a picture out of his or her squiggly line and tell a story about it.

"The Imaginary Time Machine" (Selekman, 2000, p. 129). The child is given the following directive: "Let's say I have sitting over here an imaginary time machine and once you enter it, you can take it anywhere in time, in the past or into the future. Where would you go?" Follow up questions could include: "What would you see there? With whom would you meet and talk? What would you talk about? If you and the person from the past hopped into the time machine and came back to the present day, how would this person help you out today? What advice would he or she give you? How would he or she help out with your parents? What would you bring back from there to help you out today?"

There are other ways of dramatising the past and imagining the future. Sometimes, a toddler appreciates an opportunity to pretend he is a little baby again with the parents. This is particularly helpful around the time a new sibling is a few months old and the toddler is aware of how much the baby receives from the parents in terms of attention, cuddling, and feeding. A child sometimes spontaneously "becomes a baby" again. This is an opportunity to talk about that experience together, but maybe also a time to join your child in his "being a baby again" and parent as if the child was "a baby" briefly before going back to the child's present age and discovering what might be lovely about being his own age able to do certain things.

In talking with young people, I have discovered they, too, like to reminisce about "the time when they were babies" and have the parents talk about this time. They might also like to imagine themselves in ten years, in twenty years, in thirty years' time. "What would you do if you were the mother in our house?" "What would you do differently from us?" These dialogues can be an imaginative way of improving the quality of family relationships. Also, discussions of the future can involve more thinking about now.

"I would like to be a writer when I grow up," said one young person. When asked what she wanted to write about, she said her "illness", which was anorexia nervosa. I said, "Why wait till you grow up to do that?" Last year she published her book at age fifteen. Of course, you do not always have to wait to do things when you are grown up! Marion Milner's seven-year-old son had his storybook published (Milner, 2012) and the young children of Tempo Lineare had their drawings of fairy tales published (Pasquini, 2002). If you gain sufficient support at the age you are, many more things are possible than sometimes can be imagined.

The other commonly heard subject is, "I will do something creative for myself when the children are in secondary school", or "when they leave home"; however, does it have to be impossible to find an evening once a week for parents to do something now, either separately or together if a baby-sitter is available? Life is not solely for the children! They will be relieved and inspired if they see that their parents are also fulfilling their imaginative and creative potentials.

4.   Creating special time for the children and for the parents

It is simply unhelpful and stressful to children if the burden of developing imagination and creativity is all placed solely upon them, with people vicariously getting pleasure through their achievements. Rather, it is important for each of us to consider how we promote the development of teachers', parents', and professionals' imaginative thinking, as well as providing good opportunities for the children's imaginative and creative activities to develop. Here are some ways for adults to free their own creative forces.

4(a).   Catching "butterfly sensations, feelings, and thoughts"

For adults, I can recommend reading Milner's *On Not Being Able to Paint* (1950) and Cameron's *An Artist's Way* (1995). Milner suggests that we may cling to the raft of logical thinking (Brearley, 1998) in fear of rough seas of imagination. She stresses the need for constant oscillations between merging with the object through blurring of boundaries in order to create symbols and the more logical, differentiating, practical, common sense states. She believes children without a secure internal mother may desperately cling to thinking in a rational way for security.

Milner feels one can regain lost parts of the self through use of the imagination and symbolisation. In her book, *On Not Being Able to Paint* (1950), she describes how one has to sacrifice the old self one knows and plunge into an empty space from which one develops a trust that, out of the unconscious, something new and valuable can grow. She advocates a kind of introspection that involves observing fleeting thoughts which she calls "butterfly thoughts", for they leave the mind so quickly. Milner suggests that observing and noticing fleeting thoughts through drawings or writing and becoming more deeply aware of one's sensory experiences promotes both growth of the imagination and the self.

In a similar vein, Cameron suggests that we may have our own internalised perfectionist and eternal critic who keeps up a constant stream of subversive criticism which sounds like the truth (Cameron, 1995, p. 11). In order to unblock imaginative and creative processes, she suggests that a person write three morning pages by "moving the hand across the page and writing down whatever comes to mind". She says, "nothing is too petty, too silly, too stupid or too weird to be included" (Cameron, 1995, p. 10). She suggests that through doing a kind of "stream of consciousness writing" one will "touch a source of wisdom within" (Cameron, 1995, p. 15). To avoid being self-critical, she suggests not re-reading the morning pages. The other, thoughtful introspective writing can happen after the free-flowing and unread morning pages are written.

4(b).   Using imaginative journeys and tales

Completing stories is not just an activity for children. For instance, you might be inspired to gather round with friends and older members of the family to complete the stories in Calvino's (1979) book *If on a Winter's Night a Traveller*. If you read a few lines of one of the twelve chapters you will become enticed by the story. Then the story is suddenly interrupted. You have the opportunity as a group to then create and tell the rest of the story. For example, there are stories written in the style of Borges, Chekhov, and a Spaghetti Western.

4(c).   Using spontaneous play and a "special time box"

Of course, there is a need for parents to be attentive to, and accompany, rather than interfere with, a child's spontaneous play, for the child is spontaneously telling a story of his unconscious feelings and thoughts. Strange as it may sound to you, using a special time box with toy human and animal figures can be useful for an adult on one's own or for couples, too. You might find that stories emerge from within you if you sometimes use your children's toys to imagine how you are experiencing your world at the moment. This depiction is a little like a dream showing some deeper, buried, inner experiences that you might want to consider more fully but do not have words to describe. Being a partner to your hidden self and getting close to your actual partner can occur through physical depictions using three-dimensional animal and human figures to represent your personal experiences of the moment or of the past. Trying to understand the themes present in the internal conflicts, tensions, pain, and joy, which are present in the representation of states of mind, can be a very enriching and creative activity which frees the self to exist with more vitality in the world.

5.   Appreciating the need for time, for an uncluttered safe space,
and supportive fostering of imagination

Unless we have the emotional and intellectual capacity to conceive of what does not yet exist, there is nothing towards which we are able to direct our motivation *to create* something. We all have access to imagination, the imagination required for creativity to ensue (Liu & Noppe-Brandon, 2009). What differentiates a creative person from a non-creative person is developing an *empty inner space, time, motivation, and effort* in order to develop the imagination and be creative in some way. To actually become creative, good practice doing the activity is required. Good practice is releasing the ego's hold on the situation long enough to let imagination and mistakes made in creating to guide us. Good practice involves having a safe environment where the fear of being correct is absent. A safe environment allows the creating person to learn from the experience of imagining and creating from those imaginings. (Liu & Noppe-Brandon, 2009, p. 189).

   The motivation for creativity can only come from within, but many a creative person has been inhibited by the negative, pessimistic remarks made by their family and friends. Motivation to create something from one's imaginings can be linked with the wish for recognition, approval, catharsis, validation, a challenge to mortality, sublimation of the birth instinct, excitation of feelings of passion and aliveness and a desire to make order out of chaos (Palaccio, 2008).

6.   Exploring and then choosing an area for development

Many people are multiply talented. However, to show creativity, ultimately one needs to dedicate oneself to a particular type of creative endeavour to develop in that specific area. Explore what you like doing, what your children like doing, and then find a way for them and for you to devote time and effort to that *particular activity* specific to each of you, rather than scattering one's talent. One can move on to another area, but true creativity requires depth of interest, time, and motivation to deepen the creative impulse in a particular area. Here is an example:

Leonard Bernstein said that his parents were looking after a neighbor's piano. His parents weren't particularly musical. With a child's curiosity he lifted the lid, pressed on the keys and felt the sounds vibrate from the instrument. A wave of excitement rushed through him. He didn't know why this happened but he knew then that he wanted to spend as much time as he could making such sounds. He had found his medium. (Robinson, 2001, p. 129)

Creativity is not so much a separate faculty as an attitude to spend time and effort in seeing new possibilities of perceiving and expressing oneself and *acting* on these possibilities (Robinson, 2001, p. 137).

7.   *Promoting spontaneous imagination and creativity*

Torrance's (1963) research in schools suggested that teachers could promote creativity in children by doing the following:

- treating unusual ideas or questions with respect;
- providing sufficient opportunity for self-initiated learning and non-evaluated learning, for evaluation promotes defensiveness;
- showing children that their ideas have value and encouraging self-expression.

To promote creativity, parents need to ensure that children have stretches of time for daydreaming and thinking and feeling about things other than schoolwork. Similarly, parents need time free from uncreative tasks in order to daydream.

Freud encouraged a shift to action in order that creativity would emerge from spontaneous imagination. He described how the creations of art heighten feelings of identification, by allowing opportunities for sharing highly valued emotional experiences (Freud, 1927c, p. 18). He encouraged Joan Riviere, an English psychoanalyst, to write, to get her thoughts out, and make something of her ideas so that they would have an existence independent of her.

Most importantly, the love of a good mother, accompanied by the mother's faith that the child will be a worthwhile and creative individual is the antecedent of creativity. The image of a trusting mother will sustain a child throughout his life and facilitate his struggle to endure the pains of innovative searching. Arieti says that "a longing for love" promotes an inner turmoil to expand one's own self (Arieti, 1976, p. 29).

Creating an inner space for spontaneous imagination allows transformation of extremely intense feelings into bearable and shareable states of mind. To use one's spontaneous imagination, one has to let go of facts seen or known and to look at things as though they could have been otherwise. To have an imaginative insight one has to believe in oneself, to put total trust in one's thought. "Belief in the self" is connected with internalising the good mother and father and allowing thought and feeling to freely intermingle with one another. The goal of freedom is to think thoughts that are one's own (Symington, 1990). In a book titled *Imagination First* (Liu & Noppe-Brandon, 2009), Richard Lewis asked some 7–8-year-old children, "Do you think there is a bird who could make the rain fall, or who could bring up the sun in the sky?"

What do you think they came up with? Joel, one of the seven-year-olds, wrote,

My bird comes out at night in the full moon.

He flies through the sky.

At night you can never see him. He is in you.

His name is imagination.

He lives in a place called heart brain body.

It is in everyone.

Some adults think it is childish, but it will never leave you even if you hide it. (Liu & Noppe-Brandon, 2009, p. 190)

We constrict children if we focus too much on teaching them names of things and numbers and colours before they have had the opportunity to explore freely with their hands, their eyes, and their symbolic play. We put a great deal of emphasis on the child saying words and insufficient emphasis on the fact that the powers of exploration, perception, and imagination welling up in the child need to be protected from too much clamping down with facts and words.

Grozinger (1995) suggests that the scribbling phase of a child is an important and decisive phase in which the child creates the inner space where he then receives and assimilates the world. Encouraging the child to scribble with both hands stimulates the child's sense of space and the body. The paper on which a child draws is like a body on which the child's sense of space and body crystallises. It is primarily the body that gives birth to the drawings: the trunk, hands, and feet are at work. Through engaging both sides of the child's body, both hands in drawing, the child experiences a liberation from the constriction of being kept to conceptual drawing, which is linked with language. Grozinger (1995) feels that it is good thinking to combine the drawing with limbering-up and breathing exercises. Now I understand why Wordsworth, like many poets, used to like to walk before writing. Painting with two hands can also be a way of working through psychic experiences and conflicts. Painting should not be marked or criticised, and neither should one ask what it is . . . It is what it is. It is part of natural development (Grozinger, 1995). Scribbling is like the child's babbling; it represents the child walking over the paper with the wordless rhythm of life. Premature favouring of the "proper hand" prevents the child from having a full sense of his body and the vision can be left solely to the eye. Grozinger suggests that there are phases of spontaneous expression through scribbling with both hands:

First there is 'the suckling', followed by the 'grip-ling' and only then by the 'talkling'. This means that the eye has first of all to work together with the hand, with the sense of touch, in exploring the world. Only when the hands have both reported back, like scouts, as to how far away things are, how light they are, how solid, how heavy, only when space has been crawled though, walked through and felt through, does the eye know something of the world. Then the hands and feet can rest, then the eye can ally itself to the ear and name things . . . the haptic phase of touch will be missed if one starts naming things too soon. . . . It would be useful to allow drawing to take place without a suggestion to 'draw' something in particular . . . just drawing, like skipping, singing, dancing, without colour necessarily, just lines, later the need for colour might occur . . . It is better simply to suggest that the child draw on a large surface, perhaps standing up initially so the whole body can be more involved. (Grozinger, 1995, p. 35)

What can you do? Using your thinking hat

I have shared with you seven different approaches to freeing the mind of its tightly held rituals and defences, in order to help creativity flourish. Now I have an exercise for you. You can do it alone, or with family, friends, or colleagues. I want you to step back for a moment, and think about what you believe promotes imagination and creativity. This could be at home or school, in parents, teachers, or children. In doing the exercise that follows, you will be able to think more about what creativity means for you, and what you can do to promote it.

As an added twist, let's step away from our usual thinking patterns and use a creative way to organise our thoughts: Edward De Bono's *Thinking Hats* (De Bono, 1985). Imagine that we have six hats, each in a different colour to represent different points of view. Now it is time to pick a hat. You can choose any colour you like: white, red, black, yellow, green, or blue.

White hats

White hats seek and lay out information. White hats have the task of differentiating facts from surmises. What factual information do you know about the development and inhibition of imagination and creativity?

Red hats

If you have a red hat, you focus on your intuitive feelings. You are allowed to be bold and open about them. They could be feelings of dislike about some methods or there might be strong feelings of pleasure for a particular way of allowing creativity to soar. They often say that at first people "have a feeling" and then they work out a logical reason for doing something based on that feeling. Whatever the situation is, feelings are always an essential part of thinking. What do you *feel* prompts your imagination or that of your child? Do you have feelings against the ways schools help children develop? What is your intuition about how Tempo Lineare helps and hinders imagination?

Black hats

Black hats represent caution, critically pointing out difficulties and problems with new approaches. They focus on what will not work with a new idea. Black hats might encourage reasons as to why we should focus more on learning facts and technical achievement rather than on fostering imagination and creativity.

Yellow hats

The yellow hats' thinking is hopeful, positive, and optimistic thinking about the future. Yellow hat thinking allows visions and dreams of what might be possible. Yellow hat thinkers are supportive of the idea that there are aspects of life in everyone that would profit from the creation of more time and psychological space for the imagination to develop. How would having a better house for the imagination benefit you and your family?

Green hats

Green hat thinking is concerned with generating new ideas and new ways of looking at things. The green hat symbolises fertility, growth, and a need to go beyond the known, the obvious, and the satisfactory. When you put on the green hat, you are signalling to yourself that you are setting aside time for deliberate imaginative and creative thinking to improve what already exists. Creativity involves provocation, exploration, and risks. Put on the green hat and pretend you are head of Tempo Lineare, or head of your child's elementary school, responsible for planning the weekend for your family or adding new dimensions to the use of personal space for you. What could you do?

Blue hats

The blue hat's task is to summarise what came out of this exercise of using different ways of thinking to create stronger houses for the imagination to grow. Did anything helpful come out of this thinking exercise, using many of the ingredients of imaginative thinking? What did you conclude that you could do to help promote and develop creativity?

What creativity can mean: inspirational creative acts

Volavkova (1993) tells the story of Friedl Dicker-Brandeis, an artist who hoarded materials such as scrap paper, cardboard, and wrapping to give to the children in a concentration camp, Terezin, near Prague, Czechoslovakia. Friedl went from camp to camp working with the children using these art materials. She taught the children the importance of observation, patience, the freeing of oneself from the outer world of numbing routine in the concentration camp and the inner world of dread. She told the children stories, much like Patrizia Pasquini does in Tempo Lineare. Afterwards, the children would act out the fairy tales, or stories they and others wrote, create and sing children's operas, and draw pictures. The children drew their concealed inner worlds, their tortured emotions, which Friedl was then able to enter and try to heal. Through art, she helped to restore a balance to the trembling consciousness of terrified children. Of these 15,000 children, who for a time played and drew pictures, only 100 survived.

Expressing their feelings through art and poetry was a way in which the children were enabled to moderate the chaos of their short and threatened lives. They loved drawing and writing with their teacher, Friedl. The children used the precious moments when they were alive. Here are two poems that they wrote. The first, "Illness", is by Franta Bass:

Illness

> Sadness, stillness in the room.
> In the middle, a table and a bed.
> In the bed, a feverish boy.
> His mother sits next to him
> With a little book.
> She reads him his favorite story
> And immediately, the fever subsides.
> (Franta Bass, in Volavkova, 1993, p. 30)

Pavel Friedmann wrote the following poem in 1942, while he was in Terezin:

I Never Saw Another Butterfly

For seven weeks I've lived in here,
Penned up inside this ghetto.
But I have found what I love here.
The dandelions call to me
And the white chestnut branches in the court.
Only I never saw another butterfly.
That butterfly was the last one.
Butterflies don't live in here,
In the ghetto.

(Pavel Friedmann, in Volavkova, 1993, p. xix)

When they wrote poems, the Terezin camp children told of longings to go away somewhere else where there were kinder people; there was a longing for home and a fear. Yes, fear came to them as they saw the executions and they could tell of it in their poems, knowing that they were condemned to die. Their drawings and their poems speak to us; they are "the voices of reminder, of truth and of hope" (Volavkova, 1993).

There are other, less serious tragedies which children are able to work through using writing stories. For example, one boy's father was a painter. His father gradually became blind. This boy, Peter Mann, helped his own grief and that of his father, Sargy Mann, by writing about his father and his painting (Mann & Mann, 2011). In doing so, he helped us understand something about "seeing and not seeing" which is important to our own capacity to observe, to imagine, and to create from our own experiences. Mann describes how drawing is completely about questioning and trying to understand the world as we perceive it. He describes how you need to look harder at what you see. As a seeing person, he would experiment with visualising space through walking around blindfolded for the day. I have done this with children, trying to help them become more intimate with their bodily sensations, emotions, and perceptions other than vision. Subsequently, they talked and wrote about their experiences. Walking around outside their familiar school became a new and significant adventure for them.

Sargy Mann was also an art teacher who taught psychoanalyst friends of mine. They said, "He taught us to see" (Symington & Symington, 2012). Developing imagination within the family can involve a deeper seeing, a more acute seeing, that brings all sorts of different possibilities for expression of one's experience. You can help the family to see by asking questions and trying to find answers to them. Here are some examples of what you can say.

Look at this glass. Can you see the bouncing light coming off the surface? How do you communicate sensations of bouncing light? How do you show both the colour of the illuminating light, the direction from which it has come, and then show the object on which the light has landed? You can walk around just noticing the light, how it lands, how it bounces off, how it influences the same plant in your house at different times of the day. You can learn to see light in this way.

Pierre Bonnard helps us to keep quiet while looking at a child's drawing. He says, "You can take any liberty with line, form, proportion, colour, so long as the feeling is intelligible and clear" (Mann & Mann, 2011, p. 4). Let your child find his way while drawing and allow yourself the same privilege.

Children and their parents can search for "a picture" to draw. Mann and Mann say,

> When searching for a spatial experience eyes can move very fast. It can be like flying. Your eye hits some grasses near your feet, skims the field, dipping and banking, climbs up the bushes, up and over the poplar and willows and off into the sky to circle and dive. These rushing dizzying circuits explore and build to an ever greater experience of the whole articulated space in which one finds oneself. Every point on that journey is giving off a different sensation of coloured light and requires a different colour at that place on the canvas. (Mann & Mann, 2011, p. 68)

You can experiment now, looking around, far away and close up, imagining how and where you might "frame" something you see.

When Sargy Mann became blind and unable to see details, he was a better painter than ever before! This occurred because he allowed himself an intuitive freedom with colour. Before, he was always involved in using colour to create the most convincing light. Now he was free to use colour not to express the presence of light, but, rather, he could use colour completely intuitively in order to express whatever experience he had in being with a figure, feeling its surface, and painting on the canvas. His blindness forced him to be free from his painting routine of looking for the way a light existed on an object. He now had to paint not through what he saw, but through feeling with his hands and then painting what he was feeling with his hands. You can imagine that he had an inner house for his imagination to grow and ferment, an imagination which was infused with memory and the experience of feeling what he drew without seeing (Mann & Mann, 2011, p. 212). People in the family can take turns closing their eyes, touching an object presented, and then trying to draw as Sargy Mann does. Through this, touch becomes another way of seeing.

The painting of Sargy Mann's wife, Frances, in the *Black Coat Pink Lining* (2007), was done when he was blind and using simply touch to paint her. In the painting, the top part of her head is missing, and it is not known if he planned it this way or not. What we see is a perspective from someone sitting below her, almost like a child.

Conclusion

We have been dwelling on developing a stronger house for imagination and creativity in families, schools, and in ourselves. I have been trying to encourage our minds "to stroll about hungry, fearless and supple" and to encourage our hearts "to always be open to little birds with secrets of living" (Cummings, 1991, p. 481). In doing so, I am aware that it is very comfortable to remain secure in the old routines, old ways of being together, and old ways of thinking together. I hope, though, that we shall be inspired, as was the black writer Maya Angelou, by Paul Dunbar's poem "Sympathy":

> I know why the caged bird sings, ah me,
> When his wing is bruised and his bosom sore,
> When he beats his bars and would be free;

It is not a carol of joy or glee,
But a prayer that he sends from his heart's deep core,
A plea, that upward to Heaven he flings,
I know why the caged bird sings.

(Dunbar, 1893, p. 102)

References

Arieti, S. (1976). *Creativity. The Magic Synthesis.* New York: Basic Books.

Bass, F. (1993). Illness. In: H. Volakova, *I Never Saw Another Butterfly* (p. 30). New York: Schocken.

Bick, E. (1968). The experience of skin in early object relations. *International Journal of Psychoanalysis, 49*: 484–486.

Brearley, M. (1998). Obituary: Marion Milner. *The Independent*: 10 June.

Calvino, I. (1979). *If on a Winter's Night a Traveller,* W. Weaver (Trans.). London: Secker Warburg, 1981.

Cameron, J. (1995). *An Artist's Way: A Course in Discovering and Rediscovering Your Creative Self.* London: Macmillan.

Cooper, H., & Magagna, J. (2002). The origins of self-esteem in infancy. In: J. Magagna, N. Bakalar, H. Cooper, J. Levy, C. Norman, & C. Shank (Eds.), *Intimate Transformations: Babies with their Families* (pp. 13–42). London: Karnac.

Cummings, E. E. (1991). May my heart always be open to little things. In: G. Firmage (Ed.), *E. E. Cummings Complete Poems, 1904–1962* (p. 481). New York: Liveright.

De Bono, E. (1985). *Six Thinking Hats.* London: Penguin.

Dunbar, P. L. (1893). Sympathy. In: J. M. Braxton (Ed.), *The Collected Poetry of Paul Lawrence Dunbar* (p. 102). Charlottesville, VA: University of Virginia Press, 1993.

Freud, S. (1927c). *The Future of an Illusion. S.E., 21*: . London: Hogarth.

Friedmann, P. (1993). I Never Saw Another Butterfly. In: H. Volavkova, *I Never Saw Another Butterfly* (p. xix). NewYork: Schocken.

Grozinger, W. (1995). *Scribbling, Drawing and Painting,* E. Kaiser & E. Wilkins (Trans.). London: Faber and Faber.

Jongsman, Jr., A., Peterson, M., McInnes, W., & Berghuis, D. (2004). *The Child Psychotherapy Progress Notes.* New York: John Wiley.

King, P. (2001). Openness. In: *Something Understood.* BBC Radio 4, 22 May 2011.

Liu, E., & Noppe-Brandon, S. (2009). *Imagination First.* San Francisco, CA: Jossey-Bass.

Magagna, J. (2002). Three years of infant observation with Mrs Bick. In: A. Briggs (Ed.), *Surviving Space: Papers on Infant Observation* (pp. 75–00). London: Karnac.

Mancia, M. (1999). Psychoanalysis and the neurosciences: a topical debate on dreams. *International Journal of Psychoanalysis, 80*: 1205–1215.

Mann, P., & Mann, S. (2011). *Sargy Mann.* London: S P Books.

Milner, M. (1950). *On Not Being Able to Paint.* London: Heinemann.

Milner, M. (2012). *Bothered by Alligators.* London: Routledge.

Palaccio, D. (2008). Inhibition and the creative process. Unpublished paper.

Pasquini, P. (2002). *Da Fiabe Nasce Fiabi.* Rome: Genitori e Amici del Tempo Lineare-Onlus.

Perls, F., Hefferline, R., & Goodman, P. (1951). *Gestalt Therapy: Excitement and Growth in the Human Personality.* New York: Julian.

Robinson, K. (2001). *Out of Our Minds: Learning to Be Creative.* Chichester: Capstone.

Schneider, J. A. (2010). From Freud's dreamwork to Bion's work of dreaming: the changing conception of dreaming in psychoananalytic theory. *International Journal of Psychoanalysis*, 91: 521–540.

Selekman, M. (2000). *Collaborative Brief Therapy with Children.* New York: Guilford Press.

Symington, J., & Symington, N. (2012). Personal communication.

Symington, N. (1990). The possibility of human freedom and its transmission: linked with thoughts of Bion. *International Journal of Psychoanalysis*, 17(1–4): 95–106.

Target, M., & Fonagy, P. (1996). Playing with reality: II. The development of psychic reality from a theoretical perspective. *International Journal of Psychoanalysis*, 77: 459–479.

Torrance, E. P. (1963). *Education and the Creative Potential.* Minneapolis, MN: University of Minnesota Press.

Volavkova, H. (1993). *I Never Saw Another Butterfly.* New York: Schocken.

Winnicott, D. W. (1960). The theory of the parent–infant relationship. *International Journal of Psychoanalysis*, 41: 585–595.

CHAPTER FIFTEEN

Living in a group: children learning to know themselves and others

Patrizia Pasquini

One day time was passing (Valeria, aged eleven)

One day time was passing
I told it:
"Time, give me a lift in the past,
let me go back
at least nine years,
so that I am two.
I always have it my way
because my sister is not there yet.
I cry a bit . . .
Mummy feeds me with a spoon,
daddy cuddles me,
I see Granny Isabella,
so sweet
with her forest
of thick black hair.

I have a white, pink and pale blue high chair
I play with my little rattles
I have a teddy bear
I sleep together with it:
at night I cuddle it
and it cuddles me.

I have a room all for myself,
I can see characters of stories,

Pinocchio, Little Red Riding Hood,
the Ugly Duckling.

Those were the days!
Run, run time
into the past:
fulfil this wish of mine."

(Valeria, 2008, pp. 23–24)

Every child that is born has his own time. Time that is past remains present in our mind as a memory of our experience. Time is linear because it starts at a certain point, when a child is born, and it ends at another point, when his life draws to an end. Each of us freely uses his little time-line, putting his life in it.

If someone lives a beautiful experience, he will "venture towards the infinite and . . . time will end when the world will end, when nobody will be left to think of time, when nobody will be left to think of and remember passing time" (Meltzer & Harris, 1976, p. 402).

In my peculiar experience of the Tempo Lineare school, time passes in a strange way; it is never the same, it is never boring, and it runs quickly. Everyday in this collaborative space, healthcare professionals, parents, children, and I observe the growth of children between zero and six years. I think of Tempo Lineare as a testing ground for the children to use their inter-nalised parental capacities and develop them further with the help of their relationships within Tempo Lineare. Within the nursery space, parents gain access to their children's emotional world, so that they can reach a degree of intimacy which enables them to modulate, regulate, and contain their children's very intense emotional experiences and reflect upon their own emotional experience.

In the epigraph above, Valeria, aged eleven, describes the experience of growth and her awareness of the effort involved in growing up. In every child there is a part that wants to grow up and another part that does not, that wants to stop time. This is because when growing up, a child often feels he is losing something special, he might be afraid of separation and feel that development brings anxiety, pain, distance, drawbacks, and loneliness; simultaneously, his notion of being a baby makes him feel softness, nearness, warmth, and fulfilment. For this reason a child may wish to re-enter the mother's body, an idealised womb-space. Valeria describes her memory of feeling "her majesty the child of the golden age", in which she enjoyed omnipotence, a right for every small child, a state of beatitude to which she would like to go back in order to discover more personal fulfilment. Through her poem, Valeria can fulfil a wish she will not be able to satisfy in external reality. For, in contrast to her life of inner imagination, in her external reality Valeria will discover that time does not stop, for her body cells endlessly reproduce and everything moves and changes. Children, if helped to think, understand that this is how life proceeds.

Children, living together for some hours each day in a nursery group, develop maturity as they learn to overcome the disappointment they feel when they find out that not all fantasies become reality, that daydreaming often does not come true, but can bring pleasure within the activity itself. A child grows up well if fantasy is not denied. This happens because fantasy can be beautiful, it can help a child cope in his relationship with reality, potentially, it can help him to find a balance between the pressures and conflicts of external reality, therefore assisting him to grow up. Fantasy is linked to desire: if a child desires a thing and the parent says "no", the child becomes frustrated and angry, but frustration is part of growth.

A child in nursery can learn that growth is not simply linked to a loss, but also to some excitement, pleasure, freedom, and sense of achievement. When a child learns that growing also means accepting reality as something that poses limits to some of his desires, then he understands that life is not as perfect as he imagined. He might also realise that potentially life can be beautiful because of its imperfections and endless interesting changes and challenges.

However, as parents and teachers, we need to think about what we can do when a child's growth brings about feelings of emptiness and loss to either the child or the parents. Our task is to discover how can we help children and their parents to modulate these feelings regarding separation and loss. It is important for the child and his parents to understand that with every change the loving feelings of old times are still alive. In twelve years working collaboratively with families at Tempo Lineare, we have managed to assist children in getting to "know" themselves and in developing an inner psychological space for thinking about feelings. At Tempo Lineare, the experience of being together with other parents and teachers helps parents to discover different ways of being a parent with one's child.

Being in touch with one's child

I would like to show how Sandra, Miriam's mother, become more in touch with her daughter's needs. Afterwards, this mother could become interested in the parents' group and communicate her understanding of her daughter to others. This observation, as always happens when mothers observe in Tempo Lineare, was made in my presence. In the group, parents observe and see the way their child is, the way other children are, and they understand that every person's life is different from that of someone else. Observation enables mothers to be receptive to their children's different states of mind when they are together. The mutual joy mother and child receive from one another is made possible by the mother's understanding of her child's feelings, which is developed through conversations with other parents in the parents' group.

The following passages demonstrate this ability of a Tempo Lineare parent mother to observe her daughter. This ability was strengthened through the monthly Saturday morning Young Child Observation course the mother, Sandra, followed in a small group of six, with thirty other Tempo Lineare parents, teachers, psychotherapists, and social workers.

Mother's first observation of Miriam, five months

Miriam is lying with her head resting sideways on a big pillow. I am showing her a big, colourful fish, made of various sections. Every time we come to Tempo Lineare, she adores playing with it. The fish has a plastic ring that Miriam tries to catch, While I swing the plastic fish in front of her, Miriam reaches out with one hand to try to catch the attached ring. After she manages to take the ring, she holds it with both hands and puts it into her mouth. Miriam chews the ring happily for a few moments, then she lets the fish go. We play this way for a while as she babbles with delight. Miriam does not look at me while playing with the fish and I do nothing except hold the toy and look at her.

The room is quite noisy, as the whole group of children are in it. Something falls to the floor with a loud crash. Miriam turns and looks at the other children. Then she turns towards me with a smile. We start playing again, but after a while Miriam becomes tired and remains quiet, looking at the fish. After a while, having had enough of the fish, Miriam starts looking up, arching her back and pushing her feet against the sides of the soft ring. I take her in my arms and I stand up. I kiss her cheek and I ask her what we want to do now. We move to a basket full of animal-shaped toys. I choose the black and white sheep, in which she seems most interested. I stretch her out on a sheet and try to get her attention with the black and white sheep. Quickly, I realise she is not interested in it, but, rather, in looking intently at my face. So I put the sheep away and begin to talk to her. She reaches out with one hand and touches my face. Miriam is very relaxed, her movements are slow and delicate. She looks at me with shining eyes and utters a very delicate "haiih".

This observation tells us that the mother does not need to be told what would be helpful for her to do with her baby. She is spontaneously able to be deeply in touch with her daughter, to modulate her movements, intonations, and her facial expressions. She has a deep unconscious understanding of her little girl. Working with mothers, I observed that if a woman is not supported by a big family, she can learn the hard job of being a mother in a group, where she gets enough emotional support to do her job well. I am deeply convinced that, as Stern (1995) said, a mother's work is like that of an artist who has an encounter with a baby, half as a choreographer and half as a musical composer. She is required to attune to her baby in a non-verbal way, using appropriate timing and rhythm to connect with her baby at a deep emotional level. One sees here how the mother who has written this observation attunes to her baby.

Mother's second observation of Miriam, six months

Miriam is in the soft ring, playing with a cloth cube that rattles. Beside the soft ring in which Miriam is sitting, I am seated so that I can see Miriam's face without facing her. From time to time, I bend forward to see her expression, but most of the time I remain quietly seated without interfering. Miriam is sitting with her back leaning against the comfortable ring. She holds the cube with both hands, then she finds the handle on the side of the cube and grabs it with her thumb and index finger. As Miriam shakes the cube, it makes the rattling sound. Being very amused by this, she opens her eyes and mouth wide with delight. Patrizia, the Director, places another baby, Alessandra, five months older, in front of her. While holding her cube in one hand, Miriam follows Patrizia. From time to time, Miriam puts the cloth cube in her mouth. When Alessandra is seated in front of Miriam, the two babies look at each other: Miriam is curious and attentive, but does not smile. While looking at Alessandra, she becomes calmer, and for a while she looks frozenly attentive in her movements, almost suspended, by what she is seeing.

Patrizia suggests to one of the teachers to put some music on. The music is playing just above Miriam's head and she follows the sound above with her eyes. She tilts her head back and remains with her head leaning on the side of the soft ring. She looks surprised when she hears birds singing on tape and turns her head more firmly in the direction of their chirping. Then she starts playing with the cube again, half leaning against the side of the soft ring. Alessandra's mother is sitting nearby on the sofa between the two soft rings. She has given a book with sounds to her daughter and after a while I give one to Miriam. I talk to Alessandra's mother a little about breast-feeding. She asks me Miriam's weight and I tell her that she weighs seven kilos already. I tell her that I like seeing our children growing so much on our milk and suggest that we can be proud of it. She tells me that she feels spent, exhausted by the baby. She adds that during the day her bones ache, all of her body aches, and sometimes she cannot move. She looks worried. When I turn to Miriam, I see that she's looking at Alessandra's mother. The mother returns Miriam's glance and starts talking to her, smiling. Miriam studies her face with a serious look, then smiles broadly.

Sitting in the nursery with their babies, the mothers establish bonds, and this experience helps them to take care of their children. This common experience allows them to feel that being a mother does not mean being alone. The group favours a social interaction through improvisation, adaptation, and creative relationships. Every mother understands this complex task. In the group, parents discover and develop their inner resources, they observe and think about their relationship with their children, and start to recognise mutual projections between themselves and their children. In time, the parents' group increases parents' trust, enables them to deeply experience their children's feelings, which beforehand were so difficult to stand. Parents also find the freedom to be in touch with lost parts of themselves that were unconsciously projected on their children. Day after day, the group becomes a way of learning from knowing their babies in order to further develop their parental abilities. Acknowledging how important they are as parents for the child helps build emotional bonds between the child and the parents both in the outside world and in the child's inner world, the feeling of being important for the child. These parent–child bonds enable the child to relate well to people outside the immediate family.

My role is to try to help parents understand the usefulness of the group and assist those mothers who find difficulty in participating in the group. They meet other parents anxiously and have no pleasure in doing so. These difficulties emerge also in the lack of emotional contact with their child: they cannot express themselves through their smile and voice and they are not able to be attentive enough to elicit their child's participation in an intimate mutual gaze. There follows an observation of a mother–baby interaction fraught with such difficulties.

Observation of Danilo, two months

Danilo enters the babies' room with his mother. She puts him on a big pillow. He wakes and immediately starts wailing, then screaming. His mother touches his feet, saying that he suffers from colic. Danilo becomes all red in the face as he screams louder and louder. When his mother takes him in her arms, Danilo avoids her gaze, screaming desperately. The mother strokes his back with determined strokes, but Danilo screams even more loudly. He does not seem to be able to calm down. The mother looks at her watch and wonders aloud if maybe Danilo is hungry, but she does not endeavour to feed him because she thinks it is not the right time to feed him as she looks at her watch again.

As Danilo is still screaming, I ask mother when she last fed him and she tells me that it was just two and a half hours ago. I tell her that maybe the baby is hungry, and she feels more confident to breast-feed him. When mother gives him her breast, Danilo sucks voraciously. While he is sucking, the mother tells me that he must eat every two hours, even during the night, and she is very tired. She adds that during the day when she is feeding Danilo, he is disturbed by his four-year-old brother, Pietro, who insistently demands her attention.

In such situations, I manage to help a mother feel more confident about getting in touch emotionally with her baby. Sometimes, I observe that, when a baby avoids the mother's gaze, the baby is aware that the mother finds the intimacy of the baby's gaze difficult to bear. Only after this difficulty between mother and baby is resolved does the baby find he can become more intensely involved with his mother. Then he smiles, he looks at his mother, he vocalises, he holds on to her with his gaze, and the baby's gestures elicit the mother's capacity to feel even more able to be in touch with him. In a parents' group, my task during a child's first year is to foster a good attachment, which can express itself in this phase when mother and child are face to face, in mutual communication, and when mothers start playing the peek-a-boo game. The Tempo Lineare parents have a positive experience when they feel they are compassionately kept in the observer's mind.

A neurologist, Siegel (1999), claims that psychical health is characterised by a growing complexity and interdependence of various aspects of the brain's functioning; people with psychological problems have a less complex brain structure, more chaotic, more rigid, and less organised. This emphasis on bonds and complexity recalls Bion's (1963) theories on the formation of bonds between mother and child and on the importance of the maternal containing function. Neuroscience teaches us that the brain, in particular a young child's brain, is extremely malleable. Schore (2003) emphasised that from the last three months *in utero* to the second year of life, the child's psycho-biological brain development is regulated by a mother's physiological and mental states. A mother's maternal gaze can stimulate some of the infant's neuronal circuits. This regulating function was suggested in Winnicott's (1967) idea, when he stated that a newborn cannot be considered without his care-giver and that the newborn's self-understanding develops when he sees himself reflected in his mother's eyes.

Neurological research confirms what developmental psychology says about growth and small children. Our work at Tempo Lineare is centred on support for healthy parentality and loving care-giving, but interfering conflicts have deep transgenerational roots in the human soul. We can identify this conflict in the foetus manipulating the mother's body to receive a greater supply of nutrients, at the same time releasing into the bloodstream hormones that increase blood pressure, putting the mother's health at risk. The foetus takes control of the mother's arterial system like "an astronaut piloting a spaceship".

Klein (1930, pp. 219–231) described the child's primitive aggressive phantasies and impulses. She illustrated the child's curiosity and phantasies regarding the mother and her secret interior space, the womb. Two- and three-year-olds, alone in the nursery room without their parents, might begin playing out aggressively towards me. Fear, anger, conflict, and pain regarding separation from a parent is voiced in this way. As the care-giver representing the maternal object, I can become persecutory, hated, and envied.

When playing, the child elaborates upon his current emotional experiences, exploring new solutions and expressing his phantasies as his mind evolves. Play not only represents an opening up of the child's mental life to instinctual impulses, but also it suggests an attempt to resolve conflictual and painful states of mind. As can be seen in the following observation, playing can become a creative process of discovering what one feels.

Observation of a group of children aged two and a half years

Cecilia plays with the teddy bears before she puts them all behind her and sits still without playing. After a while, I tell her, "It takes a long time before they are born!" She answers, "Yes, it takes a long time." Then she takes the bears and says, "One two, three, four, they're so many!" Two teddy bears fall. I perceive some aggressive undertone as they drop, but I say nothing. Then Cecilia stands up and falls to the ground, saying, "I'm falling too." Shortly afterwards, she comes close to me and hugs my legs very tightly. I tell her that she is afraid of falling from the minds of people who love her if she does not hold on so firmly. At this point, other children in the group start to play: Federico grabs a rag crocodile and pretends that it is eating my arm. I respond, "Help! help! It hurts!" In fact, Frederico is firmly squeezing my arm.

Cecilia looks at him and says "What's up?" and Federico continues to play. He takes a rag cow and presses its nipple with both hands on my hand, saying that milk is coming out of the nipple. He gives me a cloth deer, saying that it needs to drink the milk. Cecilia looks on while Antonio, feeling anxious about Frederico's play, approaches me, saying, "The crocodile is gone, isn't it?"

Now Marco uses a rag tiger to attack the little deer Federico left on my lap. I hide the deer under my scarf. Marco presses his tiger against my lap, saying, "The tiger wants to get in!" I tell him that it is not possible, because the door is closed. Federico repeats, "It is locked." Marco insists, but after a while he and Federico start hiding other animals under my scarf: a squirrel, a horse, a hedgehog. After hiding these objects, one of the children lets two toy cars run twice up my arm. He says that dad is in one of them, mum is in the other.

At a certain point, the play becomes more excited: the children try to attack the little animals under my scarf with the wild animals, the tiger, crocodile, and lion. I protect the hidden toys from attacks that become increasingly forceful. When a little girl hurts my arm, I have to remind the children that we are "just pretending". Cecilia aggressively shows her teeth and expresses her rage towards the hidden little ones. Federico is alarmed and grabs the cow, saying that the little ones must drink their milk. They calm down and smile while putting the aggressive animals away. When I say, "They can be born now, they're safe and there is good milk", the children say "Yes". In response, I can take the protective scarf away and put the toy animals in the basket next to me where they belong.

As you can infer from this play, one of the deepest childhood phantasies is to penetrate into the mother's body, sometimes out of curiosity, sometimes out of rage, frustration, and desire to damage inner objects. This happens when the child feels jealous and wants to steal his mother's riches. The jealousy children feel, starting from two to three years of age, is mainly due to the fact that they feel left out of their parents' relationship and worry that they will be forgotten if attention focuses on someone other than them.

The "mother's babies" damaged in phantasy by the child's aggression turn into persecutory objects and cause colossal paranoia. For this reason, the child uses play to externalise his feelings by acting them out at a distance through play characters. In the above observation, it is possible to trace conflicts that children experience in phantasy, dealing with the mother and father's relationship and the mother and father's babies. Curiosity about the mother's body promotes new conflict-free relationships and, through substitute objects, a symbolisation process can be initiated.

Creative play is, first of all, an individual activity. The child makes up some characters he can talk to and this makes him feel safer. The child has his own place, a place for himself that he has found by himself. Others witness his creativity; he uses the characters in the play to speak up instead of himself. The play reveals the child's current inner reality. The child's impulses are expressed without physical danger to others. In time, one child's play evokes the interest of another child and, in time, the group is sharing a joint phantasy, a joint play in which everyone expresses his/her own mind in a creative way.

When the separation process begins between parent and child, it is useful to help them to understand the child's reaction to separation and individuation. At these moments, the child may become fidgety, always alert, and unable to pay attention. When the child becomes more competent in regulating his own feelings and he understands more clearly what he is expressing, he feels that he is present in the adult's mind, and this helps him to establish a more secure relationship with the care-giving adults. As he feels more secure in his relationships, the child begins to let himself be known, to know himself, and the group helps him to feel that he is seen. The group phantasises that I am like a generous and omnipotent mother, able to give equal attention to all. The younger children's group play occurs in a context that is felt as free from dangers.

I conceived the Tempo Lineare school for the older three- to six-year-olds as a place where children can be educated to know themselves and others, to freely think and express themselves, to participate in school life so that they can build a democracy of differences. The child is the true protagonist and his knowledge, expressed through play, builds a real "culture" in a genuine and joyful way. Starting from the discovery of the mother's warm breast, of the milk's taste, of people's eyes and voices, the child explores the world around himself. Gradually, the things seen with his eyes, touched with his hands, are internalised, and this leads him to know the world, people, language, and rules.

The child discovers the pleasure of play, the pleasure of listening to a tale, of drawing, and he finds out the value of music and painting. Through creativity, he lets himself be known and knows the others. At Tempo Lineare, the child experiences his own environment, finding out that things and people change and that he himself has a story of growth and affections. Experiencing the care offered to him by parents, the nursery staff, and the other children, the child receives a more or less positive idea of the world, which becomes his *weltanschaung*. Every day, the child re-enacts his stories with play, the theatre of the child's imagination, and with language. When not interrupted by adults' intruding and controlling interventions, drawing can become a real artistic alphabet to express unverbalised emotions. Children work in a group that becomes a true sounding board of feelings and emotions, the place where differences can be thought out, the tool used to share and discuss issues important to them.

As for gender differences, the school does not propose male and female stereotypes: those stereotypes get to children in other ways, through parents, teachers, and other children in the group. Research shows that parents react in a different way according to the newborn's gender: they choose different words for speaking to girls or boys, nursery school teachers treat children according to gender stereotypes, and children tend to exclude and criticise other children who behave "inappropriately" with respect to their gender. When children play, they show that their idea of male and female is a caricature of adult stereotypes, and teachers tend to propose the "right" type of play according to gender: males play with Lego, females play with babies and toy pots.

At Tempo Lineare, toys are at the group's disposal: if the group plays with dolls, everyone is supposed to take care of his/her own doll. If the group plays with puzzles, every one has his/her own puzzle. There is never a toy only for girls or only for boys. Together, girls and boys think up new ways of playing together and there is no difference between them. This experience, in which gender differences are not underscored, can help every child to learn from diversity, from exchanges with the other sex, and to get to know people different from him/herself.

The parents' idea of sexual difference is revised and discussed in the parental group. Often, parents wondered whether, at Tempo Lineare, their male children with a fragile masculine identity became too "kind" to live in a world so full of aggression. Gender identity in males and females is somehow in progress and a shared experience makes everyone more sensitive and thoughtful and, therefore, stronger in facing life's issues.

Another important factor is having an adult observe the child and the group conducted by an adult. A child tries out new experiences all the time, and the function of organising, controlling, and containing the play must be thoughtfully considered by an adult. When an adult in Tempo Lineare is playing in the group, children feel that the barrier separating them from the adult world is not as strong, for the adult does not impose adult rules and does not use a language they cannot understand. The children feel they can be in another's mind all the time. Children in a group get to know each other and they certainly need to know other children to develop. The Tempo Lineare group becomes "a small protected space not far from the adult world, where one operates identifications and learns about the adult world". In the group, the children not only imitate, not only play a particular function (teacher, father, mother, child), but also represent different things (a train, a plane, the wind). In this representation, the child chooses a particular element. For instance, I think about movement and force. When a playing child becomes a moving train, he is "that force" and the adult becomes the train driver. Children recognise that an adult can guide them.

In a group, children can see themselves and others more clearly and the adult can perceive them more perceptively. While living in a group, children can see themselves and the other group members in a sort of mirror reflecting their emotional issues. The following observation of a dialogue between children shows us how children can think about what happens in the school.

Observation of group dialogue

Before I read a fairy tale to the children, as I do every day, I explain to Luigi, who is showing anger and restlessness, that he can explain to us why he is so angry. Michele, four years old, butts in, saying, "When I was angry I was not glad, now I feel happy." But Giorgio, five years old, explains, "When I was angry I was alone. If one is angry, he stays lonely. Now I can do more things and I feel better and I have lots of friends." While he is speaking, Giorgio is looking towards Francesco, and I ask him why. Giorgio explains to me that Francesco has always been nice to him and that he has been playing often with him, trying to become his friend.

Once a child enters a group, he begins to understand his own psychological functioning, thanks to identifications that arise in relation to other group members. The group mirrors back to every child aspects of himself, and this makes everyone in the group wonder about their own emotions and behaviours. Thus, a child discovers that other children, too, may have the same kind of trouble as he has and that they may act in ways prompted by anxiety or guilt. The child comes to realise that others might also need to be constantly on the move to express all this anguish. The group is also capable to take, acknowledge, and bear every child's distress, until the child himself becomes able to express what he feels.

It is for this reason that, at Tempo Lineare, we choose to work in a group, so that even the most fragile children, such as adopted children with extremely difficult histories, can ask for help, while the better regulated children can offer understanding and support, thus avoiding isolating children with difficulties and assigning them to work much of the time alone with a special teacher. Everybody is engaged in the task of sharing a certain amount of distress and the responsibility of opening oneself to accept support. Everybody is helped to recognise that one's life is enriched by staying with others and their differing personalities and experiences. The group becomes a mediating area in which children are helped to represent and regulate their own feelings. Children start to feel themselves held through games involving aggression and loving co-operation and the possibility of talking about their emotions.

This kind process is particularly present during group activities in which children try to manage their intense emotions by projecting upon their playmates their rivalrous feelings in such a way that they can name and to recognise them. An observation of such a process follows.

Observation of a group of children, three to five years old

I read to the children the tale "Wolf or sheep?" Afterwards, we begin discussing whether they identified themselves more with the wolf or with the sheep. A five-year-old boy, Sammy, says, "Patrizia, when you read the tale about Tonino, who was first angry and then became full of kindliness, I too became like Tonino who made friends with Giovanni, because I have made friends with my schoolmates. Now I have become a nicer boy because I am more kind. Don't you think so?" I answer that one is happier, when he feels he has improved his ways of being gentle and amiable, and also because he feels he is easier, like the sheep, and no longer rude as the wolf is.

A three-year-old boy, James, steps in, saying that he feels like a wolf because he is so angry with his mother since his sister Julie was born. He adds that Julie is always meddling with his toys. Five-year-old Sammy again speaks, saying that also his little brother is a messy boy. Another child, three-year-old Jude, exclaims that he wakes up at night because he is cross about finding his sister in mummy's and daddy's bed.

Sacha, aged four, says that she often feels wicked like the wolf, but that she has managed to find a solution to it: she puts all the naughty thoughts in a bag, so that they cannot escape as long as she keeps the bag closed. I ask her if she would like to tell what her wicked thoughts are. She answers that she is often angry with her mother because her mother is always spending a lot of time with her little brother since his birth, feeding him, changing him, talking to him. Sacha ends up saying "I am jealous!" I suggest that she might tell her feelings to mummy, because sometimes children are a bit jealous and also a bit sad when new ones are born, but they can tell mummy and mummy can help them to feel better about it.

Briony, a little girl of three, explains to everybody that she feels like the bad wolf when mummy marries daddy, and another girl, Susan, aged five, agrees that she feels angry like the wolf when mummy kisses daddy. I state that children would like to have mummy and daddy all for themselves, but mummy belongs to daddy and daddy to mummy, and both belong also to their sons and daughters. A girl of three, Sophie, tells me that she is jealous of daddy sleeping with mummy, and another girl, Carla, aged four, butts in, saying, "I remember you already told me that during the day mummy and daddy belong to us children."

The capacity of being able to express one's thoughts through a game enables children to reflect upon themselves and to understand their own feelings. Their play also allows them to be known and understood by others. This is a crucial issue, because it allows inner emotions to be represented and then put into words. As seen in the previous observation group, reflection on the adult–child relationship can be augmented by the children sharing their experiences in a group. As time passes, as Carla mentioned, it is possible to build a common group history of shared thoughts. The sense of belonging to a group and a more marked awareness of each child's individual feelings with the group fosters supportive interactions between the group and children within it. After these repeated daily experiences in Tempo Lineare of talking to others and being listened to by the group, it will be easier for each of these children to acknowledge in a group their feelings and difficulties.

This feeling of belonging to a group is particularly evident with the five-year-old children experiencing the last few months before leaving Tempo Lineare. At Tempo Lineare, children who are about to leave for the primary school are given opportunities to play while learning to read and to write. The children need to have confidence that they can progress into this more mature phase of being in the world. While trying to read and to write by themselves, they know there is a teacher nearby whom they can glance at out of the corner of their eyes. They need also to rely on an internalised relationship with a parent who appreciates and contains their feelings. The basis of being able to be truly autonomous is being safely contained by a secure attachment to a mother/father. Dependence on good helpful parents enables independence from them to occur (Winnicott, 1967).

Whenever I read a story, children listen to something that will help them to construct their own identity. Although our way of thinking is mainly organised by developing stories, children find their way of learning by playing the game of personifying somebody else and by reverting then to their usual self, thus learning how to get in and out of different roles and relationships in different environments. The following is an example of an exercise embarked upon with the children.

Observation of a group of children, aged five

After four to five months' work spent playing once a week with letters, numbers, puzzles, and rhymes, children have succeeded in bearing in their mind numbers and letters while amusing themselves. Now, after a tale on Springtime, children are asked to draw a spider on coloured cardboard and to stick it in their exercise books. Later on, children enjoy themselves trying to write the different insects' names that they heard during the story-telling. They show enthusiasm at this game, so they are asked to try to put together words to make some sentences about the tale, and then to draw the tale in the exercise book. Everybody works hard. The most assured and the most curious among the children write and draw without fearing to make mistakes, while the more anxious and insecure continually ask for help, which they receive.

Marta, although she has noticeably improved, is still very anxious, so much so that she writes "ladybird" without any vowels, thus making the word almost unintelligible. Nick is very insecure and timid, and unceasingly begs for consideration. We explain to him that he could try to work by himself, and that he will be helped if necessary. He looks discouraged and writes unintelligible words. The anxiety that shows on Nick's face is so considerable that he cannot write an understandable sentence. He himself states that he has not written any word that can be understood, but only spare letters that he remembers. He then talks about his anxiety about writing and suggests that he is really afraid of leaving Tempo Lineare and beginning primary school. After this, he is able to cancel all the words he has written and he succeeds in writing a correct sentence. He feels very happy about this!

Mario begins with writing a title to the story; he is the only one among the children to do this. He then proceeds to write half a page of tightly spaced text in his large exercise book. He picks up the tale's contents and he writes the story of a skipping mole, with numbered chapters and a drawing of the mole's house.

Phillip is inclined to withdraw, to get lost in his thoughts and to let his attention wander. This seems to be his way of calling for continuous attention. He has great difficulty in bringing words together and he seems to be unable to write if an adult is not near him. In contrast, Anita now has managed to understand how to write meaningful words and she, too, succeeds in writing a short tale and in drawing the story. When she is not sure about how to write a word, she asks a teacher.

Alba writes fast, neatly, and with very few mistakes. She works alone, never asking any adult's help. She has written a tale with a beginning and an ending and she has drawn a nice picture. She shows her work only after she has completed it, and she states, "I want to be a writer when I grow up!"

Beatrice, too, shows her tale when she has finished it. She has worked silently by herself, remembering what she had been told, when she still wrote words all over the sheet, about writing from left to right and from top to bottom. Today, she has succeeded in writing neatly and correctly on her sheet and, moreover, she has displayed a lot of creativity. Lorraine has succeeded in writing a short tale, notwithstanding the fact that words are still closed up on one another. Still, she has developed a lot in the past month and she is happy works gleefully. By the end of this story-writing exercise, each of the children has written and read their tales to the others. All the stories have been appreciated and talked about one by one in due course.

This observation of the five-year-old children's group shows how everybody, by himself, has succeeded in bringing words together, thanks to a training in which every child has had fun with letters and numbers and drawing and can use their learning to create something of interest to them. Such a style of learning involves a low level of control, of expectation, and involves only a minor level regarding performance anxiety. Freely creating and sharing one's stories and drawings creates their own vitality in the children's minds. The enthusiasm children have shown all through this last year towards learning how to read and to write autonomously has convinced me that a teacher can build up a relationship to help children's autonomy in learning if he gives up attitudes of being harsh, bossy, lax, and demanding. Structured spontaneity in learning creates much more eagerness in participating in the learning process.

If a child, step by step, can think and talk about his feelings, he becomes able to inwardly build a mind that can remember and think, even about the more difficult and confusing pattern of his own experiences. Tempo Lineare holds a "therapeutic role", in which, step by step, every child is enabled to accept and bear emotional experiences in learning. The child's self-awareness developed through the group activities facilitates the capacity to learn and to be creative. In turn, through these processes, the child begins to discover and develop himself as a person.

Again, school ought to allow every child to experience a space of freedom, inside the group, arousing agreement and bonds between them

I end this chapter with a short tale titled "The rose", written by Maria, a girl of eleven. Maria took part in Tempo Lineare's school project, and she now attends an experience group inside our Association courses. Unlike Valeria, Maria does not feel growth to be a change involving uncertainty and disadvantage, but thinks of it as a mystery. For Maria, the flowing of time is tightly linked with an idea of "changing" and it is "linear". The rose stands for a good aesthetic experience, that is, to meet the world's beauty, which prompts an attitude of curiosity towards nature, or Mother earth. In this story, the rose represents a good interiorised object and the compass that shows Maria the path towards her growing up:

The rose

Once upon a time during an April afternoon a girl was born, and just at the same moment in a flowerbed in her parent's garden a white rose came out. For the first years mother looked after her girl and father attended to the rose watering it every day. When the girl was six, she began to look herself after the rose, growing it, protecting it and keeping it in the sunshine. The girl and the rose grew up together and the girl, now a woman, never forgot the rose that grew luxuriant.

When the girl became a very, very old woman she died and at the same time died the rose too.

On the old woman's grave a white rose grew and never withered. Was it the old lady's kindness that allowed the rose to grow on her grave? This is still a mystery.

References

Bion, W. R. (1963). *Elements of Psychoanalysis.* London: William Heinemann [reprinted London: Karnac]. Reprinted in *Seven Servants* (1977). London: William Heinemann. Reprinted London: Karnac, 1984.

Klein, M. (1930). The importance of symbol-formation in the development of the ego. In: *Love, Guilt and Reparation and Other Works 1921–1945* (pp. 219–231). London: Hogarth, 1975.

Meltzer, D., & Harris, M. (1976). *Child, Family and Community: A Psychoanalytical Model of the Learning Process.* Paris: Organization of Economic Co-operation and Development. Reprinted in: A. Hahn (Ed.), *Sincerity and Other Works* (pp. 387–455). London: Karnac, 1994.

Schore, A. (2003). *Affect Regulation and the Repair of the Self: The Neurobiology of Emotional Development.* Hillsdale, NJ: Lawrence Erlbaum.

Siegel, D. (1999). *The Developing Mind: Toward a Neurobiology of Interpersonal Experience.* New York: Guilford Press.

Stern, D. (1995). *The Motherhood Constellation.* New York: Basic Books.

Valeria (2008). One day time was passing (Valeria, age 11). In: M. Lodi & A. Pallotti, *L'Orologio Azzurro* (pp. 23–24). Molfetta, Italy: La Meridiana.

Winnicott, D. W. (1967). The mirror-role of mother and family in child development. In: *Playing and Reality* (pp. 111–118). London: Tavistock, 1971.

PART IV

FROM ONE TALE ANOTHER TALE IS BORN

CHAPTER SIXTEEN

The children's fairy tales

Jeanne Magagna

Children are born with phantasies, both conscious and unconscious, which are given expression in everything they do. Their play of repeatedly dropping objects for their parents to pick up demonstrates their need to be reassured that mother and father are reliably present to respond to them. Later, the children build towers and knock them down, only to rebuild them. They also put blocks and toys in containers, tip them out, and put them back again. These activities symbolise the children's attempts to integrate all the various aspects of themselves. Their wish is to feel their strength, hope, and hostility are emotionally contained by the parents. Containment by the parents enables the children to develop inner strength, courage, and self-esteem.

Later on, being able to give expression to their wishes and thoughts through understanding language and speaking comes as an enormous pleasure to the children. Language usage and the understanding of language gives children another way of being intimately understood by their parents. The children express their own individuality and curiosity through saying, "I want this", or "No", or "What is that?" The children understand words, particularly the names of objects and specific action words when they are as young as three months old. Many parents have intuitively understood this and talked to their babies in their early months and told them stories about their experiences in the day, or read and showed simple picture books to them.

The children's repeated requests for a fairy tale to be read suggest that the imaginative portrayal of love, loss, jealousy, hate, courage, and hope captures the children's emotional experiences which urgently require dramatisation and thinking by the child in the security of the parents' supportive, thoughtful presence.

Patrizia Pasquini, the founder of Tempo Lineare, has fully appreciated children's urge to give expression to their emotions through listening to stories, playing with their little box of toys, as well as with each other, and listening to the fairy tales. Patrizia acknowledges that when the teacher provides experiences of sublimated gratification in a secure setting, the children at a young age accept the task of being separate from their parents who are in an adjoining room. Tempo Lineare is a nursery facility which promotes the children's individuation as well as intimacy between children, their parents, and teachers.

Tempo Lineare gives credence to the belief that children need the emotional space to discover the well of creative imagination within themselves. Patricia challenges the notion of too much structured learning and dictated artistic tasks for children at this early pre-school period of development. Through sharing spontaneous play and story-telling in the presence of an interested, thoughtful, and empathic nursery teacher, the children are keen to use their artistic potential for colour, design, and imaginative artwork.

When the children eagerly surround Patrizia as she reads the story for the day, their faces often look as though they are experiencing a sublimated satisfying feeding at the breast of a thoughtful and attentive mother. Immediately afterwards, the children rush to find paper and felt-tips to express on paper the welter of key phantasies that have been stirred within themselves as they listened to the fairy tale being read. Later, in the group, they discuss their drawings. I have observed such intensity of eagerness for the "fairy tale experience" that, two hours before Patrizia's story-telling, a four-year-old boy was vociferously eliciting votes from two- to four-year-old children regarding whether they wanted to have Patrizia read *Little Red Riding Hood* or *Snow White and the Seven Dwarves*. Afterwards, they discuss what the themes present in their drawings. Frequently, the children choose their favourite story, but sometimes an event, such as the arrival of "The Queen of Caramels" during the nursery's Carnival celebration, prompts the children to create a spontaneous fairy tale that is written down by Patrizia and illustrated by them.

What is obvious is that the children are not "taught to draw", but, rather, their imagination is profoundly touched by the shared experience of the fairy tale and their love for Patrizia. It is each child's unique phantasies augmented by imagination that spontaneously resurrect an artistic creation searching for a place on the white sheet of paper. The result is the fairy tale pictures shown in their published book, *Dalla Fiaba Nasce Fiaba* (From One Tale Another Tale Is Born) (Pasquini, 2002).

This daily experience of having one's imagination greeting a fairy tale and then creating an illustration prompted one three-year-old child to say to his parents, "When I grow up, I would like to be a writer." More important, though, is the fact that each child feels impelled to draw something important to him. The child's individuality, rather than an imposition of a teacher's assignment, is foremost in the learning process. The drawing is freely given and freely created because the child needs to give voice to some feeling linked with developmental issues that are burning *at that present moment* in the child's life.

Each child's inner vivacious creative capacities are given *a place to be* in Tempo Lineare. The children appreciate the aesthetic beauty of their creations and sometimes request "May we have the story drawn by Phillipo or the story by Romana?"

Although the children initially created the drawings for themselves, they wish to share the creation of their inner selves to be shared with their parents and other children. We hope that when you find a regular space to be together as parents and children you will delight in looking and commenting upon the pictures in the Tempo Lineare book of children's drawings, *Dalla Fiaba Nasce Fiaba* (From One Tale Another Tale Is Born) (Pasquini, 2002) as someone reads the fairy tale aloud. This can be a way of touching upon and understanding some of the inner fears, joys, and pleasures of both the child within the parent and the children themselves.

References

Pasquini, P. (2002). *Da Fiabe Nasce Fiabi.* Rome: Genitori e Amici del Tempo Lineare-Onlus.

CHAPTER SEVENTEEN

From tales to life and from life to tales

Patrizia Pasquini

T he child's experience of listening to a fairy tale, identifying with the characters, associating to the story and sharing their impressions verbally and through drawings can play a significant role in enhancing the development of thinking and creativity in the child. Psychoanalytical theories consider the mind as a stratified, multi-dimensional space where several different features may be present simultaneously. This implies that the good and the bad internal parents, hate and love, a self with capacities and the self with deficit, the self in agreement with others and the self in conflict with others, all coexist. By helping children work on the meaning of the fairy tale, they realise it is possible to impart dignity to all emotional experiences without too much fear being engendered by them. Representation of feelings, dreams, anguishes, desires, and needs occurs in the fairy tale, and drawing and naming certain characteristics in the fairy tale narrative tends to enrich each child's life.

In telling the children fairy tales each day, I have noticed on their faces feelings of both fear and wonder, as if they had gone into an imaginary wood, full of undeciphered experiences, from which it was important to start making distinctions and giving a name to their feelings. For instance, in *Little Red Riding Hood* (J. Grimm, 1919), every child listened to the narrative, which becomes increasingly lively. As we enter the wood, we become afraid, for the wolf is there, waiting for us! At this point, the children remain with bated breath, their hearts beating rapidly, their bodies immobile. Little Red Riding Hood has not listened to her mother's advice not to wander off the path; she is encouraged by the wolf to go into the forest to pick some flowers and eventually she is eaten up by the wolf just as her grandmother has been. Finally, a huntsman arrives and saves both the grandmother and Little Red Riding Hood. The children smile, looking relieved and happy, when I say the reassuring final words regarding how they lived in great joy together.

In *Little Red Riding Hood*, as in every fairy tale, there is a peaceful beginning: "Once upon a time . . .", then a problem for the characters emerges until finally there is a happy ending, where all live in great joy together. Every day, soon after each fairy tale is read, the children begin talk-ing and drawing some of their fantasies stimulated by the plot. It is clear that everyone has been moved by some part of the tale. The relationship between the teller and the listener gener-ates a shared experience, a feeling of being in the same boat, and this experience of being united in their sharing of the story makes it possible to encounter some magic and unique moments.

Having one's imagination and curiosity stimulated by this experience of listening and drawing results in some children recounting their own experiences and creating another tale. It may well happen that a child begins to tell everyone a tale that his mother told him the night before, and everyone listens to it with rapt attention. On other occasions, however, soon after a tale is completed, the children start talking about episodes of great irritation or exclusion, as when one desires to get rid of his mother or brother, or when one feels excluded by a brother, a sister, or a friend within the group. The fairy tale permits dark fears to be transformed into images and, through the identification with a character in a specific episode of the tale, the child may compensate with his own fantasy to overcome anxieties about both real and imaginary scenarios. For example, the child might imagine himself to be the hero who beats the giants, and in this way he becomes the strongest and best character. This allows him to overcome his feelings of inadequacy or sorrow. At this point, the child may find in himself a more hopeful attitude towards his relationships with others and himself. He may gain a better insight into his own feelings and start to make sense of an experience that previously had no name because he had not been able for formulate thoughts about it

The work on fairy tales with children at Tempo Lineare is composed of three phases:

1. The telling of a tale, where the child goes through an experience of "emotional intensity in the presence of others". To be attentively joined with other children "with bated breath" allows both the child and myself to establish areas of good interrelatedness where it is possible to explore one's own experiences. This shared opportunity to be curious about oneself generates harmony and creativity inside the group.
2. The drawings eagerly made by the children become the symbolic space for their own personalised narrations.
3. The group's reflections on their shared and individual emotions aroused by the fairy tale are considered.

Each child has the opportunity of finding his own message in the tale, according to his particular interests and needs. The sharing of drawings and thoughts allows each child to be simultaneously attracted and enriched by the discoveries of others. The tale generates a new emotional reality for the individuals and the group and, by giving specific names to their expe-riences, the children embark on enriching their creative potential and their emotional acumen.

In working with the children in an educative institution, I, too, have often found myself in the "wood" created by the tale, accompanying the children with their fears and desires, giving voice to intense personal experiences through reading and discussing the fairy tale. I realise that an important aspect of the "fairy tale work" with the children is to apprehend my own and the group's sentiments stimulated by the tale and to listen attentively to them.

I have also paused to listen to my voice and to think about the use of sounds and specific emotional aspects of my story telling, such as my gestures and facial expressions. I realise how

important it has been to provide the children with the experie
through story telling and listening to their expressive response
what the children are saying is not sufficient to establish a sig
"the feel" of what comes from them individually and I asses
particular moment, for I sense that what is experienced in t'
tive of their internal worlds interacting with the group. Onl'
self's internal movement and external movement within the
a deep meaning which can resound in each of us.

Developmental growth in the individual or the group may occu.
ence of the reader behind the tale is real and authentic. By re-entering the "woo
in finding a way of getting close to my feelings. Only in this way could I find the necessa.,
energy to live again something old that had been kept quiescent. The fairy tale experience,
therefore, becomes like a journey where we greet our feelings, touching them again and again
and bringing them to light. The tension stemming from this intense emotional experience
fosters more lively and true communications with the Tempo Lineare group. This approach
allows something inside ourselves to occur: a fairy tale will give rise to a new one, which will
give voice to something unconscious that will be able to be approached, thought about, and
accepted so as to facilitate our passage through life.

But from where do the fairy tales and personal narratives arise? They come from the dark-
est places of our mind, the place in which we run into figureless sensations, faceless fears, and
shapeless desires. The child needs to be contained to tackle all these novelties that life presents
to him in the fairy tale. In effect, to be together with an adult allows a child to enter the "wood"
and gain knowledge of anxieties and dilemmas, dreams and realities, face uncertainties, and
recognise that which is beautiful in our existence.

At times, when I am telling the fairy tale, the emotional impact of my words may be similar to the emotional impact of a child's mother, beautiful and loving, as she feeds and responds
to him. As he is being read to, the child may experience a joyous pleasure and praise the beauty
of the meeting: in that moment, the child may feel as if in the arms of the mother, close to her
breast. In this story-telling encounter, the child sometimes ponders over tales of the "mother-
witch" and experiences of suffering and confusion that children go through during their
growth; in doing so, that child may elaborate on feelings in such a way that he is able to re-
establish a relationship with the good, real mother. My experience with the Tempo Lineare children makes me realise that this spontaneous, creative encounter describing, drawing, and
creating new images occurs in such a way that the beauty of an encounter with the good, loved,
internalised mother replenishes the child's heart and mind.

Reference

Grimm, J. (1919). *Little Red Riding Hood*. New York: Harper Design.

CHAPTER EIGHTEEN

"The Queen of the Caramels"

Patrizia Pasquini

"I would like to be beautiful but I cannot find a dress for myself . . . I would like to be a caramel." These are the words of a little girl who could not find a way to represent herself through a costume linked with caramels on the day of a school festival. I understood the desire of this girl to be identified with a good object, "the caramel", a symbol for love created in Tempo Lineare. This little girl's words stimulated me to engage all the other children in her group in creating this fairy tale. It is interesting to observe how each of the children contributed to the discussion, which involved creating part of the tale which goes on from those words, "I cannot find a dress for myself but I want to do something about a caramel."

I started the tale by saying, "Once upon a time there was a Queen of the Caramels who lived in a castle made of caramels". The children, aged three and a half to five years, then continued the construction of the tale.

1. Julian adds, "The Queen of Caramels says, 'I am unhappy living in my castle'."

2. Martina, responding to Julian's comment about unhappiness, says, "The good Queen was happy because every morning she eats a caramel."

3. "The Queen of Caramels had a chest where she kept the recipe for the best caramels in the world, said Victoria, and then she adds: "The Queen of Caramels has two caramels on her head". Her chest is made of caramels, using a special caramel recipe."

4. I added, "She had a lot necklaces made of caramels, a crown made of caramels, and colourful dresses made of caramels too. Subsequently, Andrea mentioned, "It is all sweet, all caramels."

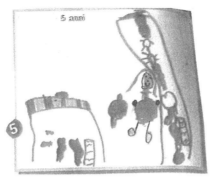

5. I added, "When the Queen of Caramels strolled around everyone could smell the caramels." Carolina continued, "The Queen of Candies put on her dress on and went for a stroll."

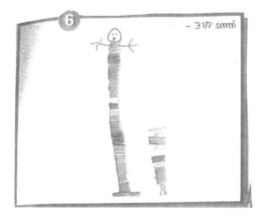

6. Then my comment was, "The Bad Queen lived close to the Queen of Caramels' castle; she had never eaten the Queen's caramels, but she was eager to taste them." Tina indicated, "There is the Bad Queen and the Good Queen."

7. I then say, "One day the Bad Queen, pretending to be a court lady, entered the Queen of Caramels' castle. Francesco then proclaimed, "The Good Queen is eating a caramel and the Bad Queen tries to grab all the caramels."

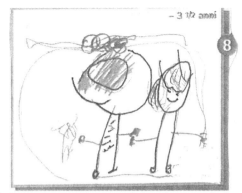

8. I continue, "The Bad Queen wanted to steal the chest with the delicious caramel recipe in order that she could be admired as the Queen of the Caramels. There is a caramel crown. The Queen of Caramels holds on tightly to the chest in which there is the caramel recipe. The Bad Queen tries to steal the chest."

9. Now I say, "The Bad Queen stole the chest and the Queen of Caramels became so sad and unhappy that everyone in her kingdom talked about her sorrow." "She is a Bad Queen!" said Giulia.

10. I say, "A Prince, who is in love with the Queen of Caramels, says, 'The Bad Queen gets the chest. There are colourful lands and the castle.' The knight puts the Queen of Caramels in jail."

11. I go on, saying, "The Prince ran after the Bad Queen and captured her with a rope. To punish the Bad Queen he locked her in a room and forced her to eat candies forever. Michele adds, "The Prince ties up the Bad Queen with a rope and takes away the chest of the Queen of Caramels."

12. I continue, saying, "The Prince brought back the chest to the Queen of Caramels. The Queen was so happy that she fell in love with the Prince." Eugenia acknowledges, "I thank the Prince who put the Bad Queen in jail."

13. Finally I say, "The Prince felt the Queen of Caramels was so sweet that he decided to marry her immediately and they lived forever in great joy together." Caterina adds, "Then little birds scream 'cip, cip' because they want their mother."

This seemed ultimately to be a fairy tale about "poverty". All the children build this tale together. It appears as if they are saying, "We are all a little bit poor, but happiness is a kind of wealth which can arrive in poverty."

PART V

THE COUPLE, THE FAMILY, THE GROUP, AND SOCIETY

CHAPTER NINETEEN

Some good reasons to support public services devoted to children

Carla Busato Barbaglio

In this chapter, I would like to reflect upon the experience of the parents participating in Tempo Lineare. The parents are regularly asked to observe children's interactions with each other, with the staff, and with the parents. They discuss their observations in the monthly parents' groups. Going through the parents' writings, I found that the working method of observation proposed by the school had already become a natural way of parenting and learning how to become a more understanding parent. This is a very important point, because to be a parent does not simply mean to have children, but it also means to observe and understand the child's development and the relationship one has with the child. Such observation and comprehension of the parent–child relationship involves a continuous reshaping of that very same relationship and promotes the conditions for genuine personal growth and reciprocity.

Now I would like to illustrate why such a school is so important for parents and their young children. The first point concerns the previously mentioned method of observation and understanding not only of the psycho-physiological growth of the child, but also of one's own way of relating to the child. Observation enables us to know who the child is now, as shown by his movements, his way of communicating, playing, and experiencing difficulties. Observation of the child–parent relationship can involve the parents in examining some of their earliest feelings about the baby, including their first phantasies about wanting a baby and their feelings about his conception. Sharing of these experiences with other parents works as a sort of "mental cradle" for the actual experience of parenting, a cradle woven with thoughts, worries, joy, uncertainties, denials, and fears.

Thinking of how observing and understanding can influence emotional experiences, I remember the drawings of good monsters made by some children. Their parents wrote their reflections saying, ". . . a mother and a father wonder about their child's monstrosity and feel relieved by those closed lines, those brilliant suns . . .". Construction and sharing of the observation of child–parent relationships with other parents allows the weaving of a fabric made of parental group relationships, which helps contain their fears, uncertainties, joys, and difficulties. A parents' group sharing observations helps to create a shared mental space where it is possible to think about the child, even when he is not very gratifying and does not fulfil the dreams one had for him.

It can be useful to confront various problems and anxieties that arise in the complex path of shared growth in the parent–child relationship. Sometimes, problems signal that there is a shared difficulty in this relationship. For example, problems may appear in eating too little or too much, frequent illnesses, insecurities in relationships, sudden outbursts, exhausting night crying, hyper-excitement, or, on the other hand, delayed mobility. To observe, to share all this, to have the opportunity to think about it together as parents is part of the Tempo Lineare project. Tempo Lineare amplifies, supports, and creates a rich and diversified set of information and interpretations of emotions and new feelings, a set of group learning and sharing experiences apt to improve the quality of the experience itself. Tempo Lineare has the primary aim of improving the relationships of each child, as well those of the parents and the educators.

The tasks imposed by Tempo Lineare require that the parents are available, very often in conflict with their working habits that existed before the birth of their child, which did not allow the space and time essential to meet the developmental needs of the child.

It is clear from the use of colour and design within Tempo Lineare that the aesthetic appearance of the school is very important. The rooms are pleasant, symbolic of the love and care which Tempo Lineare has for the children and the parents. The quality and the emotional attunement suggested by the way in which the environment is structured reflects a wish to strengthen the loving and relational connections between those who dwell within it.

Understanding early childhood relationships

To be together while growing as parents, educators, and children, each having his or her own competences, gives rise to new ways of being together, of caring for and being with children: in other words, new ways of socialising. An analysis of the parents' writing shows the establishment of reflective group dynamics and a deepening capacity to think of some relational difficulties. This process of parent–teacher reflection does not emanate from textbooks, but, rather, stems from concentrating on the present moment of the child and oneself and having the willingness to call oneself into question and learn from the group and self-reflective processes.

Psychoanalytic and neuroscientific thinking takes it for granted that establishing intimate and emotional relationships is a basic component of the human nature. Children, even the youngest ones, have a natural capacity for perceiving others, a subtle perceptive ability to discern others, and to differentiate linguistic sounds coming from different family members. Scientific contributions agree on the fact that after birth a baby develops a primary intersubjectivity, in which sharing an intention means developing a common and involving awareness, which is the basis for every understanding and learning process. Studies on feeding, for instance, show how this experience can be seen as a sort of dialogic evolution between the mother and the child. Both are involved in achieving not only nutrition, but also communication, in which the child's pauses, his sucking movements, and his position in his mother's arms cause a maternal response in the sense of a stimulation, which is actually a postural reaction to a dialogic communication interwoven in a complex and deep way with the ongoing activity.

From the second six months of their lives, babies realise that they have a mind and others have a mind; it is fundamental to attune to feelings present in a personal encounter and find pleasure and relief in shared feeling states. This is the basis of that peculiar human communication, for which the mother and her baby work hard and long, that defines the deep cognitive–affective integration of the human experience. Positive early emotions foster optimistic and healthy features of the personality, while negative emotions are at the root of depressive and anxious mental states that persist through adult life. Such influences may occur at the cerebral level, fostering growth factors or the secretion of certain molecules as a reaction to environmental stimuli, which may be very important in shaping the plasticity of the central nervous system. Thus, early social, emotional, and environmental influences may exert significant organising effects on the brain and on the physical, intellectual, social, and emotional characteristics of development. Moreover, it is a well-established finding that autobiographical memory appears around the second year of life, and until then a baby stores unconscious experiences and relationships that are fundamental for the constitution of the self. The richer, more intimate, and emotionally enlivening, with respect to affective relations, the environment is, the less likely it is that the child will develop difficulties in perceptiveness and the capacity to think. Putting one's own mind at the disposal of the child, in order for him to become acquainted with the other's mind, is part of the complex parental work required to enable healthy child development.

The development of a benign parentality

It is important for a parental couple to be able to rid themselves of an omnipotent and infallible perception of the self in favour of considering themselves as a couple growing together with their children, being able to admit mistakes, exaggerations, or unhelpful presumptions regarding their child. This issue of a mobile and vigilant parental responsibility, always called into question by reality and experiences of "the other", is a new attitude that can be instigated by and within the parents. This new, more mature approach of accepting responsibility for who one is and how one behaves as an observing and understanding parent implies a continuous monitoring of the child–parent relationship and of one's own reactions to it.

Sometimes, although married and having children, the parental couple might discover themselves to be insufficiently mature to be parents. Very often, even middle-aged parents think they are not yet ready to deal with problems in the parent–child relationship and feel that they need more time. It is as if they did not consider themselves as real parents, but as "would-be parents", though they already have adolescent children. This can occur particularly if the adult couple have not clearly separated from their parents of origin and still feel as though their identity is that of "their parents' children". A fear can arise that if they call themselves into question and even apologise to, for example, a teacher or doctor, they might lose their adult identities. There is a continuum from being a couple where "the parents are always right" to being a couple that always redefines itself with respect to the son's or daughter's point of view, seeking acceptance by the child. Maturity as a couple involves having the capacity to think about emotional experience as an adult with some wisdom and experience, as well as having the capacity to acknowledge uncertainties and mistakes.

Within Tempo Lineare, one sees the growth of a greater creativity and a greater parental ability to deal with everyday life, feelings, relationships, and to take responsibilities in relation to other people. Tempo Lineare fosters the development of mental space devoted to the certainly beautiful, but also disruptive, experience of bringing up a child. The focus is on evolving a genuine mental space for a child, a space where one can be deeply in touch with him, a space that is not filled with a plethora of materialistic objects, entertainments, and pseudo parental behaviours, lacking real, authentic parental feelings.

It might be difficult to keep one's own individuality as one is striving to mature and develop one's new identity as a parent. Being "growing parents" is one of the difficulties for a marital couple that is itself growing to live well together. We often observe couples with very conflictual, rather than complementary, attitudes to facing problems. Similarly, there is a problem when individuality disappears and two persons become one, or become trapped in adolescent states of mind.

What are the opportunities today for the family, seen as a place for acceptance, protection, memory, and narration? We always talk about the right to be parents, but not about the rights of the child. The rights of the child can be respected only if the parents are adults who can think and sustain what is unthinkable for a child. The centrality of the young child is in crisis at times, competing with the centrality of the parents: that is, taking too much care of what the adults want and need in their lives without sufficient attention to what is needed for the healthy development of the child. When will our society, reflected by workplaces, truly give sufficient value to the child's rights to be considered and respected by caring, responsible, understanding parents and to the parental tasks of caring for the child?

A school such as Tempo Lineare may help each mother and father develop an observational ability to foster development within the child and within the parents. I shall now present the young child observations of two young mothers as a testimony to the shared experience of growing together within Tempo Lineare.

A mother's observation of her son, Franco, aged twenty-six months

"Mum, let's play with the matrioskas (the set of dolls, one within the other in decreasing size)!" beckoned my son, Franco. Chatting time for parents is over in the parents' room and we have just gone back into the children's room to play with our children. Franco is really happy: this is one of the moments he likes most, maybe because he "finds me again" after we have been separated. We sit close beside one another at the small table and the play begins! Actually, rather than a simple play, it has turned into a ritual, occurring with same dynamics. I suspect Franco's gestures and words could hide a complex meaning. Franco always picks up the largest matrioska, where he knows he can find the smallest matrioska pieces. The first thing he says is, "Mum, please, help me, the first bit is too hard for me", so I open the largest matrioska, the "Russian mother" containing all the little children. While he opens the different sized dolls, Franco is eager to reach the last one, the tiniest baby, his preferred one.

I try to intervene as little as I can, so as not to interfere with his phantasies prompting his particular way of playing; however, I suggest that he doesn't create too much mess and confusion, so that the little doll pieces do not get lost. He puts his ear on the stomach of each of the dolls to listen as to whether or not there is another doll inside. "Mum! I hear it!", "Yes, darling, open it," I answer. "Here it is: WOW! It is so little!" he comments as he finds a tiny doll. I smile, thinking that every time Franco finds the smallest doll he feels as though he is finding a treasure. In effect, he soon turns to Ada's mother and tells her, "Look, it is very little!" Then he delicately takes the tiny doll in his hands and puts it close to his face, as if the baby doll were kissing him.

After a while, the play is repeated, but in the the opposite way: it is he who kisses and starts cuddling the baby doll. I say, "She is so lovely." Franco looks at me roguishly and starts brushing it on my face: "It is cuddling," he says, "It is cuddling mum." He does the same with Ada's mother's face. Then he plays a little bit and says, " I put it here inside the larger doll, otherwise it gets lost and cold." After a last glance at the baby, he carefully puts it into the larger doll, moves it around the table, and finally reaches the matrioska mother for some more cuddling.

I feel great tenderness looking at Franco repeating his ritual play activity. It is as if he could see himself in that small bit that, notwithstanding his fragility, is autonomous and bold enough to explore a "small table", to approach new people, to go far away from his mother with the awareness she is always there, ready to welcome him if he is afraid, cold, or desires a kiss.

This ritualised play is signalled as being almost over when Franco starts to put the dolls into their respective bellies, starting first with the very smallest doll, which he encloses with the head piece, and then moving to the next biggest doll to encase the slightly smaller doll. Sometimes, he gets the replacement sequence wrong and the dolls don't fit into one another, but he soon corrects himself, saying that he has the wrong belly for it is too large for the little sister . . . and so all the small matrioskas can finally sleep in the belly of their mother!

This observation shows the mother's enormous capacity for observation and introspective work. In observing and reflecting upon her observation, she has the ability to notice all the details and become curious about her son's phantasies. When Franco gets it wrong, he feels confident when he corrects himself, for he knows that his mother is with him, thinking carefully about him and all that is happening. She also adds that short sentence "Yes, darling, open it", helping the play to continue and become more meaningful. It is interesting that, while accompanying her child playing, the young mother can share the emotions of her child, which she shows with her facial expression, her eyes, her way of being together with him, and her writing style. She does not have the wish or need to disrupt his play because she is aware he is working on something with an internal plan, or phantasy, which is informing his play.

The following is an observation by the other young mother.

Observation of Laura (twenty-eight months)

We both sit at the table, close to one another. I offer to Laura the basket with the matrioska dolls and let her pick one. She chooses the largest one, covered with gold and pink designs. Laura soon tries to open the matrioska, but she needs my help to do so. After I assist her in removing the first, biggest covering head, she quickly opens all the other doll containers. When she discovers the final and smallest doll, Laura excitedly exclaims, "Little, little" as she takes the smallest figure in her hand.

We have all the doll-pieces in front of us and, after a while, I suggest that we put them together. As Laura refuses, I put together the largest matrioska and tell her that it is "the mother". When Laura sees the matrioska mother in front of her, she takes the smallest doll and puts it close to the mother matrioska as if a young child is kissing a mother's face. I say, "How lovely! She kissed her mother."

As a reaction, Laura immediately kisses the matrioska herself! Then, while keeping the smallest doll piece in her hand, she starts describing the appearance of the matrioska: her small head, her hair. She comments on everything, but as she speaks fast I can only understand the words "beautiful" and "hair".

I suggest that she might put together pieces of other figures in order to have the whole family. As Laura does not seem to be interested, I start doing that. I build one matrioska after the other, saying, "Look, that is the older sister, then there is another small brother and another again." Laura follows with great attention, and as I build the matrioskas and put them in a row according to their dimensions, she puts the smallest piece in between them, then close to the mother. I go on building the figures and ask her to help me; however, Laura just observes and intervenes only twice, changing the place of the smallest piece, putting it first among the other children and then once again placing it closest to its mother.

I start to count the matrioskas, as I know she loves numbers. I count slowly: "one, two, three . . ." until I reach seven figures. Laura counts with me "one and two, one and two, two and two" repeatedly. I am a little bit surprised, as I know Laura can count easily to four and then six, seven, avoiding five. When I realise that, I ask her, "Why do you count only up to two? There are many more! Come on. Let's count together!" Very slowly, we reach four and finally Laura exclaims "six, seven!"

Afterwards, Laura gets the smallest piece again and I ask her, "What is the place of this piece?" With a new gesture I have never seen before, she raises the tablecloth and puts the smallest piece below it. She looks at me, clearly curious to see my reaction. I am perplexed, and I say, "What a pity! The smallest piece below there?" Laura puts her hand below the cloth but she withdraws it without the figure. She looks at me and after my negative reaction says, "No, that is not its place", and takes it out. Then we start to build all the figures of the matrioska following Laura's rhythm and order: she has a sort of personal system, used for some time, when we play with the matrioskas. She puts the small figure in the belly of the closest figure and this in the next belly; then she closes them all with the respective heads. She goes on, with some interruptions, to put just the smallest pieces directly into the belly of the matrioska mother. She corrects herself and says "no", gets the small figures and looks for their right place. So, finally, we succeed in building our own matrioska.

This observation of Laura exhibits another young mother's marvellous capacity of observation and reflective functioning, which allows her to establish a deep rapport with her child's emotional experiences reflected in the play.

Fonagy and Target (1997) write about the reflective functioning that a mother needs to develop. They refer to the mother's attempt to understand and share her feelings with her child. When Laura's mother is sad, saying "What a pity! The smallest piece is there?" (because it has been put below the tablecloth), she is expressing the importance of the child's place and the child's need to be at the centre of attention, not hidden away and isolated. This simple fact communicates to Laura the importance and centrality of the child in her mind.

The Parents' Association, Associazione Amici di Tempo Lineare, organised in 2005 an observational course shared by educators, psychotherapists, and parents. It was a unique experience not only in Italy but all over Europe as well. Busato, Magagna and Pasquini introduced each meeting with topics such as problems in the development of the self-esteem, the relationship between parents and their children and between siblings. Following these introductory contributions as described in the introduction there were small young child observation seminars in which the parents and teachers presented some observations made at home or at school. This observational collaborative experience between teachers, parents and psychotherapists can become a valid educational and preventative mental health model of work in the nursery. A nursery project such as Tempo Lineare provides a new way of socializing in a small community comprising part of an urban city.

Reference

Fonagy, P., & Target, M. (1997). Attachment and reflective function: their role in self-organization. *Development and Psychopathology, 9*: 679–700.

CHAPTER TWENTY

The couple's cradle for the inner child*

Jeanne Magagna

Two people meet, form a couple, and get married or live together. That is what happens in our society. We are programmed genetically to experience sexual pleasure, which prompts procreation for the perpetuation of our species. We form loving pairs in order to feel less anxious in encountering the outside world after leaving our family of origin (Figure 20.1). Each culture has different expectations of what being a couple, being a parent, involves.

Figure 20.1. The couple with love.

---

* All drawings in this chapter are by Cecilia Campironi, 2010.

This chapter describes ways in which the couple create a cradle for each partner's inner child. In my mind, how the couple *cradle the inner child* determines how a child in the family is greeted each moment of the day.

Perhaps firm building of the cradle occurs when the extended family acknowledges the formation of the couple. At the time of marriage, there is an acknowledgement of the couple as having a particular intimacy, with some sense of their relationship becoming primary. But throughout the marriage, the continued presence of the extended family and friends, if they enhance communication, intimacy, and understanding within the couple, can provide some stability at moments when the couple's cradle rocks back and forth through the inevitable developmental crises in the couple's relationship (Figure 20.2).

Figure 20.2.   The couple forming a cradle.

For some reason, living together without marriage seems to bring different emotional experiences than being married. Couples who have lived together for a long time and then get married are often very surprised by this. For the sake of simplicity, I am referring particularly to a heterosexual married couple, although the issues I am addressing pertain to many other forms of partnership and single parent parenting (Figure 20.3).

Figure 20.3.   Coming out of the cage and dancing together.

Following the marriage contract in which the couple openly declare their commitment to support and love each other, something happens inside each of them to increase the emotional intensity in their relationship. The couple publicly assume some adult responsibility, occasioning turning to each other for sexual and emotional intimacy, consultation, and security. This necessitates that each partner separate to some extent from the family of origin as the main emotional base. It is this act of forming a new marital couple that more firmly connects each partner to his or her own internalised parents.

Internalised parents

Internalised parents are formed through relationships with the external parents; however, these internalised relationships are then coloured by the individuals' hate and love towards the external parents (Figure 20.4).

Figure 20.4. Couple with internalised parents.

So, the internalised mother can contain all the loveable and hateful qualities of the actual mother, but some of these loveable and hateful qualities of the internalised mother can be magnified by the individual's hate and love for her.

A loving external mother can be turned to a witch, through hatred of the frustrating mother (Figure 20.5).

Figure 20.5. Loving external mother turned into witch.

Alternatively, a loving external mother can be transformed into an idealised Madonna-mother through love while the person's hatred is split and projected elsewhere (Figure 20.6).

Figure 20.6.   Loving mother idealised.

A loving external mother can also be filled with fewer projections and more clearly identified with the actual external mother (Figure 20.7).

Figure 20.7.   Normal mother freed of projections.

Likewise, the external father is internalised and, in the process, can be transformed by projections of love and destructive feelings. For example, the role of the external father to provide some limits to how much of the mother's time the child can have access to may lead to a loving external father who sets limits and is hated for making firm rules about a child's access to mother during the night turning into a harsh internal father (Figure 20.8).

Figure 20.8.   The father distorted through projections of hatred and the father, freed of projections, who comes good again.

If the father is hated for setting limits, limit setting is then felt to be horrid, bad, and this may lead to parents failing to help the child obey rules for becoming socialised into family life through thinking of others, not only himself. The external mother and father, filled with projections of love and hate, become internalised parents with whom the new couple more firmly identify when they get married.

The inner child

Simultaneously and with increasing intensity as the marriage progresses, the longings and frustrations of the inner child emerge. The inner child emerges only as intensely needy and wanting in the context of an intimate, trustworthy partnership. The couple might have been studying, working hard, engaging in a lot of social activities, watching television, reading, until the later stages of the wife's pregnancy, when there is a pause in the tempo of life. Each partner can be rather overwhelmed by how much the other really needs them and wants them at this point when, simultaneously, there are so many new demands being made on each partner to become a mother or a father.

With parenthood arise all the anxieties about *changing one's identity*. Now the marital partners are really going to have some more responsibility, responsibility for a new baby. They are required to think not only of themselves and each other, but they must care for a baby who is totally dependent on them.

How to be a "good enough parent"

Sometimes, there is a rush to buy a bigger flat, or to fix up a room for the new baby, to buy a pram, a bassinet, some books on how to look after a newborn. Often, this involves more tasks being added on to an already busy life; however, there is yet another task to be carried out. This is the most essential one: becoming even more deeply aware of the increasing needs and anxieties of each other's inner child (Figure 20.9).

Figure 20.9.   The mother holding a child.

. . . As she carried
her child may she carry her soul. As her
child was born, may she give birth and life
and form to her own, higher truth. As she
nourished and protected her child, may she
nourish and protect her inner life and her
independence. For her soul shall be her
most painful birth, her most difficult child
and the dearest sister to her other children.

(Leunig, 1990)

This poem depicts how essential it is to give birth to one's inner child, to find the space to get to know the truth of one's emotional experience, to form a picture of how one feels and to then find nourishment and protection for one's inner child. This is necessary for the mother, but also for the father:

The difficulties of creating intimacy with the inner child

Work, entertainment, and the chores of life can impede developing sufficient inner space to create intimacy with the emotional experience of the inner child in oneself and the partner (Figures 20.10 and 20.11).

Figure 20.10. The hurrying men.   Figure 20.11. The abandoned child.

How does one begin to create intimacy with the inner child? Parents know they must give time to the external baby, to holding the baby, to feeding the baby, to being emotionally present for the baby, but likewise, time and emotional space must be given to each parent's inner child (Figure 20.12).

Figure 20.12.   Intimacy with the self.

How does one penetrate more deeply to find the truth about one's emotional experience? For some, saying "This is what I feel now" arises naturally in the form of thinking about one's relationships with different people during the day. For others, it is important to follow Julia Cameron's ideas, proposed in *The Artist's Way* (1995). Her suggestions include writing a few spontaneous pages in longhand each day about whatever one feels. Another way is to spend time trying to recollect a dream. The dream is important, for it illustrates and dramatises all the emotional experiences which could not be reached and thought about by the rational, conscious mind during the busy day. Other parents might choose to engage in couple or individual psychotherapy to have support in discovering the essence of their current emotional experiences. The task of discovering and looking after one's inner child is an arduous, daily experience. It requires diligence, tolerating of emotional turbulence, being curious and wondering (Figure 20.13).

Figure 20.13.

> . . . Let us pause from
> thinking and empty our mind. Let us stop
> the noise. In the silence let us listen to our
> heart. The heart which is buried alive. Let
> us be still and wait and listen carefully. A
> sound from the deep, from below. A faint
> cry. A weak tapping. Distant muffled
> feelings from within. The cry for help.

(Leunig, 1990)

This is the first phase of reflection on the inner child . . . but only the first phase. The second phase is described below.

Creating the couple's cradle

> We shall rescue the entombed heart. We
> shall bring it to the surface, to the light
> and the air. We shall nurse it and listen
> respectfully to its story. The heart's story
> of pain and suffocation, of darkness and
> yearning. We shall help our feelings to live in
> the sun. together again we shall find relief
> and joy.

(Leunig, 1998)

Figure 20.14.   Holding two hearts.

Holding the inner child in oneself and the partner is not part of a separate individual experience. Holding the inner child involves a relationship with the inner parents of oneself and the inner parents of the partner. The couple can create a cradle for their shared emotional experiences by providing a space for each other's inner child to be known, by holding the feelings of the other and by pondering over each other's emotional experience. Through this, there is the possibility of "re-parenting the inner child within". The couple's cradling each other's inner child can bring the best possibility of emotional growth in one another and help those individuals who may have had emotionally disadvantaged childhoods.

If each of the parents is enabled to get deeper into their own individual emotional experience and provide a cradle for the partner's emotional experience, they will be able to become more intimate with the variety of emotional experiences of their new baby, their growing toddler, their developing adolescent. The couple's cradling emotional experiences in the family can be so beautiful. It is not easy, though. The marital partners will need patience and understanding to listen to, to observe, and to understand their own inner child and create a cradle for each other's burgeoning inner child. This task is more complicated than any psychotherapeutic relationship, because of the couple's emotional regression that comes through sexual intimacy (Figure 20.15)

Figure 20.15.   Burgeoning emotions.

At times, the emotional baggage from previous experience that is located in the inner child can be so great that the couple collides in conflict and marital conflict and sometimes divorce occurs (Figure 20.16).

Figure 20.16.   The couple pulled apart.

Problems in cradling and containing the parental couple's inner child

As marital partners rely on each other more fully and their trust in each other deepens, life can become more, rather than less, complicated. The reason for this is that as trust deepens between the husband and wife, the hidden, encrusted aspects of the inner child feel secure enough to emerge more fully. As these aspects of the inner child emerge, there is the potential for more conflict and more psychic pain as well as more pleasure, love, and beauty in the parents' relationship.

Emerging problems in the couple's relationship

I shall describe some typical problematic areas for the parents' relationship and follow this with ways of looking after the inner child in a way that deepens the intimacy and beauty in the parental couple's relationship.

Couple overwhelmed with the burgeoning inner child

Initially, a partner may be somewhat defended in relation to the other partner, particularly if poor relationships existed within the family of origin; in fact, one partner may be very competent at work, appear very strong superficially, while in reality the person is a bit detached from his/her inner child. As trust is established between the couple, hidden tears of the vulnerable, needy, grieving baby inside each of the partners can emerge (Figure 20.17).

Figure 20.17.   Wife drowning in her husband's tears.

Both partners in the couple can feel quite shocked that the so called "strong partner" was actually using denial and apparent strength of intellectual cleverness to unconsciously hide this vulnerable, needy, sad inner child. The couple need to sit together and ponder over these profound, previously sealed off infantile feelings of each other's inner child.

Delusion of fusion

When two people "fall in love" and come together, they often have the delusion of being in some way inseparable. The wish for union with the other promotes a regressive wish for part of the self to have a permanent, parasitical residence with the other (Figure 20.18).

Figure 20.18.   Cutting apart fused partners.

> For example, a man in tears joins his new lover saying, 'I have come home at last', and 'I could never live without you.' Encapsulated in this word *home* is the suggestion that the husband has identified his wife with parents possessing an infinite capacity to meet his needs. The regression, in either partner, can result in not feeling able to survive outside the relationship because it is too painful (Magagna & Black, 1985, p. 63).

Here is another example. A woman is terrified to be left alone by her husband as he departs on a business trip. She is worried about burglars and noises outside the house. She is relying too much on her husband's protective 'big daddy" functions. Her own unmet emotional needs from her childhood and her old infantile anger about separations and disappointments from her parents have led her to regress in the marriage and turn to her husband to parent her.

While receiving and thinking about his wife's insecurity and over-dependence on him, her pain at separation, and her anger about being left alone, the husband may become aware that he is the recipient of old painful feelings and complaints towards her parents which are still residing in the wife's inner child.

Kahlil Gibran (1926, pp. 22–24) is helpful in thinking through some of the problems of fusion in the couple when he says,

> they are with you yet they belong not to you
> you may give them your love but not your thoughts
>> for they have their own thoughts . . .
> and
> Love possesses not nor would it be possessed
> For love is sufficient unto love...
> and

If you love and must needs have desires,
let these be your desires:
and
To melt and be like a running brook that sings its
melody to the night
To know the pain of too much tenderness
To be wounded by your own understanding of love
And bleed willingly and joyfully.

The jack-in-the-box marriage

If the truth be known, perhaps at times each parent experiences being imprisoned (the jack in the box) through the weight of all sorts of unwanted bits of the other's personality (e.g., weakness, incompetence, sadness, anxiety) projected into him/her). Simultaneously, the other marital partner is identified as a super-competent or calm, confident partner (Figure 20.19).

Figure 20.19. "Jack in the box" and "Jack out of the box".

This second partner (the jack out of the box) may be out of touch with his/her inner child. This partner may feel carefree, but also suffer from a feeling of emotional detachment and emptiness while focusing on work or a hobby such as watching television, sports, exercise, or dance.
Here is an example of this phenomenon.

A couple emigrated from war-torn former Yugoslavia. Before arriving in this country, they suffered physical and emotional deprivation, following the murder of many of their close family members. They jointly developed a psychic structure for surviving together. This structure was highly reliant on the notion of a strong, super-parent husband who was successful, capable, impervious to criticism or self-doubt. He learned the language of his new country and worked hard to earn money to support his wife and their new baby. His wife was depressed and remained the recipient of all his projected pain of loss of family members, old cultural habits, and language of the mother country.

In this marriage, as in many marriages, the "Jack out of the box" is the husband, who holds some of the common stereotypes of men: the husband is assertive, strong, and superficially cheerful, but defended emotionally. His wife, on the other hand, is viewed as passive, weak, dependent, and depressed. Reparation in this marriage involves providing a space in which each partner can share the feelings of the inner child. The husband, in particular, needs support to share his deeper feelings of vulnerability, pain, and loss and, thus, retrieve the dislocated aspects of himself that he looks after in their projected form inside his wife's inner child and their new baby. The wife needs to retrieve her own strength, intellectual capacity to learn the new country's language, and to develop her capacity to assert herself in social groups in the new country.

Ways of cradling and looking after the parental couple's inner child

In the ideal marital partnership, the essential ingredient is that the partners are able to think about their experiences and bear emotional pain, joy, and love without having to evacuate competent and emotionally vulnerable aspects of themselves into the other partner. In an ideal marriage, it is acknowledged that it is impossible for all the couple's emotional needs to be met within the couple. Relationships with the extended family and friends are assumed to be necessary to support the psychological maturity and stability of the couple.

It is obvious that tasks are accomplished and relationships thrive only in the context of thoughtful space being dedicated to them. For this reason, work, friends, the baby, and other children are discussed and allocated agreed-upon spaces in the life of the family. These are some of the ways that couples have found it helpful to promote cradling and looking after the parental couple's inner child (Figure 20.20).

Figure 20.20.   Holding one's own inner child rather than projecting vulnerable aspects of self into the wife.

1. *Just being together acknowledging each other's value to each other.* Sometimes, it takes courage to let go of activities and *just be together.* Some of the parents whom I see in family therapy need me to give them permission to just be together, without their children, without their friends, without any entertainment. If the marriage is in a state of disrepair, I sometimes ask the parents the question, "Tell me, just why did you like your wife in the first place? Why did you choose to marry her out of all the women around? What made you single her

out?" Similarly, I ask the wife, "What attracted you to your husband? What qualities did he show that made you take an interest in him?" Often, the couple laugh as they recount how the husband liked his wife's spontaneity, her lively enthusiasm, and she recounts her husband's bravery in fighting against the elements when skiing and sailing. I ask them about the present too . . . "What do you value in each other now in the marriage?"

2. *Experiencing the self in the marriage.* Each partner needs time to look more deeply into their roles in the marital and parental relationships. Sometimes, when I meet with a couple, I suggest that they spend some time drawing, making a collage, or writing down how they see themselves in the marital and parental relationship. Then I ask them to take turns sharing their perceptions while asking the other partner to listen without interruption, interpretation, or critical comment.

3. *Exploring styles of relating to the inner child in self and other.* It is then useful for the couple to recognise and put into words for each other the ways in which each partner relates to the inner child's different emotions. For example, I might wonder with the wife: "What do you do with your anger? How do you recognise your husband's anger? How does he show it? Is the anger denied, avoided, thus creating emotional distancing, projected, causing a sense of persecution, or used as a stimulus to solving problems fruitfully?"

    I would also explore the couple's style of relating to other emotions of the inner child, such as longings, love, jealousy, sadness, disappointment, and other feelings surrounding painful experiences (Figure 20.21).

Figure 20.21.   Couple looking after the inner child rather than projecting.

4. *How I am, what I am wanting of myself, of you, of the marriage.* Most frequently, I need to help the parental couple give themselves permission to clear away familial and work responsibilities to find space to be alone together. Then I need to help them to be intimate in their conversation with one another. Feelings of the inner child lie hidden under every sentence spoken about the weather, work, or holidays. In particular, the needs of the parents' inner child can be projected into the actual children of the parents. As a family therapist, I often suggest that, just as we set time aside for family therapy, the couple needs an uncluttered hour each week at the very minimum, preferably on a regular evening, to cradle the inner child of each other (Figure 20.22).

Figure 20.22.   Holding the partner's pain.

Cradling the inner child involves each partner making a courageous attempt to be fully honest with the other. It involves a little silence and then each partner openly sharing the feelings of the inner child while the other partner provides the cradle for the inner child. The cradle for the partner's inner child cannot be created quickly. It takes time to build through

- being receptive, but still, not talking;
- resonating deep inside oneself with the partner's feeling;
- putting oneself in the partner's shoes;
- not defending against the partner's feeling;
- just accepting emotionally what is being said;
- not criticising;
- not making it better;
- not saying the feeling is unjustified or wrong;
- just listening, feeling empathic, and trying to understand the partner's experience.

Sometimes, when the cradle of emotional receptivity and thoughtfulness is nearly built, I wonder if the parental couple might dare use social dreaming, described by Lawrence (2003). Social dreaming involves the sharing of a dream and freely associating to aspects of the dream that might provide commentaries on the ongoing marital and parental relationships in the family. The partner can simply join the dreamer in seeing how the dream can provide thoughts about emotional experiences that might not be so apparent in the day-to-day life of the couple. Here is an example:

> *Dream:* The wife reported, "There is a river, and on either side of the river were two towns. I was on one side with my father, and my mother was on the other side . . ." (Fisher, 1993, p. 162)

In this dream, the wife shares how she comes to the marriage being rivalrous with her own mother and finding herself still caught in an oedipal relationship with her father. Not letting her own internal parents remain in a partnership will make it difficult for the wife to identify with a loving parental couple in order to create a solid base in her marriage.

The gradual development of a cradle for the inner child can enable each of the marital partners to transform the inner child. Transformation of the inner child involves being emotionally present in the moment for each other, experiencing, observing, and thinking about the emotional experiences present both within oneself and each other. This marital containment for the parents' inner child provides the best cradle for the new-born baby and other children in the family.

Divorce, ex-partner, and the single parent

In divorce or separation, usually the ex-partner still remains a parent in the mind of the child. Unfortunately, one partner can criticise or damn the ex-partner, and exclude him or her from the life of the child (Figures 20.23 and 20.24).

Figure 20.23.   Couple separating.

Figure 20.24.   Person unhappy.

However, this will only create more defensiveness and a harder shell, which will make it difficult for the ex-partner to be open and receptive to the child. It will also make it difficult for the child to feel free of guilt in loving and finding a good way to relate to the ex-partner. The child still has a right to have this parent as a parent (Figures 20.25 and 20.26).

Figure 20.25.   Child with separated parents.

Figure 20.26.   Couple talking.

Unless the ex-partner is actually destructive to the child (in which case the child should not be with the ex-partner in an unsupervised way, or, in some instances, be with the parent's ex-partner at all), the role of the parent having custody of the child should be to work extremely hard to help an ex-partner to be

- reliable in coming to see the child;
- consistent in his/her roles in relation to the child;

● thoughtful about making arrangements with the ex-partner rather than directly with the child (Figure 20.27).

Figure 20.27.   Child torn apart.

Divorce does not take away the parental responsibility for making the child's needs, not the divorced parents' marital feelings, paramount. In particular, it is important to realise that the absent ex-partner is still the role model with whom the child will, in part, identify. Allowing the child to have a good, loving relationship with "a good-enough" ex-partner is part of good parenting (Figure 20.28)

Figure 20.28.   Couple thinking about their child.

I end with a quote regarding marriage (Figure 20.29).

Figure 20.29. The couple together, yet not too near together.

> . . . let there be spaces in your togetherness,
> And let the winds of the heavens dance between you
> Love one another, but make not a bond of love:
> Let it rather be a moving sea between the shores of your souls.
> Fill each other's cup but drink not from one cup.
> . . . Sing and dance together and be joyous, but let each
> of you be alone,
> Even as the strings of a lute are alone though they
> quiver with the same music.
> . . . Stand together yet not too near together:
> For the pillars of the temple stand apart,
> And the oak tree and the cypress grow not in each
> other's shadow.
>
> (Gibran, 1926, pp. 18–22)

References

Cameron, J. (1995). *An Artist's Way: A Course in Discovering and Rediscovering Your Creative Self.* London: Macmillan.

Fisher, J. (1993). Ambivalence and oedipal conflict. In: S. Ruszczynski (Ed.), *Psychotherapy with Couples.* London: Karnac.

Gibran, K. (1926). *The Prophet.* London: Pan Books, 1991.

Lawrence, W. G. (1998). *Social Dreaming at Work.* London: Karnac.

Leunig, M. (1990). *A Common Prayer.* North Blackburn, Victoria: Collins, Dove.

Leunig, M. (1998). *Why Dogs Sniff Their Tails.* Harmondsworth: Penguin.

Magagna, J., & Black, D. (1985). Changing roles of men and women. In: W. Dryden (Ed.), *Marital Therapy In Britain* (Volume 1). London: Harper and Row.

CHAPTER TWENTY-ONE

"The paternal role" in relation to siblings' love, gratitude, greed, and revenge

Jeanne Magagna

Hansel and Gretel are the young children of a poor woodcutter. The mother of the family has died. When a great famine settles over the land, the woodcutter's second wife is worried she will die of starvation, so she decides to take her two step-children, Hansel and Gretel, into the woods and leave them there to fend for themselves so that she and her husband do not starve to death. Hansel and Gretel's father weakly opposes the step-mother's plan, but she is determined to abandon the children. In secret, Hansel and Gretel are listening to the couple's discussion and after the parents have gone to bed, Hansel sneaks out of the house and gathers as many white pebbles as he can. Rejoining Gretel in her room, he reassures her that God will not forsake them.

The next day, the family walk deep into the woods and Hansel secretly lays a trail of white pebbles. After their parents abandon them, the children wait for the moon to rise and then they follow the pebbles back home. Much to their stepmother's horror, they return home safely.

When food supplies again become scarce, the stepmother angrily orders that this time her husband should abandon the children deeper into the woods. Once again, Hansel and Gretel are listening to the couple's conversation. When the couple go to bed, Hansel and Gretel again attempt to go out and gather more pebbles, but they find they have been locked in their rooms.

The following morning, the family treks into the woods. Hansel takes a slice of bread and leaves a trail of bread crumbs on the ground in order that he and Gretel might find their way home. The parents abandon the children. This time, when the children attempt to find their way back home, they find that the birds have eaten all the crumbs, making it impossible for Hansel and Gretel to find their way back.

After days of wandering as lost souls, Hansel and Gretel follow a beautiful white bird to a clearing in the woods. In the clearing they discover a large cottage built of gingerbread and cakes and having window panes made of clear sugar. Hungry and tired, the children begin to eat the rooftop of the candy house.

Suddenly the door opens and a "very old woman" emerges and lures the children inside with the promise of soft beds and delicious food. The old woman is secretly a wicked witch who waylays children in order to eat them. Afterwards the children slept in the witch's candy house.

Next morning, the wicked witch locks Hansel in an iron cage in the garden and forces Gretel to be her slave. The witch feeds Hansel regularly to fatten him up. When the wicked witch checks, by touching his finger, to see how fat Hansel has become, Hansel cleverly extends a bone. Due to her blindness, the wicked witch is fooled into thinking Hansel is still too thin to eat. After weeks of feeding Hansel, the witch grows impatient and decides to eat Hansel anyway "be he fat or lean."

As she prepares the oven for Hansel, the wicked witch decides she is hungry enough to eat Gretel, too. She coaxes Gretel to the open oven and asks her to lean over in front of it to see if the fire is hot enough. Gretel, sensing the witch's intent, pretends she does not understand what the wicked witch is saying. Infuriated, the witch demonstrates by sticking her head near the oven. Gretel instantly shoves the witch into the oven, slams and bolts the door shut, leaving "the ungodly witch to be burned to ashes". The wicked witch screams in pain until she dies. Immediately Gretel frees Hansel from his cage.

Then Hansel and Gretel discover that the wicked witch's home is full of treasures and precious stones. Putting the jewels into their clothing, the children set off for home. A swan ferries them across a wide expanse of water and when they return home they find only their father. The cruel step-mother has died. The woodcutter father, who had been mourning the loss of Hansel and Gretel, was delighted to see them safe and sound.

Hansel, Gretel and their father live happily ever after. (Grimm & Grimm, 1925)

*H*ansel and Gretel (Grimm & Grimm, 1925) is a fairy tale describing how two siblings band together, out of love for one another, to save each other's lives. The children's problems have been exacerbated by the loss of their biological mother. Their enormous hostility about loss of their biological mother is re-directed to the wicked stepmother. The wicked stepmother is also filled with their projections of hostility that belong to their father, for he does not protect them from the wicked stepmother and support them so that they can remain well and alive.

Now read this real life story, summarised from Freud, A. and Dann, 1951.

A group of four orphans had their parents killed by the Nazis. They lived in the Terezin concentration camp near Prague. Their biological needs were mainly met by adults. They bonded themselves to one another so much so that they were almost totally dependent on one another. They showed an almost complete absence of jealousy, rivalry and competition. It was as though each child felt very identified with the others, feeling them extensions of the self. No separate self-identity seemed to be present.

What are the similarities between the fairy tale of *Hansel and Gretel*, which children repeatedly ask to have read, and the true story of the Terezin orphans who came to live in the Hampstead Nurseries in London with Anna Freud and Sophie Dann?

The stories of Hansel and Gretel and the four Terezin orphans show that human love and attachment to another human being is instinctual. Neither the fairytale children nor the Terezin orphans attacked one another physically. Both groups fought the adults: Hansel burnt the

wicked witch and the Terezin orphans spat at, kicked, and bit adults, on to whom were transferred images of the Nazi prison guards (Bank & Kahn, 1982, p. 121).

How do we understand the lack of hostility between the orphans? They were adhesively
bonded together for security and survival while they experienced persecution. They used
hostile defences of kicking and spitting towards the care-taking adults who represented the
Nazi prison guards. Like Hansel and Gretel, these Terezin orphans were loyal to one another,
for they protected each other from physical and psychological attacks by "outsiders". They
were also co-operative and did things to help one another.

But do all orphaned siblings who are treated badly and deprived emotionally or physically
remain so very loving and loyal to one another? Certainly not! Some orphaned siblings go on
to abandon one another, get into terribly rivalrous squabbles with each another, and might even
kill one another.

Why are these aggressive orphaned siblings so different from the loyal and loving orphans:
Hansel and Gretel and the Terezin concentration camp orphans? The concentration camp
orphans lovingly related to one another in the Hampstead Nursery orphanage because they
were surrounded and emotionally contained by nurturing and kindly child-care workers (Bank
& Kahn, 1982, p. 124).

Loving and loyal siblings must experience nurturing and sensitive adults whom they can
value and can introject and with whom they can identify. It is on the basis of identification with
the nurturing, loving, thoughtful adults that young children can nurture and, as much as they
can at their limited age, remain sensitive to the needs of their young toddler siblings.

What factors in a family group motivate the young toddler to change the way of relating
from the orphans' state of adhesively binding themselves to one another or "getting along to
survive" to

- attacking the other sibling and being greedy for all that one can possess;
- defending oneself assertively or hostilely in relation to the other sibling's attacks;
- taking revenge?

Those are the important issues that I shall now explore. First, I describe a study of forty children by Dunn and Kendrick (1982), who looked at the relationship between the older sibling
and mother before the new sibling's birth, after birth, and when the sibling was fourteen months
old. Subsequently, I focus on the importance of the paternal role and then I use some psychoanalytic concepts and observations of children to illustrate eight different types of paternal roles.

The paternal role

Dunn and Kendrick (1982) explored the origins of the differences between young sibling pairs
in their relationships and the ways in which the different relationships within the family
affected one another. In particular, they explored the siblings' relationship with the father and
its impact on the sibling relationship. They found that the father's role was crucial in supporting the first-born's capacity to bear the presence of the newborn (Dunn & Kendrick, 1982). Four
of the key findings that emerged from their 1982 study were:

1. The older sibling's increased expression of affection and wish for cuddling seemed to be a response to the parent's interest in, and involvement with, the baby sibling. Moreover, the older siblings' showed particularly strong affection for the father in the first year of the younger sibling's birth. At the time of the new baby's birth, the older children were also more compliant with the father's requests than with the mother's.
2. When the father played with the baby, very few firstborns ignored their interaction. In their study, half of the children could accept their mother holding the baby, but were overtly jealous when father held the new baby. "One child put it very firmly to her mother, 'Daddy is *not* Ronnie's daddy'" (Dunn & Kendrick, 1982, p. 31).
3. In families where the child was reported to have an intense and close relationship with the father, there was less escalation of conflict and confrontation with the mother. Also, after the sibling was born, when there was a close relationship with the father there was not such a decrease in joint attention involving focusing together with the mother on a common item of interest (Dunn & Kendrick, 1982).
4. Parents who encouraged their first born *to take joint responsibility* and who discussed the baby as a person were more likely to have children whom they reported to be particularly interested in, and affectionate towards, the baby (Dunn & Kendrick, 1982).

The role of the father: eight different pictures

Here are eight different illustrations of the paternal function in relation to fostering love and generosity between siblings.

1.   Lack of protection from the paternal role

What did you think of "the father's role" in *Hansel and Gretel*? The wood-cutter was a weak man wasn't he? He had lost his first wife and perhaps he was still grieving for her. Deception, lies, and unpredictability were all part of the evening scene when Hansel secretly intruded upon the parents' conversations regarding how they would abandon the children in the forest. There was *no secure base* in this home!

The father might not have mourned his first wife and could have been a weak father because he was depressed. There was a famine and the family had little food, so the stepmother felt she could give no supplies of food to the children. Simultaneously, it was apparent that she had developed no love for the previous wife's children. The weak wood-cutter father was not firm and supportive to his second wife and this lack of support meant they did not work together to find ways feeding the children and meeting their emotional and physical needs. Instead, the weak father colluded with the stepmother's depriving, conniving, and cruel state of mind that dictated the family's life. Also, instead of finding a safe haven for the children, the weak father also submitted to the cruel stepmother's demand to secretly abandon Hansel and Gretel.

Ideally, the paternal function in each parent is exercised to protect the child against the dangers of the outside world and also those that originate in the child's own asocial tendencies (Bettelheim, 1976, p. 206). If a child is deprived of the protection of thoughtful paternal functioning in either parent, the child will not be able to form an identification with thought-ful, limit-setting paternal functions in the parents. Subsequently, the child will have conflictual relationships with siblings. The capacity to bear the frustration of not having and doing just what one wants in a relationship as well as the capacity to lovingly think about the needs of the other partially depends on internalising a good paternal function.

2.   The paternal function as exercised within the mother: an example of a mother's "weak paternal function"

It is understandable that a mother of two young children, baby Lauren, aged seventeen weeks, and Sandi, aged three years, would be exhausted. When there is hostility in the mother's voice, it exacerbates anxiety rather than serving to be a good, containing, paternal limit to wishes and needs of the young children.

> Mother shouted at her three-year-old daughter, Sandi, because Sandi was getting tangled up in her tights and was either unwilling or unable to put them on by herself. The baby would not stop crying, so mother gave her the breast while shouting again at her older daughter, Sandi, who laughed at her mother's anger. The baby started to cry in a piercing tone, frantically waving her arms and kicking rapidly. Mother became very enraged with the baby and yelled at her, "Don't cry!" Afterwards, as mother put the tights on her elder daughter, Sandi pushed her elbow into the baby's chest. The baby became red with distress and cried in a piercing tone.

> Mother picked up her baby, resting her on her shoulder, and said, "Ohh, my sweet girl, it is all right." The elder daughter started to tickle the baby and would not stop when requested by the mother to do so. The mother threatened her elder daughter, Sandi, in an angry tone, "After the observer leaves I am going to beat you. Enough!"

In this very distressing observation, we see that mother's limit setting is filled with her sense of persecution and hostility. She is also not using her hands to protect the baby. Physical firm-ness and thoughtful containment are required to calm the three-year-old Sandi's aggressive tickling of her seventeen-week-old sister. Mother's hostility leaves Sandi with a heightened level of fear and anger. It triggers her lower brain reactions to threat and attack (Sunderland, 2006, p. 161). Mother's weak paternal functioning makes Sandi more anxious and more out of control, for she laughs at mother's anger towards her. Repeated parental shouting and angry explosions create in the child tensions that require discharge. This emotional discharge is often in the form of hitting or bullying a sibling or shouting, screaming, biting, hitting, or breaking something. If the parent smacks, the parent is modelling to the child what to do to a sibling when she is frustrated, which is to lash out (Sunderland, 2006, p. 161). The scene with Sandi and her seventeen-week-old baby sister is one in which there is no opportunity for Sandi to introject a containing good mother with a strong paternal protective function. Sandi's identifi-cation will be with a punitive figure rather than a loving, mentalizing parent who contains frus-trations and desires for acting out aggressively.

Dunn and Kendrick's (1982) research states that the intensity of mothers' hostility in admin-istering punishment to their sons for their aggressive behaviour towards the newborn is signif-icant in determining the boys' aggression to the baby at six months. The more hostility is present in the mother's scolding behaviour to a first-born boy, if he hits the baby sibling at eight months, then, four months later, the first-born is significantly less friendly to his twelve-month-old younger sibling.

Understanding the boys' aggressive feelings, responding with *appropriate* paternal functioning and with something other than a hostile scolding, is *crucial* in supporting kinder relationships between older boys and young siblings. Dunn and Kendrick's research showed that the more aggressive the older boy sibling was, the more aggressive the mothers were in response to the first-born's action. For example, if the older boy hit or pushed the baby, the mother was more hostile to him, and then the older boy continued a trajectory of being unkind to the baby (Dunn & Kendrick, 1982).

3.   The paternal function as exercised within the mother:
an example of a mother's "good paternal function"

A young mother, who lived in a children's home in her early years and was subsequently adopted, was raising two young boys, Martin, twenty months and William, thirty-seven months. Her method of dealing with sibling rivalry was to involve both boys simultaneously in spontaneous and often very physical play activities with her. At other times, she indicated that she was with one child and the other child would need to wait his turn. She involved each of them in helping her with the other child. She also involved them in doing some household activities they could share with her when they were developmentally ready. As well as this, the mother conversed with each boy about how the other boy was feeling and, in this way, she fostered an empathic rapport between them.

Usually, the young brothers were not competing for space, for they had found a comfortable way of being together in the presence of a thoughtful, sensitive mother who was firm and clear about behaviour that was not allowed. This included being clear that the children could not cause damage to themselves, to others, or to property. The elder boy's capacity for concern about the younger sibling, "the baby", is reflected in his conversation:

> Mother holds up a bowl with some goldfish inside. Martin, 23 months, begins to crow, "Fish, fish, fish." Mother looks in the bowl and says, "Oh dear, I think one of the fish is dead." Martin repeats "dead". Mother asks 40 month old William what he feels. William looks at the observer and referring to the goldfish, he says, "Map is sad, Map is crying." (Norman, 2005, p. 74)

Here, we see that the mother and the presence of the observer have created an emotionally containing home atmosphere. In this context, William shows how he is both able to identify with the dead fish and look at the observer while acknowledging his sadness in relation to the dead fish. The capacity to have tenderness for the "mother's other babies", represented by the goldfish, is linked with an internalisation of a containing mother who supports the children while utilising a good paternal function.

The boys are encouraged to play together, and mother talks to each of them about the other. Here is another sequence.

> The baby, Martin, 8 months, is lying on the quilt. His 25 month old brother, William, gets on the quilt and rolls over by his little brother so the mother and observer can see both children.

Dissatisfied with his brother's coming so close to him, 8 month Martin crawls over to a play car and begins to slap the car bumper. William joins him and then mother joins him in slapping the car. The boys are giggling in delight. Mother decides to seat the boys side-by-side together. Mother and the observer both watch the boys admiringly. (Norman, 2005, p. 74)

It is clear that mother is convinced that her children can share their mother's attention and love. Despite William's aggressive jealousy, mother is determined to make this happen. Even eight-month-old Martin has learnt to symbolise his aggression towards his brother and mother: he moves towards the car and hits it after his brother William lands on his blanket. The boys' capacity to symbolise aggression at this early age and to share mother comes from internalising mother's love for each of them as well as from knowing that they occupy separate and unique spaces in her mind (Norman, 2005).

According to Dunn and Kendrick's (1982) research on sibling relationships, thoughtful parental support for the older sibling's capacity for concern for the new baby and ongoing parental support for affectionate sibling relationships is of great significance in facilitating sibling relationships characterised by a predominance of love and generosity.

4.   The father's role in fostering love and generosity when the second sibling is present

The "paternal function" fostering sibling love and generosity involves activating the child's thoughtful self instead of activating fear and rage through repeated parental anger and hostile criticism. In the next example, we see a father thinking with his child, Eric, about his phantasies expressed in his play, and offering his son the possibility of holding on to the good internalised parents through thinking about his hostile and loving impulses.

Symbols are needed not only in communication with the external world, but also in internal communication. Eric has some capacity to be in touch with his unconscious, some awareness of his own impulses and feelings shown in his symbolic play. Symbolic play occurs because Eric has a thoughtful father and nurturing mother, good internalised parents within him, that promote his capacity to symbolise his feelings and the ability to form symbols. However, I think that we mean more than this; we mean that he has actual communication with his unconscious phantasies. So, Eric is "deeply in touch with himself" through a constant, free, symbol formation expressing underlying primitive phantasies of love and hate. Symbolising his hostile feelings through play allows Eric to protect his younger brother by preventing his actually hurting his brother.

Eric is thirty-two months, and his brother Daniel is ten months. Most evenings, when mother has breast-fed baby Daniel, father read a story to Eric and talked with him before putting him to bed. Eric is very close to his father and his father shows pleasure in Eric's accomplishments. As we see below, father also tries to comprehend the meaning of Eric's play.

Eric is being constantly admired and followed by his crawling, ten-month-old baby brother, Daniel. Eric is feeling irritated because when he tells Daniel to go away, Daniel does not obey him. When baby Daniel crawls near the staircase, Eric tells his father, "Watch, because baby will fall down the stairs." Eric then asks his father to come into his bedroom to see an imaginary dinosaur. Father replies, "Oh no, I can't because I'm watching to make sure the baby doesn't fall down the stairs." Eric brings a teddy from his bed, leans over near his father, and throws his teddy down the stairs. Father says, "Oh, poor teddy". Eric laughs excitedly. He orders father to "go and get the teddy". Father says, "No, I'm watching the stairs to see baby doesn't fall." Eric says, "I'll go and get it." He climbs over Father and asks, "See? I'm not going to fall, am I? Eric then goes down the stairs to retrieve the teddy. In later play activities, Eric asks his father to help him mend a broken car. He calls out to the observer, "Daddy is fixing it. I'm helping." (Adapted from Magagna, 2002, p. 101.)

One of the striking features of the father–son relationship is that Eric tries to enlist his good external father to help him feel more securely held in the face of his anxieties about hostile phantasies towards his little baby brother. Eric's hostile phantasies create an internalised revengeful, frightening persecutor—the imaginary dinosaur—that at times seems to pop out from his internal world to the external world. He shifts his psychological state and attempts to repair the damage to the car, which signifies damage done internally through his hostility to his baby brother and the parents creating him.

5.   Paternal functions and the absent father

A father might be absent through divorce, separation, or over-involvement in "other activities", including work. The quality of the parents' relationship, whether married or divorced, is always a matter of fundamental significance for the quality of the sibling relationships. If the child hears only that the father is bad and does not love him, it is painful and disturbing for the child's self-esteem. If the father is absent it is useful for the child if the mother can find some way of helping the child connect with good and helpful aspects of the father (whether or not the mother despises him). It is also crucial that a mother protects the child from harmful aspects of the father. In this way, the child will be able to maintain a belief in a good paternal function in the mother who is thinking about importance of the father for her child's development, rather than simply her own feelings in relation to the father. In this way, a child feels loved by his generous mother and this enhances his chances of introjecting and identifying with a loving internal mother as he relates to his siblings.

Similarly, it is important that the father use his own paternal function of thinking about the wellbeing of the child to protect the child from harmful aspects of the mother. Feeling loved in a thoughtful way enhances the quality of the sibling relationship. As mentioned previously, Hansel and Gretel's father lacked a good internal paternal function and failed to protect his orphaned children from harmful aspects of the stepmother.

The paternal function of the father, to "support the mother through compassionate understanding, support, and sexual nurturing", is essential for the wellbeing of the mother. The paternal function of providing thoughtful, sensitive but *firm limit setting* is an essential part of loving parenting for both the father and the mother. Siblings identify with good paternal functioning in each parent and on this basis are able to gradually develop loving relationships with one another.

6.   Hostility in paternal functioning exacerbating greed

What is involved in greedily attacking the other for all one can get? There is no doubt that we see infants who appear instinctually greedy for the breast from the first weeks of life. Klein,

1957, p. 181) says, "Greed refers to an impetuous and insatiable craving, exceeding what the person needs and what the other is able and willing to give". She senses that "the infant who is so greedy for love and attention is also insecure about his own capacity to love; and all these anxieties reinforce greed" (Klein, 1959, p. 254).

> Sam, three weeks old, is crying. He latches on to the breast, strongly, greedily sucking, with no pauses, until he stops exhausted, and turns away from the breast. The mother feels persecuted by his intensely strong, painful sucking and frequent crying, which she interprets as his "wanting the breast".

Greed, though, is an emotion that goes far beyond the satisfaction of one's oral needs. The driving force in greed is to take rapaciously everything the mother has, with no concern for the state in which the mother is left. The aim is not to spoil but to get all that one needs *and wants* both emotionally and physically for oneself (Klein, 1957, p. 181).

When the mother is persecuted by the infant's need and greed, she is unable to contain the baby's anxieties and develops a rather negative response to his demands. The baby's anxieties then severely escalate. These anxieties about not being a loved and "held in mind" baby subsequently foster more greedy sucking at the breast to take all the milk. Then the anxiety of being deprived, of being robbed, and of not being good enough to be loved arise (Klein, 1959). Greed, therefore, both fosters failure and suggests that there is a failure to securely establish the good containing mother in the internal world.

A greedy person becomes insatiable for people, things, success, but is left with endless hungry dissatisfaction and the fear of being greedily attacked in return, as is represented by the image of Hansel and Gretel eating up the candy house (representing the mother) and the wicked witch revengefully deciding to eat up Hansel and Gretel.

What prompts and augments greed within the sibling relationship?

The stepmother and father abandoned Hansel and Gretel and stimulated their hatred and greed. Likewise, greedy wishes are symbolised by the witch, who decides to eat up Hansel and Gretel with no concern for them. The experience of hatred towards depriving parents stimulates Hansel and Gretel's greed and they steal the witch's jewels as well as killing her. Overwhelming oral greed also prompts Hansel and Gretel to eat up parts of the gingerbread house that might give them shelter and safety (Bettelheim, 1976).

Now the question remains: if we move to a *symbolic level*, is the stealing of the witch's jewels necessary, or does it represent the "ganging together" of two siblings filled with hostility to the wicked stepmother? "The gang" (Rosenfeld, 1971) facilitates our looking more carefully at what first simply appears as co-operation between siblings. "Ganging up" while filled with hatred against the hostile, depriving, unprotective parents can look innocuous. It is particularly prevalent and difficult to disentangle in twin siblings' relationships. "Ganging up" between siblings can look like a co-operative friendship, but it is a psychological process characterised by seeking to obliterate need, dependency, and, in particular, envy by denying the need for parents' guidance and nurturance.

> The 'gang formation' guards the inner self against the threat of emotional vulnerability. The outcome is the severance of all nurturing ties, a rupture which in fantasy feeds a phantasy of omnipotence, but in reality destroys the capacity for emotional growth. (Nitsun, 1996, p. 126)

Symbolically, Hansel and Gretel are *splitting* their love and hate towards their parents and, in effect, saying, "We don't need that nasty stepmother (represented by the wicked witch), we shall just have a relationship with our lovely daddy", forgetting that their weak father did not protect them and let them starve in the woods. If the father were stronger, he could have tried to help the wicked stepmother to become more loving towards them.

How does the father's paternal function influence greed between and among siblings?

Favouritism by adults

Favouritism by adults, particularly parents, breeds vicious rivalries and is antithetical to the growth of loyalty of siblings to one another. We need to be very careful when observing infants to keep evenly suspended attention in relation to the older sibling. We may be very much distorting the loyalty of siblings to one another when we direct our gaze solely towards the infant–mother relationship. Likewise, the parents of two children need to be able to keep in mind both children present with them. Although one child may temporarily be centre stage, the children in the room all need to be kept in the parents' and teachers' minds.

Other factors influencing greed and attack upon the sibling

Love for another can still be present when sibling conflict, aggression, and rivalry are present. Love and concern for the other, if sufficiently developed, mitigate the severity of the aggression to one another. An "inner role of the loving father" can support the child to limit his aggression, his hitting of the other, and enable him to symbolise his aggression through play, drawing, and talking.

We see from infancy onwards that a child attacks when the other child has something he wants. What enables the young child to move from being a persecuted, passive victim, simply receiving the older sibling's attack, to attacking, defending, taking revenge, or forgiving?

7.   Hostility in paternal functioning exacerbating revenge

What prompts a sense of grievance and revenge between siblings? The child's wish for revenge is stimulated by parental deprivation, separation, hurtful and hostile treatment, or lack of protection from a hostile sibling or parent. The sadistic excitement of revenge often protects one from a painful internal sense of loss of parental love and thoughtfulness. Here is such a situation.

Baby Bruno is seated near his three-year-old brother, Sam. Baby Bruno starts moving his hand along three-year-old Sam's back. Sam asks baby Bruno to stop, and he tries unsuccessfully to hit baby Bruno's hand. Then baby Bruno tries to rock himself in such a way that he can lean into Sam. At this point Sam sits up, pushes baby Bruno backwards to the floor, and laughs.

Baby Bruno starts to laugh loudly and crazily as he sits up. This time, Sam pushes baby Bruno harder down on to the floor. Baby Bruno tries to sit up a third time, but Sam pushes him even more fiercely to the ground.

Baby Bruno then tries unsuccessfully to slap and punch Sam. Sam hits Baby Bruno twice on the head until Baby Bruno laughs and then cries desperately. (Magagna, 2014, p. 202)

Revenge phantasies always create guilt and anxiety about retribution. The psychological usefulness of the fairy tale *Hansel and Gretel*'s (Grimm & Grimm, 1925) description of the wood-cutter's wife as "the wicked stepmother" is that it allows children to acknowledge, rather than repress, their hostility about the limits of parental nurturance and presence.

Through the fairy tale, children are allowed to symbolise hostile feelings through fully engaging in revenge fantasies about the wicked step-parent, without the same degree of guilt or fear in respect to the true parent who loves them, albeit with some ambivalence. The transfer of the child's hostile phantasies from the unconscious to the child's conscious mind through the use of the fairy tale, accompanied by thinking about these hostile phantasies with a parent or teacher, makes it less likely that the child will "act out" in revengeful actions towards siblings or parents.

8.   *The bounteous parental role: gratitude and generosity*

What is gratitude? Klein (1957, pp. 176–236) said that gratitude is the appreciation of goodness in others and in oneself. It is essential in building up the relation to the good object. "In the course of development, the relation to the mother's breast becomes the foundation for devotion to people, values, and causes" (Klein, 1957, p. 187).

> A child with a strong capacity for love and gratitude has a deep-rooted relation with *a good object* and can, without being fundamentally damaged, withstand temporary states of envy, hatred and grievance, which arise *even in children* who are loved and well mothered. (Klein, 1957, p. 187)

Essentially, Klein is describing the good breast assimilated and experienced as being part of one's self (Erlich, 2008).

Fonagy (2008) raises a crucial issue:

> The problem with love and gratitude is: can we keep our memories of enjoyment and gratitude, given the transience of a moment with another and the pain of mourning its loss? Constitutional differences exist between infants' ability to receive love and experience gratitude. Attachment to the loved object and the development of gratitude is interfered with by the young child's excessive aggression. Love and gratitude are made possible by the assimilation of inborn aggression. Excessive aggression will disorganize attachment to a point where caregiving will no longer have its anticipated effect. (Fonagy, 2008, p. 209)

Roth tells us that "Klein saw gratitude as the protector of loving feelings, opposing it to greed. Gratitide is the acknowledgement, recognition, and enjoyment of the fact that something good, something unique has been received—'a gift' (Roth, 2008, pp. 15–16).

How does gratitude to parents influence generosity and forgiveness between siblings? The presence of good internal parents allows feelings of internal abundance and generosity and that fosters *gratitude* to parents. Gratitude towards parents fosters *love and generosity* towards siblings, because there is an identification with loved internal parents and, on that basis, one loves the parents' other children (Klein, 1957, p. 189).

What is generosity? Abraham tells us that a generous person is identified with a bounteous mother (Abraham, 1924). O'Shaughnessy states that "the bounteous mother with whom the generous person identifies is the bestowing loved object to whom gratitude can be felt" (O'Shaughnessy, 2008, p. 82). There are two kinds of generosity, compulsive and genuine.

What is compulsive generosity? Compulsive generosity is often present in a revengeful sibling who devalues the parents, has unconscious feelings of rage and deprivation, and seeks, by taking over the sibling, to replace the parent. The sibling over-identifies with the younger sibling and increases his own righteous sense of triumph to block out disturbing thoughts and feelings such as despair, depression, and outright murderousness toward that parent (Bank & Kahn, 1982).

Compulsive generosity is described by Susan, a twin, who says, "I have no self, there is no choice; I give my twin sister what she wants, do what she wants me to do. It is not my decision." Susan's statement suggests that there is no internalised good paternal function placing thoughts or thoughtful limits on what the twin sister, Susan, compulsively gives to her sister.

What is genuine generosity? True love and generosity towards a sibling is based on an identification with internalised bounteous and loving parents. The bounteous parents with whom the truly generous child identifies is the bestowing loved parents to whom gratitude can be felt (O'Shaughnessy, 2008, p. 82). Such love fosters forgiveness when one is hurt or offended by a sibling.

A child's psychological development, coupled with generosity to siblings, is often seen in his dreams. Here is an example of a young boy who was school phobic, an anxiety linked with his intense jealousy and envy of his brother. At the end of his psychotherapy with Melanie Klein,

> Richard dreamt that he was in a caravan and travelling with him is a very happy family. The father and mother were middle-aged; there were quite a lot of children, and all of them were nice. Klein interpreted the dream as representing how Richard had all his loved people in a happy, harmonious family inside him. This meant he had loving relationships to her other patients and his brother Paul. (Klein, 1961, p. 430)

Conclusion

This chapter has described how aspects of the parents, the father's role in the family, and the paternal function in the mother promote love and generosity between siblings or exacerbate greed and revenge between siblings.

What the child cannot hold he cannot process. What he cannot process he cannot transform. What he cannot transform haunts him. It takes the parents' minds, the paternal function, to help the child heal the anguish of sharing the parental space with other siblings. Then the child's mind and heart can grow and re-grow the capacities to form intimate, loving, and pleasurable relationships with other siblings within the family.

References

Abraham, K. (1924). A short study of the development of the libido. In: R. V. Frankiel (Ed.), *Essential Papers on Object Loss* (pp. 73–93). New York: New York University Press, 1994.

Bank, S. P., & Kahn, M. D. (1982). *The Sibling Bond*. New York: Basic Books.

Bettelheim, B. (1976). *The Uses of Enchantment*. London: Penguin.

Dunn, J., & Kendrick, C. (1982). *Siblings. Love, Envy and Understanding*. London: Grant McIntyre.

Erlich, H. S. (2008). Envy and gratitude: some current reflections. In: P. Roth & A. Lemma (Eds.), *Envy and Gratitude Revisited* (pp. 50–62). London: Karnac.

Fonagy, P. (2008). Being envious of envy and gratitude. In: P. Roth & A. Lemma (Eds.), *Envy and Gratitude Revisited* (pp. 201–210). London: Karnac.

Freud, A., & Dann, S. (1951). An experiment in group upbringing. *Psychoanalytic Study of the Child*, 6: 127–168.

Grimm, J., & Grimm, W. (1925). *Hansel and Gretel*. London: Hodder and Stoughton.

Klein, M. (1957). Envy and gratitude. In: *The Writings of Melanie Klein, Vol 3: Envy and Gratitude and Other Works* (pp. 176–235). London: Hogarth Press.

Klein, M. (1959). Our adult world and its roots in infancy. In: *The Writings of Melanie Klein, Vol 3: Envy and Gratitude and Other Works* (pp. 247–263). London: Hogarth Press, 1975 [reprinted London: Karnac, 1993].

Klein, M. (1961). *Narrative of a Child Analysis*. London: Hogarth Press, 1975.

Magagna, J. (2002). Three years of infant observation with Mrs. Bick. In: A. Briggs (Ed.), *Surviving Space: Papers on Infant Observation*. London: Karnac.

Magagna, J. (2014). Envy, jealousy, love, and generosity in sibling relationships: the impact of sibling relationships on future family relationships. In: B. Maciejewska-Sobczak, K. Skrzypek, & Z. Stadnicka-Dmitriew (Eds.), *Siblings: Rivalry and Envy-Coexistence and Concern* (pp. 172–193). London: Karnac.

Nitsun, M. (1996). *The Anti-Group*. London: Routledge.

O'Shaughnessy, E. (2008). On gratitude. In: P. Roth & A. Lemma (Eds.), *Envy and Gratitude Revisited* (pp. 79–91). London: International Psychoanalytic Association.

Rosenfeld, H. (1971). A clinical approach to the psycho-analytic theory of the life and death instincts: an investigation into the aggressive aspects of narcissism. *International Journal of Psychoanalysis*, 52: 169–177.

Roth, P. (2008). Introduction. In: P. Roth & A. Lemma (Eds). *Envy and Gratitude Revisited* (pp. 1–18). London: Karnac.

Sunderland, M. (2006). *The Science of Parenting*. London: Dorling Kindersley.

CHAPTER TWENTY-TWO

Men in the nursery: a discussion–play group with fathers and their infants and toddlers

Carl Bagnini

Fathers and mothers both attend Tempo Lineare and are very involved with their children and the parents' group. This chapter is included to highlight some rather important issues regarding the role of the father in the development of young children.

Since the 1980s, women and men have become more interested in how men approach parenting in light of the rapid shift in family values with the attendant stresses on traditional roles. Both men and women became more involved in discussing how the division of labour in child-rearing arrangements, employment out of the home, and gender redefinitions were influencing men as parents. At this time, I also began pursuing the subject, and in the process discovered questions surfacing that were at first unsettling. As a parent to two young daughters, I wondered if I parented that differently from my wife. While I concluded I was different as a parent, I had not considered if my parenting style was based on my maleness, my personality, my professional training in mental health and psychotherapy, or rooted in my parents' influences on my early development.

The men I knew did not generally discuss their parenting, while the women I knew seemed to speak regularly about child rearing with other women, including their mothers. Could generations of men have assumed parenting was a secret endeavour, learnt by a secret process not requiring the company of other men? How did men learn to parent? Was it by observing women, or through grandfathers that had more time for it after retirement? I felt a little guilty, as though I had no right to enquire into a secret society. An absurd idea came to me: maybe men did not parent, but instead relied totally on the traditional division of labour between men and women. I knew better, however, for social values and trends were shifting towards requiring equal family roles, although economic forces were moving slowly, in snail-like fashion, regarding equal pay for both genders.

I was teaching sociology at the time and decided to do a small piece of empirical and experiential investigation on the subject of fathers as parents. I needed a spontaneous, relaxed setting to observe youngsters with their fathers or perhaps without them. I decided to observe the spontaneous play of children in a naturalistic setting and subsequently interview them regarding parenting influences on their play activities.

The other approach to studying male parenting was more ambitious and required planning and the co-operation of a community agency. The purpose would be to observe fathers along-side one another interacting with their young children in a nursery. Later, the fathers would review their experiences in a group discussion with one another. The play with children followed by a group discussion could provide a "males-only" experience so I might observe the similarities and differences in the men's parenting of their infants and toddlers.

My hunch was that traditional child rearing was essentially left to mothers and grand-mothers, while fathers had limited contact with babies and toddlers. Men learnt parenting through instruction by women essentially, not by the involvement and mentoring of other males. I wanted to isolate the men to get as *in vivo* a sense of their styles, concerns, ideas, and aims for their very young children, especially when the communication was through play, since verbal skills at the infancy and toddler age would not be the basis for gaining attunement to baby's needs. The men would be on their own, without their wives, and have to sense what their babies needed on the basis of their emotional responses, which were usually identified as being part of their more feminine capacities. I also wanted to test an assumption that men did not naturally take to active parenting until their children, sons for the most part, were old enough to walk around and at least throw or kick a ball.

First, I decided upon the simpler task of observing children's spontaneous play in a play-ground attached to my daughter's nursery and subsequently interviewing the children. I did not complete the second part of my study of fathers with their children for several years because there was no nursery in my vicinity that provided fathers with an opportunity to spend unstructured time with their youngsters. In the rest of this chapter, I discuss some of the ideas gained through observing and meeting with the children and the fathers.

My observations and interviews with pre-schoolers describing their versions of how their mummies and daddies parented them were revealing; for example, a little girl of three and a half explained how "daddy climbs up the monkey bars to show and teach climbing." She described how this contrasted with what happened when mummy and she were alone in the playground: "Mummy watches me climb and tells me to be careful." Her daddy appears to be bold and physical, hands on, and instilling confidence and a sense of adventure.

Upon reflection, I thought that the fathers' parental motives were based on an internalised male sense of responsibility for building strong, independent children prepared for social and economic "climbing up the ladder" prescribed by the world outside the playground. Looking back on the modest experience with the young children, my conclusions about motives underlying male parenting appear obvious and stereotypical for that time; however, to this day there is much to support these conclusions. Men have traditionally, in spite of the feminisation of child rearing, continued to represent a responsibility to raise and prepare children *to be strong* in order to sepa-rate from the security of home and succeed in the "cold, cruel world". The concurrent worldwide fighting in wars tends to support some of this thinking about what children need to survive.

My curiosity lingered about how men parent and how indispensable fathers are in the development and identity formations of their children. This issue brought to mind how our culture tends to view father as a playmate or substitute baby-sitter for the child. I regard such references as pejorative to the male parent in relation to his child. Male parenting is a matter addressed by earlier psychoanalytical writings, but in relation to the oedipal triangle between the mother and father and child. Magagna's Chapter Twenty-one and the fathers' contributions in Chapter Twenty-four describe other roles of the father; however, the theories of the Oedipus complex tend to emphasise the father as initially the rival male with whom the child is a competitor for the attentions of the mother. The father is viewed as a biological/cultural stereotype as an exciting and temporal object, specifically contrasted with mother, who is defined as the formal organiser of the holding, containing environment. However, I believe that the father's influence is multi-faceted and not subject to reductionist portrayals. Defining a father's influence with the child requires more than the accumulation of actual time spent with the child. I am aware, however, that the actual time spent with the child is very important for internalising a father as a person. Two parents often have precious little time with their children, so that the quantity of time *vs.* the quality of the time spent with the child is better studied with both parents. How mothers express their feelings about their husbands, both as mates and as parents, has great impact on how children identify with both parents' qualities.

I want to turn to clinical practice, to discuss another dimension of the importance of the male parent. The repressed theme of "father-hunger" emerges in many of the antisocial depressed and alienated boys and girls with whom I work. Mothers in psychotherapy with me, individually or in a family context, often refuse to speak about their divorced or deceased spouse, as though the spouse never existed. They incorrectly believe their children would be harmed if the mother spoke openly about the father and the marriage. Another related fear of single mothers stems from the anxiety of breaking down, losing control, and appearing weak, which conflicts with the requirement of having to be the strong parent if there is only one parent present within the home. Often, the children feel torn in their loyalty to mother and fear offending or hurting her if they were to talk about father with any positive feelings.

Whatever the circumstances surrounding loss of the father, whether through death, abandonment, or divorce, the loss is a family experience of tragic proportions, and the need to process feelings, memories, and perspectives regarding loss of the father is a crucial psychological task for all the family members. The children's mental health is at risk if they do not develop the capacity to mourn loss of the father and find ways of rebuilding trust in adults, and males in particular, and look to the future with hope and optimism.

Returning to how men parent, the capacity of men to care about and for their babies and young children is multi-determined. I will take up one influence that is not discussed by men in general that is central to the development of the father's capacity to care effectively for young children: being in the company of other caring fathers.

The men's nursery group was the setting for observation and discussion of what men feel, do, and talk about with other fathers with respect to their babies and young children. The men's group consisted of eight fathers, aged 26–38, each having at least one child under the age of thirty months. The youngest child was six months. Some of the fathers had two young children. The format consisted of a free playtime with the children for sixty minutes in the morning, followed by a men's discussion group. In the first meeting, the fathers were introduced to each other and each other's children. An open carpeted play space was provided with appropriate soft and hard toys, books, playpens, and changing tables. The fathers were told that the time could be spent in any way they chose to be with their child.

All eight fathers signed up for this activity after seeing an advertisement in the local newspaper describing this ten-week play and talk group for fathers and their youngsters. Five fathers were Caucasian, comprising two Italian-Americans, two Jewish, and one from Nepal, India. Two others were from Guatemala, and one was African-American. The range of socioeconomic backgrounds was diverse: several men had master's degrees and were professionals, one was a solicitor, another a long-distance lorry driver. There was also a car mechanic, a landscaper, a high-school teacher, and a social worker.

The second part of the morning consisted of a ninety-minute fathers' discussion group with me as the leader. Three male baby-sitters were available for childcare in the same room as the fathers' discussion group. The children played within twenty feet of the discussion group and thus had immediate access to their fathers as needed. The fathers could excuse themselves, attend to their child, and return to the ongoing group discussion. The mobile children could make contact with their fathers and then return to play with the other children and the childcare staff. Within four weeks, the children and fathers had settled down into separate spaces in the room, allowing for more continuity of the fathers' group discussion.

The most significant feature of the "Play and Talk Father's Group" was the proximity of *men with other men* enjoying the experience of caring and playing with their children. The men took to each other within the first hour, at first assisting each other in small ways, such as passing a diaper along, or soothing another child, or handing a toy. As the men played with their children, a playful banter began among the men and between the children in the shared space. I expected that men might try to create a separate group activity consisting of the older children, but that did not happen.

Each father was content to be with his own child and appeared to savour the facility and time to be with the children. I observed that the fathers were motivated to demonstrate how capable they were in the eyes of the other men. At first, in the large and new setting, the soothing of children was the first emotional challenge as, in the adjustment period, the children's different ages and temperaments required some time and patience. I noticed how the men observed each other's approaches to the children, later occasionally emulating one another without comment. There was a quiet rubbing-off of the fathers' different holding styles, preferred cuddling, examples of more verbal, or less verbal, approaches, and play choices; these provided a rich variety of parenting styles for the men to observe and try out for themselves.

During the discussion periods, many important themes emerged. As the facilitator, my role was to offer a simple beginning to the group by enquiring about what it was like for fathers to parent their babies and young children. I referred to the play hour to ask what it was like being with each other and the other fathers' children. At another time, I asked if we could discuss how they learnt to parent. A few concerns emerged: several stated their wives were the main source of information and direction. As this theme evolved, fathers indicated they often felt they were not allowed enough time alone with their baby, especially when the mother-in-law was present. At first the men said they got a break when in-laws were involved, but after a while resentment was expressed in the group. Other fathers encouraged a more assertive approach. It was felt that men were too often considered baby-sitters, rather than parents.

As for their styles of parenting, one father brought in how he and his wife differed in parenting styles. The fathers described how some of their wives appeared to feel compromised if their husbands were able to give a good account of the baby's mood, or needs, or describe a good experience the child had with them; this was felt as competitive, especially when discussions took place in front of in-laws. It was as if the women felt they had to demonstrate to their own mothers a total competence, so that when the husband participated with good instincts, or could soothe the baby better in a situation, differences in parenting approaches created conflict between the parents.

The fathers also supported each other's feelings of sadness when they were away on business. The long-distance lorry driver described how he really missed his baby and tears were shed in this poignant discussion of missing the babies. It took a while for the men to realise it was "manly" to miss one's child.

The following story gives an example of how the men thought about their parenting.

> Father took sixteen-month-old Jimmy in the pram for a stroll. Mother, for reasons we might conjecture, looked out of the window for a peep. The carriage sped by mother. There was a shrieking, ecstatic child holding on to the sides of the pram with no father in sight. Of course, the child was strapped in the pram. A few feet behind the pram ran father, laughing as loudly as his little son, Jimmy. This, the men concluded, was how fathers take a walk with their child.

As the fathers became bonded and mutually trusting of each other, I began to receive phone calls from several of the wives enquiring if they could attend the men's group. I would ask about their interest and was surprised to hear that the husbands were becoming more assertive at home and owning their input into the child's care. They seemed to experience more enjoyment in their parenting. Several of the wives were feeling both impressed and somewhat less in charge of the parenting.

When I brought these comments into the group, the men wanted to complete their fathers' group experience without their wives present. The men did recognise that at first the wives felt the group idea was great, since they could get a break from children. Now that the husbands had returned home with ideas, confidence, and assertiveness, the wives experienced some anxiety about the parents' changing psychological identities and roles. Some roles previously held solely by the mothers were now being shared by the fathers. Parenting knowledge had previously been the domain of the wives. The husbands were expecting more acceptance in their parenting roles and were prepared to earn this acceptance. There had to be a reworking of the unexpected changes in the parenting system to make room for the men's desire to take on enhanced roles as parents.

To summarise the experience, the men's group and their marriages survived very well. In many of the homes there was an integration of the father's changed expectations of family life that promoted a psychological blending of male and female involvement in the parenting. I came to believe that the children were gaining the benefits of affectively attuned fathers all along. The fathers' input needed more visibility because the couple and extended family relationships seemed most stuck in the past divisions of labour. In many families, men have been raised exclusively by women, and that factor might be the most decisive traditional influence on "father-hunger" in men; however, when men try to make a difference in their own babies' lives, they seem destined to fall behind unless two important insights emerge.

First, women and their mothers need to make room for men to learn from their own experience of hands-on parenting.

Second, men need the company of men to support and nurture the earliest emotional connections to their babies and toddlers.

———

CHAPTER TWENTY-THREE

Welcoming and listening while wor
children, parents, and nursery staff

Patrizia Pasquini

I n a time when what we produce and consume in a hurry is often prioritised, this book has
the purpose of acquainting people with the experience of the Tempo Lineare school, whose
aim is to offer a space and time for people to think together over the quality of children's
first experiences and of the arms holding them. From this perspective, parents, staff, and
psychotherapists have wondered what, in the experience of this school, makes family life easier
and what, instead, makes it harder and causes damage to children's growth. We have tried to
reflect upon not only the parent–child relationship and the children's and teachers' group
dynamics, but also upon the whole Roman environment surrounding children. In these years,
all the people taking part in the project have worked hard to become increasingly familiar with
the observation, not only of the child, but also of motherhood, fatherhood, the couple, the
family, and the educational model inside Tempo Lineare.

Tempo Lineare, with its two separate schools, one for 0–3-year-olds and the other for 4–6-
year-olds, helps families to feel less lonely in Rome. For a couple, the birth of a child can sometimes be surrounded by "a heavy fog". How can the "the heavy fog" be ameliorated in order
to preserve the beauty of such an important event as having a child? The answer depends on
the parents' wish to preserve the beauty of infant–parent relationships and their wish is influenced by the experience which they, as children, had with their own parents. My task as the
Director of Tempo Lineare has been to work with the "heavy fog" families would bring me.
Giving space to observing and listening to the experiences involved in having a young child or
being a young child seems to lessen some loneliness within the family. I have also attempted
to be curious about, and to try to ameliorate, the impediments to developing more happiness
within the family.

Tempo Lineare was created with an aim of helping parents to become inquisitive as they
consider how they are in the relationship with their children. The school has the accompanying
aim of supporting the harmonious development of very deep emotions through observing and

ile helping if necessary, mothers and fathers in their encounters with their child. are gives continuity to a learning process and takes children's needs and emotional ent into consideration, but it is also a place where parents can reflect upon their chil- growth. This experience is shared within a Tempo Lineare community that gives life to an otional experience, produces transformations, and creates ties among families. The child's first steps in development take place inside a relationship with the parents. The parents' experience of meeting with other family groups, where being a mother and a father is a source of reflection and sharing, becomes very interesting and crucial for parents' development. In the parents' groups, the parents begin to show their solidarity to each other in their attempt to voice their fears, hopes, thoughts, and recollections of their childhood. This process of getting to know oneself and others enables mothers and fathers to further develop their new parental identity and simultaneously encourages new forms of socialisation within Tempo Lineare parents' group.

Winnicott (1958, p. 29) describes how the capacity to be alone is one of the most important signs of emotional development. Supporting the child's capacity to separate from the mother is an important task in the first years of the child's life. The child can only separate without too much anxiety through having the experience of a reliable, emotionally containing mother who shares her time with her child in a constant but discreet way, and acts in the background without taking away his own initiative. If the child internalises a compassionately containing relationship with his parents, he can later expect this positive experience to be present outside the family and, thus, bear being separate from his parents. The *capacity to be alone*, holding good internal parents, enables individuals to modify their state of loneliness in favour of a state of creative solitude.

Supporting a mother's inner maternality

Welcoming and listening to people is one of my primary activities as the Director of Tempo Lineare. This openness to others will be illustrated through my two meetings with a young mother and her two-month-old child. On the phone, she told me that she was having negative thoughts, sort of "woodworms" eating into her loving maternal feelings. Also, she indicated that she was afraid something might happen to her and her children. Her child could not sleep and overwhelmed her with his continuous crying. She went on to say that she had an urgent need to talk to me and we agreed to meet.

Selina was an attractive, twenty-nine-year-old, slim, not very tall woman, with brown hair, dark blue eyes, regular features, and a beautiful smile. Her baby, Stefano, greatly resembled her. At the beginning of our meeting, she described her "strange thoughts" as being like destructive "woodworms" which frightened her and she feared she could not control them. She said, ". . . one day, when I was nine months pregnant, I became haunted by these thoughts." From her description, it was clear that all the negativity felt as though it arrived from foreign bodies, "the woodworms", outside of her mind, making her feel confused and afraid. These strange thoughts arrived again after Stefano's difficult delivery, and then twice more after his birth. Selina worried that these "woodworms" might cause damage to her child.

When I asked her if she could share her worry with anyone else, she told me she had talked with her husband, who had been unable to reassure her. While she was telling me this, she held her sleeping child tightly in her arms. Immediately afterwards she tried to excuse her husband by saying that he was a weak man who was easily frightened.

Meanwhile, Stefano opened his eyes and looked at me for a moment while keeping very still in her arms. Then he put a finger into his mouth and started to suck it, but shortly afterwards he began to whimper. His mother responded by standing up, finding a dummy, and placing it in his mouth. Stefano calmed down for a few seconds. Shortly afterwards he started to cry again, until his mother put the teat of the bottle to his mouth and fed him. Stefano started to suck in a rhythmic way, while his mother, in a very loving way, looked at him and stroked him. After she began talking about Stefano's birth, his mother paid him much less attention.

She gave a long account of the arduous delivery of Stefano and his difficult breast-feeding, which was ended after a few weeks. Then, all of a sudden, Selina began to talk about a miscarriage she had had six months before this second pregnancy. She was still suffering psychologically from her miscarriage, which had been caused by a rare placenta disease. I suggested that she was describing something really painful that might have made her experience a lot of anxieties. Selina went on to say that for the whole of Stefano's pregnancy she had been wondering whether everything was fine inside her tummy and if her child would be born healthy. I told her that these were frightening thoughts and Selina added, "Especially when you haven't got anybody to whom you can talk."

Later on in the discussion, I remarked that Stefano was healthy. His mother replied, "Yes, he's healthy and beautiful too." While standing facing me, she looked at him cradled in her arms. She continued to look at me fervently while remaining silent for a while.

When I wondered if she might feel like telling me more about her own story, Selina told me that she was the sixth of eight children. She said, "My father died when I was nine and after that I lived in more than ten relatives' and sisters' houses." Her childhood was a life of abuse and privation. Her mother was absorbed in her job, which was necessary to support the family, and she seemed to give insufficient care and protection to Selina. Subsequently, Selina had a difficult and troublesome adolescence. She was still standing opposite me cradling her baby as she told the long narrative of her life. I noticed that she was very anxious and I became aware that I was to feel the weight of all her suffering.

Afterwards, Selina told me about the time when she was an adolescent and met her husband-to-be. He had problems similar to hers, for his father had also died young because of his diabetes. In addition, all her husband's siblings had diabetes and she feared her husband might also get diabetes in the future.

She then went on to describe her current family situation, saying they lived in a very small flat near Tempo Lineare. She was isolated from other mothers and spent her days at home with her children. I asked her, "But what do you think prevents Stefano from sleeping?" while helping her notice that her baby was sleeping in her arms. Selina looked at me and said, "If he isn't in my arms I can't hear him. I'm worried he could cry and I wouldn't hear him. I am afraid he might stop breathing and I won't realise this." I told her that her fear was probably connected to the idea that something could happen to her baby. Selina began to cry and told me that I was perfectly right because she was always thinking he could die, always thinking that if she did not hold him tightly enough and did not protect him, something destructive might happen to him. Stefano woke up. His mother cradled him more firmly. I told her that maybe what made her child wake up and prevented her from sleeping were those negative thoughts, maybe the "woodworms" she had told me about. Selina looked pensive as she heard this.

Before our meeting came to an end, she flashed back to her childhood, saying, "You know, my sisters and I vied with each other to see who would wake up first in the morning. We only had one pair of trainers and the first one who awakened could wear them, while the others had to do without." Then she told me she often thought about all the things she had never had, and that she was sorry when she did not have the money to buy her children the clothes and toys she would like to get them. She described her tiny, dark flat, to which she did not dare to invite her daughter's schoolmates because she was ashamed of it. Her daughter was upset that her mother felt so ashamed that she never picked her up at school. But, mother added, she had taken her daughter to a dance course for a few days and she herself had recently begun attending a spinning course.

At the end of our meeting, I remarked that now she had a pair of trainers to go cycling, that she had her own flat, maybe tiny and dark, but still a flat, and I highlighted this contrast with her past. The woman smiled and kept on going around the room cradling Stefano, who had fallen asleep again. At this moment, I suggested she might lay her child on some cushions placed on the floor. She did so, looked at me, then touched her baby and put a cushion next to him. After a while, Stefano awakened. Selina was on the point of picking him up when I suggested she gave him a dummy so that he could fall asleep again. Stefano spat the dummy out and whimpered. The woman picked him up again and said: "I can't stand him crying" and I replied that when Stefano cried, she got in contact with her own inner crying child. She nodded; then, after a short pause, she told me that talking about these things had made her feel a sense of relief.

As I pondered over the session, I realised that Selina could not keep hold of the positive things in her life. What she described in our first meeting was a world of darkness. At least spinning was something lively in her life. Selina was lonely and disappointed because she did not have anybody close to her who could give meaning to her experiences. She could not imagine trusting someone to understand her, but then, during our meeting, there seemed to be a gleam of hope and confidence in me: she looked into my eyes and shared her feelings with me. I tried to welcome and contain what she had told me and to help her to understand what was happening to her in this particular moment of being a mother after having had a miscarriage.

This first meeting presents a good example of how even a few meetings can provide understanding of buried feelings and mark the onset of change. In the second meeting, the change in Selina was heralded by her holding Stefano inside a baby-carrier and not in her arms. During this conversation, she informed me she had not had any "bad thoughts" since our first meeting. While she talked, Stefano, while sucking his dummy occasionally, slept quietly for a long time. Selina looked at her baby from time to time and smiled at me as she saw his peaceful repose. I responded, saying that Stefano seemed to be sleeping well and that she seemed to be able to let him sleep.

Selina explained that after our meeting her baby had slept quietly, six hours a night without ever waking up. She said, "Now he never wakes up crying any more . . . maybe my thoughts about death had made him wake up." This second meeting consisted of Selina elaborating on her anxieties and fears linked with maltreatment as a depressed and impotent child. These feelings still lingered, and she was worried about her own child experiencing the same fate.

When Stefano awakened, Selina emphasised how she was getting on well with him, talking to him a lot, and she was pleased that he responded to her. This left her feeling she had a lot of fun with him. I suggested that she had understood and been able to meet Stefano's needs and now she need not be so terribly worried about looking after him. While Selina and I were looking at Stefano, sitting in his mother's arms, he began looking around while pausing now and again to focus either on me or the lamp next to me. Selina subsequently bottle-fed her baby and kept on looking at him, talking to him, and stroking him, even when she was talking to me. This was a marked contrast to last time, when she had seemed to forget about him. She told me that Stefano was still sleeping in her bed, but now she did not hold him as tightly as she had done before.

When Stefano finished drinking his milk he smiled, looked at me, his mother, and sometimes around the room. Now mother was more capable of keeping in contact with her child, who was facing her, and he was a more communicative baby. Feeling less anxious about bad things happening, Selina was able to respond to her baby's needs and to let him sleep. With my supportive, welcoming presence there had arisen a new positive emotional atmosphere between mother and child; mother, assisted by my compassion, had begun to be a protective, responsive parent who did not feel compelled to project her painful past on her baby.

"Ghosts in the nursery" (Fraiberg, Adelson, & Shapiro, 1975) suggests that a mother's imaginings and recollections may contribute to a baby's possible difficulties. The authors indicate that parents' unremembered thoughts about their past experiences might revisit them as unconscious "ghosts". These "unexpected visitors" are more likely to arrive near the time of the child's birth. If bonds of love and protection for the child are created between the parents and their baby, then these unwelcome ghosts can be sent away from the place in the parents' minds where a child plays and sleeps. These ghosts, coming from past generations, could damage a child's life in the present. By engaging in a thoughtful dialogue with parents, they are helped to realise the important role played by these internalised past experiences, now in their current unconscious, which are influencing their present family interactions. In lending some thought to some of these internalised experiences, parents can become protective parents who do not repeat their painful past relationships.

One sees that Selina found it difficult to acknowledge her underlying feelings and face her external reality. The birth of Stefano had awakened a lot strong feelings and with them came the ghosts of the total childhood chaos, abuse, and trauma from which she had been unprotected by her parents. Selina felt at a loss, not knowing what to do with these experiences that arose within her.

Our conversations enabled her to express her sense of inadequacy and her ensuing sense of threat when her child cried. She could not stand his cries. After our first face-to-face meeting, Selina was able to feel more in contact with her child and she began to find the courage to look at and comprehend her own feelings and behaviour. Selina's ghosts concerning death, having found a place to be examined within a meaningful dialogue about them, have moved to the background, so they do not prevent her from being an adequate mother. Feeling welcomed, listened to, and understood by me, Selina gradually was able to be present for Stefano in a very different way.

Facilitating thoughtfulness in the staff and parents' groups

I would like to go on reflecting how we can help parents and teachers to develop their capacity hold emotional experiences and lend thought to them in such a way as to prevent or modulate suffering. It takes a considerable amount of time to gain the confidence of the parents and teachers. The teachers feel themselves to be the recipient of powerful projections of feelings issuing from both the children and the parents. They erect defences of denial and blame which can interfere with the teachers' ability to think clearly. For this reason, not only do I have parents' groups, but I also spend a considerable time in a work discussion group with the teachers. I also need to be supervised by a mentoring psychotherapist to understand my experience as Director of Tempo Lineare, whose task it is to create a climate of containment of teachers, parents, and children's anxieties.

Facilitating acceptance and understanding of the projections reverberating within the relationships between parents, teachers, and children promotes a state of reflectiveness and increased maturity in facilitating the children's upbringing (Fonagy & Target, 1996). The work discussion group prompting reflection enables the teachers to find relief from anxiety as they acknowledge their own feelings of inadequacy, but also understand that the parents may be projecting into them unbearable feelings of parental failure when the parent critically says such things as: "You don't understand me."

The work discussion reflective group is designed to enable the teachers to tolerate these unbearable feelings and identify with what it feels like, also as a parent, to look after a young child with anxieties and unmodulated feelings. Providing a regular reflective space for careful observation and understanding of processes of interaction within Tempo Lineare potentially assists the staff group to become less defensive, more welcoming, receptive, and curious about what is taking place in the various interactions within the groups of older and much younger people within the institution.

These words of Michael Rustin's (1989, p. 66) support our way of working:

> The observers can only understand the central relationship between mother and baby if they are able to experience some of the impact of the baby on mother. Various processes of identification are involved in this, from feeling anxiety and distress in response to the baby, to identification with the mother's different responses to the baby's needs. Being able to remain receptive and calm while with a baby and mother, so as to be able to take in their different states of mind, is the key to this. Descriptions of a mother–baby couple's delight in each other, of a baby's distress, or a mother's emotional withdrawal, though they may seem straightforward are only possible because the observers were able to take in feelings and subsequently remember and reflect on them. The observer has to be a receptive register of emotions in others and herself.

In the following example, the reader will notice the teachers' awareness of very intense individual and group feelings, activated by their relationships with others within Tempo Lineare.

Irma, twenty months old, attends Tempo Lineare with her mother and, from time to time, with her father. During one of our meetings, Irma's mother told me about her great difficulty in weaning her daughter, who is still breast-fed. Irma is a thin, pale little girl who rarely smiles and, when she does, her smile is as sad as her eyes. Sometimes, she moves slowly around the room, but most of the time she clings to her mother and reads books. Irma plays very little and she does not show much curiosity for what the other children in the group are doing. Eyes lowered, her mother often sits next to her. Here is an observation.

Irma, aged twenty months

Irma's mother, after she had entered the room, told me she had stopped putting her daughter to sleep by breast-feeding her. Later, at snack time, Irma started asking her mother for a biscuit: at that moment the assistant standing beside the mothers and children was offering milk, biscuits, and fruit juices. Irma, after placing the first biscuit on her napkin, went on asking for more biscuits until she had four of them, but she did not eat them. The assistant did not say anything, either to the mother or to the child, and let the mother deal with her child's requests.

I said something only when Irma stood up, holding her biscuits in her hand. I told Irma that biscuits had be eaten sitting at the table with the other children and made her observe that she was holding four biscuits in her hand but she was not eating any of them. Irma started complaining. Her mother stayed still even when her child tried to make her mother her ally. I told Irma that her mother could not take decisions on her own in this place for here, together with her mother, there was also me. Irma started complaining even more, pulling her mother's hair and hitting her on her shoulder.

I told her she was angry but there was no reason for it because she had four biscuits. Irma pointed at the biscuit box as if she was telling her mother she wanted some more. Her mother felt uneasy and told her daughter, "Listen to what Patrizia is telling you."

Irma tried to leave with the biscuits she was holding in her hand, but her mother stopped her and pulled the biscuits out of her hand. Irma started yelling, but then she sat down, took her biscuits again, and, without complaining, ate them. Soon after her snack, she approached me, took a toy minibus with six children inside (like the six children of her group in the room), pulled them out of the minibus and gave them to me. The mother observed her daughter and smiled. I told her that maybe she felt I could hold all her anger, in the same way as I could hold all those children now. This game was repeated several times by Irma during that morning.

While we were thinking about this particular moment of the morning, my assistant said, "I didn't even see the little girl had had four biscuits from her mother . . . If I think about it, I feel I couldn't have intervened because I couldn't stand Irma's complaint." I realised that Irma was experiencing the withdrawal of her mother's breast-feeding at night and she was protesting. I also noted how difficult it is for us to stand the child's anger and hatred when these feelings overcome his love. On the other hand, acknowledging the existence of such feelings and bearing, rather than placating, a child's anger is extremely important in our roles of teachers and parents. If we accept a child's anger, we show the child it is safe to have strong feelings and we indicate that we can reflect upon them together and feel close in our comprehension of what it feels like to be the child.

Parents often need a person ready to help them, in the same way as a child needs an adult ready to welcome his emotions, to observe and bear them, so enabling his growth and development. In the same way, a teaching assistant needs a supportive teacher to facilitate thoughtfulness and reflection upon his actions.

Stern's work (1995) highlights the importance of the parents' representations of their child and of themselves as parents: he suggested that one needs to observe the baby in the mother's arms, but also the baby as represented in the mind of the mother. Likewise, it is important to understand the baby as represented in the mind of the father. Stern (1995) also emphasises the importance of not only what the parents consciously feel, but also to take into consideration their phantasies, their fears, hopes for their child's future, and their dreams. More precisely, starting from the experience of the child–parent interaction, to arrive at the personal experience of "being with" another person. This interaction experience can be real or imagined, but in any case it is an interaction that exists since it happens to the self when it is in relation with others.

Allowing spontaneous interaction between inner an outer experiences

Getting in touch with another human being is the basis of my everyday work. I aim to establish an intimate contact with each of the participants while I am listening to, and observing, the child–parent relationship. Such a profound rapport enables the creation of significant ties between the parents and me, which support their maternal and paternal functions that are most helpful to the child's emotional and intellectual growth.

I am grateful to Professor Paolo Perrotti, who for many years supported me in my way taking care of other human beings. His words perpetually remain with me to support spontaneous fluidity between a person's inner and outer experiences:

> I find myself in my house by the sea, a house I bought when my children were little. I managed to come here in a moment when none of them were here. I did not want to see them grown up: I came here to see them little again. And so I saw them again and I played with them. This morning I have identified with a father of two children, a little girl and a little boy, who were playing with him and building a sand castle. I followed their movements; I suggested, inside me, some building devices.

> I stroked the Adriatic sand, so subtle, soft and motherly, the sand of my childhood . . .

> The sand has brought my mother's image back. . . . I see her again moving on the beach. . . . She dries me when I get out of the water, she presses a little hat down on my head to protect me from the sun; she lays a cloth on a table taken to the beach and places a smoking soup tureen on it at lunchtime.

> In front of me, when I was child, there was the sea, as calm as it is now: quiet, almost still. . . . A white sail on the horizon, always the same, as if it was fixed on the blue sea board, a typical example of all the sails from the Adriatic, of all the colourful sails from the Elba island. (Perrotti, 1997, p. 151)

References

Fonagy, P., & Target, M. (1996). Playing with reality: I. Theory of mind and the normal development of psychic reality. *International Journal of Psychoanalysis*, 77: 217–233.

Fraiberg, S., Adelson, E., & Shapiro, V. (1975). Ghosts in the nursery. *Journal of American Academy of Child Psychiatry*, 14(3): 387–421.

Perrotti, P. (1997). Improvvisamente . . . in un nero agosto. *Psiche*, 5(1): 147–154.

Rustin, M. J. (1989). Observing infants: reflection on methods. In: L. Miller, M. E. Rustin, M. J. Rustin, & J. Shuttleworth (Eds.) (1989). *Closely Observed Infants* (pp. 52–79). London: Duckworth.

Stern, D. (1995). *The Motherhood Constellation*. London: Karnac.

Winnicott, D. W. (1958). The capacity to be alone. In: *The Maturational Processes and the Facilitating Environment: Studies in the Theory of Emotional Development* (pp. 29–36). New York: International Universities Press.

PART VI

PARENTS CREATING AND COLLABORATING

CHAPTER TWENTY-FOUR

The parents speaking

The ABC of emotions, by Alberto, Francesca's father

My daughter left Tempo Lineare two years ago and has been going to elementary school. I am part of the Tempo Lineare Parents Association, formed by parents whose children have left Tempo Lineare. We wanted to continue some of the thinking about the whole of our children, their hearts, their souls, their intellect, their creativity, and the whole of our family, as we had done in Tempo Lineare. In the elementary school during the past two years, music, painting, and drawing are the only moments of relaxation and fun, more or less time-fillers when the children take a break from their serious schoolwork or some teacher is absent, or there is a holiday such as Christmas or Easter. Then the instruction is: "Now make a nice drawing", or "Let us sing this song".

My daughter and her peers had grown up in the experience of Tempo Lineare along with all the tools, all the necessary acts and sacred places of creativity: techniques, measurements, sounds, silences, colours, love of materials, disciplined reading of the world and of emotions. If these children in primary school do not have enough of an alphabet for emotions or thoughts, then they will not have the ability to talk and communicate with themselves. This might last for ten years, because, paradoxically, only at around 16–18 years old will a very few fortunate ones have language writing fluent enough that they will be able to find the road back to their true selves. Music, painting, and writing are, above all, exercises in silence and listening.

In a certain sense, in primary school, my daughter is learning to become illiterate with regard to her feelings, although fluent in speaking and writing skills about academic subjects learnt at school. It is not a coincidence that, as teenagers, they throw themselves into music so desperately and happily. Obviously, without fluency in language and without art, writing itself loses much of its magic and creativity.

In looking back at the experience of Tempo Lineare, I realise that Patrizia Pasquini, the Director, gave central importance to all the elements: in fact, the experience, the discipline of shapes and colours, of varied sounds and signs, the incredible alphabet of the soul, much of which the confining and rote learning of primary school will erase. For example, in the second year, my daughter was asked to illustrate a story of an imprisoned little girl who escapes and runs for freedom. My daughter drew the girl with red hair, a projection of herself with red hair. Fabulous! Fabulous and moving, if it were not for the fact that the teacher had written on the side of the picture an admonition that the protagonist of the story had black hair. I imagine that my daughter identified with the protagonist of the story and "her error" was an illumination for me and for her, a precious indication *to follow her* in *her* escape.

I then realised that in primary school, after her time in Tempo Lineare, my daughter did not love colours any more in the way she had previously. In the two years of primary school, the only true instruction in art she received was to colour by filling in the lines of an already drawn figure. At the moment, my daughter writes like a girl in the second year of school and does not have much capacity to have a verbal dialogue with herself. Her emotions are not assuming more shape and visibility. They are not becoming idols and myths, as on the walls of a cave: she draws with that very sickly mimetic ability and show of skill of the best in the class, making trees, houses, and children who are nothing else but trees, houses, and children. It feels bleak to me, as if I have a mute child in front of me. She also does not have the grammar of music with which she can resolve and transform into sound in flight and into illusions of life.

Sometimes, I get the distinct impression that our responsibility as adults and educators is to ensure the incommunicability of youth, the anguist of being illiterate, of finding oneself desperately unable to transform, as the Italian poet, Ungaretti, in *L'allegria*, would say, the days and the pains into singing and knowledge. He spoke of poems and of songs as a *buried harbour* (1931, p. 23).

A few days ago, my daughter was a little sad, or at least it seemed so to me, not that I, as an adult, am more literate than she. I approached her and asked her what was wrong: "What is it my love?" I tried to sing a song, wondering if she did not want to tell me. Then, very dramatically, I realised that she did not know *what* to tell me. First, does she not know what to say even to herself? I gave her a piece of paper and a pencil, saying that she could try to make a drawing and I left her at the table alone.

A little later she came to me and asked, "What must I draw?" as if to say, "What do you want, what do you desire?" She suggested to me that she had learnt, from a friend at school, how to draw a cat from behind. I told her that was fine: "Yes, go for the cat seen from behind", hoping that through a sign, a slip, a smudged colour, perhaps she would transform the cat into a message in a bottle, or into a self-portrait, or into scribbled poetry escaping from the deep.

I received my daughter's drawing of the back view of a cat: to the right and to the left of his profile came two fountains of tears from his eyes. When she gave me her drawing, we looked at the paper and burst out laughing as I exclaimed, "But this cat is despairing!" "Yes", she was saying, and both of us dreamily bent over the paper to contemplate the sorrow that we were not able to understand, but that we could at least look at.

Becoming a mother, by Eleonora, Helena's mother

I have been waiting for almost ten years to become a mother and I have been "officially" Helena's mother for three and a half months. Now I can say that, despite my wish to be a mother, it is not as automatic and natural as we expected and the maternal instinct is not so instinctive. I do not know whether or not that is linked with my being an adoptive mother, but I have become aware that creating a relationship with our child is as difficult as beginning a lasting relationship with a friend or partner. A mothering instinct may exist, but automatic relationships do not.

We adopted Helena in Krakow. About ten days after our return, just when I was running out of energy to improve my relationship with Helena, Mrs Durham, the psychologist from the family guidance centre supporting us, said, "It will be a useful experience for both of you to visit Tempo Lineare." Mrs Durham thought Tempo Lineare offered Helena a good opportunity to become part of a new social environment with other children, experiencing a different reality from the one in which she had been living. I believe Mrs Durham also thought, "Go and see how other mothers experience being a mother." For three years, Helena and I have participated in the activities of the group of 4–6-year-old children within Tempo Lineare.

After being at Tempo Lineare for two and a half months, Helena had become integrated within the group and was enthusiastic about the "glue", "Paticha" (the Director), and the "babies". By this, I mean that this group experience seemed to hold Helena together psychologically and she looked forward to being at Tempo Lineare. On the other hand, I experienced rather different feelings. It is true that I was pleased because Helena was happy. Also, this school was important to me, for it helped me understand some of Helena's behaviour and particularly her play. The problem in experiencing the pleasure of being a mother was that I found that I was comparing myself with other women who had become mothers.

I made comparisons through observing other mothers' behaviours, attitudes, and gestures towards their children. The result of my observing such good mothering and my keeping their relationships with their children in my mind sometimes depresses me and makes me doubt if I can be a good mother for Helena. When I see a mother's attitude that is different from mine in a particular situation, I wonder, "Is it me who is wrong?" Despite this difficulty of comparing myself to other mothers, I keep on going to Tempo Lineare. It is a long and difficult journey I take in trying to become the best mother I can be with my adopted child Helena. Who knows if I can put a stop to my insecurities?

Going to school with a big tummy, by Maria, Jacobo and Ricky's mother

I heard about Tempo Lineare a year ago from a friend of mine. She had already been attending this school with her children. Unfortunately, it was not immediately possible to enrol our child at Tempo Lineare because there was no place available at the time. I agreed to Patrizia, the Director's, suggestion that while I was waiting I could take part in a weekly afternoon group for pregnant mothers. These meetings provided an unexpected opportunity to consider some aspects of the relationship between my mother and me. As the meetings progressed, I discovered that I could release and think about some of my anger and resentment towards my mother. She had never helped in looking after my children as much as I had expected and deeply desired. This experience in the mothers' group taught me how to accept my mother as she was, with all her limitations and her own difficulties. I hope that developing this understanding will help me to recognise my own difficulties in mothering my children.

After I attended the group for pregnant mothers, we enrolled Jacopo in Tempo Lineare and my younger child, Ricky, was born. I received great support from Tempo Lineare when my younger child was hospitalised at the age of three months. It was a really hard time for my husband and me. Even if my little baby recovered very soon from his physical problems, we were psychologically overwhelmed and required a lot of emotional support and affection. Thanks to the sensitivity, competence, and reliability of Patrizia's thoughtful conversations with us as a couple, we were greatly supported to re-engage with life-enhancing ways of being with our children and stop dwelling on our anxieties connected with this sad and painful experience of our son Ricky's hospitalisation.

It was not just Patrizia's help which was important though; it has been extremely helpful to be able to discuss with parents how to deal with both big and little everyday problems in raising a family. Thanks to these parents' formal and informal group discussions about children's upbringing, my husband and I had the chance to understand and work through problems concerning certain events that had happened to us as children. We also had the opportunity to learn to observe our children's behaviour, to be more receptive to their feelings, and to understand more fully some aspects of our children's personalities and behaviours.

My relationship with Tempo Lineare has also been overshadowed by some difficult feelings. I often felt a sort of resistance to attending the school twice a week. I somehow feared that I would be judged badly with regard to my ability to be a good mother. At times, I tended to hide in a corner and isolate myself from the other parents. Thanks to Patrizia, the Director, who has always been very attentive, but also discreet, I have been encouraged to mix more with the parents and appreciate the value of having a social relationship with them. I realise that both I and our children gained many advantages from my being an integrated member of the parents' group.

Becoming a father, by Michele, Susanna's father

Being a father has been for me a perpetual meandering between intertwined joys and fears, achievements and shortcomings, pressure and defences, temptations and escapes. It has been everything I imagined and, at the same time, everything I feared it would be. It has also been the source of discovery, mystery, surprise, and disorientation. Is there a contradiction in all of this? Yes. But I believe that in this subject of fatherhood contradiction is quite normal. That incoherence is part of the framework and skeleton of the relationship with one's children. With the birth of my first child, who was intensely desired, I immediately experienced a sense of disbelief, a sense of the incapacity to consciously live with such an extraordinary novelty in my life. The pilgrimage of two months back and forth to a "plastic box", the incubator, where my baby Susannah "resided" with determination, covered in needles and tubes, has certainly contributed to this slow awakening of fatherhood. I really struggled to feel my part in this period when she was in intensive care in the incubator. For many days and weeks, caresses were the only material element I could share with my daughter. For this reason, my imagination consisted only of these daily caresses.

Immediately afterwards, when Susannah left hospital, the "full immersion" period set in, day and night exclusively living to meet her needs. My time with her went from almost nothing during the first many days in hospital to the totality of the first weeks when she was at home. A real shock! In any case, it was something very different in my life. It did not feel either ordinary or normal.

During the first months of my initiation into fatherhood, I have been on a roller-coaster ride of emotions, conscious of both the beauty of life and the fear of my baby's death, feelings that made this experience of being father to my daughter very special. I do not know if what I feel is out of the ordinary, but it certainly feels different from what I have frequently heard other fathers describing. Over time, my role as a father has stabilised. In all honesty, I could not say if it has stabilised in the best possible way, but certainly life felt as a father and husband had a certain rhythm.

However, this did not last very long, for after little more than a year there has been another earthquake! The arrival of the second child!! Here, everything has been much more simple on the material level, but incredibly more difficult on the psychological one. Right from the start I had a true reaction of rejection. I did not feel ready yet to change my life even more in order to release the time and energy a newborn baby would inevitably require. On top of that, I did not yet want to share my time with another child besides my daughter.

It has been very tough. It has been almost impossible to escape the self-blame I inflicted upon myself regarding my negative reactions towards a new baby arriving, a situation that generally is considered to be a "wonderful" one. Even during my wife's pregnancy a tough battle ensued between me and my son: I who "kept him at due distance" and he who inevitably entered my life. For a very long time I had a horrible vision of myself as a beast. I frequently punished my own consciousness, blaming myself for the negative feelings that were spontaneously arising within me.

Painful weeks and months passed. They were filled with my trying to reason with myself about the matter of a second baby, but in the end I found myself overwhelmed und drowned in a sea of violent contradictions.

Today, my son has conquered me completely: he has won hands down! I have always thought that a good parent is essentially one who finds within himself satisfaction and happiness which could then be passed on to the children. Basically, the battle was obviously between meeting the needs of my children, my wife, and myself. To find the right balance between myself and my children was not simply an issue regarding the *quantity of time* spent with each child; it was, rather, an issue regarding the *quality of the time* spent together. The very moment I discovered this extraordinary truth, this essential point of equilibrium, right in that moment my inadequateness started to take shape and lasted for months. There remains a scar from a period gone by in which I was not adequately present for my children … a period that will never return and that therefore represents an outright failure. I do not think that I have been much different from other parents. However, I believe that the achievement of a certain consciousness could have led me to different ways of behaving, to very different choices and feelings.

It is not worth describing what has been missed, especially since what a father is capable of withholding from his child is directly proportional to what that very child is incapable of realising from his or her own potential. Of course, the primary remorse is that I have been distracted, that I have missed a lot of the small moments of my children's experiences that form part of their lives. Until recently, these shortcomings have certainly made my fatherhood absolutely unsatisfactory, unenjoyable even.

Actually, though, fatherhood is not an expression of an activity limited in time; therefore, it is certainly possible to feel a new current of emotions about this experience. What I now understand is that it is certainly not possible for anyone to draw a definite conclusion about what it is to be a father, for the simple reason that, quite differently from many other aspects about our being, fatherhood is an experience subject to radical changes, improvements, erosions, losses, and recoveries across our entire life span. I am saying this because now I am in a quite different situation emotionally in relation to my fatherhood. Even if I have been shaken by difficult and sometimes unhelpful choices regarding how to be as a father, I am actually living my role as a father with great pride and depth. I feel, perceive, and am subject to a much deeper relationship within the mutual exchange of feelings between the children and myself. This is also the result and the cause of some profound changes in my life, but undoubtedly it represents a new equilibrium on which my children, by being who they are with their love, their needs, and their personalities, have imposed the essential parameters necessary for being a good father without much ado, but with great determination instead.

Today, as opposed to yesterday, being a father is not only a consciousness, but a reality that occupies and determines all of my choices, that is continuously measured against my life, altering quite frequently the way I spend my time and the way I act as a father. I do not know why this is happening today and not yesterday. I only know that today it could not be any different, just as it seemed impossible yesterday to accept that somebody, whoever that might have been, could really have had such a great influence on my decisions and on my time. Today I *really am a father*, less present in terms of time, but much more *inside* the days, the decisions, and the lives of my children.

It has not been just anyone inviting me to write down these thoughts, but the very person to whom I have given both my children in a wicker basket, asking her to help me during the times when I felt I could not make it or I just would not understand. Given that this person has the great gift of having brightened the faces of my children with a splendid smile, while I have seen so many tired faces in the expressions of other children that did not have the good fortune to meet her, and given that this woman is evidently endowed with a trace of "lucid folly"—all of us writing such words owe her a lot. This person is Patrizia Pasquini the Director of Tempo Lineare.

How to say thank you? Thankfulness towards a person, Patrizia Pasquini, the Director, and to Tempo Lineare for teachers, parents, and children working together, which has turned into much more than that, into a project well under way, towards a reality that will always be assured of our fidelity and recognition. In the end, what every one of us would actually want for our children is that they could have a "Tempo Lineare" ("linear time"): a linear life, a linear future!

The answer, by Rosa, Bernardo's mother

My life changed forever on the tenth of March, the day I discovered I was expecting a baby. After a first moment of bewilderment, fear, and joy all mixed together, I took my decision: I was keeping the baby. "Heavens, I thought, I am so young to be a mother." But on the whole I did not regret my condition; on the contrary, I exhibited my belly with ease, and I did not feel at all embarrassed going around with a naked tummy.

Unlike what some parents-to-be imagine, I considered the period of my pregnancy as a really good one. I felt perfectly at ease in my body and in my mind. Expecting a baby was the most natural and beautiful experience of all my life. I was not worried; I was relaxed and happy. At last, thanks to my son, I had succeeded in slowly healing a very painful wound.

To be more explicit, I was born and then forsaken by my birth mother when I was only two months old. Having been forsaken by my original mother branded me forever. The fear of being forsaken is always inside me. Now that I have grown up, this fear has been reduced considerably, but I feel somehow that it will never completely disappear. During most of my twenty-three years of life I have tried in every way to find an answer to this question: "How can a mother forsake her child?" For a long time I have been brooding over a feeling of primeval rage against my birth mother, pouring it out on my adoptive mother. Notwithstanding my boundless love for my adoptive mother, it was as if she, too, had to pay for my abandonment by my birth mother and father.

What answer could there be for my question about how a mother could abandon her child? I found none, especially as I saw how much love came from my adoptive parents and with what sweetness and patience they were trying to heal my wound. Only now that I, too, am a mother have I found an answer to my question and discovered some peace inside. I can realise now that it is because a mother loves her child more than herself that she sometimes is compelled to make so cruel and painful a choice as that of leaving her child to someone who can mother the child better than she can. As for me, I am sure of one thing: I shall never leave my son.

Returning to the story of my becoming a mother, the time of giving birth to my son was slowly approaching. At last, on the second of December, Bernardo was born: he was not as I had imagined him, for he was much more beautiful. Spontaneously, I became a mother in every way. I think that being a young mother is great fun; one has a little more spontaneity that makes life's tasks less burdensome; perhaps a young mother cares less about the minutiae of daily life than an older mother.

Of course, my life was not all roses, living as a young single woman without the security of living with a partner or being married. It was not easy to reconcile the demands of my university studies and social life with meeting the baby's needs to have a good life. Also it was not easy to maintain all my previous friendships, and neither was it easy to grow up and suddenly face so many responsibilities for another being's life. I had to transform my identity in a very short time; I had to grow up so quickly compared with the many years it usually takes young people to find their feet as adults. Sometimes, I feel confused, due to the overlapping of my roles: I am still a daughter, living at home with my parents, but I am a mother, too; I am a mother but yet still a daughter. Am I both? How am I to behave?

Thanks to the help of Tempo Lineare's staff, I am developing a clearer and more responsible self. I can remember very well the first time I visited the nursery. It was summer; I was so favourably impressed that I can even remember how I was dressed. Patrizia, the Director, showed me the schoolrooms for the children and for the parents. She immediately appealed to me because she seemed a very warm and nice woman. She often smiled and at times she was humorous. Sometimes I laughed as I saw her with all those children crowded around her like bees sucking honey out from a flower. I thought, if the children find her nice, then she must be a kind person, because people say children have a sort of sixth sense.

When my son, "Bernie", was only a few weeks old, we began to stay in the Tempo Lineare babies' room with the other new mothers. Everything was so calm and relaxing there and very soon Tempo Lineare became a nest for my "Chicco", and for me, too. Inside Tempo Lineare's babies' room I felt I was safe from all the outside confusion. Patrizia, the Director, became a very important person in my life. Her receptivity allowed me to experience her as a sort of container in which my fears could be left. At the same time, she reassured and helped me with precious advice and support to discover ways of understanding and helping my son to develop. Every time I think of her, of "Pizia", as Bernie says, there comes to my mind the image of a great matrioska, a Russian doll with many smaller dolls inside, a teacher containing many emotions, many children, all different but all having the same value.

The second and third months after "Bernie's" birth were the most difficult for me: I really felt alone. "Bernie's" father, in fact, was increasingly less present and weighing heavily upon me were the responsibilities both of a being a mother and of having to contend with the absence of a partner and father for "Bernie". I felt I had to do everything by myself. Luckily, I have a wonderful family with a father, mother, and brother, and for this reason many of my fears and my loneliness have virtually disappeared. Fortunately, I belong to a supportive place like Tempo Lineare. At Tempo Lineare, besides becoming acquainted with other mothers whom I can ask for advice, or with whom I can exchange opinions, I began to share with them a healthy way of listening, observing, thinking, and talking with our children.

Sure enough, by being present frequently with all these teachers and parents, I no longer felt alone! I enjoyed finding a second family at Tempo Lineare. It provided developmental challenges for both me and my son, who is loved and supported by many people, even if he can no longer count on his father to be near him.

Life wins, by Giovanna, Silvia's mother

I am Silvia's mother. Silvia had her first birthday party three months ago. I began to attend nursery with her towards the end of September, a few weeks after her discharge from hospital. Silvia was born before I ended the sixth month of pregnancy, on a fine day at the beginning of spring. I was told that the chances that she could survive and that she could lead a life within the boundaries of "normality" were ten per cent. Immediately after her birth, Silvia was transferred to a neonatal intensive care unit.

When, three days later, I succeed in joining her, I ask the nurses to show me the incubator from a distance. All of a sudden I am afraid to go near her; I want to approach slowly, to have even a short time to get accustomed to what awaits me. As I see her, the shock is terrible: nothing in that little being lying in the incubator makes me think of wellbeing or normality. A long waiting has started. Day after day, slowly but inexorably, the situation is getting worse, many complications, much suffering, always less hope. I am not able to resist seeing that this small life is passing away. Our main contact is my little songs and lullabies to her, but now my voice fails me. Anguish is overwhelming me. The doctors have always encouraged me to touch her, to speak to her, saying that parents' nearness is a powerful stimulus to the baby to stay alive. But now she is so weak that my caresses on her little arms disturb her precarious equilibrium, the control parameters jump, the alarms ring. It is better not to excite her. I can still reach her with my voice. I must struggle repeatedly with a cynical thought of death. It is the only thought that makes me able to stay near her: I am not in danger, whatever may happen, I will survive anyway, therefore I must act. I sing softly, for her and for me, leaning against the side of the incubator.

I am grateful that I have still the emotional strength to stay with her; with all my might I want to stay with her for it might be my only solace for the future. The head physician sends for me and I must prepare myself for the worst. I bear the brunt of the worrying news I receive from him and I return home. Hours go by, the night passes, and then morning, but the telephone does not ring, the worst is not coming. At this point, having exhausted every outward sign of vitality, all of a sudden Silvia succeeds in breathing by herself! Once again they have tried to extubate her; the oxygen is no longer artificially reaching her lungs, instead she is breathing it from the mask by herself, even though she has little strength.

She gets through the first hours of the new day, she reaches afternoon, overcomes the night, another day begins. And she makes it! Now at last, for the first time, I can lift her out of the incubator and take her in my arms. For the first time I can hold her near my breast. Two months and four days have passed. It has been a time of acute suffering, hot red sensors, ringing alarms, blood samplings, transfusions, tubes, medicines, heart stimulations, and specialists' examinations.

She will still have much to endure, but from that moment on the way is towards life. At last the discharge day comes,: in all, four months have elapsed. I am in heaven! We have been at home for a week now, it is a fine afternoon at the end of summer and we go to a park: my husband plays with Stefano, our first born; I walk up and down the alleys without my feet touching the ground.

I feel like a little girl who has gained from an aunt the privilege of pushing the pram for a few steps with a "real" newborn cousin inside. The experiences I am having belong to the world of my childhood. I feel a bit embarrassed while walking among other people: is one allowed to be so happy?

In a short while, we begin to attend Tempo Lineare. It is the first time I am outside home alone with her, and I am worried. What if something happens? I try to calm down; I repeat to myself that the doctors would not have discharged her if she were in danger. I drive carefully, holding out my finger for her to grasp quietly. I do not know whether it is that she is needing me more or that I am needing to be comforted by the warmth of her body.

At Tempo Lineare, it seems they have been awaiting us all the time. I see smiling faces, cosy and tidy rooms. I hold Silvia in my arms. She is close to my breast; we both are warmly cuddled and attended to by the staff and parents, whom I already know because Stefano is in the older group there.

Silvia is growing up little by little, she looks around and she smiles at the teachers and at the other mothers. She is leaning against the cushions; she is aware, participating, and capable of strong communication. Doctors are optimistic about her motor and cognitive development, even if she is still a child they need "to follow up". And I am happy with what I see. What is more beautiful than her open smiling mouth every time I meet her eyes? I do not ask her for more, it seems to me one cannot and must not ask for more. She has been alone in hospital for months, my daily visit lasted two hours; how was the rest of the day for her? Now it is right to hold her in my arms, to cuddle her, to fill that emptiness.

Once I read a phrase to describe the mark left from these experiences of early detachment from the mother: it is "congenital distress" and it weighs on me like a stone. I am not able to separate from her; I must touch her.

As time goes by, I become aware of being at a crisis point, and the Tempo Lineare staff prompt me to notice this. Exchanges of beaming glances and smiles continue between me and my daughter, but the first steps towards the development of her autonomy are not coming. If I put her on the ground, she cries and stiffens. I cannot resist her appeal; I am holding her in my arms all the time, and this is the classical vicious circle. A feeling of discomfort in me begins and becomes very intense inside the nursery. The experiences I suggest to her are monotonous; there is progression in our relationship. On her birthday, during the little party at the nursery, I feel bad. Silvia has been going to two physiotherapy sessions a week for several months, and these are conducted amidst tears and non-stop wailing. The physiotherapist seems to be in trouble, notwithstanding her unmistakable professional skill, and acknowledges that she has never met with such stubborn resistance to her efforts.

Weariness and uneasiness prompt me to reschedule tasks and I ask my husband to take Silvia, once a week, both to nursery and to the physiotherapist's office. After these changes, a week later, she is not crying any more during physiotherapy, she is becoming interested in toys, she is moving inside the nursery room, and she is crawling away from me, whereas she once used to show signs of moving some steps only in order to reach me!

Since then, we have entered a new phase, but I know I must be aware. There is always something looming up, which will soon be repeated at the next important development stage. What will it be? Anguish, sure enough, but what kind of anguish? I am still not able to say. One thing is clear, though: during all the present school year Silvia never had any illness, except just a few colds, no temperature, no allergies, no intolerances of any kind. Silvia is a really strong little girl.

The little shoe, by Roberto, Marco's father

It's Tuesday morning: a different way to spend time with my son, a time to play all by ourselves. While I walk to Tempo Lineare, I notice that my son, Marco, aged one and a half years, in my arms, is excited. He laughs and utters sounds of surprise, such as "uuuh, uuuh!". I get the impression that he recognises Tempo Lineare and he knows where we are going, even if the school year has just begun. In fact, when I go to Tempo Lineare, I don't feel as if we are going to a school or to a crèche. Rather, I feel as if I am being greeted, with Marco, in a wider project that provides a way of thinking that all of our family considers with pleasure and curiosity.

We climb the stairs leading to the main door; I take Marco's little hand, pressing it to the bell, he pushes, it rings, he looks at me and smiles. We are greeted by Ileana, kind and attentive as usual, and we enter. The chair where Marco usually sits while I undress him is empty, waiting for us to perform what looks like a rite of passage, from the outside to the inside, that we prepare to meet. As I put our bag on the wooden rack, I realise that Marco is wearing only one shoe. "We lost it!" I tell Marco. I am convinced that he took it off in the car and I am certain we will find it there when we go back home. I take Marco's hand and we go into the children's playing room.

Elisa and her mother say hello, and so does Sacha, a "new" child, while playing with wooden blocks. Marco pulls my hand, leading me towards the toy kitchen cabinet, where he begins to open and close the doors. He is surprised to find some red cups inside. Alex joins us on all fours, followed by his mother. He climbs to a standing position and begins to make a clatter with the little pots. Marco looks at him without stopping his play. Alex's mother takes some plastic food from a basket and puts them close to the two children, who keep on touching, manipulating, and exploring the utensils hanging in the play kitchen. Alex crawls away from Marco, who, holding on to the kitchen door, stops, blushes, frowns, and looks at me: he is doing a poo.

This is not the first nappy I have changed, but it is the first time I have changed Marco's nappy at Tempo Lineare. Lying on the changing table, Marco lets me change him without struggling. He sucks on a plastic fish that is a part of the play activity he just interrupted and is going to resume once we go back to the playing room.

At this point, Leon and his mother arrive in the room, while Elisa dances around Marco holding some teddy bears. From time to time she puts them to sleep under a blanket. After a while, Elisa, too, slips under the blanket, pretending to sleep like the teddy bears. Leon smiles, he reaches for Marco and caresses him. Then he looks at me and caresses me too. I greet him warmly; he smiles and gives me a toy car. Marco and Leon, also one and a half years old, take turns handing each other the wooden fire truck for a while, but this shared play doesn't last for long. Almost simultaneously they get up and move towards more solitary activities.

From time to time Marco lets go of my hand and departs to explore new toys and corners of the room. He then turns to look at me, as if he wants to be reassured that I am there, and he begins to play again. After a while he moves toward the soft armchairs that divide the older toddler's room from the babies' room. Marco looks very attracted to the babies' room; he smiles and points. He climbs on an armchair, peeping into the room, and he meets Toni, another child, who is sitting on the border between the two rooms and seems to observe both the newborns and the toddlers.

Marco understands that he cannot get into the babies' room and just when he starts to get nervous, the morning snacks come and he exclaims "din dins!" This is not the first time I have noticed that Marco is the first one to sit and the last to leave the table. He eats everything with pleasure; he sits calmly while I feed him, though he needs to keep a spoon in his hands, too. Lorenzo cries and hints that he wants to get off the chair. The other children are noisy and lively, and Marco looks at them with a biscuit in his hand. He seems to wonder "Why are these children so fussy? Now it's time to eat!"

After the meal, we go to the bathroom to wash our hands, in another ritual marking the time of our morning together, signalling a passage to a new phase. Patrizia arrives and brings music with her. Every time the doorbell rings, Marcos becomes still, while standing and looking at me. I note that he also behaves like this when his nanny comes or in the evening when I get home early from work and his mummy arrives.

While I am thinking about this, Patrizia sits on her usual chair and Marco says "Mummy!" Everyone is "mummy" for Marco: not really everyone, but, rather, "mummy" is his word for adults. Patrizia, the Director, has quickly become one of them and Massimo seems to "feel" something strongly towards her. The music is on, a good rhythm and blues piece, and Marco dances, flexing his knees in rhythm. All the children, amused, dance around the room in an improvised choreography. Marco takes my hand, as he wants to be helped to stand, and again he goes towards the babies' room. He would like to get in and he gets quite agitated knowing he can't do that. Patrizia notices this frustration and takes a toy from the babies' room, handing it to Marco. He sits to examine this new object and quiets down. After a while, Marco asks me to take him up in my arms, he rubs his eyes and touches his hair; I realise he is tired and we say goodbye to the whole group of adults and children.

As I go back to my car, I look down at the ground, hoping that the pavement will give us back the little shoe we lost. We don't find it, neither on the pavement nor in the car, as I had hoped. When we get to our door, I realise that Marco is asleep in my arms. Not yet defeated, I ask the tobacconist, the doorman, and the barman whether by chance they found a little blue shoe. A spontaneous "neighbourhood committee" is born, participating in our dismay about the lost shoe. An old man passing by encourages me: "Why don't you go back all the way? Maybe you'll find it."

I say goodbye to Marco and his nanny and go all the way back to Tempo Lineare. A bit fed up, I park the car, and, as I walk along Via Vespucci, the road to the school, I see, on the edge of a wall, the lost, now newly found, little shoe. The first time I looked for it, I just looked at the ground and for this reason I couldn't find it. I imagine that a benevolent passerby put it on the wall to help me find it. And then I realise that a "third person" has helped me to change perspective, my point of observation, the way I look at things. So I decide to write down this simple morning adventure, to give it further consideration, to fix it. I have the impression that I did not record everything, maybe because what I see is how I see, but I am grateful to Patrizia Pasquini for the passion driving her Tempo Lineare project and because she encouraged me to "see".

"I've been naughty", by Helena, Anna's mother

Anna and I used to call Tempo Lineare "the little school". Anna is my daughter, almost three years old, who was adopted by us when she was twenty days old. We found out about the existence of Tempo Lineare thanks to the advice of the psychologist who followed Anna's period of adaptation into our family. Since we enrolled at Tempo Lineare, I have been able to discover more about my experience as an adoptive mother with its specific and unique differences from being a birth mother. We were thrown into a turmoil of emotions when our baby girl arrived, a child for whom we had waited and wished for so long and so much. Our uncertainty about the best place and way for her to grow up was great. Despite our uncertainty, I must admit that the psychologist's advice to attend Tempo Lineare felt like a sort of "prescription", which annoyed me a little.

Uncertainty about how one is going to parent a child exists for every couple at a child's birth, but this is especially true for an adoptive couple who, at least in my experience, have a continuous need to show that they are worthy of the gift of the child they received. The first pressure, however, was Anna's way of being and my feelings about how I could mother her.

But I soon found out that this choice of what to do for her also concerned what I could do for me: finding a place and time to live and improve my relationship with my daughter together with other children and families in Tempo Lineare. The result of choosing what was right for me as well as what was right for Anna is that Anna is not the only one happy to go to the little school. I am also pleased, as is, I believe, her father. Also, Anna is not the only one who works hard to learn the dynamics of a group, its rules and methods of evolving as a better group. All the parents, including my husband and me, work hard as well and we do so because we perceive our effort is valuable.

So, what is the value of working within Tempo Lineare? I can give one response: learning to look at children with pleasure. I will give some examples: when, one year later, a second adoptive child arrived at the school, everybody noticed an instinctive attraction between the new little girl, Mariella, and Anna, and they started to play together. The teachers and their assistants observed the two girls from their points of view, while I looked at them with the emotions of a mother. I cannot build up any theory about that attraction between the two girls occurring; I can only say that Anna and I think Mariella, the other adopted girl, and her mother, too, experienced an especially close feeling which enriched us.

I also experienced pleasure with Patrizia Pasquini, the Director, who, observing Anna taking a particular interest in playing with dolls and looking after them, found a dolls' house for them. In the second year, there was another particularly appealing experience. The children and parents made special toy boxes together and an individual "special time game" evolved of having the child play with the box filled with toys the child and parents had selected. On the first morning when children played with the special time box, we parents were a bit nervous. After all, it was the first activity our children did while we were not there. When our children came out of school, Anna told me, "I've been a bit naughty." Patrizia and the assistants did not tell me anything about what she meant. Some weeks after, I read an observational report about that particular day: Anna had cut off the puppet-mother's head and she then threw it away. Later, at Patrizia's request, Anna picked up the doll-head and fixed it by spreading it with glue.

I thought the glue might have been intended to glue the doll together, with a reparative motive, but the glue was spread all over, like paint, which is very similarly held in a tube and can be confused with glue. But Anna's confession seemed to me more reparative than the use of glue. Thanks to our relationship and the support we had both received from the little school, Anna was able to show aggression to the mother doll, representing me, and then to look for complicity with me for what she had done. Initially, it seems very difficult within the closed family environment keep one's mind open to the meaning of one's child's play while observing it. It is necessary to have the support of a thoughtful group of teachers and parents such as those working together in Tempo Lineare. I say this despite all the social relations we can have as a couple, despite all the relatives and friends who can enrich our daily life.

In conclusion, I want to say, Tempo Lineare is a good school, but only for parents who have lots of spare time. I have a demanding job, and my husband does, too. If I had been told some years ago that I would have to plan my life with three mornings off, I would have categorically stated that this was impossible. After a while, I thought I could do it by working hard during the hours I was at work. The result was that I did so and sometimes without any great effort. I somehow learnt to face the necessity of putting a limit on the invasion of my job engagements on my necessary parental duties to my child, Anna.

Growing together, by Annabelle, Asia's mother

I am the mother of a child, Asia, whom my husband and I adopted when she was aged three, from a Cambodian orphanage. I would like to describe the experience of a child who has left family, orphanage, and country of origin to find herself in an Italian family in which neither she nor we had any shared words. The trauma of being without familiar care-givers and a familiar language was greeted with many physical expressions of distress. I shall share our experience of finding a way of understanding Asia's non-verbal communication with us and helping her develop a loving, dependent bond with us, her parents. Developing a shared Italian language for communication was just one part of deepening our relationship with one another. Her drawing allowed us to experience the richness of her emotional life, which would take a longer time for even a child much older than Asia.

Brief history

We found Asia living in a group of thirty children who had very serious disabilities. They were being looked after by a group of five nuns in extremely impoverished circumstances. She had been living among the cries of tearful children for ten months, after living in two other institutions. She had been abandoned from birth.

Asia was described as being "a rebel" who interrupted the conversations that the nuns had with other children. When we met her, she threw herself into our arms, while at the same time she was visibly frightened and looked at our faces intensely, scrutinising us to see what we were like as people. After showing her immense vitality and humour, it was clear that Asia had a great wish to possess someone who would look after her and only her. After meeting Asia, we spent a week living near the Cambodian orphanage. Asia was willing to accompany us to various places in her city Phnom Penh, but she fearfully refused to stay with us at night.

A week later, we flew from Cambodia to Rome, where we live. Asia was fascinated with the aeroplane journey and when she began to speak, the aeroplane journey became the way of marking time: "before the aeroplane trip" and "after the aeroplane trip" were phrases she often spoke.

Arriving at a strange new home with a "foreign" language

We arrived in Rome with a child who had changed dramatically from the child we first saw in the orphanage. Although she intensified her extroverted way of approaching people, she was increasingly aggressive, kicking us at times. She scratched, spit, and wet her pants. Within our home, we noted that Asia faced many unknown experiences alongside not knowing Italian. She was unfamiliar with many objects, but felt at home with water, with which she played incessantly. She had such fascination for watching it appear and disappear and loved being bathed while experiencing my sole attention.

Immediately, we became aware that although she "threw herself into our arms" when we went to select a child at the orphanage, Asia had a profound lack of faith in any dependent relationship. This was understandable, since she had been abandoned at birth, but her persecution and rejection was very painful and confusing for us. One moment she expressed a great joy, and the next moment she was persecuting or in a rage with us. Her anxiety and confusion was accompanied by spitting, vomiting, and urinating, particularly during the night.

Meeting a new group of young people and adults in Tempo Lineare

We chose Tempo Lineare as a support to help Asia and us develop an intimate, trusting relationship. Asia went to the nursery two or three mornings per week. Here was another new set of adults and young children, all of whom spoke Italian, a language diverse from Asia's. Recognising the difficulties, Patrizia, the Director, had recommended a gradual transition into the nursery.

Asia's experience of encountering new adults and children in Tempo Lineare, although I was always present with her, seemed to evoke all sorts of behaviours that perhaps expressed an anxiety that she was just being left "back in the orphanage", having to "fend for herself". It is unclear what Asia felt, but I sensed that any possibility of separation from me was terrifying . . . as shown by her behaviour. It seemed that her aggression and hitting had many underlying feelings including:

- aggression, expressing her need to hold on to some personal strength for dear life;
- aggression to me as a way of distancing herself from frightening, new people

Tempo Lineare's philosophy is very clear and strictly enforced: children are not allowed to hit or be hit. As a way of helping Asia express her explosion of different feelings, the Tempo Lineare teacher gave her paper and pen to "draw out" her feelings rather than simply inhibit them. These drawings seem to trace an evolution in her state of mind that her use of language did not yet reflect.

Settling into the Tempo Lineare community

Both my husband and I, as well as Asia, became more familiar with the staff and families at Tempo Lineare. This enabled me to work together with the Director, Patrizia Pasquini, to develop a way of handing Asia over to her. This transition seemed extremely important to help Asia realise that there were adults always present for her. She did not always have to use her own rigid protections against anxiety.

The journey of understanding and communicating continues

Asia and my husband and I are still on "our journey" of discovering how we can be with one another. For our part, we have learnt from Tempo Lineare how to observe sequences of interaction, to try to put ourselves in Asia's shoes and give voice to her experiences.

Too close, too far, by Belinda, Marianna and Nicola's mother

How does one exist as a mother of two children, finding room for both of them in my heart and in my mind? I think it all depends on the state of the mind and heart. If they are free and strong enough, there is room for everyone. But it is difficult to find mental space and strengthen its capacity to bear feelings, which means to become a mature adult, a good mother. As I look back on my story and that of my children, I think of how it hard it has been for me, and for them as well, to find room inside oneself for everyone. Indeed, it took time, effort, and sometimes difficult choices for me to become a mother. The beginning of our family life, with Marianna's birth, was marked by uncertainty: a father and a mother who were not too sure of what they were doing, living in different cities, rather busy with their jobs. Apart from overwhelming love for my daughter, I could not help feeling that I was not very capable as a mother. But bit by bit, day by day, the growth of my beautiful child heartened me.

However, for a long time I have had a problem of distance from my daughter: we were either glued together, or too far apart, never at the right distance. Separation has been a slow torture for both: it took years. In the meantime, we changed cities twice, I left my job to live in Rome with her father, I gave birth to a new child, Nicola, I found a new job, then another. The most important choice was made when we, the father and I, decided to give life to our second child, Nicola: we, Marianna, Nicola, Vittorio, my husband, and I, then became a family and still are. Marianna found it very hard to accept the arrival of the new baby, Nicola.

My extreme closeness to Marianna, the first-born, worsened the situation. I am a first-born and my earliest childhood memories are linked to the painful jealousy I felt towards my little sister, who was born when I was a little over two years old, the same age as Marianna was when Nicola was born. I think that there was a moment of confusion between Marianna and I. I couldn't bear the idea that Marianna would suffer jealousy, feeling left out, worried about her place in my mind, because I knew how much she could be suffering. I felt her so close to me, that I was so identified with her, because I, too, was a first-born. For some strange reason, I tried to keep her at a distance. This was the state in which Marianna arrived at Tempo Lineare: she was suffering because of a newborn sister and because of a mother who could not keep the right distance from her, or, in other words, I was not so sure of my ability as a mother.

The parents of Marianna's playground friend told us about Tempo Lineare and about the new 3–6 years project that was about to open. We registered Marianna without a second thought, after an ominous experience in a private nursery school. For two long years, Marianna cried and had fits in front of Tempo Lineare's door before entering. At the beginning, she was really scared by separation; later, perhaps, she needed me to feel her pain of separation. I know my daughter's capabilities and I knew that she was perfectly able to enjoy school. But I also know what happened to Marianna: she felt abandoned and betrayed by me in a moment of extreme difficulty. How can I explain to her that I had confused her with me, that it was too hard for me to bear? And above all, what is her problem and what is mine? As Patrizia says, one needs to be able to bear things. Now, after working in the Tempo Lineare parents' group, I can bear intense feelings and think about them, but maybe in the past I couldn't.

Nicola arrived at Tempo Lineare for 0–3-year-olds at sixteen months of age, right after Marianna started Tempo Lineare for 3–6-year-olds, after I had decided to interrupt her attendance at the council nursery school where she went for a few months. The time we spent together, Nicola, I, and her father, too, at the "little school" has been extremely important. I could, or, rather, I *had to* look at my daughter, and there was someone teaching me how to do it. I could, or, rather, I had to, think about her but also *about both children*, with the adult mind of a mother, not with a self overwhelmed with anxiety.

Separation from Nicola at Tempo Lineare was not painless, but I remember I always thought that she could make it. I had a confidence in her, and in myself, that I had not had with Marianna. Thanks to my experience with Marianna at Tempo Lineare, and thanks to a school where Nicola learns to sort out good from bad, pain from joy, to utilise her strength, slowly the wounds of separation begin to heal. I see Nicola growing and finding confidence in her own abilities, I see Nicola dealing with her envy of her elder sister, and having a world of her own, with her own relationships with other children. Now it seems that maybe she has a boyfriend. I say, maybe, because Nicola, so small, is a bit of a boaster, just like her alleged boyfriend, Roberto, while her sister Marianna is, in fact, deeply in love, a love returned, with a certain little boy Michelle, whom she met at school.

Now, did I have to pay a for it with sorrow and intense and painful thinking? Just a little bit.

One of the many good things at Tempo Lineare is the joy children feel in doing things, and the opportunity offered to the parents to share it: for instance, thinking together of a costume for Carnival, or following them in one of their outings ("you know mummy, we are going to the market with the rope," Anna told me excitedly last week). I recall the funny moments of the "little bird", who, in the younger children's school, gives a sweet to each child at noon, at the end of school time, only if they are able to wait together for it, sitting in silence. The first time, Anna grabbed her sweet and ate it without thinking too much about it, the second time, as soon as she heard "the little bird is coming!", she was sitting still and silently on the couch. The third time, at less than eighteen months old, she learnt how to unwrap the sweet on her own.

And there are other good feelings that arise: a few days ago, my daughters asked me to paint at home. I was sitting there watching them paint with great concentration, without blotting the table, handling their brushes with an ability I have never had in over forty years of life. I didn't expect this from Anna, who is three. This capacity to enjoy painting is thanks to Cecilia, who teaches painting to children who adore her. And more, only parents at Tempo Lineare have the chance to eat the good bread kneaded and cooked by their two- or three-year-old children. In short, children are wonderful, but parents' lives are so filled with activities that it sometimes appears that activities are created on purpose to create an excuse to forget the children. Luckily, there is Tempo Lineare, which reminds fathers and mothers of how wonderful it is to have children.

Slow and steady development, by Laura, mother of Johannes and Maria

We know very little about the first months of the life of our adopted Brazilian son, Johannes, apart from the fact that he spent his first three months in intensive care to recover from severe prematurity. When he was eight months old, he was abandoned by his biological mother, who was encouraged to do so by her own family. We adopted Johannes when he was thirteen months old and throughout these past eight years I often noticed some behaviours that made me aware that he was conceivably neglected or ill-treated. We tried to help him ourselves as well as providing him with psychotherapy and a place in Tempo Lineare, where many sorrowful emotions could be worked out. However, old wounds still bleed, particularly when the old fear of being left by us arises and compels Johannes anxiously to seek reassurance that he is not being cast aside. Johannes struggles against this fear in quite an obvious way, but other and more hidden signs also reveal his uneasiness.

At Tempo Lineare, older children help the younger ones. Johannes himself had been supported by an older peer and, although he knew quite well how the support system worked, he often acted with indifference towards the younger children, disregarding them or getting annoyed when they cried. He sometimes lacked the capacity to get in touch with a smaller child's cries of distress or request for support. This happened not only in regard to other people's requests, but also in connection with their intentions: in fact, we noticed that until he was about seven, Johannes failed to distinguish between an intentional foul and an accidental clash during a football game. If someone accidentally collided with him, he got very angry or cried, blaming the playmate who had accidentally collided with him.

We remember Johannes as a very confused little boy about everything concerning "good" and "bad", but Tempo Lineare helped him to unravel these knots: the fairy tales Patrizia reads every day to the children were often dedicated to such themes, and so were the suggested games, such as the one with "good" and "bad" animals, or the game of disguise with carnival or theatrical costumes. It was difficult for Johannes to identify good and bad characters either in a story-telling or in a television cartoon, and he often sided with the negative character. I recall that when he was about three, he watched a Robin Hood cartoon and developed a strong liking both for the villain, Price John, and, most of all, for his sneaky counsellor, Sir Biss, the snake! It is true that the hero is a thief, but anyway . . .

I think that Johannes's muddled moral attitudes, his inability to understand other people's minds, and his lack of judgement about their being malevolent or hostile, are all consequences of his having been neglected during the first months of his life. This might also be the reason Johannes forgets people, such as his psychotherapist, who was a good influence on his life. Johannes never asks about him, and yet I know he feels very attached to him. Probably because, as a little child, Johannes did not have anybody who was seriously interested in him, nobody who tried to attune with his needs in a significant and steady way, he is often lacking in awareness about himself and about others.

Johannes has difficulty perceiving his own physical and emotional feelings. He still sometimes does not take off his sweater when it is hot, and struggles to express his feelings. Often, his feelings emerge in a violent, uncontrolled, or even twisted way, as in the past when he sometimes attacked little children if they cried loudly.

Johannes began to speak when he was about three and still, at age seven, he often is unable to express verbally what he is experiencing; sometimes this results in his feeling overwhelmed. For instance, he becomes quite anxious if he has too much homework. He does not ask for help when he is not able to do his task and he has raging fits, throwing away pen and rubber if we mention that he has made a mistake. When this happens, we find it important to comfort him, making him feel that we appreciate him, as we learnt to do with Patrizia and the teachers at Tempo Lineare.

Up to last year, Johannes had never said which job he would like to do as a grown-up, almost as if his internal fragmented self would not allow him to project himself into the future. Some months ago, at last, he spontaneously said that he would like to be a palaeontologist: obviously, he will change his mind lots of times, but the important thing is that he has succeeded in thinking of himself as someday being a grown-up person, with a life and a job. It is interesting that he wants to explore life in the past.

The difficulty of projecting himself into the future recalls Johannes's almost non-existent interest in symbolic play, that is the game of "let's pretend . . .", and also a scant interest in assuming a role, for instance in a Carnival masquerade or a theatrical play. Some weeks ago, I had to help him study the lines of the play they are learning at school. The teacher had told me that he had not studied his part, but I soon realised that he did not have a memory problem. Johannes knew all his lines by heart, but he was unable to enter his part: for him, those lines were only strings of words to pronounce at the right moment, without intonation or dramatisation. I had to remind to him that his role was that of a king, that he had power and authority, and I went through the script with him to let him understand how to perform his character.

Afterwards, I thought again about an adaptation of *Alice in Wonderland*, which Johannes and his classmates performed. Johannes knows very well, almost by heart, the Disney cartoon film of *Alice*, and, therefore, he knows very well the king's character. All the same, he seemed unable to mimic him, that is, he seemed unable to understand the internal structure of the character, his good and bad sides and his comic ways. Johannes also had difficulty choosing which character in a play he would like to act. In fact, during the first rehearsals, roles are not assigned, children learn all of them and perform them in turn. I asked then which character he would have liked to play, and he answered that he would like to be a card, one of the Queen's soldiers—that is, the most anonymous and static role!

However, we believe that is possible to heal some of Johannes's difficulties. We are aware that he has an aesthetic appreciation of life. We often draw his attention to the beauty that we can find in the world around us and we ask him how he experiences what he is seeing or hearing. Ever since he was very young, we have carried on pointing out to him the loveliness of a landscape, or of a sunset at the seaside. We have been going with him to art exhibitions, even difficult ones, such as those featuring Giotto's or Van Gogh's work; we discuss buildings' and churches' harmonic lines, and also merely his tastes with regard to common objects, smart cars, fine trinkets, clothes, or just nice drawings.

As a result, we may say that Johannes can observe all that is around him with a great deal of interest. I sometimes bring Johannes and some schoolmates of his home in my car, and Johannes may point out either a seagull flying low near our car, or he describes the unusual colour of a tree, which now has become "our tree", at Porta Capena. In these moments, my son's internal world shows itself, exactly as when, in his bed, at last relaxed just before going to sleep, he succeeds in talking about his feelings during the day.

Notwithstanding all kinds of help and all his considerable developmental progress, Johannes sometimes gives the impression of being a boy with little confidence and little capacity to dream about his future life. Much of his life is spent trying to manage the day and needing to concentrate upon himself and protect himself to get through it. At the same time, he often thinks he needs material and immediate rewards to fill up some internal voids: he asks to have gifts, of little value, such as figurines or gadgets, but he wants them immediately, as if in recompense for alleged wrongs or ill-treatments: for instance, as compensation for the fact that, at dinner, I served his little sister before him.

Johannes has begun to work on some of his difficulties and to grow up more rapidly after our second adopted child, a girl, entered our family. Many had told us that this occurrence would worsen his problems, and perhaps made him regress. But it has been on the contrary, for his teachers at school told us that this year Johannes has shown better achievements in his study, he is more active, more able to organise his work, and more self-assured. So, apart from experiencing some jealousy towards his sister, Sophia, Johannes seems to have begun to secure a more distinct role in the family, and to develop a more defined personality. He also seems more able to express some preferences; for instance, when he was asked about what family holiday he would like to take, he expressed a wish to visit Egypt.

I was also happy to see that he agreed to go to the Carnival feast at Tempo Lineare, his old school, which his sister now attends. He wore a mask and went to the feast, saying later that he had enjoyed himself. I thought that within Tempo Lineare he must have re-discovered a large part of his life. Moreover, it seems to me that since then Johannes and his sister, Sophia, have begun to build something together. No doubt it was important for him to share with his sister a pleasurable gathering at Tempo Lineare, a place that both of them and us acknowledge as being important in their lives. There we all have experienced special help with our respective feelings and difficulties.

Dinosaurs and necklaces, by Stefania, Aaron and Alicia's mother

I heard about Tempo Lineare from a friend whose daughter was attending the school when my elder child, Aaron, was a little more than two years old. I put Aaron's name on the school waiting list and I waited a few months until the end of the Easter holidays. Meanwhile, I had gone to the school Carnival party and I had had a couple of talks with Patrizia Pasquini, the Director.

I was particularly worried about Aaron because, at the age of two, he had already experienced his sister Alicia's birth and was having some difficulties, as shown by his rejecting solid food for a long time and his wanting only to be bottle-fed. I felt rather impotent and very guilty, for I saw accepting food as being linked with accepting one's mother, inhibiting chewing as inhibiting aggression to the mother, being able to tackle solid food by chewing and swallowing it as connected with a desire and ability to approach life and get involved more fully in it. I had already tried to persuade Aaron "kindly" to eat through playing with him, through distracting him with cartoon films, through depriving him of food for many hours in order that he might eat it. Then I showed him my rage about his not moving on to solid food . . . all with no success at all.

When Aaron began to attend Tempo Lineare, it was immediately evident that he had to work on his eating and whatever it represented emotionally. As soon as Aaron went into the schoolroom, he would generally rush to the box of wild animals and play with dinosaurs, lions, crocodiles, and whatever other animals could devour, mangle, open their jaws, sink their teeth into somebody, and tear someone to pieces. He very rarely could sit at his table at snack time and have a biscuit. I remember with joy when, in June, at the end of a beautiful trip to Villa Borghese, everyone was sitting on the lawn and Aaron rested in Patrizia Pasquini's arms. Everyone else, parents, teachers, and children were eating heartily, for they were hungry after the long walk and the sultry weather. While I was taking a picture of him, Aaron tasted a little bit of yogurt on a teaspoon that Patricia sensitively put to his mouth.

As I had expected, play experiences within the nursery school, which were observed and compassionately understood, the lunch with other children, and Aaron's maturational growth have slowly, very slowly, enabled him to work through his aggressive and loving feelings sufficiently to resolve his eating problems. Even today, when he is too old for Tempo Lineare, Aaron asks to go to "Patrizia's little school", which, in the meantime, has become his sister Alicia's nursery school. When Aaron visits Tempo Lineare, he is very happy to display his improvements, which suggest that he has grown up. He also demonstrates how he can finally play in a variety of ways with the animal toys, not only aggressively with wild animals, but also with the young farm animals, which he has the farm animal parents nurture and protect.

My second experience at Tempo Lineare has been with Alicia, who began attending the baby group with me when she was one year old. Now she is in a group for those children between three and six years old. Her relationship with the "little school" has always been good and her personality is definitely less complex than her brother's. I remember her mentioning her school friends Tito, Rocco, Antonella, and the others while we were travelling by car during the summer holidays. Especially this year, Tempo Lineare is referred to by Alicia as "my school" and "Patrizia", the Director, is also mentioned at home as the one to whom Alicia has to show or tell this and that.

Tempo Lineare is where Alicia is supported to become autonomous, competent, sociable, and independent, to build that inner self-confidence which will make her strong, as she gets older and prepares to start the "real school" next September. So far, this is in the last four months Alicia has attended "the little school", more with the au pair than with me. Only after the Christmas holidays, as I have been with her more, has she has started coming in and going out from her classroom, to say "pick me up", or indicate that I should follow her into the classroom, saying "mummy come".

My third experience at Tempo Lineare is mine. This was the discovery, even if I was working, of a new way of being with my children—not in the park, not at some friends' home, not at the playschool, to which, however, I had never thought to send my children. Tempo Lineare fostered in me a committed and attentive way with all the ambivalence this implies: hard work, a constant rush, sacrifices, frustrations, and "performance anxiety" when my little girl was not able do something. At times, when I could not go to Tempo Lineare, I would feel guilty. I compared myself with other mothers and found that some of them had easier relationships with their children, I also compared Patrizia Pasquini's teaching with other pedagogical methods, which, in the meanwhile, I had taken into consideration. Within Tempo Lineare, I also witnessed the parents' and teachers' deep sense of devotion to the children.

This led me to a serious reconsideration of my job. At this point in the children's lives it was too involving and not compatible with the children's needs. Maybe it was time to look for another job. I asked myself, "Why not?" I have not succeeded in involving my husband, their father, who is too busy at work, but I find joy in being able to tell him our children's improvements, little events in their lives, his daughter's everyday life with her schoolmates.

In the past few weeks, Tempo Lineare has become a way of life, a very important meeting point for parents, teachers, and the children. It is different from those gatherings of parents and children in the park or at school parties. Through writing about our experiences as parents involved in Tempo Lineare, I hope that a lot of mothers and fathers will receive *a little seed* to nurture new potentials for creating closer relationships with their children, their children's teachers, and each other.

A shared and exclusive time, by Leandra, Enrico's mother

It is a privilege for a parent to be able to attend Tempo Lineare, although hardly any parents joining this project are likely to be fully aware of the importance of their choice. It is probable, instead, that the initial decision—despite all the advice, explanations, talks, and forms to fill in—originates more from an instinctive choice, an intuitive response from parents wanting to fully understand crucial moments of their experience with their children.

I remember very well the moment I first stepped into Tempo Lineare, and the feeling of quiet, tranquillity, order, and competence I experienced in being in the school with the teachers and other parents. What impressed me most was the attention Patrizia Pasquini, the Director, paid to my personal story about me and my new family. This made me feel comfortable and reassured me in my search for good and suitable experiences for my son. By observing her way of illustrating her project and her manner in being with me, I found a concordance between her and my aspirations, albeit a bit confused. In her attitude, I perceived an energy I no longer had. At that time, I did not realise I was also looking for some enriching experiences for my partner and me. I must say that the decision to attend that school was made almost instinctively because it fulfilled our family needs, about which we were not yet fully aware. Eventually, with time, having undertaken active roles in the project, we realised our deeper reasons for participating in Tempo Lineare.

The real strength of Tempo Lineare is that it gives everybody—mothers, fathers, and children—*an exclusive time* when we can observe interactions and get to know each other by thinking and talking together, playing together, and doing creative activities. In this particular cultural moment in society, when "nuclear" families are usually advised to use "substitutes" to look after their elderly people, houses, animals, and children, it is very important to find a school which returns parents to their central position in the lives of their children and society in general. Tempo Lineare is a school that helps us become more responsible for our relationship with our children. The experience at Tempo Lineare reveals straight away that the journey to become a good parent, although potentially filled with much joy, is long and difficult. Everybody, without distinction, is faced with problems that need to be considered in relationships with family, work, and everyday life. The work done in the Tempo Lineare parents' groups, with Patrizia Pasquini's support, is aimed especially at sharing experiences, listening to and supporting each other. In doing this work, parents come out of the isolation and bewilderment they often experience after a child's birth. They discover a way of being more in contact with their child from an emotional point of view. The group shares a greater awareness of the vital life-giving opportunities of the family and the importance of both the father's and the mother's roles.

From time to time, the school asks the parents to work together on projects. In working collaboratively with each other, the parents can overcome some of their lack of self-confidence, develop new skills, and find the happiness, thoughtfulness, and tenderness they have lost in the experience of being isolated in a big city and weighed down by the burden of parental responsibilities and anxieties. Moreover, the parents discover that the more they can be coherent and devoted to the nursery group projects on behalf of the parents and their children, the more they will be motivated in their family life and closer to their children.

What is striking is that compared to other children of their age, the Tempo Lineare children are often more spontaneous and creative in the way they show more affection and attachment towards their schoolmates, including both the older and younger ones, and listen to and take part in school activities. The bond of affection children build up day after day with Patrizia Pasquini, the other teachers, and children at Tempo Lineare actually becomes an important and steady landmark, which often remains unchanged even when they grow up and reach six years, the age required for compulsory education. For this reason, in 2002, parents attending Tempo Lineare decided to found an ONLUS parents' association to support this project. In the following eleven years of activities, the parents' association was able to hold yearly conventions discussing children and parenting which professionals and parents from various parts of Italy attended. The parents also actively participated in the creation of Tempo Lineare Two, the school for children aged 3–6, self-published its own fairy tale book with Tempo Lineare children's drawings entitled *Da Fiabe Nasce Fiabi* (Pasquini, 2002), produced a film based on the schoolchildren's pictures, organised seminars and child observation courses for the Tempo Lineare parents, and participated in the writing, translation, and publication of the Italian version of this book, *Tempo Lineare* (2007). But, above all, the parents' association, of which I was the president for a period of time, succeeded in the pursuit of its aim, which is supporting Tempo Lineare, a unique project in Italy which feels essential for the sixty families that have children in the school and is a reference point for the other 400 families whose children have attended the school.

I believe that nowadays we really need schools in which parents, teachers, and children creatively collaborate as they do in Tempo Lineare. Schools like this need to be visible to the public and open to everyone. They need to be a real and effectual support and landmark for families to which parents can return at any time to think more about their children and support other parents with their younger children. This project makes us aware of how vital it is to find a school that is always able to create and mend strong and valuable ties between children, teenagers, and their families, a place which has the potential of being a stable, permanent meeting point in the community for all the parents and their growing-up children, on both an affective and an emotional level. At the same time as such a place as Tempo Lineare is able to foster good emotional connections, it also places value on individual freedom and respects families' independence.

What Tempo Lineare means to me, by Annamaria, Monica's mother

My encounter with Tempo Lineare was a physical, almost obligatory one, as I was located very close by it, in the same street, Via Vespucci 41, where I have lived since I married and moved from Sicily to Rome. I discovered Tempo Lineare at precisely the same time as I was expecting Monica, my second child. This occurred one day as, walking through the courtyard, I saw, for the first time, the front door of this school open. The school, with the inscription "Children's House", had always aroused my curiosity. I thought to myself, "What a marve! It is a pity it is not so busy." On that very day, renovation work began. In short, I saw this place, located in a block of flats, come alive bit by bit. I kept looking at "the little school" until its opening day, when I read the plate posted up next to its door and saw the leaflets posted on the garden walls.

I remember the curiosity of the people from the neighbourhood: at the tobacconist's, at Salvatore's food shop, at the baker's, in the park, everybody was talking about Tempo Lineare and wondering what it was all about, what its purpose was and how it worked. Some people said it was a playschool where mothers from the area would go and look after babies alternately. Some others said, children go to the playschool with mummy and daddy? What is the aim of all this then? It does not solve the problem of working mothers. In conclusion, I was very curious and puzzled too, even a bit suspicious, as if I were facing something unknown.

I talked about Tempo Lineare with my husband. With his usual attitude of attention, curiosity, and interest in anything new taking place in our society, he had already had many talks with Patrizia Pasquini, the Director of the school. She had explained the purpose of Tempo Lineare's project to him. We put our child to be, Monica, on the waiting list and here we were, ready to live this experience thoroughly, with fewer doubts and growing confidence that the experience at Tempo Lineare would be something important for our daughter.

The first time we were invited to the school was on the occasion of the Carnival party and Monica, who was now eleven months old, and I "went to see the little children". "Going to see the little children" was the phrase I had been using with Monica during the first year when we walked by the schoolyard. The Carnival party was the first occasion for us to be inside Tempo Lineare. After some time, we received a telephone call saying that there was a vacancy for us to attend the school. It was a small group of male children and Monica, eleven months, was not only the only girl, but also the youngest child.

Fairly quickly, Monica began to approach school with such confidence and competent control that everyone was surprised. She used to play, laugh, and address the other children as if she were at home, winning adults' favour with her friendly manners. This is what was said by the Director, Patrizia, or, better, "Pacicia", as Monica called her: "Monica, at the age of eleven months, can talk like an eighteen-month-old baby girl. I've seen her grow up from being the very tiny baby I saw walking in the courtyard with her father." I was surprised and moved by the support and affection Patrizia showed when talking about a little girl she had just met.

I did not always feel at ease in Tempo Lineare, for I did not know which role I should take, how I should behave with other parents, and with the school's assistant teachers. I found myself in a group of parents who had already been meeting regularly for six months. It was not easy, but I tried to do my best. I even managed to create some relationships with some parents outside the school hours. In one of the parent group meetings with Patrizia, I mentioned that I was still breast-feeding Monica but, as it was coming near her first birthday, I was trying to stop. Patrizia thoughtfully responded, "You'll be able to stop little by little." Addressing the rest of the group, she said, "Mothers, you could ask your husbands to help you in this difficult task."

Then something unexpected happened in my family: my husband fell ill and was forced to stay at home for several days. I had to deal with everything outside the house. Little by little, Monica, staying at home with her father, began to accept the bottle from him. After a few days she stopped breast-feeding and drank only from the bottle or a cup. I remembered Patrizia's words, "Ask your husbands to help you." My second painful separation from my little girl had taken place.

When the end of the school year arrived, we decided that the following year Monica would stay with a new group of young children as she was too young compared to the children moving up. The second year at the little school started at the end of September. I had to go back to work—I am a teacher and I had been away from teaching for two years. Monica began her third painful separation with unexpected tranquillity. She stayed with the baby-sitter when I was not at home and seemed to cope without me very well. On the other hand, I was nervous and worried. Monica, who was now two years old, wished to go to "the little school", as she called it, to play with toys *with me* and not so much with the other children. I tried to explain to her that she was supposed to play with the other children, but she only wanted to play with me. At home, she had to share mummy with Jonathan, her brother. At Tempo Lineare, she could have me to herself.

Monica used to play one game repetitiously. It consisted of taking all the baskets full of plastic cakes and food and feeding me, Patrizia, the teaching assistants, Paola and Isabella, and some mothers. She continued to resist playing with the other children. She was becoming increasingly more unsociable and less agreeable in following daily living routines at home. She often cried because she could not accept limits to what she wanted. Gradually, Monica became unwilling to go to school; she said that the children were ugly and she would not play with them.

At a certain point, Monica started a different game that she played repetitiously. She used to put a family together with whatever toys she had in her hands and repeat all the time: mummy, daddy, Monica, and Jonathan. Her repetitious games consisted of feeding and putting her family together. I became aware that Monica had been deceptively "good" at controlling her pain in separating from me, while simultaneously experiencing inside herself a lot of resentment which she was having the confidence to release in her play bit by bit. Patrizia said that she shared the same perception as mine and we discussed what Monica might be worried about. By the middle of April, just after Monica had turned two, she began to have lots of troubles. She would cry when I was going to leave home or her little school. When "the little bird carrying a sweet for each child" was coming at the nursery, she was frightened, since she knew that straight after that I would leave to go to work.

There are no words to express the pain I felt when working through this separation, touching it so personally in a place like Tempo Lineare, where I was required to observe my child and face what was happening inside her while she felt so abandoned by me. While I was going through this period, I sometimes thought that Patrizia, Isabella, and Paola, the teachers, did not help me as much as I wished. And what about the other parents? I rarely felt them to be sympathetic to my pain. I often saw them concentrated only on their children. I wondered: what am I doing here, then?

But, when I regained some inner tranquillity, I understood that things could be done differently from that for which I was hoping. At Tempo Lineare, walking along the way with somebody could involve gently supporting him in silence. Little by little, we got over this critical moment. Monica was willing to go to "Patrizia's school" again to tell her this and that. And at the end of June, before school was over, she felt happy to wait for the "little bird bringing her a sweet" . . . the marking of the end of a school year. At that very moment I felt the pleasure of the presence of the group: we were all excited and clapped our hands.

This year, the last one, is the most tiring one for me. From time to time I still do not feel at ease, not in the right place. And now I have doubts and uncertainties I have not had before.

Tempo Lineare is very demanding. Space and time are sometimes constrained and oppressive. There are doubts and uncertainties. I feel tired and want to give up; I am frustrated. My daughter cannot cope with the school, the other children can. I cannot go on any more, the other mothers can. The others, how difficult it is to stay with the others sometimes.

Why? What is the matter? And is there really a problem? Or is it I who must face reality in a rather small place, where I have to share my time and space with my child, compare myself with the others, often support and be supported, get on well with the others or be in conflict, leave space for the others to be heard because I am not the only one in that place? In the parents' group, we often talk with Patrizia or we listen to her thoughts about difficulties in relationships, which sometimes make me nervous but often make me reflect and understand that there are no specific solutions to the problems concerning the mother–child separation. Every child is different from the other child, with unique phases in growing up, which must be respected and accepted with love.

We have walked part of our way and are still walking together, Anna and I, and also Bernardo, her father. Now that this experience at Tempo Lineare has almost come to an end, I do not feel like judging those parents who send their children to state playschools because of family or money problems. They have no choice. But I strongly hope that adequate attention will be given to such an important issue by our lawmakers in order to give more parents willing to spend more time with their children the opportunity to stay at home with them or to go to places like government funded Tempo Lineare, where parents are involved with their children while they are in the nursery school. This is not and must not remain an oasis of peace and growth for a few lucky families, but should be the first of a whole series of Tempo Lineare school projects. I say this in order that parents will create more space for thinking about their children, finding new perspectives to explore, and to find more time to be deeply together with their children. Tempo Lineare can support parents to realise what is happening them and to their child who feels abandoned.

References

Pasquini, P. (2002). *Da Fiabe Nasce Fiabi.* Rome: Genitori e Amici del Tempo Lineare-Onlus.
Ungaretti, G. (1931). *L'allegria.* Milan: Preda.

GLOSSARY

The following pages describe some key psychoanalytic concepts used in this book. Further exploration of psychoanalytic concepts, including these terms with relevant current references, can be located in *The New Dictionary of Kleinian Thought* (2011), edited by E. Bott Spillius, J. Milton, P. Garvey, C. Couve, and D. Steiner.

Containment: This concept is based on the model of a mother as a container for the infant's projected feelings, needs, and unwanted aspects of the self. Using reverie, the mother receives the baby's projections and conveys to him the sense that his anxieties and communications are bearable and have meaning. It is through the internalising of a mindful care-giver that the infant gradually develops the capacity for mentalization.

Countertransference: This concept refers to the whole of the person's feelings and unconscious reactions occurring in the encounter with the young person or the family. It is one of the most important therapeutic tools for thinking about the young child and the family. The counter-transference can provide valuable information about the unconscious that is not yet in symbolic form suitable for talking to and thinking with the therapist to take place.

Denial: The process of denial can involve disposing of limitations of the self and the importance of the people upon whom one depends. It can also involve obliteration of perceptions particularly of bad parts of the self or the other.

Dissociation: This refers to a partial or complete disruption of the normal integration of a person's consciousness. Dissociation can be a protective response to trauma, for it allows the conscious self to distance itself from overwhelming experiences that are too much for the psyche to process.

Inner world and internal objects or figures: There is the external world with external family figures, school figures, and peers and there is the internal world of internal objects or figures formed by the introjecive identification with external loved and hated important figures who are distorted by one's phantasies and feelings projected on to them. The person's internal world provides the impetus for re-enactment in relation to external figures.

Introjective identification: This concept describes a process of being in a relationship with someone and taking in aspects, qualities, or skills of the person in such a way that they are gradually identified with and inform the character of an individual. This process is the way by which a child develops in an emotionally healthy way with a capacity to think about emotional experiences.

Mentalizing: This is an act of mental activity in which one imagines what other people might be thinking or feeling. It implies perceiving and interpreting behaviour as combined with intentional mental states. It involves analysing one's emotional experiences (Bateman & Fonagy, 2006, p. 2).

Omnipotence: This is a concept referring to a notion that one's thoughts have the power to protect the self from harmful anxieties. For a child using primitive omnipotence, there is a turning to one's phantasies as powerful and controlling protections. The child's omnipotence is used rather than facing the reality of one's persecutory fears and depending on care-givers necessary for one's emotional development. This sense of omnipotence is characterised by "doing it oneself", although others may be needed to support one emotionally.

Phantasy: "There is no impulse, no instinctual urge or response, which is not experienced as unconscious phantasy" (Isaacs, 1952, p. 83). "Unconscious phantasy is in a constant interplay with external reality, both influencing and altering the perception or interpretation of it and also being influenced by it" (Box, Copley, Magagna, & Smilansky, 1994, p. 258).

Projective identification: This process is part of normal development in parent–child and teacher–child relationships. Through the way he is being or speaking, a child or adult puts parts of himself into the other person so that the other person (teacher or parent, for example) may feel and understand those experiences and be able to contain them, enabling them to lose their unbearable quality. The problem comes when one loses unwanted parts of the self in the other and then fears the other person (such as a teacher or parent) is relating with those projected parts of self; however, good parts of the self may also be projected into the other. For example, projecting hostility may lead one to fear being criticised by the teacher.

Re-enactment: "An essential element in this concept is replacement of recollection (or any form of mental realization) by a blindly repeated pattern of events" (Britton, 1994, p. 86).

Regression: This is a process involving emotionally returning to an earlier stage of psychological development rather than handling an emotional crisis in an age-appropriate way.

Reparation: When the object loved is also seen to be the same object as the object hated, then some integration of the personality can occur and there is some feeling of responsibility to repair harm done to the good object.

Reverie: This concept refers to a state of mind in which one is open to receiving emotions and experiences of others regardless of whether they involve love or hate, pleasantness or unpleasantness.

Splitting: This process occurs as part of normal development, but also in later life. It involves separating the gratifying experiences linked with an attuned experience with a person and keeping them apart from the persecuting, frustrating negative experiences. This leaves an idealised object and a hostile persecutory object relation until the splitting is replaced by integration of the good and bad aspects of the object.

Transference: Transference implies that there are impulses and phantasies that are aroused and made conscious during the progress of the therapy. A transference experience is part of an ongoing internal relationship to internal figures that is being re-experienced in relation to the therapist or teacher in the nursery school or others in one's life.

Working through: The process of repeating, elaborating, and amplifying understanding. It is believed that such working through is critical for emotional development. Understanding will allow the person to apply rational thought and conscious awareness to an emotion that previously had been hidden by defensive mechanisms in the personality. Distortions of current experiences that occurred through projection can be mitigated in this way and the person will be able to relate better to a current situation. Working through can occur when a person comes up with a "thing", be it written, a piece of art, music, verbal, or some other form, that was previously buried in the subconscious or unconscious mind. This "thing" is then used to understand an event occurring in the person's internal drama and perhaps also from a person's past.

References

Bateman, A., & Fonagy, P. (2006). *Mentalization-Based Treatment for Borderline Personality Disorders: A Practical Guide*. Oxford: Oxford University Press.

Bott Spillius, E., Milton, J., Garvey, P., Couve, C., & Steiner, D. (2011). *The New Dictionary of Kleinian Thought*. London: Routledge.

Box, S., Copley, B., Magagna, J., & Smilansky, E. (Eds.) (1994). *Crisis at Adolescence: Object Relations Therapy with the Family*. Northvale, NJ: Jason Aronson.

Britton, R. (1994). Re-enactment as an unwitting professional response to family dynamics. In: S. Box, B. Copley, J. Magagna, & E. Smilansky (Eds.), *Crisis at Adolescence: Object Relations Therapy with the Family*. Northvale, NJ: Jason Aronson.

Isaacs, S. (1952). The nature and function of fantasy. In: M. Klein, P. Isaacs, P. Heimann, & J. Riviere (Eds.), *Developments in Psychoanalysis* (pp. 67–121). London: Hogarth.